ON THE LAW OF SPEAKING FREELY

This book tackles the most pressing problems of contemporary free speech law by examining where the idea of free expression came from in the first place, applying the lessons of the past to address the challenges of the present.

Free speech cannot be taken for granted – it needs to be fought for. But its champions will be successful only if they understand what they are defending. For free speech is a deceptively simple principle.

How should it guide us on the bounds of what is acceptable to say? Should we be free to preach hatred, or to spread fear or fake news? Can media freedom be balanced against the right to privacy? How does free speech work online? Can the internet be made a safe space without compromising freedom of expression?

This book offers not just insights but answers to these and other such vital questions by roaming widely over the law of free speech, from English common law to the European Convention on Human Rights via the US First Amendment.

In rescuing free speech from the culture wars in which it has become embroiled, Adam Tomkins restates its values, its complexities, and its enduring importance, in prose that is as passionate as it is clear-sighted. Even-handed, informed and authoritative, this is a major, timely work from one of the UK's leading constitutional scholars.

On the Law of
Speaking Freely

Adam Tomkins

·HART·

OXFORD · LONDON · NEW YORK · NEW DELHI · SYDNEY

HART PUBLISHING

Bloomsbury Publishing Plc

Kemp House, Chawley Park, Cumnor Hill, Oxford, OX2 9PH, UK

1385 Broadway, New York, NY 10018, USA

Bloomsbury Publishing Ireland Limited, 29 Earlsfort Terrace, Dublin 2, D02 AY28, Ireland

HART PUBLISHING, the Hart/Stag logo, BLOOMSBURY and the Diana logo are
trademarks of Bloomsbury Publishing Plc

First published in Great Britain 2025

A catalogue record for this book is available from the British Library.

A catalogue record for this book is available from the Library of Congress.

Library of Congress Control Number: 2025930949

ISBN: PB: 978-1-50997-210-4
       ePDF: 978-1-50997-212-8
       ePub: 978-1-50997-211-1

Typeset by Compuscript Ltd, Shannon

For product safety related questions contact productsafety@bloomsbury.com

To find out more about our authors and books visit www.hartpublishing.co.uk.
Here you will find extracts, author information, details of forthcoming events
and the option to sign up for our newsletters.

PREFACE

A striking number of the ideas central to modern constitutional law have ancient roots. Democracy is perhaps the best-known example. Today's practices of adult universal suffrage date back only to the early twentieth century (in the United Kingdom, to the Representation of the People Acts 1918 and 1928). But the idea of democracy as a means whereby the exercise of political power may obtain legitimacy stretches back two and half millennia, to the Athenian city-state of Plato and Aristotle, in the fourth century BCE. Several of our most dearly held constitutional ideas date from medieval times. The idea of constitutional monarchy – that the king is bound by fundamental rules of constitutional behaviour – can be traced in English law back to Magna Carta in 1215. The idea of sovereignty – perhaps the central idea of the British constitution – was forged in the late Middle Ages and crystallised in the early modern period. The modern notion of the separation of powers was formed only in eighteenth-century France and America but it developed out of a much older one, traceable all the way back to ancient Rome, that a stable constitution combined three different modes of rule (each given an old Greek name) – monarchy, aristocracy and democracy – the rule of the one, the rule of the few and the rule of the many.

The idea of free speech, by contrast, has no such roots in our deep past. Despite its centrality to modern conceptions and practices of constitutionalism, at least in liberal constitutions, it arrived only recently. It is true that there are two ancient Greek terms, used in Athens in particular, which have been translated into English as 'freedom of speech'. But neither of them is in fact analogous to what we understand by free speech today. The first, *isegoria*, was a notion more of equality than of expression, signalling the equal right of citizens to participate in certain forums of public debate. The second, *parrhesia*, signified something resembling the modern civil service notion of 'speaking truth to power': the idea that counsellors and advisers must have the courage to tell the rulers of the moment what they do not wish to hear.[1] That is an important principle, for sure, but it would be a mistake to see it as today's universal right to free speech in embryonic form.

---

[1] Teresa M Bejan, 'Two Concepts of Freedom (of Speech)' (2019) 163 *Proceedings of the American Philosophical Society* 95. See further, Richard Sorabji, *Freedom of Speech and Expression* (New York, Oxford University Press, 2021) ch 1.

There are at best only the faintest and most distant echoes in the ancient world of what, more than two millennia later, would become our modern-day doctrine of free speech. Free speech is not an idea with ancient roots, which were then treated to two thousand years of careful nurturing, in order to allow them to ripen and blossom. Rather, *isegoria* and *parrhesia* were distinct cultural practices of a time long ago, which were later compared (by some scholars) with modern free speech, but which in no sense provided the source from which our modern conception of free expression sprouted. It is not true, then, as is sometimes claimed, that Socrates was the first free speech martyr. He was tried and sentenced to death in 399 BCE for 'not duly acknowledging the gods in which the city believes and of introducing other, new divinities ... [and of] corrupting the young'.[2] It is easy to see why later generations would seek to recruit a figure as colossal as Socrates to the cause of free speech, but the truth is that such roots as free speech has are to be found only in the modern world, and not in the ancient.

This book is concerned with contemporary controversies pertaining to free speech, whilst seeking to locate today's concerns in the context of the idea's foundations, both as a political aspiration and as a matter of legal doctrine.[3] This is for several reasons. First, as we shall see, today's problems are not new. Free speech may not have a long history, but the story of its emergence and development nonetheless shines light both on the nature of the problems it faces today and on the strengths (and otherwise) of the various approaches we may take to tackling them. The technology of speech may be new – communications technology has been moving at breathtaking pace in the modern world – but this does not mean the problems the technology creates for free speech are all novel.

Secondly, it is a mistake in constitutional or legal analysis to start from (what the author asserts to be) a fundamental principle without excavating something of where that principle comes from. In the United Kingdom especially, where the constitution, like the common law generally, owes so much of its authority to the past, it is an error to assert first that 'here are the principles upon which the constitution is based' and then to proceed to measure the merits and demerits of current constitutional practice against the standards of the asserted principles. The constitution may well be 'based on' certain principles, but you cannot simply start from the principle as if it is self-evident or axiomatic. Principles have to be grounded and, in order to grasp anything of their foundations, we have first to understand

---

[2] Janet Coleman, *A History of Political Thought* (Oxford, Blackwell, 2000) 50.

[3] In this book 'free speech', 'freedom of speech', 'free expression', 'freedom of expression' and 'speaking freely' are used interchangeably. No aspect of the argument in this book hinges on any perceived difference between 'speech' and 'expression'.

something of their past. Accordingly, this book starts with the history of the idea of free speech. Free speech is not an abstract principle that landed from nowhere. It had to be fought for – argued for. And without a clear sense of the struggle for free speech we can never hope to comprehend where free speech should sit in today's affairs.

The struggle for the idea of speaking freely can be divided into three chapters, which I call the 'age of heresy', the 'age of sedition' and the 'age of offence'. None of these ages is over: even now we still live in them. They emerged, however, in that order. The age of heresy came first and was then, at least to a degree, eclipsed by the age of sedition, which was, in turn, overtaken by the age of offence. The three 'ages' are best understood not as blocks of time, with discrete beginnings and ends, but as modes – or even moods – of expression, of liberty and of their curtailment by censorship, punishment and censure. The first struggle for free expression was that of heretics against the established church. The first of the great European institutions to be concerned about the dangers of free speech was not the state, but the church. Only later did the state start to learn from the church about how free speech could endanger its interests, as the struggle for free expression moved into the age of sedition. In England, this shift occurred around the time of John Locke, at the end of the seventeenth century and the beginning of the eighteenth. If the century between the Glorious Revolution (1688) and the French Revolution (1789) was the coming of the age of sedition, by the mid-Victorian era of the nineteenth century the struggle for free speech had moved again into territory on which it continues to fight to this day. For this was the age of offence, when speech could be censored and when its consequences could be censured not because it was held to damage the interests of the powerful – whether priests or kings – but for its social harms, its tendency to deprave and corrupt, its ability to cause hurt, upset, alarm or distress.

Of course, the story of the struggle for free speech is more complicated than this. Modern ideas of church and state are exactly that – modern – and in the sixteenth-century age of heresy the two were far more mutually entwined than has tended to be the case in post-Enlightenment Europe. Nonetheless, even before Henry VIII's schism with Rome, it was clear that papal authority, on the one hand, and the rulership of kings and emperors, on the other, could be distinguished from one another, even if they overlapped, and even if the lines separating their respective powers were not always distinctly drawn. It is in this world where our story starts, the world of the Reformation, the world of the Tudor court, the world of Martin Luther. It was a world where free speech was neither celebrated nor practised. Books were publicly burned, as were heretics. The printing trade was licensed and it was to rail against licensing that the first arguments towards freedom of expression were made, by John Milton in the middle of the seventeenth century and later, towards its end, by Locke. Their arguments are considered in detail in chapter one.

Chapter two opens at the dawn of the Enlightenment. The first fully secular argument for free speech in England was made by the radical Whigs, John Trenchard and Thomas Gordon, in a number of their co-authored *Cato's Letters* (1721–23). Not all their contemporaries were convinced that free speech was as uncritically to be welcomed as Trenchard and Gordon maintained. The most resonant notes of scepticism were sounded first by Jonathan Swift, author of *Gulliver's Travels* (1726), and then by Samuel Johnson. Their competing contentions are set out and explored in chapter two, as are the ways in which the English courts started to grapple with them, not least in cases concerning John Wilkes, John Entick and the troublesome law of seditious libel. It was not until the early nineteenth century that sedition came to be understood more as a offence against public disorder than a crime of illicit expression. By the time John Stuart Mill came to write the most famous essay ever written in English about free speech – *On Liberty* (1859) – he saw that social censure, pursued as a crusade against offensiveness, posed just as grave a threat to free expression as criminal sanction. Mill's great argument for human flourishing, and its moment of eventual triumph in the 'liberal hour' of the 1960s and 1970s, is where chapter two closes.

Chapter three moves from the struggle for the *idea* of speaking freely to the struggle for the *law* to adopt it. Its story starts in the United States, where the US Supreme Court played such a central role in turning freedom of speech into an enforceable right. The First Amendment to the US Constitution now offers the most sophisticated and most ardently protective free speech law in the world. But it was not always so, and the story of the long struggle to 'awaken' the First Amendment is told in chapter three. The contrast with the rather dismal view the English common law took in the twentieth century to freedom of speech is considerable. That story, too, is told in chapter three, as is the influence brought to bear on the common law by European human rights law. The case law of the European Court of Human Rights on the Article 10 right to freedom of expression[4] was, as the twentieth century came to a close, impressive. Regrettably, though, the Strasbourg court has lost its way in more recent years. The decline of its commitment to free speech can be seen in cases surveyed not only in chapter three, but also in chapter four (on media freedom) and chapter five (on offensive and hate speech). It is one of the most worrying findings of

---

[4] European Convention on Human Rights, Article 10. In this book, ECHR means the European Convention on Human Rights and ECtHR means the European Court of Human Rights (which sits in Strasbourg).

the book: that Europe's premier human rights court seems to have lost its grip on the importance of the right to free speech.

Chapters one, two and three comprise part I of the book, 'the struggle for free speech'. Chapters four, five and six comprise part II, 'free speech today'. Each chapter in part II examines a different aspect in which free speech today is problematic, seeking to analyse the issues in the light of the legal and historical stories told in part one. Thus, chapter four concerns media freedom, chapter five concerns offensive and hate speech, and chapter six concerns online safety and how free speech can be navigated in the modern world of internet search engines, algorithms and social media.

Chapter four starts with licensing – not of the press, but of broadcasting. It argues that even if sweeping broadcasting regulation was justified when the technology was in its infancy, in today's landscape of satellite TV, cable and streaming services, the breadth of legal restrictions imposed on broadcasting is ever harder to justify. In the United States this was understood 40 years ago but it has yet to be grasped in Britain and Europe. Especially onerous are the UK's rules prohibiting political advertising in the broadcast media, rules which have been interpreted so broadly they are disproportionate. The press, too, operates under the burden of legal restrictions which can be hard to justify, notably as regards the ways in which courts in the United Kingdom have extended rights to privacy to an extent far greater than Parliament intended when it enacted the Human Rights Act in 1998. This is a tougher argument to make, though, than that regarding broadcasting, because of the woeful behaviour of (elements of) the press in the 1990s and early 2000s. Where the Leveson report (2012) leaves press freedom is where chapter four ends.

Chapter five is on hate speech, examining the matter not only in the United Kingdom but in Canada, in the United States and in European human rights law. It argues (contrary to the dominant position in the United States) that some restriction on hate speech can appropriately be imposed but, equally, that the restrictions enacted in England and Wales – and even more so in Scotland – go too far in their punishment of speech and should be liberalised. This applies not only to the stirring-up offences (which are analysed in depth) but also to the communications offences, which are too often overlooked in this context. The law here can be complex – and there is much unavoidable devilry in its detail – but a model hate speech law is set out and defended, as a benchmark against which to assess rules currently in force not only in the United Kingdom, but elsewhere too. With Mill's prescient warning in mind, the chapter considers not only the criminal law relating to hate speech but also the ways in which employment law is having to come to terms with how individuals can be pilloried and subjected to intense social censure for expressing themselves. How the law responds to 'cancel culture' is critical to how it seeks to set limits to hate speech.

The book closes with online speech. Chapter six asks how speech is different online and how, given its differences, it needs bespoke legal regulation. It examines problems of 'fake news' and disinformation and finds that, even if the technology is new, the problems are not. There is much that the likes of Jonathan Swift said about speech in the eighteenth century which can help guide us through the maze of internet regulation. As such, chapter six acts much like a coda, bringing a number of the book's arguments to a conclusion.

If this book is concerned mainly with free speech in the United Kingdom, it seeks to place both historical and current disputes in comparative perspective. Britain's struggles for – and against – free speech cannot be understood in splendid isolation, after all. The Reformation (and Counter-Reformation) were Europe-wide. Printing came to England from Europe. So, during times of domestic repression, did books (notably from the Netherlands). The book trade was exactly that – an aspect of trade, of transnational commerce. Likewise now: the United Kingdom is hardly the only country in the world to be grappling with media freedom, hate speech or online safety. Appreciating the strengths and limitations of British legal and policy approaches to these matters is aided by assessing them in the light of what is happening in other comparable jurisdictions. For a British free speech lawyer, the two most important comparators are the United States and the case law of the European Court of Human Rights. The book includes extensive treatment of both.

This book is intended for anyone with an interest in free speech, whether expert, beginner or anywhere in between. Whilst I hope that other academic lawyers may enjoy it, it is certainly not written for academics or lawyers alone. Policymakers, journalists, political commentators, students, activists and others all need to understand what free speech entails – and what it does not.

In neither Britain, nor in the United States or Europe, is free speech today in a good place. Elements of the political left appear to have given up on it, regarding it as little more than a bastion for bigots, or a haven for populist kleptocrats. Elements of the right seem to regard it as a political football, to be kicked about as a weapon in the culture wars. Both are doing immense damage to the idea of free speech. If this book can help those who would like to see free speech rescued from the culture wars, it will have a served a large measure of its purpose. Forty years ago lawyers who wrote about free speech in Britain tended to be civil liberties lawyers who had authoritarian governments in their sights. As the twenty-first century dawned, liberal internationalists could write about free speech as if it were a Western value to be globally exported: the West telling the rest how to live and be governed. The election and re-election of Donald Trump to the US presidency, the Brexit vote and the rise of authoritarian populism in Eastern Europe and elsewhere, have well and truly shot the arrogance of that particular fox, dividing the West in on itself and shattering its misplaced self-confidence. More recently, commercially produced books on free speech have tended to contribute to the culture wars, rather than to rescue free speech from them.

This book is different and is aimed as a sort of corrective. I believe very strongly in free speech, but I am absolutely not a free speech absolutist. Free speech is vital – absolutely vital – but properly understood, it has limits. Our commitment to it is tested not by our preparedness to defend expression we agree with, but by our willingness to defend expression we not merely disagree with, but dislike or find objectionable. Likewise, our support for censorship or for the sanctioning of speech is tested not when expression we disapprove of is censured, but when speech we would like to hear is silenced.

My own interest in the law of free speech was first kindled when I was in the final year of my undergraduate studies. It was 1990, the time of the *Spycatcher* saga (on which see chapter three), the *Satanic Verses* and Salman Rushdie being forced into hiding. I wrote a dissertation on these matters, and on the Thatcher Government's broadcasting ban relating to Northern Ireland (which led to the *Brind* case, also considered in chapter three).[5] Like any UK lawyer interested in free speech, my first debt is to Eric Barendt's book, *Freedom of Speech*. I read its first edition when I was an undergraduate, and the current edition has never been far from reach on my shelf as I worked on this book.[6] After Barendt, the next most influential book on my thinking about speech and law was Simon Lee's short work, *The Cost of Free Speech*, which I read right at the beginning of my academic career.[7] Both its argument and, even more so, its way of writing accessibly about topical debates in law have stayed with me ever since. As a young academic my research and writing thereafter moved away from free speech, tackling other aspects of constitutional and public law instead. My eventual return to the law of free expression came not in the academy, but in the Scottish Parliament. I stepped back from full-time academic life for a five-year period, whilst I served as a Member of the Scottish Parliament (2016–21). In my last six months as an MSP I worked on two bills which related directly to free speech: namely, the Defamation and Malicious Publication (Scotland) Act 2021 and the Hate Crime and Public Order (Scotland) Act 2021. The latter is considered in chapter five.

---

[5] For a rather more recent essay on Salman Rushdie and freedom of speech, see Adam Tomkins, 'Words and Weapons', *Law and Liberty*, 17 May 2024 (available at: lawliberty.org/book-review/words-and-weapons-in-salman-rushdie/).

[6] Eric Barendt, *Freedom of Speech* (Oxford, Oxford University Press, 2nd edn 2005).

[7] Simon Lee, *The Cost of Free Speech* (London, Faber & Faber, 1990).

The experience of working on those bills made a lasting impression and led me to start thinking about writing this book.

After returning full-time to academic life in 2021, I have had the opportunity to rehearse some of the ideas and arguments in this book with several audiences. At my home university, the University of Glasgow, I delivered the 2021 James Wood Lecture on 'Free Speech and Hate Speech', for which I am grateful to my colleagues, Professor James Chalmers and Professor Jane Mair. Friends and colleagues at the Antonin Scalia Law School, George Mason University, Virginia; at the Harry Radzyner Law School, Reichman University, Herzliya; and at the Jagiellonian University, Kraków helped me sharpen my arguments. Back home, a roundtable on the Online Safety Act, hosted by Glasgow's public law research cluster, was invaluable to the development of chapter six, and I thank Martin Kretschmer, Stefan Luca, Claire McDiarmid, Micheál Ó Floinn, Philip Schlesinger and Konstantinos Stylianou for their insights. I thank my colleagues Ana Cannilla and Michael Foran for their expert comments on an early draft of part of chapter five. I also thank my editors at the *Herald* and at Liberty Fund's *Law and Liberty* website for giving me platforms to write about free speech. I owe a particular debt to the Liberty Fund, and to all the scholars I have been privileged to meet through its work. My friends Sarah Skwire and Brian Smith know how much I appreciate this, I hope. For ongoing support, companionship, friendship and counsel, I thank Eddie Barnes, Lionel Bently, Stephen Bogle, Donald Cameron, Emilios Christodoulidis, Timothy Endicott, Lindsay Farmer, Michael Foran, Marco Goldoni, Liam Kerr, Alex Schwartz and David Womersley, all of whom helped me as I worked on this book. Most of all I thank my family – my rock – my parents Karen and Bill, my partner Susan and my children. It is to my children that this book is dedicated: to Oliver, Leo, Phoebe and Jasper. May they always speak freely.

Adam Tomkins
Glasgow
30 November 2024

TABLE OF CONTENTS

PART II
FREE SPEECH TODAY

PART I

The Struggle for Free Speech

1

The Age of Heresy

I. From Reformation to Civil War

A. 'In the Beginning was the Word'

Martin Luther, erstwhile law student, monk at Erfurt, and professor of theology, both wrote and spoke about the ways in which he disagreed with the teachings and practices of the church. Whether or not it actually happened, his most infamous act was the nailing of his Ninety-Five Theses to the Wittenberg church door in 1517.[1] In retrospect, this moment came to be seen as the 'opening salvo' in the Reformation's great 'challenge to the medieval Catholic order'.[2] What is certain is that Luther's preaching and writings were central to that challenge. Luther was no proponent of free speech as we would understand it today. He presided over book burnings himself, not least the public burning in Wittenberg of the papal bull by which he had been excommunicated (in 1520, the same year in which Luther's own books had been publicly burned in Rome). But, strikingly, at the heart of the Reformation lay the sacred importance of the Word of God and the belief that an individual's salvation could lie only in the Word of God – in the scriptures themselves – and not in any intervening act, ritual or rite of priestcraft.

Words, and free access to them, were the very point of the Reformation, one of whose foundational texts was the opening line of St John's Gospel: 'In the beginning was the Word, and the Word was with God, and the Word was God.'[3] Luther believed that the only route to salvation was by faith

---

[1] There is no doubt about the Ninety-Five Theses, but it may be a legend that Luther nailed them to the church door: see Walter Stephens, *How Writing Made us Human* (Baltimore, Johns Hopkins University Press, 2023) 294 and Quentin Skinner, *The Foundations of Modern Political Thought* (Cambridge, Cambridge University Press, 1978, vol 2) 3.

[2] Francis Oakley, 'Christian Obedience and Authority, 1520–1550' in JH Burns and Mark Goldie (eds), *The Cambridge History of Political Thought 1450–1700* (Cambridge, Cambridge University Press, 1991) 164.

[3] John 1:1. On the importance of these extraordinary words to the issues surveyed in this chapter, see Robin Vose, *The Index of Prohibited Books* (London, Reaktion, 2022) 10–13.

alone – *sola fide* – and that divine grace could be obtained only through the scriptures, not through public works, or via the authority of a priest or the mediation of the church. This, in the view of the (established, Catholic) church, was heresy. But, for Luther, the church, properly conceived, was not an institution, still less a hierarchy, but the communion of Christian souls. As it developed through the early 1520s, his argument became less that the powers of the church had been abused and more that the church had no right to claim powers over Christian souls at all.[4] The sacraments of the church offered no hope of salvation, for salvation could come from faith alone. Grace could come not from the priestly interventions of the church, but only from God directly, mediated by Christ and through scripture alone.[5]

This was a profound set of challenges not only to the church's teachings, but to its power. The sale of indulgences, for example, by which souls could be released from torment in purgatory, was a key source of revenue for a church intent on building gigantic, awe-inspiring cathedrals. Luther, who condemned such practices as 'clerical confidence tricks',[6] craved a simpler Christianity: a return to the message, in particular, of Paul, that Christians should focus on love, charity and compassion rather than worry about worshipping idols or paying homage to relics. At the heart of this message was loving thy neighbour,[7] the 'fruit of the Spirit' being love, peace, gentleness and meekness.[8]

Luther's works reached England in 1519, whereupon Henry VIII promptly banned them.[9] For his repudiation of Luther,[10] Henry was named '*Defensor Fidei*' by the pope, a title ('Defender of the Faith') still borne by the reigning monarch of the United Kingdom. Yet, in England as elsewhere in Europe, Luther's theology met with support, as well as – at least to start with – official opposition. Despite the brutal treatment of heretics – as 'society's worst enemy'[11] they were liable to be burnt at the stake – there

---

[4] See Skinner (n 1) 13.

[5] As Sheldon Wolin notes, Luther's most fervent belief was that 'the Word of God, which teaches full freedom, should not and must not be fettered' (see *Politics and Vision* (Princeton, Princeton University Press, expanded edn 2004) 128). Everything standing between God and man – all intermediaries – must be removed: 'the only true mediators were Christ and Scripture' itself (ibid 134).

[6] Diarmaid MacCulloch, *Reformation: Europe's House Divided* (London, Penguin, 2004) 15.

[7] Romans 13:9.

[8] Galatians 5:22–23.

[9] Among Luther's most vociferous and vehement critics was Thomas More, who would be Henry's Lord Chancellor from 1529 to 1532. More called Luther 'a mad friar-let and privy-minded rascal with his ragings and ravings, with his filth and dung'. See Alister McGrath, *In the Beginning: The Story of the King James Bible* (London, Hodder and Stoughton, 2002) 82.

[10] In *The Assertion of the Seven Sacraments* (1521).

[11] Susan Brigden, *New Worlds, Lost Worlds: The Rule of the Tudors 1485–1603* (London, Penguin, 2001) 84.

had been heretics in fifteenth-century England, as there continued to be in Henry's reign in the sixteenth. The Lollards, inspired by the ideas of the fourteenth-century theologian John Wyclif, met together in houses rather than in churches to read the scriptures – the Gospels and Epistles of the New Testament – in English, aloud. This was illegal, the English Bible having been outlawed since 1409.[12] The Lollards were the spiritual forebears of the puritans. For them, as for Luther, the Word of God was everything. They regarded Catholic devotion as superstition and Catholic veneration as idolatry. Their gravest heresy, perhaps, was to doubt the miracle of transubstantiation: 'Lollards believed that to worship the consecrated Host was idolatry, as was the veneration of images and crucifixes'.[13] For them, it was not only idolatrous but 'socially iniquitous' to devote time and money to serving saints' images rather than to serving the poor.

There is doubt about how far and wide Lollardy spread but, whatever their numbers, they never posed a serious threat to the established order.[14] Reformation succeeded[15] after 1517 whereas earlier theological protests had withered for two main reasons: one technological and the other intellectual.[16] The first was the coming to Europe of the printing press. Johannes Gutenberg commenced printing in Mainz in the 1450s. The Englishman William Caxton learnt the trade in Cologne in the early 1470s, bringing his knowledge home in 1476. The first book he printed in England was Geoffrey Chaucer's *The Canterbury Tales*.[17] Across Europe, the growth of printing was meteoric: there were only four printing workshops in 1462 but 1,700 by the end of the century. In that period (of less than 50 years) something like 13 million books were produced in Europe, more than the Continent's scribes had been able to produce in the previous millennium.[18] Reformation theology and technological innovation marched hand in hand. Luther's Ninety-Five Theses sparked an immediate pamphlet war, being circulated as rapidly in print as were the many counter-arguments it spawned.[19] As Diarmaid MacCulloch notes, Protestantism 'would prove to be good business for printers' just as 'printing turned out to be good for

---

[12] ibid 86.

[13] ibid 88.

[14] See John Guy, *Tudor England* (Oxford, Oxford University Press, 1990) 25–26.

[15] 'Succeeded' in the sense that it endured, not in the sense that it overcame or overthrew Catholicism. Dividing western Christianity and unleashing centuries of religious warfare in Europe may, to some readers, appear an odd measure of 'success'.

[16] As we shall see, in England there was also a third reason: King Henry VIII's desire for divorce and remarriage.

[17] See Adam Smyth, *The Book Makers* (London, Bodley Head, 2024) ch 1.

[18] See Jacob Mchangama, *Free Speech: A Global History from Socrates to Social Media* (London, Basic Books, 2022) 63.

[19] MacCulloch (n 6) 124 and 152.

Protestantism'. After all, 'a religion of the book needs books'.[20] It was not only the *availability* of books which was revolutionary, though: it was also that printing changed *how* people thought about the written word and the authority it may carry. Medieval scribes copied. Each copy was a one-off: if it was lost in a fire, it was lost forever. The work was painstaking. The industry it required privileged accuracy over anything else. Those who devoted long hours to copying had – by definition – neither time nor incentive for original thought. What was important was that copies of the same thing (most often, of course, the Bible) were made over and again, being the only insurance available against loss. The dominant culture was to guard, not to spread, knowledge.[21] This is the world that the printing press turned inside out.

If printing was the technology which underpinned the Reformation, it owed a similar debt to the power of ideas: in particular, to humanism and to its central figure, Desiderius Erasmus. Humanists were 'lovers and connoisseurs of words'.[22] They saw words as 'containing power' which could be used to 'change human society' for the better, and they found them in ancient texts – not only in Plato, Aristotle and Cicero, but in the Bible.[23] Taking a lead, as would Luther, from Paul's Letters, Erasmus' great ambition was to spread the Word not only to the educated, but to everyone. For Erasmus, 'true religion lay in righteous conduct, not fatuous ceremonies'.[24] Erasmus was hugely popular both across the Continent and in England. Among his readers was Thomas More, whose *Utopia* (1516) is in part a response to Erasmus' work *In Praise of Folly*, an early draft of which was written whilst Erasmus was More's guest in London.[25] Erasmus translated the whole of the New Testament and published parallel Greek and Latin texts in 1516. The translation 'created a sensation'[26] yet, even so, the Bible was still 'locked up in Latin, mediated by priests'.[27] In England, William

---

[20] ibid 72. As MacCulloch records, had printing technology been available to him, the Czech Jan Hus (who died in 1415) might have been the central figure in the European Reformation, rather than the men who lived a century after him, Luther, Zwingli and Calvin. Walter Stephens makes the same point: Stephens (n 1) 298.

[21] MacCulloch (n 6) 74.

[22] ibid 77.

[23] ibid 77–78.

[24] Brigden (n 11) 90. Erasmus was no Lutheran. The two men may have agreed on the need for the Bible to be made more widely available but, thereafter, they agreed on little else. Indeed, Erasmus was recruited to rebut Luther, as in his 1524 tract *On the Freedom of the Will*. On this tract, and on Luther's impassioned response to it in *The Bondage of the Will* (1525), see Skinner (n 1) 4–5. Erasmus remained Catholic all his life – if the church needed reforming, he thought, it should be reformed from within. When he died (in 1536) he did not feel his career had been a success: MacCulloch (n 6) 105.

[25] Brigden (ibid) 92.

[26] Lucy Wooding, *Tudor England: A History* (New Haven, Yale University Press, 2023) 105.

[27] Brigden (n 11) 93.

Tyndale wanted to go further. For him, as for the Lutherans, Christians should believe 'nothing' without the authority of God's Word: 'Scripture enshrined all religious truth. They believed that from the freedom to read the Word followed another: the liberation from priestly authority.'[28] Luther's German translation of the Bible was published in 1522; Tyndale's English translation of the New Testament was available in London in early 1526.[29] The authorities were horrified. The Bishop of London banned the book, summoned London's booksellers, and warned them against it. Having found as many copies as he could, the bishop arranged yet another public book-burning.[30]

B. Henry VIII: Regime Change

Yet within a decade the official view of England's regime changed. In 1534 Henry VIII became the first monarch in Europe to break decisively with Rome. He did so less because of theological differences with the pope and more because he wished to terminate his marriage to Catherine of Aragon and wed Anne Boleyn instead. This the pope refused to permit. Parliament passed the Act of Supremacy 1534, which separated the English church from Rome and consolidated vast power in the English Crown. The king, his heirs and successors, said the Act, 'shall have full power and authority from time to time to visit, repress, redress, reform, order, correct, restrain, and amend all such errors, heresies, abuses, offences, contempts, and enormities, whatsoever they be.'[31] Thus began the Henrician Reformation and the establishment of the Church of England, a development which would set England at odds not only with papal authority, but with the course Protestantism was to take on the Continent. England's Reformation was top-down, implemented by the Crown and for the Crown.

Alongside the Act of Supremacy Parliament also passed the Treason Act 1534, the first major revision of the law of treason since 1352.[32]

---

[28] ibid 98. Freedom to read the Bible in the vernacular, however, did not mean freedom to read a book that preached the virtues of free speech. The Word of God contains many more warnings about the dangers of speech than it includes statements that tongues should be unbridled. Among numerous examples are the following: 'Thou shalt not revile the gods, nor curse the ruler of the people' (Exodus 22:28); 'Curse not the king, no not in thy thought' (Ecclesiastes 10:20); 'Keep thy tongue from evil, and thy lips from speaking guile' (Psalms 34:13). For discussion of these and other, similar, warnings, see David Cressy, *Dangerous Talk: Scandalous, Seditious, and Treasonable Speech in Pre-Modern England* (Oxford, Oxford University Press, 2010) ch 1.

[29] See McGrath (n 9) 80.

[30] ibid 83.

[31] Act of Supremacy 1534. See JR Tanner, *Tudor Constitutional Documents 1485–1603* (Cambridge, Cambridge University Press, 1930) 47.

[32] Guy (n 14) 136.

No longer was the offence confined to 'compassing or imagining (ie, intending) the king's death' or to 'levying war against the king' (as the law had provided since 1352). Now, in addition, the subject was a traitor if he failed to follow the king in matters of religious belief, or in the changes he made from time to time in the status of his various wives. Moreover, by this Act mere words were made a treason: calling the king a heretic (or even a schismatic) was punishable by death, not by being burnt alive (that particular torment was reserved for heretics) but by being hanged and, whilst still (just about) alive, drawn and quartered. The phrase 'on pain of death' was meant quite literally. Executions were unspeakably savage.[33] The Treason Act 1534 provided as follows:

> if any person or persons ... do maliciously wish, will, or desire by words or writing, or by crafty images invent, practise, or attempt any bodily harm to be done or committed to the King's most royal person, the Queen's, or their heirs apparent, or to deprive them or any of them of the dignity, title, or name of their royal estates, or slanderously and maliciously publish and pronounce, by express writing or words, that the King our Sovereign Lord should be heretic, schismatic, tyrant, infidel, or usurper of the Crown, ... then every such person or persons, ... their aiders, counsellors, consenters, and abettors, being thereof lawfully convict according to the laws and customs of this realm, shall be adjudged traitors.[34]

To compound all this, an Act of 1536 for 'extinguishing the authority of the Bishop of Rome' made it treason for any clerical or lay official to refuse an oath to renounce all papal authority and to support the king's supremacy.[35] This was the first time that 'a spiritual instrument of commitment had been used as a political test'.[36] Among those who were caught in its net of repression was Thomas More. In 1535 he was tried for and convicted of treason, and executed.

The new Church of England was no Lutheran sect. Rather, Anglicanism would evolve into a strange, indeed unique, hybrid between Catholic traditions and Protestant practices. There would still be bishops, hierarchy and priestly vestments: 'the English national church would have an essentially Catholic structure ... while adopting a basically Protestant set of beliefs ... The settlement was a compromise, and was widely recognised as such'.[37]

---

[33] In the 1530s some 63 people were executed in England for speaking treasonous words: see Rebecca Lemon, *Treason by Words: Literature, Law and Rebellion in Shakespeare's England* (Ithaca, Cornell University Press, 2011) 10.

[34] Treason Act 1534 (see Tanner (n 31) 388–89). Trial by 'the laws and customs of this realm' meant, in the case of treason, that accused persons were entitled only to limited legal representation and that they could not compel witnesses for their defence. Prosecutors, by contrast, laboured under no such restrictions (Tanner 421).

[35] ibid 379.

[36] Brigden (n 11) 121.

[37] McGrath (n 9) 125.

Only three of the seven Catholic sacraments were considered necessary – baptism, the eucharist and penance – the others being 'passed over in silence'.[38] Henry was still Defender of the Faith; he saw it as his role both to identify and to defend orthodoxy. To this end he commissioned Thomas Cranmer, Archbishop of Canterbury, to prepare a statement of church doctrine. Cranmer's Ten Articles would, in time, evolve into the Thirty-Nine Articles which, since the beginning of Elizabeth I's reign, have been appended to the *Book of Common Prayer*.[39] One, earlier, iteration of Cranmer's text was converted by Parliament into statute and given the apt title of 'An Act abolishing diversity in Opinions'.[40]

As well as an official statement of doctrine and a prayer book, the Church of England also needed a Bible. Anne Boleyn was a keen supporter of the vernacular Bible: 'she sponsored Tyndale's forbidden New Testament, and interceded for those persecuted for its sake'.[41] Cranmer wanted an authoritative translation in English, as did Thomas Cromwell (Henry's principal secretary and chief minister until his fall in 1540), under whose order in 1538 an English version of the Bible was to be placed in every parish – quite the reverse of the official position when Tyndale's translation of the New Testament had first appeared in the shops and stalls of the London booksellers. The Tudors were among the first to appreciate that the power of the press could be harnessed to serve the authorities' interests. Cromwell invested both his own money and the Crown's resources in paying London's printers to produce thousands of copies of the Bible.[42] Cromwell's mission proved so successful that Henry took fright, ordering after Cromwell's death that 'only upper status groups in society, presumably deemed less excitable', should be allowed to read the Bible for themselves.[43] Henry saw the Bible as a bulwark of the Crown's power, not as source from which his preferred doctrine could be challenged. He explained his position to Parliament in 1545 in the following terms:

> [A]lthough you be permitted to read Holy Scripture and to have the Word of God in your mother tongue, you must understand that it is licensed you so to do, only to inform your own conscience, and to instruct your children and family; and not to dispute and make Scripture a railing and a taunting stock against priests and preachers, as many light persons do.[44]

[38] DL Keir, *The Constitutional History of Modern Britain 1485–1937* (London, A & C Black, 1938) 70.

[39] The *Book of Common Prayer*, prepared by Cranmer, was first introduced in 1549 and was revised in 1552. Queen Mary withdrew it, but, thereafter, Queen Elizabeth restored its use in substantially the same form as the 1552 version.

[40] Statute of Six Articles 1539: see Tanner (n 31) 95.

[41] Brigden (n 11) 114.

[42] Guy (n 14) 182.

[43] MacCulloch (n 6) 203.

[44] See Wooding (n 26) 257.

There was no one authoritative – still less, formally authorised – English translation. There was Tyndale's New Testament (1526) and his translation of the first five books of the Old Testament (the Torah, or Pentateuch) (1530). And then there were several different versions of the whole Bible published (in English) in quick succession: the Coverdale Bible of 1535, the Matthew's Bible of 1537, and the Great Bible of 1539. Later in the century the most widely read Bible in England, as in Scotland, was the Geneva Bible of 1560. This was the Bible Shakespeare knew, but its popularity came despite official opposition to it rather than because it had been authorised by either church or Crown. In the end, an Authorised Version of the Bible would come only in the next century: the King James Bible in 1611.

As is evident, the English Reformation did not herald an age of free speech. Henry was as determined to impose the new orthodoxy on his nation as he had been to defend the Catholic regime so threatened, earlier in his reign, by Luther and his ilk. The new Royal Supremacy was to be insisted upon every bit as rigorously as had been the old order, before the schism with Rome. Heresy was still an offence in England, albeit now a criminal offence executed by lay tribunals rather than, as before, a matter for the ecclesiastical courts.[45] As Susan Brigden notes, 'the break with Rome had never been meant to augur the end of persecution'.[46] Yet, in the main, the laws were meant to terrify without having actually to be used. The new settlement may have given the king 'alarming new powers over conscience' but they were 'kept as a threat which was usually unfulfilled'.[47] Later Tudor reigns were bloodier.

C. Reformation, Counter-Reformation and the Anglican Establishment

Henry died in 1547 and was succeeded by his son, Edward VI. Young Edward was only nine years old when he became king and he never reached maturity, dying aged 15 in 1553. His short reign – which was, throughout, a regency – was marked by attempts to draw the Church of England

---

[45] See Keir (n 38) 70.

[46] Brigden (n 11) 133. John Stuart Mill caustically noted in *On Liberty* (1859) that 'those who first broke the yoke of what called itself the Universal Church were in general as little willing to permit difference of religious opinion as that church itself'. See John Stuart Mill, *On Liberty and Other Essays* (John Gray (ed), Oxford, Oxford University Press, 1991) 12. Mill's views on free speech are discussed in ch 2.

[47] Brigden 163–64. Keir was of the same view: 'the rest of [Henry's] reign witnessed little systematic persecution' (Keir (n 38) 70).

further away from Catholicism and nearer to continental Protestantism. It was during his reign that Cranmer's *Book of Common Prayer* was first published. His reign also saw rapid growth in England's printing and book trade. This may have had something to do with a number of Henry's controls on printing being lifted, but it may have had more to do with the sudden intensification of the persecution of Protestants on the Continent (particularly in the Low Countries) and the consequent migration of printers from Antwerp to London.[48]

Edward was succeeded by Mary, Henry's daughter by his first wife, Catherine of Aragon. She was, like her mother, an avowed Catholic and she sought to restore England to the Catholic faith. Her reign is notorious for its bloodthirstiness. Between 1555 and 1558 alone, some 300 heretics were burnt at the stake. Among them was Thomas Cranmer. We should be cautious about her notoriety, though. That she is even now known to school children as 'Bloody Mary' is testament to the enduring power of Elizabethan propaganda. Viewed in European perspective, her 'inquisition' was 'small scale'.[49] Throughout, Mary's aim had been not to burn heretics but to convert them; every burning was a public and brutal admission of failure.

Mary fell ill and died in 1558, to be succeeded by her half-sister Elizabeth.[50] In the first decade of the new reign there was far less persecution and fewer tests of faith. Elizabeth famously 'desired no windows into her own soul nor into those of others'.[51] Her hope and expectation was that the sheer passage of time would simply atrophy 'the traditional faith'. It was not to be. A Catholic uprising in the north of England, inspired in part by the presence on English soil of Mary Queen of Scots, was met with violent retribution: more than 700 men were hanged under martial law.[52] In response, Pius V issued a papal bull in 1570 excommunicating Elizabeth and declaring her to be no queen, commanding all Catholics to withdraw allegiance and placing every Catholic in the realm under a moral obligation to dislodge her from the throne.[53] In 1571 the House of Commons, excluded of Catholics who could not in conscience swear the required oath, extended the treason laws to include all those who imported papal bulls. Persecution returned with a vengeance, and not only in England.

---

[48] Compare, eg, Wooding (n 26) 292 and MacCulloch (n 6) 256.

[49] Guy (n 14) 227.

[50] Elizabeth was Henry's daughter by his second wife, Anne Boleyn.

[51] The remark is widely quoted: see, eg, Guy (n 14) 296 and Brigden (n 11) 237. Guy attributes the words to Francis Bacon.

[52] Wooding (n 26) 458. Mary Queen of Scots fled Scotland in 1567 to seek refuge in England, where she was kept prisoner for 20 years before Elizabeth reluctantly but finally agreed that she be executed. Throughout that period she was heir presumptive to the English throne. She was avowedly Catholic and became a focal point for Catholic disloyalty in England.

[53] ibid 459, 464.

In the 1572 St Bartholomew's Day Massacre, as many as 5,000 Huguenots (French Protestants) were butchered and slaughtered. The bloodbath shook all Europe and outraged the House of Commons. Inevitably, repression was met with repression. In 1577 Cuthbert Mayne became the first of more than 200 Catholics to be martyred in Elizabeth's England.[54]

From the perspective of speech and its unfreedom in the Age of Heresy, one of the most significant consequences of the Protestant Reformation was the creation (and subsequent expansion) of the *Index Librorum Prohibitorum*: the Index of Prohibited Books. This was a list of authors and their works, maintained by the Vatican, which were prohibited to Catholics. A recent study of the Index suggests it was,

> arguably the most important, longest-lived and least understood institutional exercise in censorship that has ever been attempted. At some times and in some places, it did incalculable harm to the history of human creativity. It was also in many ways a failure.[55]

The Index is 'what full-blooded ideological censorship looks like'.[56] It dates from 1559 and, astonishingly, it was maintained for more than four centuries, being formally abandoned only in 1966. The Papal Index of 1559 was not the first such list of banned works. In 1529 Thomas More had drawn up an earlier list for Henry VIII.[57] The theology professors of the University of Paris compiled an index of prohibited works in 1544, their counterparts at the University of Leuven following suit two years later. The Spanish Inquisition used its own index, which dated from 1551, and for centuries the Spanish index existed alongside the Vatican's (the Spanish Inquisition was permanently closed only in 1834).[58] There was much overlap between them but, at the same time, some books (or authors) were prohibited in one index but not in the other. After the English Reformation there was nothing like such a scheme of censorship in England. Heresy was a crime, as we have seen, but its scope never came close to matching that of the Index.[59]

The 1559 Papal Index ran to 70 printed pages and prohibited some 1,100 works. It was printed in an easily portable format, akin to a modern paperback, and was designed to be readily used across Catholic Europe.

---

[54] Brigden (n 11) 266.

[55] Vose (n 3) 7.

[56] Debora Shuger, *Censorship and Cultural Sensibility: The Regulation of Language in Tudor-Stuart England* (Philadelphia, University of Pennsylvania Press, 2006) 62.

[57] Among many grim ironies of the Index, More's *Utopia* (1516) was prohibited by the papal Index.

[58] The Spanish Index included even Jesuit texts and banned all Spanish books printed outside Spain. It also forbade Spaniards from studying abroad: see MacCulloch (n 6) 299.

[59] See Shuger (n 56) 63. As we shall see, in seventeenth-century England, it was the domestic *printing* of books, rather than access to them as such, which was licensed.

It was 'extremely onerous, especially in its proscription of entire categories of books that might in fact have no heretical content whatsoever'.[60] Thus, all books written by heretics,[61] all books printed without an author's and a publisher's name, and all books produced by a printer who had in the past published a heretical work were included on the Index. It was not only Lutherans and later Protestants whose works were banned: Erasmus himself was placed on the Index from the beginning: all of his works were prohibited.[62]

Once established, the Index needed to be maintained: as the publishing industry grew, keeping it up to date required considerable institutional infrastructure and personnel. Updates in the 1590s doubled the number of prohibited works. By the middle of the following century the Index was no longer a convenient paperback, but a huge and cumbersome work of reference designed to be relied upon by local censors when deciding what to license for printing, and what to suppress. It was not long before the Index, at least in some places, was counterproductive, undermining the very purposes for which it had been compiled. In 1627 the head of the Bodleian Library in Oxford reprinted the Index not as a list of banned works, but as a 'bibliographical resource ... of all the greatest works of Protestant scholarship', using it as a guide for librarians as to what should be collected and preserved on their shelves.[63]

Despite being easily satirised in this way, huge resource was poured into maintaining and updating the Index. Its reach was extraordinary. Copernicus, Galileo, Isaac Newton, Mercator (as in the famous *Atlas*), Machiavelli, Bodin, Grotius, Hobbes, Pufendorf, Locke, Spinoza, Leibniz, Montesquieu, Voltaire, Diderot, Rousseau, Hume, Kant and John Stuart Mill were just a few of the authors whose works were prohibited. Thus were several of the core and classical works of the European Enlightenment, of scientific discovery, and of political theory banned and, for prolonged periods, made effectively unavailable in Italy, Spain, Portugal, their colonies and elsewhere. In the nineteenth and twentieth centuries the Index was used as an instrument of suppression ranging far away from the context of Protestant heresy which had first inspired it. Catholic censorship in the sixteenth and seventeenth centuries was onerous. But in England, too, repressive laws underscored and extended the state's intolerance of anything it considered to be heretical or treasonous.

---

[60] Vose (n 3) 62.
[61] Debora Shuger notes that 'the crucial feature' of the Index was its grounding in heresy law: 'this link between the regulation of the press and the repression of heresy was explicit from the beginning'. See Shuger (n 56) 56.
[62] MacCulloch (n 6) 277.
[63] Vose (n 3) 87–88.

In Elizabethan England it was not only Catholics who were persecuted, it was Presbyterians too. Elizabethan Anglicanism, rather like the Church of England of her father's reign, found that it had to fight on two fronts, Calvinists being little more tolerated than those who were loyal to Rome. The invention of Anglicanism may have drawn on both Catholic traditions and Protestant beliefs, but its unique hybridity was in no sense a liberal compromise, nodding to the righteous virtues of each. It was, rather, its own version of authority, which required 'emphatic championing'.[64] This required not only its careful explication in works such as Richard Hooker's *Laws of Ecclesiastical Polity* (1593) but, where perceived to be necessary, repression. Following the violence of the early 1570s, it was Catholics who were the most hounded in England. By the 1590s 'the erosion of parish Catholicism was largely complete'.[65] English Catholics were fined recusancy fines;[66] some suffered long imprisonment; they were excluded from Parliament, from office-holding and from university education; and, after 1593, they were not even permitted to travel more than five miles from their homes without a licence. By the end of Elizabeth's reign, even if Catholicism 'survived as a living faith', it had been well and truly 'broken as a political force'.[67] Diarmaid MacCulloch has noted that 'England judicially murdered more Roman Catholics than any other country in Europe', which, as he says, 'puts English pride in national tolerance in an interesting perspective'.[68] It also puts Elizabethan propaganda about 'Bloody Mary' in interesting perspective.

Presbyterians and puritans, in contrast, were a growing force politically – a development that would continue, with devastating effects, in the following century. Indeed, their presence in Elizabeth's House of Commons marked an important moment in the development of the idea of free speech as a constitutional principle in England. Since the Bill of Rights 1688, it has been a cardinal rule of British constitutional law that freedom of speech is a parliamentary privilege.[69] Puritan MPs such as Peter Wentworth began to talk of the 'freedom' of their 'speech' as early as 1576,[70] always, it seems, in the context of debates 'touching ecclesiastical government'.[71] In the 1587 Parliament, a bill had been introduced seeking to reform the governance of the church and offering a replacement prayer book (puritans considered

[64] Wooding (n 26) 488.

[65] Guy (n 14) 301.

[66] ie, they were fined if they refused to attend Church of England services.

[67] Brigden (n 11) 335. MacCulloch agrees: by 1600, he says, English Catholicism had 'fossilised as a largely upper-class and faintly exotic sect' (MacCulloch (n 6) 393).

[68] MacCulloch (ibid) 392.

[69] Bill of Rights 1688, art 9: 'The freedom of speech and debates or proceedings in Parliament ought not to be impeached or questioned in any court or place out of Parliament'.

[70] Wooding (n 26) 233.

[71] Tanner (n 31) 557.

the *Book of Common Prayer* to have retained too many hangovers of Catholic ritual). The queen intervened, commanding the Speaker not to allow the bill to continue. Wentworth attempted to raise the question of MPs' freedom of speech, that is, the freedom of MPs to initiate debate and discussion on any subject. For the audacity of doing so, he was sent to the Tower, and his questions were not moved in the House, the queen having on previous occasions made it clear that the House of Commons was not to meddle in matters of church government. As Tanner puts it, quoting Sir William Anson,

> the view of the Crown was that the Commons were summoned merely to vote such sums as were asked of them, to formulate or to approve legislation or topics of legislation submitted to them, and to give an opinion on matters of policy if, and only if, they were asked for one.[72]

Elizabeth had warned the Commons off three topics in particular: religion, foreign policy and trade. Wentworth's offence, in her eyes, was a serious one. He may have been unsuccessful in securing its enforcement in his lifetime – Wentworth died in the Tower in 1596 – but in his call for the freedom of MPs' speech to be recognised and protected, Wentworth pioneered an argument which would prove triumphant, albeit not for another century.

There is one final aspect of Tudor government relating to free speech to note. It is an aspect of the regulation of speech and printing which was to become central in the tumult of the seventeenth century: it is licensing. There was no freedom to publish in Tudor England: no freedom of the press. When printing came to England for the first time, the Crown simply assumed for itself the right, as a matter of prerogative, to control and regulate it.[73] The Crown's authority to do so was unlimited, and remained unchallenged throughout the Tudor period. The first person to mount a serious and sustained challenge to the power of the state to license the press was John Milton, in 1644, to whose work we shall soon turn. The institutions through which Tudor governments controlled the press were the Privy Council and the Star Chamber (ie, not the common law courts) and the vehicle by which they did so was royal proclamation (rather than Act of Parliament). Printing was a privilege, granted by the Crown, often in the form of a monopoly. From 1538, all printing – whether of religious works or otherwise – was subject to licensing.[74] Printers who published in breach of licensing conditions were liable to be fined or imprisoned or both; and, in practice, they were (such liability was not merely theoretical).

---

[72] ibid 555.

[73] Frederick Seaton Siebert, *Freedom of the Press in England 1476–1776* (Urbana, University of Illinois Press, 1952) 21.

[74] ibid 49.

In 1557, during the reign of Queen Mary, a charter was drawn up for the incorporation of the Stationers' Company. Under its terms, all printing within the realm was prohibited except by members of the Stationers' Company, a practice designed to preserve the monopolistic position of the men who, as officers, controlled the company.[75] It was not only the law which impeded press freedom: printing was expensive. To establish a press required significant outlay: type was not cheap; and ink and paper also needed to be purchased. Ink was inexpensive, but paper was costly (and had to be imported as England's first paper mill supplying the printing trade was not established until 1670).[76] Despite these difficulties there were, by 1600, some 50 presses operating in London which, during Elizabeth's reign, had produced more than 7,000 different titles.[77] As John Guy puts it, as the seventeenth century dawned, the power of the 'printed word was potentially explosive'.[78] Tudor governments had an acute sense of that power. They sought to repress it when they considered it necessary. They sought to control it via systematic state licensing. And they also sought to harness it for their own ends. Among the many legacies of the Tudors is the lesson that we need to be as alert to how officials manipulate and channel information as we must be to their attempts to block and censor it.[79]

D. Censorship and the Stuarts

The Tudor line came to an end when Elizabeth died in 1603 and was succeeded to the English throne by the Stuart, King James VI of Scotland. As England's new king, James inherited what had become a remarkably stable system of government. Modern ideas of free speech had yet even to be

---

[75] ibid 69.

[76] See Wooding (n 26) 320–21.

[77] See Guy (n 14) 416.

[78] ibid.

[79] The Tudors were so successful in this last regard that, even now, much of the way we understand early-modern English history is shaped by it. 'Bloody Mary' is one example. Two others could usefully be borne in mind. When Henry VII defeated Richard III at the Battle of Bosworth and became king in 1483, inaugurating the period of Tudor rule, he had only the barest, weakest claim to the throne; yet the Tudors are remembered for uniting the Houses of Lancaster and York, for ending the Wars of the Roses, and for securing the succession. The truth is that after Henry VII's death in 1509 the succession was anything but secure: it was, in fact, fraught with insecurity in 1553, 1558, 1603, 1688 and 1714, insecurities to which the Tudors had in large measure contributed. Comparable is Elizabeth's propaganda about Spanish Armada (1588), presenting its defeat as the providential and once-and-for-all extinction of any hope of Catholic restoration in England. Had England in fact considered itself to be secure in its Anglicanism (or Protestantism), the seventeenth century would have looked unrecognisably different. Indeed, even into the eighteenth century Britain had to face down significant threats of Catholic insurrection, not least from Jacobites in 1715 and 1745.

voiced, let alone accepted or put into practice. But in England both expression and its freedom had nonetheless begun to assert their importance. The Tudors bequeathed to their Stuart successors a polity in which the written word – and arguments about the written word – were of unprecedented importance. Books played a greater role in society than they had ever done before: 'the *Book of Common Prayer* and English editions of the Bible had transformed English religion; literary epics like Edmund Spencer's *Faerie Queene* and chronicle histories like Holinshed's ... had helped construct an English national identity'.[80] Such was the combined legacy of technology, humanism and Reformation. James I also inherited a well-established system of state licensing and a Parliament which, even in the earliest years of his reign, would become increasingly self-confident and vocal, not least about its freedom of speech.

Both the technological and the theological breakthroughs spawned instruments of fear and repression, in church and state alike. As we have seen, heresy and treason were capital offences, capable of being committed by words alone, whose scope had been enlarged, not diminished, in the years of Tudor rule. James' reign saw the last ever burnings at the stake in England for heresy (the executions of Bartholomew Legate and Edward Wightman, in 1612).[81] But there could be a sizeable gap between theory and practice. The full, terrifying savagery of the law could be brought to bear on puritans and Catholics alike but, even in the sixteenth century, there had been periods of calm when the terrors of the law were potential rather than actual, persecution paused rather than pursued. During James' reign, though, Catholic repression only hardened. After Guy Fawkes' Gunpowder Plot (1605) and the murder in Paris of the French King Henri IV (in 1610) all Catholics remaining in England were 'identified as potential terrorists'.[82] Not only were recusants more heavily fined, but their land and property could be confiscated.[83]

James, as monarch, relied even more than the Tudors had on the printed word to broadcast his own views about kingship, rulership and government. Of all the United Kingdom's monarchs, James I wrote most learnedly and intelligently about monarchy. His *Trew Law of Free Monarchies* was first published in Scotland in 1598 and his *Basilikon Doron* in 1599. Both tied the authority of the king to the authority of the printed word, in a manner

[80] Cyndia Clegg, *Press Censorship in Jacobean England* (Cambridge, Cambridge University Press, 2001) 8.

[81] These were not the last executions in Britain for crimes against God. That honour goes to Thomas Aitkenhead, who was hanged for blasphemy in Edinburgh in 1697. The last Catholic to be martyred in England was Oliver Plunkett, in 1681, who was hanged.

[82] Clare Jackson, *Devil-Land: England Under Siege 1588–1688* (London, Penguin, 2022) 131.

[83] ibid 116.

no subsequent monarch has repeated.[84] At the same time, King James relied on the system of licensing and on the habit of ad hoc book burning he had inherited from the Tudors: 'James skilfully wielded the press as a propaganda tool and created bonfires out of books that crossed him or his international allies'.[85] For James, books licensed by the state obtained 'a quasi-official status'.[86] This may help to explain why he suppressed books perhaps twice as frequently as had Queen Elizabeth: during the 45 years of her reign there had been 23 legal actions to suppress objectionable books; in the 22 years of James' reign, there were 25 such actions.[87] Employing even the most conservative estimates of how many books were published in Jacobean England, however, efforts at suppression or punishment were targeted at less than one per cent of printed works.[88]

James died in 1625 and was succeeded by his son, Charles I. The new administration was more oppressive: indeed, 'the licensing regime of the 1630s was stricter than that of any other decade in the seventeenth century'.[89] Whereas James had been keen to turn to print to justify his conception of kingship, under Charles I even works which supported the Stuart conception of the king's divine right to rule, such as Sir Robert Filmer's *Patriarcha*, were suppressed. The very idea that kingship needed to be justified by words could not be conceded, it seems.[90] Opposition to Charles' rule was led by Parliament, the House of Commons in particular. The escalating disputes between the Crown and Parliament focused on two matters: whether the Crown could raise money, via either taxation or forced loans, without parliamentary consent; and the governance of the church. If freedom of speech played any role in these disputes, it was as yet a marginal one and, even then, it would have been limited to the freedom of MPs to contribute to parliamentary debates without fear of arrest and detention at the king's pleasure in the Tower of London.[91] Ancient liberties certainly featured in these disputes, but freedom of speech was not among them. It was arbitrary arrest and detention without trial on which Parliament's common lawyers, such as Sir Edward Coke, focused. The Petition of Right (1628), drafted by Coke, sought to restate and reassert the

---

[84] Clegg, *Press Censorship in Jacobean England* (n 80) 9.

[85] Randy Robertson, *Censorship and Conflict in Seventeenth-Century England* (Pennsylvania, Penn State University Press, 2009) 3.

[86] Shuger (n 56) 242.

[87] Robertson (n 85) 3.

[88] Clegg, *Press Censorship in Jacobean England* (n 80) 19.

[89] Robertson (n 85) 3.

[90] ibid 31. He was no more enthusiastic about speaking (perhaps because he suffered from a stutter). He told his first Parliament in 1625 that it was not 'in my nature to spend much time with words': see Jackson (n 82) 193.

[91] See Adam Tomkins, *Our Republican Constitution* (Oxford, Hart Publishing, 2005) 77–83.

ancient liberties of Magna Carta, but freedom of speech was not included, not even as a parliamentary privilege.

After Charles dissolved Parliament in 1629 he was not to call another until 1640. During this period of 'the personal rule', the king and his Archbishop, William Laud, used the Star Chamber to enforce their political and religious agenda, its most notorious case, from a free speech perspective, being the persecution there of William Prynne. Prynne was a puritan, who wrote and published in 1632 a near-unreadable, 1,000-page omnibus diatribe ostensibly targeted at the theatre but, under the surface and in reality, an attack on all the trappings, pomp, ceremony and ritual of the Caroline court and Laud's vision for the church. For writing this book, *Histrio-mastix*, Prynne was prosecuted in the Star Chamber, where he was found guilty of seditious libel. He was 'fined, disbarred, imprisoned, and condemned to lose his ears'.[92] As if that were not enough, he was then 'made a spectacle in the pillory'.[93] Remarkably, none of this stopped him. He continued to write and in 1637 he found himself on trial in the Star Chamber again. Once again the verdict was severe. Prynne was pilloried, mutilated and imprisoned: 'the executioner sheared away what remained of Prynne's ears and branded his cheeks with the initials "S.L.", for seditious libeller'.[94]

II. The First Stirrings of Free Speech: Milton and the Levellers

When a new Parliament was finally called in 1640, it immediately set about dismantling the institutional architecture of the personal rule, as well as taking proceedings against its leading personnel. But, as in earlier debates, if free speech played any role, it was hardly in the forefront. As in the 1620s, the key parliamentary concern had more to do with the ancient liberties of due process than with any sense that writers and publishers should be free to print what they wanted. It was that Prynne had been made a public example of, and that liberties had been taken with regular and established judicial procedure, which angered the newly gathered House of Commons, rather than that his writings had been censored.[95] This, as much as anything, is why the Long Parliament legislated to abolish the court of Star Chamber in 1641.

[92] Robertson (n 85) 58.
[93] ibid.
[94] ibid 66.
[95] Cyndia Clegg, *Press Censorship in Caroline England* (Cambridge, Cambridge University Press, 2008) 215.

One of the effects, even if not one of the purposes, of that legislation was to contribute to an explosion of more or less unlicensed printing in early-1640s London. Since 1637 the Stationers' Company had lost its regulatory powers of oversight and enforcement of print licensing to the Court of Star Chamber (and to the Court of High Commission, which was likewise abolished by Act of Parliament in 1641). This meant that, from 1641, even if licensing remained a feature of the printing trade as a matter of form, breaches of licensing conditions were essentially unenforceable as a matter of practice. The legislation of 1641 did not begin the extraordinarily rapid increase in publishing in the early 1640s, but it helped to accelerate it. Above all, growth was driven by demand.[96] England was on the brink of civil war (hostilities having already broken out in Scotland). Political and religious debates alike spurred unprecedented demand for polemics and pamphlets. Before the actual war commenced in England in 1642 there was first a war of words, a propaganda battle. And it was in the midst of that blizzard of print that the first great defence, even if a partial and in some respects flawed defence, of free speech appeared. This was John Milton's tract *Areopagitica*, written and published in 1644.

Milton, author of course of *Paradise Lost* (1667), was not only a colossus of English poetry, he was also one of the seventeenth century's finest and bravest political pamphleteers. His *Tenure of Kings and Magistrates* (1648) was a defence and justification of regicide. His *Ready and Easy Way* (1660) was a heartfelt plea, published on the eve of the Restoration, not to revert to monarchy but to persevere with the 'free commonwealth'. Much earlier, his first political pamphlets were a tirade of anti-episcopalian attacks on the bishops of Laud's (and Charles I's) church. He then wrote about reforming the law of divorce and about education, before turning his attention, in *Areopagitica*, to the licensing of the press.[97] His immediate cause for doing so was Parliament's decision, in 1643, to reinstate a system of licensing based on the hated scheme that had been in place from 1637 until Parliament had abolished it in 1641. During the personal rule it had been the king's ministers and Laud's bishops who had acted as the censors. Now it was to be the Presbyterians in Parliament. Milton, not merely sympathetic to but actively supportive of the republican cause in the Civil War, was no royalist. But, for him, no government of any persuasion should take upon itself the task of seeking to 'bridle pens' or to decide which books could – and which could not – be read.

---

[96] On average, 624 books had been published each year in Britain during the 1630s, whereas in 1642 alone some 4,038 were published: see Jackson (n 82) 23.

[97] These tracts and pamphlets are conveniently collected in a modern edition in John Milton, *The Major Works* (S Orgel and J Goldberg (eds), Oxford, Oxford University Press, 1991). All references below to *Areopagitica* are to this edition.

Areopagitica is a remarkable essay, and is justly famous. Anna Beer, in her biography of Milton, does not exaggerate when she describes it as 'a unique piece of writing, one of the most powerful and inspirational works in the English language'.[98] As Randy Robertson has stated, the tract is a 'canonical text in the history of Western liberalism'.[99] It ranks alongside John Stuart Mill's *On Liberty*, which it predates by more than 200 years, as one of the leading essays on freedom of speech ever written in English. And yet it is, as noted above, both partial and flawed. It is partial because, whilst it attacks pre-publication licensing, it endorses post-publication censorship. And it is flawed because it clearly denies even freedom from licensing to Catholics. How, then, are we to read it? There is much to be said for Robertson's approach:

> Modern scholars often dwell on the tract's shortcomings: *Areopagitica* denies freedom to Roman Catholics and perhaps even to royalists, and it allows for the suppression of books that prove 'monsters' upon publication. Yet the pamphlet's plea for the 'liberty of unlicensed printing' was radical enough in context: many parliamentarians believed they were fighting against the king and his 'popish' advisors, not to mention the Irish papists; Milton could scarcely have addressed a tract to Parliament that supported their enemies' right to vent war propaganda.[100]

Areopagitica, then, is a political pamphlet of its time but, simultaneously, it is an impassioned plea for an unlicensed press deploying a range of arguments that span the ages. It is of its moment and yet, in the same breath, it has a certain timelessness about it. In passages it is sublime. We are, after all, in the hands of one of the great poets of our language.

Within his essay, Milton makes a whole series of different claims for free speech. These contentions overlap and, whilst they are introduced sequentially, Milton often goes back to them before moving on. *Areopagitica* is not written in the style of a systematised philosophical argument: it is written in the style of speech to Parliament (and it is written by a poet, albeit a classically educated one, not by a philosopher). What follows is an account of Milton's argument. He starts from the perspective not of the writer, but of the reader. Milton's reader is educated, of course, and is 'worthy': a man of 'virtue'.[101] He has the means whereby he can distinguish for himself the pure from the impure, good from evil, sound arguments from bad. He has no need of the government to do this for him. Reading impure words or unsound arguments is not like eating rotten meat, Milton says.

---

[98] Anna Beer, *Milton: Poet, Pampleteer and Patriot* (London, Bloomsbury, 2008) 165.
[99] Robertson (n 85) 100.
[100] ibid.
[101] *Areopagitica* (n 97) 246, 252.

Individuals may well need legal protection from food that would poison them, but they have no similar need of protection from ideas that would corrupt them: even 'bad books ... to a discreet and judicious reader' may serve to allow the reader 'to discover, to confute, to forewarn and to illustrate'.[102] Bad food cannot nourish the body, but all books – even bad ones – may serve to nourish the mind. Indeed, for Milton, to read in this manner is not merely a freedom, but a duty. It is both a Christian duty and a requirement of becoming a virtuous citizen. We do not bring innocence into the world, says Milton. We bring impurity. What purifies us is trial, and what allows for trial is to be confronted with that which is 'contrary'.[103] Licensing takes all this away, depriving us of the means we need in order to prove our virtue.[104]

If the argument from virtue is Milton's first, his second is an argument from truth. The purpose of reading books 'promiscuously', as he puts it, is to enable the truth to emerge from all its possible sources.[105] The more we read, the closer to the truth we will get and, at the same time, the more we read, all the more easily and quickly will we be able to identify what is false and reject it. He cites as an example the work of John Selden, a lawyer sitting in Parliament, whose work on 'natural and national laws proves ... that all opinions, yea, errors, known, read and collated are of main service and assistance toward the speedy attainment of what is truest'.[106] The truth, says Milton, is 'strong': 'she needs no policies, nor stratagems, nor licensings to make her victorious'.[107] This, as we shall see in the next chapter, is also a key contention made by champions of free speech in the eighteenth century. The truth will out and, in the battle of the marketplace of ideas, the truth will defeat the false. The truth can be trusted – trusted to be strong, trusted to rise to the top, trusted to drown out the false. This is a frequent refrain even now in debates about free speech, despite the weight

---

[102] ibid 246.

[103] ibid 248.

[104] The idea of virtue was central to seventeenth-century English republicanism, as it was to Machiavelli (the classic work is JGA Pocock, *The Machiavellian Moment: Florentine Political Thought and the Atlantic Republican Tradition* (Princeton, Princeton University Press, 1975)). Milton's reliance on it in *Areopagitica* is no accident. See generally, David Armitage, Armand Himy and Quentin Skinner (eds), *Milton and Republicanism* (Cambridge, Cambridge University Press, 1995) and David Norbrook, *Writing the English Republic: Poetry, Rhetoric and Politics 1627–1660* (Cambridge, Cambridge University Press, 1999) 118–39. In ch 3 we will encounter Holmes and Brandeis JJ's view, expressed in US Supreme Court case law in 1927, that 'to courageous and self-reliant men' freedom of speech poses little 'clear and present danger'. There are echoes in this famous and influential formulation of Milton's 'virtue'.

[105] *Areopagitica* (n 97) 248.

[106] ibid 246.

[107] ibid 269.

of evidence showing it to be a claim rooted more in hope than experience, and we shall return to it several times in this book.

Milton's third argument is that licensing is futile. He likens it to 'the exploit of that gallant man who thought to pound up the crows by shutting his park gate'.[108] Censorship by licensing, says Milton, is 'vain and impossible'.[109] It is 'fruitless'.[110] It is bound only ever to frustrate the ambitions of those who undertake it, and yet it will cost them dearly in terms both of time and effort. Neither 'evil manners' nor 'evil doctrine' can be stopped or corrected by licensing as, even without books, they are so prevalent as to be commonplace.[111] The futility (as well as the great expense) of licensing can be seen, says Milton, by examining the fate on the Continent of the Index of Prohibited Books, which required not only huge official effort, but which demonstrably failed to improve the manners of the Italians and the Spanish: they are not 'one scruple the better, the honester, the wiser, the chaster, since all the inquisitional rigour that hath been executed upon books'.[112] Licensing is not merely futile: it is ridiculous, Milton contends. If Parliament were really to want to control and correct evil manners, it would have to license not only books, but dancing, music, gluttony, drunkenness and even the garments we wear:

> [I]f we think to regulate printing, thereby to rectify manners, we must regulate all recreations and pastimes, all that is delightful to man. No music must be heard, no song be set or sung ... There must be licensing of dancers, that no gesture, motion or deportment be taught our youth ... [Likewise licensers will have to] examine all the lutes, the violins and the guitars in every house; they must not be suffered to prattle as they do ... And who shall silence all the airs and madrigals that whisper softness in chambers?[113]

Milton's next argument is to propose an alternative to licensing. Manners and doctrine are best regulated not by censorship, he says, but by education: specifically, by 'virtuous education [and] religious and civil nurture'.[114] These, he says, are 'the bonds and ligaments of the commonwealth, the pillars and sustainers' of the political order and of the law.[115] Far better, claims Milton, to nurture the growth of one virtuous man than forcibly to restrain 10 vicious men. In this claim, as in his argument from truth, Milton prefigures one of the key contentions made today in support of the right to free speech: that a well-educated public is far better able to

---

[108] ibid 249.
[109] ibid.
[110] ibid 251.
[111] ibid 249.
[112] ibid 254.
[113] ibid 251.
[114] ibid 252.
[115] ibid.

distinguish truth from falsehood (or virtue from vice) than can ever be engineered via systems of licensing and suppression. The censor's hand dishonours the 'privilege and dignity of learning' both from the student's and from the teacher's point of view. Let the state 'be my governors', says Milton, 'but not my critics'.[116]

Most of these arguments apply every bit as strongly in contemporary society as they did four centuries ago when Milton penned them. One that has not worn quite so well, by contrast, is Milton's occasional foray into nationalistic argument (or jingoism, to use a word Milton would not have known). He cannot resist the temptation to suggest that licensing was a matter for the countries of the Inquisition, and not for the 'happy … place of philosophic freedom' he had supposed England to be.[117] We need pursue this line of argument no further, but Milton was hardly the first, nor indeed the last, to deploy a slice of unnecessary nationalistic exceptionalism in order to make a political point.

He was on firmer ground when he sought to identify the harms licensing causes. Of these he focused on two, which might be called the individual harm (a harm done to the writer) and the collective harm (a harm done to the reader). The former is that for the state to presume to license books is 'so far to distrust' a man's judgement and honesty that it is 'the greatest displeasure and indignity to a free and knowing spirit that can be put upon him'.[118] Licensing is a blanket policy. It does not matter how learned a man is. It does not matter that he has never before offended. It does not matter that he is in no way corrupt. Yet, even such a man – that is to imply, even a man such as John Milton himself – may go to print only after his work has been examined, 'lest he should drop a schism'.[119] Licensing is an affront to dignity. The collective harm is similar. 'Nor is it to the common people less than a reproach', he says,

> for if we be so jealous over them as that we dare not trust them with an English pamphlet, what do we do but censure them for a giddy, vicious and ungrounded people, in such a sick and weak estate of faith and discretion as to be able to take nothing down but through the pipe of a licenser.[120]

Trusting the people takes courage, and to be courageous, says Milton, is exactly what we should aspire to. Licensing is for the weak, the 'timorous', the 'suspicious' and the 'pusillanimous'.[121] Again, this is a theme which echoes through today's debates about freedom of speech. It is an aspect of

---

[116] ibid 256.

[117] ibid 258.

[118] ibid 255.

[119] ibid.

[120] ibid 258. This, says Robertson, is Milton's 'principal objection to licensing' – namely, that it 'infantilises authors and readers'. See Robertson (n 85) 110.

[121] *Areopagitica* (n 97) 259–60.

Milton's argument which, to twenty-first-century eyes, is remarkably fresh and modern.

His final argument is quite different, and takes us back to the particular time in which he was writing. It is his most theological argument. Mankind sins. Divine truth once walked the Earth, but He has now ascended. The Christian duty now is to seek the truth or, at least, to seek to come as close to the truth as we can, given our sinful nature. Licensing obstructs that endless search for truth for which it is the duty of Christians to strive. If it is the human condition to search endlessly for scientific truth, says Milton, it is the Christian condition to search likewise and always for theological truth. This, he says, is 'the golden rule' of theology: 'to be still searching what we know not by what we know, still closing up truth to truth as we find it'.[122] This, of course, is a profoundly Protestant argument: that salvation may come via Scripture and that God's grace is revealed through his Word.

Milton concludes with a great flourish, in which liberty is placed centre stage, and in which Parliament is held both as the source and as the guarantor of English liberty. It is Parliament, he says, which has set England free. Parliament's 'own valorous and happy counsels have purchased' us a 'liberty which is the nurse of all great wits'.[123] This liberty, Milton claims, has 'rarefied and enlightened our spirits like the influence of heaven' and has 'enfranchised, enlarged and lifted up our apprehensions degrees above themselves'.[124] Having liberated us in this way, Parliament cannot by reintroducing licensing

> make us now less capable, less knowing, less eagerly pursuing of the truth … We can grow ignorant again, brutish, formal and slavish, as ye found us; but you [ie, Parliament] then must first become … oppressive, arbitrary and tyrannous.[125]

He concludes thus: 'Give me the liberty to know, to utter, and to argue freely according to conscience, above all liberties'.[126] This may be stirring stuff, but it failed. Licensing survived.

Milton's plea for an unlicensed press did not succeed in his own day, but several elements of his argument have shaped debates about free speech in the centuries since. That the price of free speech is that the public must be well educated; that censorship causes harms to readers and writers

---

[122] ibid 264. Robertson sees this argument as a 'salvo against certainty', a 'sceptical strain' running throughout the tract whereby 'Milton contends that the elusiveness of truth enjoins toleration of diverse viewpoints'. Robertson (n 85) 113. Again, we will find echoes of this when we turn to Oliver Wendell Holmes in ch 3.

[123] *Areopagitica* (n 97) 268.

[124] ibid.

[125] ibid.

[126] ibid.

alike; that censorship is in any event futile; that it obstructs truth; and that, whilst censorship has a tendency to infantilise, its absence may require of us not only the wit and wisdom to distinguish sound arguments from 'fake news', but may also require us to grow thick skins, to be robust and courageous both in what we read and in what we write. Each of these notes was sounded by Milton and, as we shall throughout this book, every one of them continues to reverberate.

War ended in 1646. Parliament, although victorious, was bitterly divided. Peace was short-lived. Civil war broke out again and, once more, the king was defeated. He was executed in 1649. The Cromwellian regime which governed thereafter tightened press controls as the 1650s wore on.[127] It was an echo of the 1630s, except instead of Charles I and Archbishop Laud now it was Oliver Cromwell and his secretary of state John Thurloe, who played the role of state censor.[128] Parliament's attempt to rule without the king proved as unsuccessful as the Crown's earlier attempt, during the years of the personal rule, to govern without Parliament. By 1660 it was clear that England needed both the Crown and Parliament, albeit that the terms on which they were to govern together continued to be contested and debated until they were finally resolved – through an altogether different sort of revolution from that seen in the civil wars of the 1640s – in the Glorious Revolution of 1688 and its constitutional settlement, the Bill of Rights.

Amid the turmoil, freedom of speech as Milton had defended it never gained prominence in the long battle of constitutional ideas and experiments. It is there, of course, in the Bill of Rights, but only as a parliamentary privilege, not as a liberty to be enjoyed generally by writers and readers. Even the most radical and progressive of political campaigners in the seventeenth century – the Levellers – did not focus their energies on freedom of speech. In the unsettled years after the end of the first Civil War but before the Regicide (that is to say, in the years before Cromwell's grip on government tightened), the Levellers produced a blizzard of tracts arguing for a written constitution, inalienable rights, a radical expansion of the franchise (removing all property qualifications from a man's right to vote), and a House of Commons both truly representative and sovereign.[129] Freedom of conscience and an entitlement to dissent was

---

[127] Milton's ever-changing relations with Cromwell are expansively and expertly treated in Blair Worden, *Literature and Politics in Cromwellian England* (Oxford, Oxford University Press, 2007) 154–398.

[128] See Robertson (n 85) 128.

[129] See David Wootton, 'Leveller Democracy and the Puritan Revolution' in JH Burns and Mark Goldie (eds), *The Cambridge History of Political Thought 1450–1700* (Cambridge, Cambridge University Press, 1991) 412. For a selection of Leveller tracts, see Andrew Sharp (ed), *The English Levellers* (Cambridge, Cambridge University Press, 1998).

claimed in a number of Leveller tracts[130] – and a commitment to freedom of speech was thereby implicit – but such matters were never their focus. The Levellers were concerned above all with popular sovereignty, with the idea that political authority should rest upon consent, with representative democracy, and with the right to vote. That they managed to publish so widely in the years from 1646 to 1649 shows that Parliament's system of licensing had broken down, but even in this chaotic environment its leaders such as John Lilburne and Richard Overton, found themselves arrested and imprisoned.[131] Once Cromwell had the power to do so, he crushed the Leveller movement. As a political movement, they were finished by 1649, even if some of their ideas survived to influence later generations.

In 1649 England did away with its king, even with kingship. But Parliament maintained in force a law of treason. After the king's execution it became treason to say 'by writing, publishing or openly declaring' that the new commonwealth was 'tyrannical, usurped or unlawful'. Further laws in 1654 and 1656 made it treason to 'compass or imagine the death of the Lord Protector' (ie, of Cromwell). Likewise, it was treason 'by writing, printing, openly declaring, preaching, teaching or otherwise' to assail Cromwell's authority. The treason laws that had protected Tudor and Stuart monarchs were copied and pasted to protect the new regime in the same terms.[132] After the Restoration they were copied and pasted all over again to protect Charles II.

III. Locke and Licensing

The Restoration regime of Charles II was as committed to state censorship – to the pre-publication licensing of the press – as Charles I and Laud, Cromwell and Thurloe had been. Censor-in-chief was Roger L'Estrange, surveyor of the press, who, like his predecessors, relied on spies and agents in the Stationers' Company to enforce his 'energetic assault on unauthorised printing'.[133] His reach was fearsome. General warrants, granted by the king's secretaries of state, authorised widespread search and seizure (without any need, of course, to show reasonable suspicion of an offence having

---

[130] 'No man' should be 'imprisoned for his religion' said Overton in *A Remonstrance of Many Thousand Citizens* (1649), for example. Likewise in *An Agreement of the Free People of England* (1649): 'we do not impower or entrust our said representatives to continue in force, or to make any Lawes … whereby to compel by penalties or otherwise any person to any thing in or about matters of faith'. For the originals, from which these quotations are taken, see: oll. libertyfund.org/page/leveller-tracts.

[131] Both were imprisoned in 1646: see Wootton (n 129) 427.

[132] See Cressy (n 28) 197.

[133] See Robertson (n 85) 18.

been committed). It would not be for another century that the courts would put a stop to such warrants (in the great case of *Entick v Carrington* (1765)).[134] Within the Stationers' Company it became an offence to neglect to inform the authorities of a secret press. Meanwhile, L'Estrange's secretariat had a monopoly on the news and controlled the post. With his team of censors 'L'Estrange pried into every corner of the book trade'.[135]

The Licensing Act 1662 contained provisions familiar to anyone with knowledge of the regulation of the press since the reign of Henry VIII. Thus, the Act made it illegal to print anything heretical, seditious or schismatic, or any opinion contrary either to the Christian faith or to the doctrine and discipline of the Church of England. It required all books to be licensed, either by the Stationers' Company, by the Bishop of London, or by one of the chancellors or vice-chancellors of the universities. There is no doubt that the Act suppressed the printing trade. Whereas some 2,700 titles appeared in England in 1660 and some 1,600 more the following year, by 1666 the number had fallen to a mere 630 (although the Great Fire of London, which destroyed so much of the city in 1666, may also have had something to do with that). Throughout the 1670s the number of books produced in England was in the region of 1,000–1,200 titles each year. It was not until the Licensing Act lapsed, in 1679 (on which see below), that the number exceeded that for 1661.[136] Alongside the Licensing Act stood the Act of Uniformity 1662, which required all clergymen and all teachers (from village schoolteachers to fellows of university colleges) to conform to the liturgy of the Church of England, as prescribed by the *Book of Common Prayer*. At the same time, old, Elizabethan laws against recusants remained on the statute book.[137]

The Restoration was popular, at least to start with. The puritan bans on Christmas, maypoles, the theatre and suchlike had never been widely liked. Charles II found it easy to capitalise on the renewed popularity of making merry. He enjoyed enjoying himself, particularly in public; he loved little more than a day at the races, led a merry (if not debauched) life himself, and played up his role of appearing as all things to all men and women. Early in the 1670s, however, old fears started to return, none more so than the fear of 'popery and arbitrary government'.[138] Charles II fathered no fewer than 14 illegitimate children but he and his queen could produce

---

[134] See Adam Tomkins and Paul Scott (eds), *Entick v Carrington: 250 Years of the Rule of Law* (Oxford, Hart Publishing, 2015) and see further ch 2.

[135] Robertson (n 85) 19.

[136] See Tim Harris, *Restoration: Charles II and his Kingdoms 1660–1685* (London, Penguin, 2006) 70.

[137] ibid 53.

[138] The classic text is Andrew Marvell's pamphlet, *An Account of the Growth of Popery and Arbitrary Government in England* (1677).

no heir. Upon his demise the Crown would pass to his brother, James, Duke of York. And herein lay the problem. James was widely suspected and, from 1673, known to be a Catholic. To use decidedly twentieth-century terms for a moment, Catholics were 'folk devils' and in the 1670s a vast 'moral panic' was whipped up that England would be forcibly returned to Catholicism, English liberties being abandoned and replaced by arbitrary government.[139] This was not mere sectarian bigotry: Catholicism was truly feared. 'Bloody Mary' had not been forgotten. Neither had the Spanish Armada. Nor had the Gunpowder Plot. Everyone worried that a Catholic monarch would be unable to work with Parliament and would have to rule with a standing army instead. English liberties were genuinely on the line. Fears were made all the worse by the news from France, where Louis XIV was persecuting the (Huguenot) Protestants, closing their schools, excluding them from their trades, subjecting them to higher taxes, and seizing their estates.[140]

Parliament's first response was to pass a Test Act in 1673, requiring all office-holders under the Crown to take a series of oaths of supremacy and allegiance, swearing, among other matters, to uphold the doctrines and disciplines of the Anglican church. This, of course, Catholics of good conscience could not do (and neither could dissenters). The Act succeeded in identifying a number of Catholics, including the Duke of York, but it did little to quell fears of popery. Such fears reached their crescendo at the end of the decade, in the scandal of the Popish Plot.

The Popish Plot is an important episode in the struggle for free speech in Britain because it reminds us of a theme we will return to several times in this book: namely, the problem of 'fake news'. The Popish Plot was a tissue of lies. It was, as one historian has recently put it, a 'hoax' from beginning to end.[141] At the same time, it was a politically manipulated struggle for power, in which a group of leading Peers of the Realm (led by Anthony Ashley Cooper, the Earl of Shaftesbury) campaigned to exclude the Duke of York from the line of succession, in which perhaps as many as 30 wholly innocent Catholics were killed – 17 of them by means of execution following conviction (although 'judicial murder' would be a more accurate phrase) – and which led directly to the emergence for the

---

[139] The terms are Stanley Cohen's, who used them in relation to Mods and Rockers: see his brilliant *Folk Devils and Moral Panics*, first published in 1972 and now available as a Routledge Classic.

[140] See Harris (n 136) 150–52. The Huguenots were expelled from France in 1685. Many settled in England, cementing yet further the idea of Britain as a Protestant nation, surrounded by Catholic threats: see Linda Colley, *Britons: Forging the Nation 1707–1837* (London, Pimlico, 1994) ch 1.

[141] Victor Slater, *Hoax: The Popish Plot that Never Was* (New Haven, Yale University Press, 2022).

first time in British politics of something resembling political parties. The first Whigs were those who, like Shaftesbury, wanted to exclude the heir to the throne from the line of succession and the first Tories were those who opposed them, fearing as they did a return to the civil wars of 40 years previously. In the event, such a war was avoided when the Tories abandoned James[142] and joined with the Whigs in seeking to have him replaced as king by his son-in-law, who in 1688 became King William III: this, of course, was the Glorious Revolution.

The Popish Plot, then, despite being a contrivance of the most outlandish fiction, was a moment of great consequence not only for the story of the struggle for free speech, but for the very shape and identity of the British state. The plot, in short, was a claim that Catholics in general and Jesuits in particular were conspiring to assassinate Charles II and to provoke a civil war in which Louis XIV of France would intervene, returning the country to Catholic rule. The claim had its foundation not in reality but in the malevolent and scheming minds of its authors, principally Titus Oates and Israel Tonge.[143] That they managed to weave their web of fabrications to the extent that dozens of innocent Catholics were sent to their deaths was due to two factors. The first was the febrile atmosphere of 1670s England (and of 1670s London, in particular) in which the credulous were only too willing to believe the anti-Catholic nonsense they heard in coffeehouses, inns and alehouses. This was a time of great suspicion and fear, in which all fingers pointed to popery. The frenzy was by no means confined to the lower orders. It spread all the way up the establishment.[144] Chief Justice William Scroggs, who presided over many of the trials which sent the plot's victims to the scaffold, loathed Catholics. Secondly, and perhaps even more importantly, the plot was useful beyond measure to those, such as the ruthless Earl of Shaftesbury, who were so determined to block the Duke of York's accession to the throne that they would think nothing of conspiring to send a couple of dozen Catholics to the gallows as wrongly convicted traitors. Shaftesbury was a man whose ruthlessness was even greater even than his ambition – a lethal combination if you were a Catholic in his way.

---

[142] Charles II died in 1685 and was succeeded as king by his brother. When James' second, Catholic, wife gave birth to a son, also named James, and a Catholic succession seemed assured, Whigs and Tories joined forces to have James and the Stuarts ousted in favour of William of Orange and his wife, James's older daughter by his first marriage, Mary. Both William and Mary were, of course, safely Protestant. At the time of the Glorious Revolution, William was fourth in line to the throne and Mary was second. William's forces invaded (by invitation) in order to secure that Mary's inheritance would not be denied to her by the newborn prince (who was to become known, in the next century, as the Old Pretender).

[143] The full, grisly story is briskly told in Slater (n 141).

[144] Although not, at least to start with, to the king himself. Charles II was the supposed target but, at least on Slater's account (ibid), he was sceptical from the beginning that there ever was a Jesuit plot to topple him.

In the short term, indeed, in his own lifetime (he died having fled to the Netherlands in 1683), Shaftesbury failed. A second Test Act, passed in 1678 to extend to members of the House of Lords the requirement to take the oaths of supremacy and allegiance, expressly excluded the Duke of York from its scope. It did have the effect, however, of excluding Catholics from the Upper House: they were not to return to the House of Lords for 150 years. Two attempted Exclusion Bills failed. Each would have removed James from the line of succession. Upon the death of his brother in 1685, James did become king albeit, as we have seen, only briefly. In the longer term, by contrast, it was the Whig view which prevailed over the Tory. By the end of the century it was clear not only as a question of theory, but by force of written constitutional law (in the Bill of Rights 1688 and the Act of Settlement 1701), both that the *powers* of the Crown were for Parliament to determine and that the very *identity* of the monarch was a matter over which Parliament had control. When Elizabeth died in 1603 parliaments were called by and exercised their limited powers subject to the will of the Crown but, a century later, both propositions had been effectively reversed.

At the height of the Exclusion Crisis, when the fever and hysteria of the Popish Plot were at their most inflamed, in 1679, the Licensing Act lapsed. Among other consequences, this meant that Sir Roger L'Estrange needed a job, or at least a means of earning an income. He found one as a Tory propagandist and his *History of the Plot*, published in 1679, was one of the first works openly to challenge the lies of Titus Oates and his fellow travellers. There ensued a propaganda war, not just as regards the plot itself, but ranging across the whole of the constitutional and political argument that divided the Whigs from the Tories. In its midst, that great censor of his time, L'Estrange, put his finger on one of the great dangers of free speech. These are his words:

> The world is so miserably divided betwixt some that will believe everything, and others nothing, that not only Truth, but Christianity itself is almost lost between them, and no place left for sobriety and moderation. We come to govern ourselves by dreams and imaginations, we make every coffeehouse tale an article of our faith, and from incredible fables we raise invincible arguments.[145]

The trouble with an unlicensed press was not merely that it had put Sir Roger L'Estrange out of employment. The deeper trouble was that, if any old rogue is free to write and print whatever lies he wishes, truth suffers as it is drowned in a flood of fabrications, fantasies and fake news. You do not have to have worked as the state's censor-in-chief to consider this to be a real problem and, as we shall see, some of the eighteenth century's

---

[145] Roger L'Estrange, *A Further Discovery of the Plot* (1680), cited by Slater (n 141) 234.

finest writers (including Jonathan Swift and Samuel Johnson) would, in time, make much the same point as L'Estrange. It remains a real challenge for all advocates of free speech and a free press.

The lapsing of the Licensing Act triggered a doubling of the number of books and pamphlets published each year in England. About 1,100 had been published in 1678, whereas there were 1,700 in 1679, 2,100 in 1680 and another 2,000 in 1681. Historian Tim Harris has claimed that, 'taking into account contemporary print runs, somewhere between five and ten million pamphlets must have been in circulation in 1679–81'.[146] The news and views reported and discussed in this blizzard of publishing were by no means restricted to the literate. Newssheets could be (and were) read aloud in coffeehouses and alehouses and, in addition, they would find their ways into sermons, plays at the theatre, poems and ballads. London, in particular, had never been so awash with words and speech.[147]

England's most important writer of the 1680s, however, was not in London. Like his patron the Earl of Shaftesbury, he had fled to the Netherlands and would not return to England until 1689, a momentous year for this author – John Locke – as it saw the publication in English not only of his *Letter Concerning Toleration*, but of his *Two Treatises of Government*. Locke's *Second Treatise* is perhaps the single most significant work of political theory ever composed in English, for it sets out more compellingly than any other text the justification and the reasons for the Glorious Revolution, that is, the circumstances in which a body politic, a commonwealth, may overthrow and replace its ruler. Locke's masterpiece is justly revered as one of the foundational texts of modern political liberalism. Our focus here, however, will be on two other interventions Locke made, each of which enjoyed a lasting influence on the ongoing struggle for free speech. These interventions will be treated in reverse chronological order, starting with the role he played, having returned to active life in England, in the final abolition of state licensing 1694–95. Thereafter we will look briefly at his *Letter Concerning Toleration*, first published in Latin a decade earlier (and then published in English in 1689), as it is Locke's arguments in this text which pave the way, as we shall see, for the move away from the age of heresy into the next age of the struggle for free speech: the age of sedition.

The Licensing Act 1662, as we saw above, lapsed in 1679. It was revived in 1685, when James succeeded his late brother to the throne. In 1694 a committee of the House of Commons was appointed to inquire into and

---

[146] Harris (n 136) 142.

[147] As Harris has written, during both the Exclusion Crisis and the Glorious Revolution itself, 'members of the political elite (of all political persuasions) certainly made every effort to exploit the medium of print in order to woo public opinion' (ibid 16).

to report on which laws should be allowed to expire and which should be revived or continued. When the resulting legislation reached the House of Lords, their Lordships proposed that the Licensing Act should be continued. The Commons disagreed and charged Edward Clarke, MP for Taunton, with the task of setting out the reasons why the Act should be allowed to lapse. Edward Clarke and John Locke were close and lifelong friends, and Locke was instrumental in furnishing the MP with the arguments he needed to ensure the will of the Commons prevailed over that of the Lords.[148]

Locke's starting point was that licensing harmed scholarship. The monopoly enjoyed by the Stationers' Company resulted in poor quality books being made available at high cost, both of which features of book publishing were contrary to the interests of scholars. Locke was vitriolic about the 'lazy, ignorant' members of the Stationers' Company, those 'dull wretches' who abused the system for their own gain and who produced books that were 'scandalously ill-printed, both for letter paper and correctness'. This, as many have noted, is an argument rooted in concerns about restraint of trade, rather than freedom of the press (or free speech), but it was no less effective for that. Neither Locke nor the House of Commons overlooked in their entirety arguments based on freedom: Locke referred to the 'liberty to print' and the Commons to fears that a 'great oppression' could return, depending on the identity of the licensors, but such arguments played only a supporting role from 1694 to 1695 and were never the main thrust of opposition to the continuation of licensing. Even absent licensing, the Commons (and Locke) noted, there would still be ample room for the law to punish 'treasonable and seditious' books and pamphlets. Action could be taken in the common law courts against any publication that was libellous or blasphemous, for example.

What Locke wanted in England was what he had experienced in Holland, in his years of self-imposed exile. He wanted high-quality, affordable books, and he considered the Licensing Act to be an impediment, preventing the London book trade from enjoying what the Dutch had been profiting from for some years. These arguments prevailed and when the Licensing Act lapsed in 1695 it lapsed forever. It had expired before, only to be brought back to life. But now it was gone for good. Since 1695 English law has controlled the printed word not via ecclesiastical or state-sponsored

---

[148] The surviving text of Locke's Memorandum on the matter is published in full at (2010) 27 *Cardozo Arts and Entertainment Law Journal* 555–72. For commentary, see Ronan Deazley, 'Commentary on the Licensing Act 1662' in Lionel Bently and Martin Kretschmer (eds), *Primary Sources on Copyright 1450–1900*, available at: www.copyrighthistory.org, and John Willinsky, *The Intellectual Properties of Learning: A Prehistory from Saint Jerome to John Locke* (Chicago, Chicago University Press, 2018) ch 12.

schemes of pre-publication censorship, but through a range of legal actions available to those (including church and state) who consider that something which has been published or said ought not to have been. We owe a great deal of that to John Locke, even if the arguments he mustered to secure this outcome had little to do with free speech and more to do with his attack on restraint of trade. Amidst his 1694 Memorandum on the Licensing Act, Locke did, however, write the following:

> I know not why a man should not have liberty to print whatever he would speak; and to be answerable for the one, just as he is for the other, if he transgresses the law in either. But gagging a man, for fear he should talk heresy or sedition, has no ground than such as will make gyves necessary, for fear a man should use violence if his hands were free.

We do not put manacles on someone just because they might otherwise punch and fight. Likewise we should not be in the business of censoring someone just because the words they use might be heretical or seditious.

Locke's influence endured not only in the abandonment of licensing, but in what was to replace it after his death: namely, the emergence of a law of copyright. Towards the end of his life (he died in 1704), Locke came to see what he called the 'whole stock of human knowledge' as something held in common. Individuals could make progress through their own endeavours and studies, as Locke had done throughout his own life, but even the greatest of them always owed an intellectual debt to those who had 'made the ways passable', as he put it.[149] Moreover, it was 'the very business of learning to create a public record' of those who brought truths to light. Locke cared greatly that the public record was not only accurate but accessible and, as such, public. The Stationers' Company did not rest easy upon the end of licensing. They lobbied many times for its reintroduction. In time, their arguments about needing to protect the economic business of book production, for writers and printers alike, evolved. Even if the state would not return to licensing, something needed to be done, they insisted, to guard against piracy. It was neither fair nor reasonable that any rogue printer could rip off a writer's work. Thus developed the beginnings of an argument for the legal protection of copyright, which Parliament eventually enacted into law in the so-called Statute of Anne in 1710.[150] And here, as elsewhere, we can see Locke's influence for, as well as conferring exclusive rights to publish, the Statute of Anne also granted powers to fix the price of books, outlawed restrictions on the import of books, and imposed

---

[149] See Willinsky (ibid) 306, citing from Locke's *Reasonableness of Christianity as Delivered in Scriptures* (1695).

[150] See Brad Sherman and Lionel Bently, *The Making of Modern Intellectual Property Law* (Cambridge, Cambridge University Press, 1999) ch 1.

duties on publishers to deposit their books in the great libraries of England and Scotland, not only the university libraries, but elsewhere too, including the library of the Faculty of Advocates in Edinburgh (whose most illustrious Keeper, later in the century, was David Hume, one of the leading figures in the Scottish Enlightenment).

Before we leave Locke, there is one final area relevant to free speech where his work and thought had an enduring and determinative influence: namely, freedom of conscience. This brings us full circle: this chapter started with Luther and the Protestant Reformation and it closes, 150 years later, with the emergent Enlightenment argument for religious toleration. This framing is quite deliberate because it shows that no account of free speech can divorce itself from freedom of conscience. Even now there are echoes which continue to reverberate, reminding us of where free speech came from, of its first struggles against the powers less of state than of church. When writers in our own age offend against religious sensibilities they may find their freedom of speech comes under the most impassioned challenge, with only the most ardently secular of liberals prepared to defend them unreservedly. Witness, for example, how lonely Christopher Hitchens sometimes appeared to be – even in the company of other so-called liberals – in the robustness of his defence of Sir Salman Rushdie, after the publication of *The Satanic Verses*.[151] (Witness also, as we shall see in the next chapter, how the authorities could still persuade juries to convict for blasphemy even after it had become much more of a gamble to seek a conviction on a charge of sedition.)

John Locke's *Letter Concerning Toleration* was, as his modern editor Mark Goldie has put it, 'one of the seventeenth century's most eloquent pleas to Christians to renounce religious persecution'.[152] Locke was not alone in making this argument in late seventeenth-century Europe. Baruch Spinoza and Pierre Bayle, among others, also advocated toleration and did so, moreover, even more fervently than Locke.[153] Like his forerunner John Milton,

---

[151] The notorious clip from BBC television's *Question Time*, of Hitchens condemning the failure of his fellow liberal panellists (including Boris Johnson and Shirley Williams) to offer Rushdie their full-throated support, can be seen at this link: www.youtube.com/watch?v=gEVA4EAP_S0.

[152] Mark Goldie, 'Introduction' in John Locke, *A Letter Concerning Toleration and Other Writings* (Mark Goldie (ed), Indianapolis, Liberty Fund, 2010) xi. References below to Goldie, and to Locke's *Letter*, are to this edition.

[153] Spinoza (1632–77) was born in Amsterdam and lived in the Netherlands. Born a Jew into an émigré Portuguese family, he was excommunicated from his synagogue in the 1650s. His major work, *Tractatus theologico-politicus*, was published posthumously in 1677. Despite being officially suppressed, it had significant influence. It is one of the key texts of the Radical Enlightenment. Bayle (1647–1706) was a French Huguenot who fled to the Netherlands in 1681. He was perhaps the first person in Europe to argue for unlimited freedom of conscience.

Locke did not think that Catholics could be included within the scope of the freedom he advocated, whereas neither Spinoza nor Bayle were so sectarian.[154] Locke offers three arguments for toleration. His first is that the policing of religion is not a matter for the state. Government cannot save souls, so it should get out of the business of pretending that it can. Church and state, for Locke, are 'perfectly distinct and infinitely different'.[155] The business of the state is the protection of life, liberty and property: government should confine its attention and focus its powers accordingly.

Locke's second argument is that persecution is ineffective. Coercion simply cannot bring people to believe that a particular conviction is true. What one believes is a wholly internal matter: it can never owe its weight to pressure of external force. Moreover, he added, persecution was ineffective also because different rulers in different states persecute different groups of believers. Its target is not those who are in religious error, but those who are politically weak. It is a tool not of the virtuous to deploy on the lost, but an instrument of the powerful to use on the powerless. Locke's third argument is one of mutual respect. Goldie summarises it as follows:

> [C]onscientiously held beliefs are to be respected; or, rather, believers are to be respected, even if we regard their beliefs as ill-founded. We may agree that a sect is blighted by errant conscience, but freedom of conscience must take priority over (our own conception of) truth.[156]

Locke is firm in his own Christian convictions but believes nonetheless that 'we must tolerate error'. What matters for him is 'the sincere pursuit of truth, however tangled and tortuous the paths people take'.[157]

Putting it this way explains why Locke could not extend toleration to atheists or Catholics: because they were not 'sincere' in their 'pursuit of truth'. Keeping promises is one of the very 'bonds of human society': it is a mark of sincerity.[158] An atheist cannot be trusted because he lacks any fear of divine punishment. Promises, oaths and covenants are therefore meaningless to him. As society cannot function without such commitments, a society cannot tolerate atheism. Locke's problem with Catholics was similar.

---

[154] In modern scholarship, Bayle and (even more so) Spinoza are presented as foundational figures of the 'radical' Enlightenment. Locke was foundational to more 'moderate' Enlightenment figures (such as Montesquieu, Hume and Voltaire). See Jonathan Israel's monumental tetralogy: *Radical Enlightenment* (Oxford, Oxford University Press, 2001); *Enlightenment Contested* (Oxford, Oxford University Press, 2006); *Democratic Enlightenment* (Oxford, Oxford University Press, 2011); and *The Enlightenment that Failed* (Oxford, Oxford University Press, 2019).

[155] Locke, *A Letter Concerning Toleration* (n 152) 24.

[156] Goldie (n 152) xviii.

[157] ibid.

[158] Locke, *A Letter Concerning Toleration* (n 152) 52–53.

Not only could the pope depose heretic rulers and require his followers to withdraw allegiance, but so too was it a canon of Roman Catholic law that 'faith need not be kept with heretics'. In other words, those rules of honesty and promise-keeping which were so central to Locke's conception of 'sincerity' need not apply when Catholics dealt with heretics. This, in Locke's view, could not be tolerated. It is worth noting, then, that it is not Catholicism as such which is excluded from the scope of Locke's argument for toleration. Rather, as Goldie explains, it is any believer 'who holds that ordinary moral laws are trumped by the superiority of religious truth'.[159]

Spinoza and Bayle may have pushed the argument further, but it was the more limited Lockean conception of toleration that was successful in shaping public policy. The Toleration Act of 1689, for example, whilst it exempted protestant dissenters from some of the penalties against them enacted under earlier legislation, repealed 'not a single penal law'.[160] The Test Acts remained in force. Dissenters were relatively free to worship but, as far as public life and political office were concerned, they remained very much second-class citizens. Neither Locke's argument for toleration, nor indeed public opinion, would stomach anything further.[161] This was not yet even close to being a time of religious indifference and, as John Stuart Mill was to note more than 150 years later:

> So natural to mankind is intolerance in whatever they really care about, that religious freedom has hardly anywhere been practically realised, except where religious indifference, which dislikes to have its peace disturbed by theological quarrels, has added its weight to the scale.[162]

Yet, as Diarmaid MacCulloch has pointed out, the Toleration Act was hugely significant: less because it marked the beginning of a long journey away from religious discrimination and more because it signalled the formal surrender of the established church's insistence that its version of Christianity was the only one which could officially exist.[163]

IV. Conclusion

The religious question had been neither removed nor divorced from European politics and government by the end of the seventeenth century,

---

[159] Goldie (n 152) xix.
[160] E Neville Williams, *The Eighteenth Century Constitution: Documents and Commentary* (Cambridge, Cambridge University Press, 1960) 6.
[161] ibid.
[162] Mill (n 46) 12.
[163] MacCulloch (n 6) 532.

but some of the toxicity had been taken out of it and it began – for the first time in 150 years – to slip down the list of political priorities. The age of heresy was not exactly over but it had started nonetheless to recede as the age of sedition dawned. Toleration was neither universal nor full but it had at least emerged not only as an aspiration of political liberals, but as an embedded feature of the law. Over the course of the ensuing century its roots would deepen. By 1700 printing was, at last, unlicensed in Britain and the first arguments against censorship had been voiced. None of this meant that speech was free – the battle to secure it still lay in the future – but Locke's influence was to endure and Milton's was to be revived. The struggle for free speech was under way.

2

Sedition and Offence

I. Faith, Reason and *Cato's Letters*

The European Enlightenment, which emerged at the end of seventeenth century and flourished in the eighteenth, was the age of reason. One of its defining motifs, carried forward by the brilliance of such luminaries as Voltaire, was the war it declared if not on religion itself then at least on priestcraft and on all manner and form of ecclesiastical authority. 'Theological debate', says Jonathan Israel, lay 'at the heart of the early Enlightenment' – all its controversies 'hinged on the now thoroughly destabilised and problematic relationship between reason and faith'.[1] In this regard England and Scotland were no different from France, Germany and the Netherlands. If, in England, the Revolution Settlement of 1689 'extracted the poison from the religious controversy' which had dominated English politics since the break with Rome 150 years previously,[2] so too, in Scotland and on the Continent alike, did European thinking strive to move away from a focus on considerations of religion towards a framing based instead on progress, commercial society and, above all, reason. This is as true for Montesquieu, whose *Spirit of the Laws* was published in France in 1748, as it is for David Hume, whose *Essays, Moral and Political* was first published in Edinburgh in 1741.

In this climate, it is not surprising that the focus of those who campaigned and advocated for freedom of speech shifted, with more attention paid to the state and rather less to the church. The first to make an avowedly secular argument for free speech against the state were the authors of *Cato's Letters*, a series of radical Whig newspaper columns published weekly from 1721 to 1723 in the *London Journal*, one of the capital's leading opposition papers. Written by John Trenchard and Thomas Gordon, there were 138 *Cato's Letters*, of which four focused particularly

---

[1] Jonathan Israel, *Enlightenment Contested* (Oxford, Oxford University Press, 2006) 65.
[2] E Neville Williams, *The Eighteenth Century Constitution: Documents and Commentary* (Cambridge, Cambridge University Press, 1960) 7.

on freedom of speech.[3] Trenchard and Gordon were to leave a powerful legacy which enjoyed considerable influence, not least across the Atlantic, but they were outliers in their day. The argument for free speech still had to be made and, as we shall see in this chapter, it was to face numerous opponents yet, including from some of the eighteenth century's wittiest and most intelligent writers, Jonathan Swift and Samuel Johnson among them.

It should not be thought, then, that the early eighteenth century was a time of new-found free expression. Just because licensing (ie, the pre-publication state or church censorship of books) was now a thing of the past did not mean that the press was all of a sudden free. It was not, and very few thought it should be:

> Throughout the early eighteenth century, it was the view of Whig and Tory governments alike that an unbridled press represented a constant and considerable threat to political stability and order. No minister of either party, and hardly any writers, ever seriously doubted the rights and responsibilities of governments to correct and check what were generally regarded as notorious abuses of the press.[4]

And yet, when compared with the Continent, there was, even in the early eighteenth century, remarkably more freedom of the press in England than was the European norm. David Hume in 1741, for example, could write that:

> Nothing is more apt to surprise a foreigner than the extreme liberty, which we enjoy in this country, of communicating whatever we please to the public, and of openly censuring every measure entered into by the king or his ministers.[5]

Hume was exaggerating but he was only half wrong. The extent of the liberty of the British press was indeed the envy of Europeans, but it stretched neither to the freedom to communicate 'whatever we please' nor to the right of 'openly censuring every [government] measure'.

In the decades after the lapse of the Licensing Act the government possessed – and exercised – at least four different means of seeking to restrict speech and control the press. The first was statute. A new Blasphemy Act was passed in 1698 and a new Treason Act followed in 1707. Both created criminal offences targeted at expression. The second was tax. A Stamp Act passed in 1712 imposed heavy levies on popular print,

---

[3] *Cato's Letters* is available today in only one modern edition: John Trenchard and Thomas Gordon, *Cato's Letters* (Ronald Hamowy (ed), Indianapolis, Liberty Fund, 1995, 2 vols). The four *Letters* on which we will focus are Nos 15, 32, 100 and 101. All references below to *Cato's Letters* and to Hamowy are to this edition.

[4] PBJ Hyland, 'Liberty and Libel: Government and the Press 1712–1716' (1986) 101 *English Historical Review* 863.

[5] David Hume, 'Of the Liberty of the Press' in David Hume, *Essays Moral, Political and Literary* (Eugene Miller (ed), Indianapolis, Liberty Fund, 1987) 9.

although the legislation was poorly drafted and proved relatively easy for the press to circumvent.[6] The third was censorship, albeit not of publications but of performances: the theatre was subjected to licensing under the Stage Licensing Act 1737, which remained in force until the Theatres Act 1843, which in return remained in force until the Theatres Act 1968. The fourth means – and by far the most significant – which the state enjoyed to control and limit speech was the common law: in particular, the law of seditious libel. This made it an offence to incite 'by words or writings disaffection' towards the state or constituted authority'.[7] This was expression which fell short of outright treason but which was nonetheless criminal despite the fact that it was not of itself violent (although it might lead to violence).

Seditious libel was not a new offence, but its scope was significantly broadened after 1695. It left its moorings in the law of defamation to become a crime in its own right, with its own precedents. It was extended to cover writings whether they were published or not (or, indeed, whether or not they were even intended for publication). And its reach was extended again in 1704 when Chief Justice Holt determined it to be seditious libel 'to bring scandal upon a government by defaming the government in general as well as by defaming particular persons within it'.[8] According to Holt CJ, 'If men should not be called to account for possessing the people with an ill opinion of the Government, no Government can subsist; for it is very necessary for every Government, that the people should have a good opinion of it'.[9] Seditious libel would be tried by jury, but the role of the jury was severely limited. Until 1792 its role was simply to decide whether the accused had indeed written (or printed or published) what he had been charged with having written (or printed or published). It was not for the jury to determine whether the matter was defamatory or seditious or not: that was a question of law for the judge to rule on.

'Inciting disaffection of constituted authority' and 'possessing the people with an ill opinion of government' are not exactly precise definitions of the scope of criminal liability and several authors tested their limits. This had great literary advantages as writers of genius such as Daniel Defoe and Alexander Pope, Jonathan Swift and Samuel Johnson developed the arts of satire and irony: their 'shared condition', says Thomas Keymer, was 'as writers forever navigating the vexed, indistinct boundaries of seditious libel'.[10]

---

[6] Hyland (n 4) 864.

[7] See Roger B Manning, 'The Origins of the Doctrine of Sedition' (1980) 12 *Albion* 99, 101.

[8] See Philip Hamburger, 'The Development of the Law of Seditious Libel and the Control of the Press' (1985) 37 *Stanford Law Review* 661, 735.

[9] ibid.

[10] Thomas Keymer, *Poetics of the Pillory: English Literature and Seditious Libel 1660–1820* (Oxford, Oxford University Press, 2019) 106.

Those convicted of seditious libel could be imprisoned, of course, but they could also be sent to the pillory. Being required to stand, normally for three periods of one hour each, in various locations, with your head and hands locked into wooden stocks, was not merely humiliating but potentially extremely dangerous. The pillory was a deliberately public form of ridicule, and if the assembled mob was opposed to you, you could find worse than mere rotten fruit and vegetables being thrown in your direction. The days were gone when your ears would be nailed to the pillory and sawn off by the hangman – that had been Prynne's fate in the seventeenth century, as we saw in the previous chapter – but even in the eighteenth you could be badly beaten in the pillory. You might even lose an eye, if the mob ran riot, even if you could expect to hold on to your ears. Of course, the crowd might be the opposite of hostile. When Defoe was pilloried in 1703 the legend was rapidly established (by his friends in the press) that the mob came to him with flowers. The iconography of Defoe's time in the pillory came even to resemble that of Jesus' crucifixion.[11] Yet Defoe was no free speech martyr; for him, as for Swift, censorship was a weapon to be evaded oneself but used against one's enemies.[12] Nonetheless, the risks to the state of the pillory becoming a moment not of ritual humiliation but of martyred celebration were real.

Trenchard and Gordon have seditious libel firmly in their sights in the *Cato's Letters* devoted to freedom of speech. Their argument can be analysed as having four main components. It starts from – and plainly rests upon – the Whig view, derived from Locke, that the role of government is to safeguard and to act upon the interests of the people. The government must be regarded as 'the trustees of the people ... for whose sake alone all public matters are, or ought to be, transacted'.[13] As such, rulers and magistrates have not only the interest, but ought also to have the ambition, say Trenchard and Gordon, 'to have their deeds openly examined and publicly scanned'.[14] A government that acts for the people and in the people's interests is a government that must, by definition, allow the people to enjoy the freedom to scrutinise and, where necessary, to criticise it. Conversely, and at the same time, a people can show that it is free only if it has the freedom to scrutinise and, where necessary, to criticise, its government. In what appears to be a direct rejoinder to Holt CJ, Cato puts it thus: 'That men ought to speak well of their governors is true, while their governors deserve to be well spoken of; but to do public mischief without hearing of it, is only the prerogative and felicity of tyranny'.[15] In a nice phrase,

---

[11] ibid 132–48.
[12] ibid 139.
[13] *Cato's Letters* (n 3) 111.
[14] ibid.
[15] ibid.

Cato observes, 'freedom of speech is ever the symptom, as well as the effect, of good government'.[16]

This is the constitutional root which grounds Trenchard and Gordon's entire conception of free speech. That conception, they announce at the beginning of their treatment of it, is as follows:

> Without freedom of thought, there can be no such thing as wisdom; and no such thing as public liberty without freedom of speech: Which is the right of every man, as far as by it he does not hurt and control the right of another; and this is the only check which it ought to suffer, the only bounds which it ought to know. This sacred privilege is so essential to free government, that the security of property and the freedom of speech always go together; and in those wretched countries where a man cannot call his tongue his own, he can scarce call anything else his own. Whoever would overthrow the liberty of the nation must begin by subduing the freedom of speech, a thing terrible to public traitors.[17]

We can see from this passage that freedom of speech was not an 'added extra' for Trenchard and Gordon – it was not a bolt-on. It was fundamental – as basic a building block as even the right to property. We can see also, however, that it is not an absolute. Trenchard and Gordon acknowledge both that speech can cause 'hurt' and that this should set the 'bounds' of its freedom. Liberty does not extend to the right to cause others hurt (albeit that, at least in this passage, the notion of hurt has yet to be defined). It is noteworthy that one of the modern common law's favourite things to say about free speech is found also in this passage: namely, that tyranny begins in an attempt to overthrow free speech. This is reminiscent of Lord Bridge's famous dictum in one of the *Spycatcher* cases, that 'freedom of speech is always the first casualty under a totalitarian regime'.[18] *Cato's Letters* got there first: 'freedom of speech', Trenchard and Gordon write, 'is the great bulwark of liberty: they prosper and die together'.[19]

If this is the first component of Cato's argument for free speech, its second relates to truth. This is a facet of free speech upon which John Stuart Mill would also focus, more than a century after *Cato's Letters* although, as we shall see, he did so for different reasons and to different effect. For Trenchard and Gordon, freedom of speech exposes truth and, for them, it is as simple and as straightforward as that. Only the guilty need dread it, for free speech drags guilt 'out of its lurking holes and exposes its deformity and horror to day-light'.[20] Truth is the necessary and automatic outcome of freedom of speech: 'misrepresentation of public measures is easily

---

[16] ibid.

[17] ibid 110.

[18] *Attorney General v Guardian Newspapers* [1987] 1 WLR 1248, 1286: see further ch 3.

[19] *Cato's Letters* (n 3) 114.

[20] ibid 111.

overthrown by representing public measures truly', Cato assures us.[21] For as long as 'all opinions are equally indulged and all parties equally allowed to speak their minds, the truth will come out', they insist.[22]

It is to their credit that Trenchard and Gordon do not seek to deny that free speech carries with it vices as well as virtues. Libels, they say, are inevitable: 'as long as there are such things as printing and writing, there will be libels: it is an evil arising out of a much greater good'.[23] Libel, they accept, is an 'abuse'.[24] But, by libel, they mean the defamation of a private individual, not the crime of sedition. Libelling, according to *Cato's Letters*, is 'a sort of writing that hurts particular persons without doing good to the public'.[25] The exposing of 'public wickedness', on the other hand, 'is a duty which every man owes to truth and his country', and, as such, 'can never be a libel'.[26] That libel and the abuse of free speech are inevitable, however, is no argument against free speech. It is 'ridiculous', they say, to argue that just because something can be abused it should be destroyed.[27] They illustrate the point as follows:

> As to those who are for locking up the press because it produces monsters, they ought to consider that so do the sun and the Nile; and that it is something better for the world to bear some particular inconveniences arising from general blessings, than to be wholly deprived of fire and water.[28]

Cures can be worse than diseases. Fire and water, just like free speech, can have monstrous and devastating effects. Yet we would not be without them, for all the havoc they may wreak. This, say Trenchard and Gordon, is simply part of the human condition:

> There is scarce a virtue but borders upon a vice and, carried beyond a certain degree, becomes one. Corruption is the next state to perfection: Courage soon grows into rashness; generosity into extravagancy; frugality into avarice; justice into severity; religion into superstition; zeal into bigotry and censoriousness; and the desire of esteem into vainglory. Nor is there a convenience or advantage to be proposed in human affairs, but what has some inconvenience attending it.[29]

Inconveniences need to be remedied, where possible, and not merely tolerated with a blithe shrug of the shoulders. The best way of escaping

[21] ibid 114.
[22] ibid 714.
[23] ibid 232.
[24] ibid 714.
[25] ibid 228.
[26] ibid.
[27] ibid 714.
[28] ibid 232.
[29] ibid 715.

'the virulence of libels', according to *Cato's Letters*, is not to deserve them.[30] But Trenchard and Gordon acknowledge the naiveté of this: they know that 'innocence itself is not secure against the malignity of evil tongues' and that it will be necessary for the law to have the means of punishing those who abuse free speech.[31] But it does not follow, they insist, that 'the press is to be sunk' just because some authors will inevitably abuse it.[32]

This leads directly to the final noteworthy component of the argument in *Cato's Letters* for free speech. Even for Whigs as radical and independent as Trenchard and Gordon were when they wrote the *Letters*, free speech is far from unlimited. 'Decency, good manners, and the peace of society' would all 'forbid' that.[33] The freedom of speech they advocated was explicitly a liberty bounded by 'manners and discretion'.[34] We may justly resent 'the impertinence of a factious scribbler or the impotent malice of a turbulent babbler'.[35] That is to say, we would be right not only to be irritated by impertinent controversialists or malicious gossips, but to use the legal means available to us to secure justice against them. This, say Trenchard and Gordon, is the best we can do. Free speech is a 'general blessing', whereas its abuses are 'particular inconveniences'. The latter will have to be tolerated and – where appropriate – punished, but not to the point that the former is jeopardised, let alone jettisoned. To the variety of arguments they have made in support of this contention, summarised above, they add just one more at the end of what was to be their final *Letter* on free speech. We know, they say, there is no better approach because previous methods 'to prevent real libels have proved ineffectual'. That is, licensing and censorship do not work. Such methods

> only prevent the world from being informed of what they ought to know … The subjecting of the press to the regulation and inspection of any man whatsoever can only hinder the publication of such books as authors are willing to own and are ready to defend; but can never restrain such as they apprehend to be criminal, which always come out by stealth … And dangerous and forbidden libels are more effectually dispersed, enquired after, and do more mischief than libels openly published.[36]

The argument in *Cato's Letters* for free speech was remarkable. No one before Trenchard and Gordon had ever put forward 'an essentially secular ideal of free speech as an individual political right'.[37] Their declarations

---

[30] ibid 234 (and compare 716).
[31] ibid 234.
[32] ibid.
[33] ibid 717.
[34] ibid 721.
[35] ibid 720.
[36] ibid 722.
[37] Fara Dabhoiwala, 'Inventing Free Speech: Politics, Liberty and Print in Eighteenth-Century England' (2022) *Past and Present* (supplement 16) 39, 40.

about free speech were 'extraordinary – almost everything about them was unprecedented'.[38] Their argument set out a defence of freedom 'unmatched for its breadth and vigour in the literature of the period'.[39] And yet, if one wants to be critical, there was little genuinely original about them. In the main, all Trenchard and Gordon did was to lift relatively well-established arguments about freedom of conscience and apply them to political speech. They were polemicists, 'brilliant popularisers, rather than original thinkers'.[40] Yet they were all the more successful for that. Once *Cato's Letters* started appearing in it, the *London Journal* 'soon surpassed all its competitors in influence and importance'.[41] Circulation soared, and reached far beyond the capital alone. They were regarded as the authoritative voice of opposition to the administration. Collections of the *Letters* were bound together and sold as books in their own right: there were at least six editions by the 1750s.[42] Across the Atlantic, their influence in the American colonies was immense, surpassing that even of Locke himself. Their impact in America was in no sense limited to their arguments about free speech but, as both lawyers and historians have noted, '*Cato's Letters* did much to popularise the idea of a free press in the American colonies'.[43] Indeed, Cato's most splendid phrase, that 'freedom of speech is the great bulwark of liberty' was copied and pasted directly into Virginia's influential declaration of rights and was used also by James Madison in his draft Bill of Rights.[44]

In England, the government did not take *Cato's Letters* lying down. Numerous attempts were made to suppress the *London Journal*. Moves were made in May 1721 to have Trenchard and Gordon called in for libelling the administration but, somehow, they avoided arrest and the matter was dropped.[45] Two months later, though, the *London Journal*'s 'office was raided, its printing press smashed, and its staff arrested'.[46] This did not deter Trenchard and Gordon, and the *Letters* continued to appear. There followed a change of tack on the government's part, perhaps because 'the raids had only increased Cato's reputation as a fearless truth-teller, rather than as a poisonous, rabble-rousing spreader of malicious and scandalous

---

[38] ibid 51.

[39] Ronald Hamowy, 'Introduction' in Hamowy (n 3) xxiv.

[40] Dabhoiwala (n 37) 57.

[41] Hamowy (n 3) xxxv.

[42] ibid. Caroline Robbins wrote that *Cato's Letters* were 'among the most widely read and important polemical works of the reign of George I': *The Eighteenth-Century Commonwealthmen* (Cambridge MA, Harvard University Press, 1959) 111.

[43] Hamburger (n 8) 745, citing Leonard Levy, *Freedom of Speech and Press in Early American History* (Cambridge MA, Belknap Press, 1963).

[44] See Dabhoiwala (n 37) 72; see further ch 3.

[45] See Hamowy (n 3) xxxii.

[46] ibid.

libels'.[47] The government's new policy was to bribe political writers rather than to take legal action against them. The owner of the *London Journal* reached an accommodation with the government. *Cato's Letters* found a new home in the *British Journal* but, by then, Trenchard's health was declining. After he died no more *Cato's Letters* appeared and Gordon, like many before him, found himself reaching a settlement with his erstwhile enemy, prime minister Robert Walpole, who awarded him the sinecure of becoming First Commissioner of Wine Licences.[48] His later translation of Tacitus was dedicated to Walpole. Revisiting the question of free speech in 1728, five years after the last of *Cato's Letters* had appeared, Gordon adopted the orthodox approach of rulers and magistrates – that in general it was 'safer to let the people grumble than forbid it – yet for them "tumultuously ... to publish their mutual discontents and wrongs, and to inflame one other" was insupportable'.[49] Trenchard was dead and Gordon had been bought off, silenced not by the law courts but by the bribes of the ministry of which he had once been a critic but in whose pay, says one historian, he was to grow 'rich and fat'.[50]

II. A Sceptical Note: Swift and Johnson

That historian – Fara Dabhoiwala – offers in his recently published analysis of *Cato's Letters* a trenchant critique of the worth of Cato's arguments for free speech.[51] Among his most compelling points is the following:

> *Cato's Letters* ignored the problematic reality of how mass media really worked. Aside from glancing references to the past evils of licensing, and the imperfections of the current libel laws, its free speech model made no mention of the taxation and harassment of newspapers, their cut-throat competition for readers, the government's monopoly over the postal network, the toxic spread of political lies, the problem of media partisanship, the difficulty of sifting truth from fiction, or the ways in which money and power continually undermined even the possibility of free and honest public communication.[52]

There is much to agree with in this critique. Trenchard and Gordon are certainly blithe about the connection they assume between free speech and truth. Their argument presumes that, as long as governments do not seek

---

[47] Dabhoiwala (n 37) 56, citing an anonymous government informant.
[48] Hamowy (n 3) xxxiii–xxxiv.
[49] Dabhoiwala (n 37) 70, citing Gordon's *Works of Tacitus* (1728).
[50] ibid 69.
[51] Dabhoiwala (n 37).
[52] ibid 64.

to suppress speech, the truth will always out; truth will not only be readily distinguishable from falsehood, but will prevail over falsehood.

We know it is not so simple. Dabhoiwala's point is: so did Trenchard and Gordon. Contemporaries of theirs certainly did, and the early eighteenth century is notable not only for the advances that were made in the struggle for free speech, but also for the notes of scepticism – even dissent – which were sounded along the way. There were those, even then, who saw remarkably clearly the dangers of free speech: that the truth could be manipulated, that in the hands of a skilled writer falsehoods could be all too easily disguised as truths, that the weeklies and newspapers in which Cato thrived were highly partisan, that the printing trade was not merely an industry (motivated by profit as much as by the search for truth) but a political economy (motivated by powerful forces whose interests did not necessarily align with the truth). Among the first to see this was one of the eighteenth century's greatest writers, Jonathan Swift. (We will see in chapter six that much of what Swift wrote about the problems of a free press in eighteenth-century Britain fits remarkably with very twenty-first century problems of speech online.)

Two of Swift's earliest works, *The Battle of the Books* and *A Tale of the Tub*, which were published together in 1704 but written in the mid-to-late 1690s, saw him give voice to concerns about the implications for free speech which were to stay with him for much of his writing career, including in his masterpiece of satire, *Gulliver's Travels* (1726).[53] *The Battle of the Books* is ostensibly a fable relating to the so-called 'ancients and moderns controversy', which was raging in both England and France in the 1690s. *A Tale of the Tub* is a complex piece of literary, political and religious satire, hard to categorise but, in the main, an allegorical parable about the development of Christianity in Europe. Both pieces contain various prefaces, introductions, letters dedicatory and digressions, in which Swift takes aim at the proliferation of 'Grub Street' scribblers whose inferior works, after the lapsing of the Licensing Act, were pouring from the London presses. In *The Battle of the Books* he writes that

> ink is the great missive weapon in all battles of the learned, which, conveyed through a sort of engine called a quill, infinite numbers of these are darted at the enemy by the valiant on each side, with equal skill and violence, as if it were an engagement of porcupines.[54]

---

[53] For a modern edition of Swift's work, which includes both *The Battle of the Books* and *A Tale of the Tub*, see Jonathan Swift, *Major Works* (Angus Ross and David Woolley (eds), Oxford, Oxford University Press, 1984). The authoritative edition of *Gulliver's Travels* is now Vol 16 of the *Cambridge Edition of the Works of Jonathan Swift* (ed David Womersley, paperback edn 2022).

[54] Swift, *The Battle of the Books*, ibid 4.

He imagines a character, representing Criticism, with her parents Ignorance and Pride sitting either side of her. Alongside them are her sister Opinion, 'light of foot, hoodwinked, and headstrong, yet giddy and perpetually turning'.[55] In front of them play her children, Noise and Impudence, Dullness and Vanity, Pedantry and Ill-Manners. Criticism explains that:

> Tis I who give wisdom to infants and idiots; by me, children grow wiser than their parents; by me, beaux become politicians, and schoolboys judges of philosophy; by me, sophisters debate and conclude upon the depths of knowledge; and coffeehouse wits, instinct by me, can correct an author's style and display his minutest errors without understanding a syllable of his matter or his language.[56]

Swift, unrivalled wit that he was, used irony as his most potent weapon. But underlying the humour of his satirical style lay a deeply serious point: Swift was appalled by what he read. The end of licensing had created a 'cultural swamp' in which 'imaginations did not so much soar as sink' and where prose lacked all form, 'like bilge'.[57] It was not just the 'literary mediocrity' of Grub Street[58] that irritated Swift: it was also that the new fashion for free speech was based on a profound error and that its consequences were likely to be highly dangerous.[59] The error, in Swift's view, was to imagine (as *Cato's Letters* did) that what went for freedom of conscience should go likewise for freedom of speech. Swift was an Anglican – a theologian, an ordained priest and, for 30 years, Dean of St Patrick's in Dublin. He understood conscience to mean the 'liberty of knowing our own thoughts', a liberty 'no one can take from us'.[60] Conscience, for him, was wholly internal: it 'properly signifies that knowledge which a man hath within himself of his own thoughts'.[61] Swift was opposed to the 'quite different' meaning which, in his day, conscience had come to acquire:

> Liberty of Conscience is nowadays not only understood to be the liberty of believing what men please, but also of endeavouring to propagate the belief as much as they can and to overthrow the faith which the laws have already established, to be rewarded by the public for those wicked endeavours.[62]

---

[55] ibid 12.

[56] ibid 13.

[57] Randy Robertson, *Censorship and Conflict in Seventeenth-Century England* (Pennsylvania, Penn State University Press, 2009) 167–68.

[58] ibid 175.

[59] See David Womersley, 'Swift and Free Speech' in Robert Ingram, Jason Peacey and Alex Barber (eds), *Freedom of Speech 1500–1850* (Manchester, Manchester University Press, 2020).

[60] Jonathan Swift, 'Sermon on the Testimony of Conscience' in Swift (n 53) 381.

[61] ibid 380.

[62] ibid 381.

This, he said, was the view of 'fanatics' who, it is to be noted, show not the slightest 'public spirit or tenderness' to those who disagree with them.[63]

The expansion of liberty of conscience into freedom of speech was not only mistaken: it was fraught with peril. In particular, it was dangerous to public order and to the established authority of church and state. This danger Swift alluded to in his preface to *A Tale of the Tub*, where he refers to 'the wits of the present age being so very numerous and penetrating, it seems the grandees of Church and State begin to fall under horrible apprehensions'.[64] Swift was aghast that the slightest murmur against a minister of the Crown could lead directly to jail, whereas displaying 'your utmost rhetoric against mankind', telling them 'we are all gone astray', was regarded as the delivery of 'precious and useful truths'[65] no matter how destabilising it was to peace, order and good government. If these views were Tory – indeed, Hobbesian[66] – in character, it did not follow that Swift thought the state could or should return to the old ways of suppression. Swift knew which way the river was flowing and he was more than astute enough to realise that any official attempt to obstruct it would be futile. When he urged his friend, the editor of the *Tatler* magazine 'to make use of your authority as Censor, and by an annual *index expurgatorius* expunge all words and phrases that are offensive to good sense, and condemn those barbarous mutilations of vowels and syllables', he knew full well it was never going to happen.[67]

Gulliver's depiction of the language of the Houyhnhnms in Book IV of his *Travels* tells us their use of speech was uniquely for purposes of understanding, 'to receive Information of Facts'.[68] There is no word in their language for lying or falsehood and they appear to have no conception of opinion, controversy or disagreement. Their language has no terms for power, government, war, law or punishment. Even if Gulliver is tempted to recommend such a way with words (and such a way of life) to his human

---

[63] ibid. In Book II of *Gulliver's Travels*, Swift has the King of Brobdingnag tell Gulliver that 'he knew no reason, why those who entertain opinions prejudicial to the public, should be obliged to change, or should not be obliged to conceal them. And, as it was tyranny in any government to require the first, so it was weakness not to enforce the second. For a man may be allowed to keep poisons in his closet, but not to vend them about as cordials' (Jonathan Swift, *Gulliver's Travels* (1726), Bk II ch vi).

[64] Swift, *A Tale of the Tub* (n 53) 79.

[65] ibid 85.

[66] The debt Swift owes to Hobbes has been noted by several commentators, including Robertson (n 57) and Womersley (n 59). The latter astutely observes that Swift was a 'secret sharer' with Hobbes in terms of his views about free speech. In chapter 18 of *Leviathan* (1651) Hobbes had remarked that 'it is annexed to the sovereignty, to be judge of what opinions and doctrines are averse, and what conducing to peace; and consequently, on what occasions, how far, and what men are to be trusted withal in speaking to multitudes of people'.

[67] Jonathan Swift, 'Letter on the Corruption of our English Tongue' in Swift (n 53) 254.

[68] *Gulliver's Travels*, Bk IV, ch 4.

readers, Swift surely is not. Swift's purpose seems rather to show that human civilisation, flawed as it inevitably is, can escape falsehood no more readily than it can corruption. All we can hope for is that we may from time to time possess powers of reason sufficient to distinguish the false from the true, the corrupt from the virtuous. Swift is not so optimistic about humankind as to consider that such momentary flashes of reason will be more than merely occasional. Gulliver's voyages reflect darkly on mankind: freedom of speech may be a reward we do not deserve.

It was noted above that, whilst the licensing of the press never returned to English law, the licensing of the theatre was reintroduced by Act of Parliament in 1737. The theatre had been used several times to satirise government, drawing dramatic attention to ministerial sleaze. John Gay's *Beggar's Opera* (1728) is perhaps the best-known example today but other plays of the period attracted more aggressive repression from Walpole's administration, including Gay's follow-up, *Polly* (1729), which was not permitted to be performed and was produced only in book form. Because it had been banned from the theatre, sales soared.[69] A further play, *The Fall of Mortimer* (1731), was suppressed as a 'false, infamous, scandalous, seditious, and treasonable libel' and resulted in the Little Haymarket theatre being forcibly closed down for several months.[70] Whether the authorities had the legal power to stop performances of such plays, however, was dubious. Hence the 1737 Act, to put the matter beyond doubt. The first play banned under the new legislation was *Gustavus Vasa* (1739) which, as Thomas Keymer describes it, 'gave a vaguely Jacobite inflection to the liberation rhetoric of its hero, a sixteenth-century Swede, and featured the assassination of a royal favourite'.[71] The play's banning had at least one enduring (if unintended) literary consequence: it caused Samuel Johnson to write his ironic essay, *A Compleat Vindication of the Licensers of the Stage* (1739).[72]

Johnson (like Swift and Gay) was a vocal critic of Walpole's administration. In the *Compleat Vindication* he assumed the persona of a government insider. The essay appears to defend licensing but, in reality, Johnson is mercilessly ridiculing it. The essay runs two main lines of argument: first, that authority should simply be accepted and not challenged; and secondly, that licensing can never in fact go far enough, ie, we will always need more of it, not less. Johnson starts by remarking how it is 'generally agreed' that 'few crimes are equal, in their degree of guilt, to that of calumniating a

---

[69] See Keymer (n 10) 182.
[70] ibid 183.
[71] ibid 185.
[72] For a modern edition, see Samuel Johnson, *Selected Essays* (David Womersley (ed), London, Penguin, 2003).

good and gentle ... administration'. He notes that the only virtue cited by the ministry's critics is their appeal to 'posterity', a 'chimera' which has led them to a position of 'contempt of authority and an irreverence for any superiority'.[73]

The purpose of legislating to confer upon the Lord Chamberlain the power to license the stage, says Johnson, was not to dispense justice, still less fairness. Rather, it was 'to bring poets into subjection and dependence: not to encourage good writers, but to discourage all'. There is no obligation on the licensor to permit a play to be performed, no matter how excellent it is. Moreover, no reason need be given by the Lord Chamberlain for refusing permission: after all, the government had always had the power to censor a play if it had good reason to do so. What the Act of 1737 did, says Johnson, was to extend the power even where there was no good reason: 'our intention was to invest [the Lord Chamberlain] with new privileges, and to empower him to do that *without* reason, which *with* reason he could do before'.[74] This censure, Johnson suggested, should not be confined to

> those lines in which liberty, natural equality, wicked ministers, deluded kings, mean arts of negotiation, venal senates, mercenary troops, oppressive officers, servile and exorbitant taxes, universal corruption, the luxuries of a court, the miseries of the people, the decline of trade, or the happiness of independency are directly mentioned.[75]

Rather, the 'vigilance of the licensers' should extend

> to all such speeches and soliloquies as tend to recommend the pleasures of virtue ... for though such strokes as these do not appear to a common eye to threaten any danger to the government, yet it is well known to more penetrating observers that they have such consequences as cannot be too diligently obviated.[76]

Nothing should rest beyond the reach of the censors. Otherwise, he insists, 'the mere force of artless honesty' on the part of the people will be able to 'surmount all the obstacles which subtlety and politics can throw in their way'.[77] Reaching his climax, he asks,

> how much would this single law lighten the mighty burden of state affairs? With how much security might our ministers enjoy their honours, their places, their reputations, and their admirers, could they once suppress those malicious invectives which are at present so industriously propagated, and so easily read?[78]

---

[73] Samuel Johnson, 'A Compleat Vindication' in Johnson (ibid) 498.
[74] ibid 501 (emphasis in the original).
[75] ibid 506.
[76] ibid 506–07.
[77] ibid 507.
[78] ibid.

Quite literally anything and everything inconvenient to the government should be subject to their censorship.

Indeed, he would go further. The only news which the public should be able to read should be that officially published in the government-sanctioned *Gazette*. How much happier would the state then be 'than those perpetual jealousies and contentions which are inseparable from knowledge and liberty, and which have for many years kept this nation in perpetual commotions'?[79] What is needed, Johnson concludes, is 'the pleasing tranquillity of ignorance'. And this can be secured, in the end, not merely by licensing what we see on the stage and read in the press, but by regulating even what is permitted to be taught in schools. Thus 'it may be made a felony to teach to read, without a license from the Lord Chamberlain'.[80]

Johnson's *Compleat Vindication* is satire. But its argument was put forward in all seriousness by members of the government. The Lord Chancellor, Lord Hardwicke, said in the House of Lords that 'if the liberty of the press consists in defamation, it were much better we were without such liberty'. And as for 'the freedom which some gentlemen think themselves entitled to in censuring the conduct of the superiors', he continued, this 'is a freedom unknown to our constitution, and subversive of our known statutes'.[81]

Johnson's ironic temper in the *Compleat Vindication* is withering in its contempt, Swiftian in its menace. It was a style he grew out of. The *Compleat Vindication* is an early work of Johnson's: it was before the *Rambler* (1750–52), before the *Dictionary* (1755) and long before the *Lives of the Poets* (1779–81). Johnson's most political essays appeared in two phases of his career: 1739–45 and 1770–75.[82] Like many, the older he became the more comfortable he grew with his Toryism. Towards the end of his life, he reflected with greater maturity than he had done in the *Compleat Vindication* on the strengths and limitations of free speech. His later position was more nuanced, alive both to the dangers inherent within unbounded speech and to the harms caused by censorship. This is what he has to say about *Areopagitica*, in his treatment of Milton in volume one of the *Lives of the Poets*, first published in 1779. It is both remarkable and complex, and it deserves to be quoted in full:

> The danger of such unbounded liberty, and the danger of bounding it, have
> produced a problem in the science of Government, which human understanding

---

[79] ibid 508.

[80] ibid 509. In *Areopagitica* Milton had made much the same point: that, if we are to regulate printing, why would we not also seek to regulate music, dancing and gesture. See ch 1.

[81] See Keymer (n 10) 188.

[82] For an overview, see Thomas Kaminski, 'Politics' in Jack Lynch (ed), *The Oxford Handbook of Samuel Johnson* (Oxford, Oxford University Press, 2022).

seems hitherto unable to solve. If nothing may be published but what civil authority shall have previously approved, power must always be the standard of truth; if every dreamer of innovations may propagate his projects, there can be no settlement; if every murmurer at government may diffuse discontent, there can be no peace; and if every sceptic in theology may teach his follies, there can be no religion. The remedy against these evils is to punish the authors; for it is yet allowed that every society may punish, though not prevent, the publication of opinions, which that society shall think pernicious; but this punishment, though it may crush the author, promotes the book; and it seems not more reasonable to leave the right of printing unrestrained, because writers may be afterwards censured, than it would be to sleep with doors unbolted, because by our laws we can hang a thief.[83]

Johnson is clear in this passage – as he was in the *Compleat Vindication* – that, if we are a society which seeks truth, we cannot have pre-publication censorship, for censorship collapses truth into power. But, at the same time, the absence of licensing causes harms of its own: harms to settled authority, harms to public order and harms to religious authority, too. Hence the need to retain causes of legal action which can be taken against authors whose work is seditious. And yet, as Johnson surmises, this does not always work. For one thing, going after a book which is seditious may serve only to amplify that book's ability to broadcast its message and, for another, it is no more logical than encouraging a burglar to steal your possessions knowing that you can take legal action against him after he has done so. For Johnson, these appear to be problems of good governance which admit of no solution. If we want free speech, we will just have to put up with its vices, its drawbacks and its inconveniences.

David Hume sketched a very eighteenth-century way in which, he thought, such vices, drawbacks and inconveniences could and should be minimised: through manners. We should strive to be polite and judicious, Hume suggested, as we should seek to avoid rudeness and impertinence. We owe it not only to ourselves, but to society at large, to seek to cultivate a higher and more refined taste. Such good manners, such refined taste, should frame our actions as they should qualify our speech. We may have 'liberty of the press', as Hume boasted, but we should exercise the freedom that comes with it only politely and judiciously. Such, at any rate, appears to be his suggestion.[84]

---

[83] Samuel Johnson, 'Milton' in Samuel Johnson, *Lives of the Poets, Vol 1* (Arthur Waugh (ed), London, Oxford University Press, 1906) 77–78.

[84] See David Hume, 'Of the Delicacy of Taste and Passion' in Hume (n 5) 3–8. This is the opening essay in Hume's *Essays*; it is immediately followed by his essay 'On the Liberty of the Press'. It is impossible to avoid the impression given by this sequencing that 'delicacy of taste' is understood as qualifying the 'liberty of the press'.

Be that as it may, the legal orthodoxy of the mid-eighteenth century was authoritatively set out by Sir William Blackstone in his *Commentaries on the Laws of England* (1765–69). According to Blackstone, seditious libel, blasphemous libel and all the other common law causes of action that could be commenced in respect of the published word left the 'liberty of the press, properly understood' wholly intact. They 'by no means' either 'infringed or violated' it.[85] This is what Blackstone had to say:

> [T]he liberty of the press is indeed essential to the nature of a free state, but this consists in laying no previous restraints upon publications, and not in free-dom from censure for criminal matter when published. Every freeman has an undoubted right to lay what sentiments he pleases before the public: to forbid this is to destroy the freedom of the press. But if he publishes what is improper, mischievous or illegal, he must take the consequence of his own temerity.[86]

Blackstone continued as follows:

> [T]o punish (as the law does at present) any dangerous or offensive writings, which, when published, shall on a fair and impartial trial be adjudged of a pernicious tendency, is necessary for the preservation of peace and good order, of government and religion, the only solid foundations of civil liberty. Thus the will of individuals is still left free; the abuse only of that free will is the object of legal punishment. Neither is any restraint hereby laid upon freedom of thought or enquiry: liberty of private sentiment is still left; the disseminating, or making public, of bad sentiments, destructive of the ends of society, is the crime which society corrects.[87]

Thus, for Blackstone, 'to censure ... licentiousness' is the price that must be paid (albeit not by him, of course) 'to maintain the liberty of the press'.[88] In his conclusions on the topic, Blackstone quotes an unnamed 'fine writer on this subject', who says that 'a man may be allowed to keep poisons in his closet, but not publicly to vend them as cordials'.[89] The law may no longer worry all that much about what you think (within the privacy of your mind) but once you start making your views known to the public, you had better be sure that what you are saying is wholesome and not noxious. Blackstone does not identify the writer but it is, of course, Jonathan Swift: the quotation is from *Gulliver's Travels* and was cited above.[90] An early

---

[85] Sir William Blackstone, *Commentaries on the Law of England* (1765–69) vol 4, 151.

[86] ibid 151–52.

[87] ibid 152.

[88] ibid 153. To modern ears this all sounds a bit too much like *Spiderman*: 'with great power comes great responsibility'. Yes, the liberty of the press gives you great freedoms, but you had better be damned careful about how you exercise them. Use your freedom well and wisely – and we will reserve to ourselves the right to tell you, only after the fact, if we think you have.

[89] ibid 152.

[90] Above (n 63).

illustration, perhaps, of law and literature, and a coded suggestion, maybe, that Blackstone shared the satirist's broader concerns and reservations about unlicensed speech?

The key line in Blackstone's account is that if you publish what is 'improper, mischievous or illegal' you must 'take the consequence' of your own 'temerity'. By the middle of the eighteenth century the common law was still dangerously vague about what would be deemed 'improper, mischievous or illegal'. Its approach was very much 'publish and be damned' except, for 'damned', read 'run the risk of ruin'. If you wrote, printed or published something which the authorities considered to be dangerous – to their own reputations, to public order, or to religious authority – you could very well find yourself having to face the possibly ruinous, indeed possibly even fatal, 'consequences' for your temerity. Better to keep quiet, you might think. Better not to rock the boat. Better not to take the risk. In the century that separates Blackstone's account from John Stuart Mill's (in *On Liberty* (1859)) three things started to happen. First, the law tightened up and clarified what it understood by those all-too-vague terms, 'improper', 'mischievous' and 'illegal'. Secondly, the law loosened what Johnson, Hume and Blackstone would have understood to be appropriate 'consequences'. And thirdly, the law eventually relaxed its former disapproval of the 'temerity' of writers, printers and publishers. None of these moves was complete by 1859. Indeed, as we shall see, some of them were not complete even by 1959. And some of them, even if they reached their peak in the 1960s and 1970s, may have regressed since then. But if this gives us a sense of where we are going, let us not get ahead of ourselves. In the eighteenth century it was far from clear that this would be the path pursued.

III. Testing the Limits: Wilkes and Paine

In the second half of the eighteenth century the extent to which government in Britain would tolerate what I have termed the 'vices, drawbacks and inconveniences' of free speech were most sorely tested in the 1760s by John Wilkes and in the 1790s by Tom Paine. Both periods saw a flurry of state trials, including trials for seditious libel, a number of which reveal not only the prevailing political mood as regards the limits of free speech, but also the judgment of the courts as to the weight the common law should accord to notions of free speech.

Wilkes was an iconoclast, an MP, a pamphleteer, a supporter of Pitt and an outspoken opponent of the administration. He was charming, intelligent and uncompromising. He was also greatly in debt, licentious in his personal behaviour, crude to the point of obscene, and a terrific wit. The government was unpopular; Wilkes was the opposite.[91] His principal vehicle was the *North Briton*, a weekly propaganda sheet that sought to defend Pitt and attack the government, which was headed by Lord Bute, the North Briton (or Scot) of the paper's title. Wilkes' strident opposition to the Cider Tax (a policy of Bute's so unpopular that it caused riots and had to be withdrawn) was just one of the fields in which Wilkes made his name. The *North Briton's* most famous number was No 45, of April 1763, in which Wilkes attacked not only the administration but the king himself, effectively accusing him of lying in his speech extolling the Treaty of Paris, which had brought to an end the Seven Years' War. The peace had brought with it severe economic depression, compounded by a succession of bad harvests and made yet worse by declining trade with America. Unemployment was growing; prices were rising. The rabble would have been roused in any event, but Wilkes lost no opportunity in making sure, just in case.[92]

The ministry, which had thought about but had decided against taking action in respect of earlier numbers of the *North Briton*, could tolerate Wilkes' assault no longer and, proceeding via a general warrant, they prosecuted Wilkes for seditious libel. The previous year, as every constitutional lawyer knows, they had acted similarly with regard to Wilkes' fellow pamphleteer John Entick, with respect to what Entick had written in another opposition weekly, *The Monitor*. Entick's arrest and detention, the searching of his house and the seizure of his papers, in the execution of the secretary of state's warrant, led to Lord Camden's justly famous decision in the great case of *Entick v Carrington*,[93] one of the landmarks of British constitutional law's commitment to the rule of law.[94] It was in *Entick v Carrington* that Lord Camden, chief justice of the Court of Common Pleas, ruled that the warrant of a secretary of state was no authority for lawful arrest, search or seizure: just because the secretary of state wanted something done, the agents of the state had no power to execute his wish unless the law of the land provided them with the requisite authority. The blizzard of cases which the ministry's actions against Wilkes, Entick, the *North Briton* and the *Monitor* generated tell us a great deal not only about

---

[91] The best biography is Arthur Cash, *John Wilkes: The Scandalous Father of Civil Liberty* (New Haven, Yale University Press, 2006).

[92] See Ian Gilmour, *Riot, Risings and Revolution: Governance and Violence in Eighteenth-Century England* (London, Pimlico, 1993) 305.

[93] *Entick v Carrington* (1765) 19 St Tr 1029.

[94] See generally, Adam Tomkins and Paul Scott (eds), *Entick v Carrington: 250 Years of the Rule of Law* (Oxford, Hart Publishing, 2015).

the rule of law and the limits of executive power, but about the state of free speech in 1760s England.[95]

With regard to the warrants in respect of the *Monitor*, it was not only John Entick who was arrested and detained, whose property was searched and whose belongings were seized. The same fate befell his collaborator, the lawyer Arthur Beardmore, as well as their printers, Wilson and Fell. Nothing seditious was found in the search of Entick's papers and the action against him was dropped.[96] As is well known, he sued in the law of trespass the four king's messengers (led by Nathan Carrington) who had arrested and detained him, searched his property and seized his papers. In a trial in the Court of Common Pleas presided over by Pratt CJ (who later became Lord Camden), the jury awarded Entick damages of £300 on condition that the messengers had acted unlawfully. It would be a year and a half later before Lord Camden eventually handed down his great judgment that they had acted unlawfully: this is the judgment we know as *Entick v Carrington*. Beardmore also sued the messengers. He was awarded damages of £1,000. So did Wilson and Fell. They were awarded £300 each. As well as suing the messengers for trespass, they also sued the secretary of state – Halifax – for false imprisonment. Again these suits were heard in the Court of Common Pleas; again Pratt CJ presided; and again the claimants were successful, with additional awards of damages being made.

Meantime, Halifax issued warrants also in respect of the *North Briton*. Wilkes' property was searched and Wilkes himself was arrested and detained in the Tower. Wilkes alleged that Wood, Halifax's under-secretary of state, was present during the search of his property. The messengers (named Money, Watson and Blackmore) also entered the premises of a printer, Dryden Leach, and arrested him and his colleagues. This, it turned out, was a serious mistake, as Leach and co were not in fact the printers of No 45 at all. Wilkes sought habeas corpus in the Court of Common Pleas, Pratt CJ once again presiding. The chief justice gave judgment for Wilkes, but only on the narrow ground that, because he was an MP, he was protected from arrest for sedition by virtue of parliamentary privilege.[97]

---

[95] The summary account which follows is derived from and owes a debt to the brilliant and pioneering contributions of David Feldman, Tom Hickman and Jacob Rowbottom to Tomkins and Scott (ibid), all of whom go to strenuous lengths to make sense of the complex litigation which ensued: see David Feldman, 'The Politics and People of *Entick v Carrington*'; Tom Hickman, 'Revisiting *Entick v Carrington*: Seditious Libel and State Security Laws in Eighteenth-Century England'; and Jacob Rowbottom, '*Entick v Carrington*, the Propaganda Wars and Liberty of the Press'.

[96] As Hickman speculates, it may be that no prosecution was ever intended, the ministry's aim being instead simply to intimidate and to disrupt the *Monitor's* production: see Hickman (ibid) 59.

[97] Parliamentary privilege could not protect an MP from arrest for treason, felony or breach of the peace. Pratt CJ's judgment in this case is important, from a free speech point of view,

As he left the court, the crowd was rapturous, and the first chants of 'Wilkes and Liberty!' were heard on the streets of London.[98] Parliament thereafter resolved that No 45 was 'a false, scandalous and seditious libel' and ordered it to be burned by the common hangman. This was another error. The assembled crowd was firmly with Wilkes and pelted the officials with mud, preventing the burning from taking place. The House of Commons also resolved to expel Wilkes from Parliament; and the crowd could do nothing to prevent that.

Meanwhile, actions for unlawful arrest and false imprisonment brought by Leach and his printer colleagues were successful, and resulted in large awards of damages.[99] Wilkes himself sued Wood for trespass and was awarded £1,000 in damages (again this was in the Court of Common Pleas and again Pratt CJ was presiding).[100] Such success went to Wilkes' head, however, and now it was his turn to make a serious mistake. He sought to reprint the infamous No 45, along with an obscene publication of his, the *Essay on Woman*. For this, he was prosecuted for both seditious and obscene libel. He was convicted in the Court of King's Bench (presided over by Lord Mansfield CJ), as were his printers. As well as being expelled from Parliament, Wilkes was outlawed and, as David Feldman puts it, thereafter he 'spent some years in grave personal and financial difficulty'.[101] He fled to France, and would not return to England for four years.

Three conclusions can be drawn from this (necessarily summary) account of the Wilkes and Entick, *North Briton* and *Monitor* cases. First, they are a collective case-study of how the government was prepared to act against the opposition press, using the law of seditious libel not merely to seek convictions, but to intimidate the press and to disrupt the production of newspapers and propaganda sheets critical of its policies. Secondly, they demonstrate that very different sorts of results could be obtained in different courts. Entick, Beardmore, Wilson, Fell, Wilkes and Leach all secured important wins – and generous awards of damages – in the Court of Common Pleas. The result of their litigation was that the government lost the ability, which it had previously enjoyed, to use warrants in the name of the secretary of state to disrupt the activities of the press. But the victories came at a cost. Wilkes, as we have seen, was both expelled from Parliament and outlawed. He lived in exile for some years and, upon his

---

for ruling that sedition was not, of itself, a breach of the peace. Feldman reports that the Lord Chancellor of the day, Lord Henley, considered Pratt's judgment 'mad': Feldman (n 95) 35. For a report of the judgment, see (1763) 19 St Tr 981.

[98] See Gilmour (n 92) 307.
[99] *Leach v Money* (1765) 19 St Tr 1001.
[100] *Wilkes v Wood* (1763) 19 St Tr 1153.
[101] Feldman (n 95) 40.

return to England, he was imprisoned and fined.[102] Lord Mansfield and the Court of King's Bench come out of this story rather differently from Lord Camden and the Court of Common Pleas. Yet both judges were – at least to a degree – playing politics from the bench.[103] Pratt CJ (Lord Camden) was a close ally and old schoolfriend of Pitt. Wilkes, as we noted above, used the *North Briton* vociferously to defend and support Pitt.

Mansfield's King's Bench was 'rather different'.[104] Mansfield was a Scot whose family had been Jacobite – his father had supported the Old Pretender. He had, says Feldman, 'rather authoritarian inclinations'.[105] Nonetheless, Mansfield made notable contributions to the development of the law (especially commercial law) and is justly famous for his seminal decision in *Somerset's Case* that slavery had no basis in the common law.[106] But on questions of free speech, Lord Mansfield was the opposite of liberal. He agreed with his predecessor Holt CJ[107] that in a trial for seditious libel it was necessary in order 'to avoid anarchy' that the question of sedition not be put to the jury[108] (the jury's role being confined, as we saw above, to the narrow question of whether the accused had written what he had been charged with having written).[109] Mansfield believed fervently in the 'vigorous enforcement of the seditious libel laws as a way of supporting the government and arresting what he saw as a decline in the moral condition of the country'.[110] In a case decided in 1783 Lord Mansfield ruled that 'the licentiousness of the press is a Pandora's box, the source of every evil'.[111] In an earlier case he had ruled that satires even on deceased kings could still be actionable under the law of seditious libel (prompting the quip that this was to make history itself a libel).[112] As Tom Hickman has noted, it is remarkable to observe the 'preparedness of the courts to develop the law to provide an effective tool for the government to use against the dissemination' of writings it deemed subversive.[113] Gilmour agrees: Wilkes, in

---

[102] Gilmour's verdict is that prison was 'probably the best for him' (Gilmour (n 92) 318). His fine was paid by his supporters and, in prison, he was sent a mass of gifts, not least from his American supporters, and protected from accusations of fomenting riot.

[103] With characteristically diplomatic understatement, Feldman puts it as neutrally as he can: 'judicial independence of government was far less well established in the mid-eighteenth century than it became subsequently': Feldman (n 95) 12.

[104] Another instance of Feldmanian understatement: ibid 16.

[105] ibid 16–17.

[106] *Somerset's Case* (1772) 98 ER 499.

[107] See above, text at n 8.

[108] See Hickman (n 95) 50.

[109] This remained the legal position until it was changed by legislation in Fox's Libel Act of 1792: see below.

[110] See Norman Poser, *Lord Mansfield: Justice in the Age of Reason* (Montreal, McGill-Queens University Press, 2013) 244.

[111] See the *Dean of St Asaph's Case, R v Shipley* (1783) 21 St Tr 847, 1040.

[112] See Keymer (n 10) 169–70 (the quip was Horace Walpole's).

[113] Hickman (n 95) 51.

his view, was perfectly justified in calling Lord Mansfield his 'personal enemy'.[114] Gilmour recounts how Mansfield had told the king that 'no man had ever behaved so shamefully as his fellow chief justice, Pratt, in denying His Majesty justice' in cases concerning Wilkes and the *North Briton*.[115] Gilmour's conclusion is damning: 'Mansfield, great lawyer in other spheres though he was, consistently behaved in the Wilkes affair more as a member of the government than as an independent judge'.[116]

The final conclusion to note is that even Lord Camden was orthodox in his opinion about press freedom: he 'took what is, by today's standards, a very limited view'.[117] *Entick v Carrington* may have been a breakthrough judgment in other important respects, but its dicta on free speech 'fit' absolutely 'with the dominant view' of its time.[118] Lord Camden closed his judgment in the case with some ringing words. He said the following: 'all civilised governments have punished calumny with severity, and with reason', for such publications 'debauch the manners of the people; they excite a spirit of disobedience, and they enervate the authority of government'. Licentiousness cannot be tolerated, for to do so would place liberty 'in the utmost danger'. Tyranny, 'bad as it is, is better than anarchy'.[119]

The 1760s was a period of considerable political unrest in Britain, although the succession was secure and there was never any real danger of rebellion. The 1790s were even more fraught. There was palpable fear that the revolutionary fervour unleashed in France in 1789 would cross the Channel. Many yearned for precisely this. Some actively agitated for it, none more so than Thomas Paine, well-known author of *Common Sense* (1776) and *Rights of Man* (1791–92). Paine, unlike Wilkes, was a genuine revolutionary. He fought on the American side in their war for independence from the Crown and became friends with both George Washington and Thomas Jefferson. In the 1790s he wanted to see the English Crown go the way of the French, with a wholly new constitution based on popular sovereignty replacing the settlement according to which England had been ruled since 1688. Paine, in short, wanted to import not only the revolutionary ideals but the new constitutional orders of the American and French revolutions into Britain. Pitt's government was terrified, not least because sales of *Rights of Man* were stratospheric. Paine was prosecuted for seditious libel. He fled to France and was convicted in his absence. He only narrowly escaped a worse fate in Paris: after Robespierre came to power Paine was extremely fortunate to evade the guillotine. He never returned

---

[114] Gilmour (n 92) 310.
[115] ibid.
[116] ibid 339.
[117] See Rowbottom (n 95) 99.
[118] ibid.
[119] (1765) 19 St Tr 1029, 1074.

to England, moving in 1802 to the United States, where he lived for the remainder of his life.[120]

Much of the revolutionary fervour of the early 1790s dissipated when Revolution turned to Terror and when Britain found herself once again at war with France. Paine was far from alone in his sense of bitter regret as to how his revolutionary hopes had come so brutally to be dashed on the rocks of the Terror. The Romantic poets, Robert Southey, Samuel Taylor Coleridge and William Wordsworth felt the same way, as did thousands of others.[121] The 1790s marked the beginning of the end for seditious libel. That may appear a counterintuitive, if not an audacious, claim given that the offence was not formally repealed in English law until 2009.[122] But, whilst it is certainly true that the offence was still prosecuted well into the nineteenth century, the 1790s marked the beginning of its last hurrah.[123] This is for two main reasons.[124] The first is Fox's Libel Act of 1792, which finally conferred on juries the power, denied them by Holt CJ and Mansfield CJ, to determine whether a publication was libellous or not. This rendered the use of seditious libel far more of a gamble for the government than it had been in the days when it could rely on sympathetic King's Bench judges to secure the desired result. It should not be thought, though, that 1792 marked a moment of general liberalisation for free speech in England. The same year saw Pitt's government issue a proclamation against 'wicked and seditious writings'. As John Keane puts it: 'Magistrates up and down the country were ordered to search out the authors and printers of such materials and to submit details' to ministers. Without saying so in terms, 'the proclamation was in fact designed to suppress' Paine's *Rights of Man*.[125]

The second reason for the decline after the 1790s of libel as the government's preferred route for tackling dissent is that, by the turn of

---

[120] See John Keane, *Tom Paine: A Political Life* (London, Bloomsbury, 1995).

[121] See Jonathan Bate, *Radical Wordsworth: The Poet who Changed the World* (London, William Collins, 2020).

[122] Coroners and Justice Act 2009, s 73.

[123] It was a repressive last hurrah, none the less. There were in the region of 200 prosecutions for treason and sedition in the 1790s. This compares with about 120 such prosecutions from 1702 to 1756 and about 70 between 1760 and 1789. See Philip Harling, 'The Law of Libel and the Limits of Repression 1790–1832' (2001) 44 *Historical Journal* 107, 108.

[124] In addition to the two reasons outlined below, Keymer (n 10) offers an intriguing third, which is that the courts denied the copyright protections conferred by the Statute of Anne 1710 to works which were seditious, on the basis that 'there can be no property in what is publicly injurious' (Keymer 269). If 'no profit, indeed no livelihood' could be made by writing or publishing seditious works, rather less of it would be written and published: see Keymer 271. It is true that there is no copyright in seditious (or immoral) works, but intellectual property lawyers would be surprised by Keymer's claim. They tend to think that the absence of copyright protections made the dissemination of seditious or immoral works easier. See, eg, Lionel Bently and Brad Sherman, *Intellectual Property Law* (Oxford, Oxford University Press, 2001) 105–07.

[125] Keane (n 120) 334.

the century, the authorities had started to see sedition more in terms of public behaviour than published writings – and so had juries. After 1820 the written word tended not to be regarded as seditious unless it more or less directly caused a breach of the peace.[126] What replaced seditious libel as the government's preferred means of using the criminal law to respond to dissent was the emergent common law offence of unlawful assembly. The period from the mid-1790s to 1819 is when this shift occurred. Ever since 1820 sedition has been seen much more as a public order problem – and as a public order offence – than as a problem relating to speech and expression.[127] The Blasphemous and Seditious Libels Act 1819 redefined sedition. Whilst it did not narrow sedition quite as far as to require that it must cause a demonstrable breach of the peace, it removed the capaciousness of earlier notions that anything 'possessing the people with an ill opinion of government' could constitute sedition.[128] The Act defined seditious libel as material 'tending to bring into hatred or contempt the person of His Majesty ... or the government and constitution of the United Kingdom'. At a time when constitutional reform had become a legitimate, if hotly contested, subject of debate, this was in practice a tighter redefinition of the offence than might appear on paper. One of the dominant political issues of the 1820s – in the run up to the Great Reform Act 1832 – was parliamentary reform and the expansion of the franchise. Making arguments for or against parliamentary reform was not seditious: it was perfectly legitimate. What constituted sedition, after 1820, was not arguing in the press about reform, but rioting in the streets over the cause of reform.

What had a greater impact on the freedom of the press than the scope of the offence of seditious libel were the consequences of another piece of legislation enacted in 1819: the Publications Act. This was a revenue law (like the Stamp Act of 1712, although it was far more effective than that earlier measure).[129] The Publications Act stipulated that 'periodicals must either conform to the legally-specified size for newspapers and carry a 4d newspaper stamp, or conform to the specified size for pamphlets and appear no more ... than once a month at a minimum price of 6d'.[130] This, as Philip Harling has noted, put an end to the radical two-penny press, at least for the time being.[131] As Thomas Keymer puts it, 'there was little need

---

[126] See Michael Lobban, 'From Seditious Libel to Unlawful Assembly: Peterloo and the Changing Face of Political Crime 1770–1820' (1990) 10 *Oxford Journal of Legal Studies* 307, 350.

[127] The authoritative legal account is Lobban (ibid), whose argument is reinforced by Harling (n 123).

[128] See above, text at n 9.

[129] See above, text at n 6.

[130] See Harling (n 123) 131.

[131] ibid.

to prosecute seditious libellers when the most dangerous media forms they inhabited could instead be taxed out of existence.[132]

There is no doubt, however, that free speech in Britain in the 1820s stood not where it had in the 1720s. If the vagaries of seditious libel had required the best writers of the early eighteenth century to develop the fine arts of irony and satire, the best writers of the early nineteenth could afford to be far more cutting and direct. Thus Wordsworth could write, of the French Revolution, that 'bliss was it in that dawn to be alive' and Shelley could write in 'The Mask of Anarchy' of ministers who 'murder' and in his sonnet 'England in 1819' of an 'old, mad, blind, despised, and dying king'. It is true that these words of Shelley's did not appear in print until after his death; but it is also true that that was only because of the poet's wastefully early demise in a sailing accident in 1822.[133]

This does not mean that speech was free by the early nineteenth century. As we shall see, that was not true even in countries (such as France and the United States) in which rights to free speech had been constitutionally proclaimed. And it certainly was not the case in the United Kingdom where, of course, there was no such constitutional pronouncement. But it does mean that the struggle for free speech had shifted gear – had moved into a new register. It had entered its third age: the age of offence.

IV. The Age of Offence: Blasphemy, Obscenity and John Stuart Mill

If the struggle to free one's conscience from the orthodoxies of the established church was the first age in the battle for free speech (the age of heresy); and if the struggle for political free speech was the second (the age of sedition); the third age was – and still is – the age of offence. This is the age in which both church and state continue to play a role, for sure, but in which the principal struggle for free speech is societal, rather than ecclesiastical or official. It is an age in which the enemy of free speech is the public shaming of those whose words are deemed to offend against the moral values of society. It is a censorious age, but it is an age in which the censor-in-chief is neither pope nor archbishop, neither secretary of state nor Lord Chief Justice. The new censor is public opinion and the great threat to free speech is social censure. It is an age which emerged in the disapproving and

---

[132] Keymer (n 10) 241.

[133] For a selection of the more political poetry of the Romantics, see Jonathan and Jessica Wordsworth (eds), *The New Penguin Book of Romantic Poetry* (London, Penguin, 2005) 617–81.

haughty high morality of the Victorian era. It is an age which, for a brief moment, we appeared to be growing out of in the 1960s and 1970s. But if those decades were the high-water mark of free speech and tolerance, we have receded some way back in the years since. Cancel culture is the censor of our times. It may be modern, but it is not recent.

The Pillory Abolition Act of 1816 marked the end of pillorying for seditious and other forms of libel. The pillory was last used in London in 1830 and was abolished altogether (in Britain) by Act of Parliament in 1837.[134] But the sense of public shaming inflicted upon those who write or say the unacceptable or the unwelcome has never gone away. Being disgraced today may come in the form of a social media pile-on or in being hounded out of your job. When this happens, people are being pilloried for their views and opinions – not literally with their head and hands in the stocks – but metaphorically and every bit as dangerously. Eyes will not be gouged out, nor ears sawn off, but even now people can drown in the mud flung at them. Livelihoods can be lost and lives ruined.

In the nineteenth century the guardian-in-chief of public morality was the church. The role of organised religion in the 1800s was not the same as it had been in the 1500s. This was not the age of heresy redux. But, as Ian Gilmour put it, it was 'divine cement' which held the social order together: the church was 'vastly influential in promoting social stability'.[135] If the sixteenth-century church had been focused on what men were allowed to believe, punishing with ruthless brutality those who dared challenge the church's teachings and dogma, the nineteenth-century church was a different sort of policeman. It was the guardian less of ecclesiastical orthodoxy and more of accepted social norms – public *mores* rather than religious doctrine.[136] In this role it competed, and sometimes cooperated, with a range of powerful voluntary associations and organisations. This is one of the hallmarks of the age of offence: that the policing of speech is undertaken as much by vigilante social groups as it is by officials of established church or state. We can see the emergence of this as early as in the 1790s, when loyalist organisations such as the Association for Preserving Liberty and Property against Republicans and Levellers sprang up in reaction to the spread of reform

---

[134] See Keymer (n 10) 225.

[135] Gilmour (n 92) 438.

[136] A similar evolution can be seen in the changing role of the Vatican's Index of Prohibited Books (which we encountered in ch 1). In the nineteenth century such literary figures as Dumas, Zola, Balzac, Flaubert and Victor Hugo all found themselves, or their works, listed on the Index; as did, in the twentieth, André Gide and Jean-Paul Sartre: see Robin Vose, *The Index of Prohibited Books* (London, Reaktion, 2022) 211. It was not only the French who were singled out for inclusion on the Index, but they do seem to have been particularly targeted.

(and revolutionary) societies, such as the London Corresponding Society and the Society for Constitutional Information.[137]

When Richard Carlile was prosecuted in 1819 for republishing Paine's *Age of Reason* and *Rights of Man*, it was at the instigation of the Society for the Suppression of Vice (Carlile was convicted, and spent the next six years in jail). The Vice Society, 'reflecting its origins during the Revolutionary and Napoleonic Wars', was 'a patriotic conservative movement, exercised by vice as a force of social disorder, and not simply an evangelical movement'.[138] Carlile's offences were compound: if *Rights of Man* was seditious, Paine's *Age of Reason* was blasphemous. This was an offence – blasphemous libel – which prosecutors found juries were more likely to convict for than the riskier offence of seditious libel. As the age of sedition waned and as the age of offence emerged in its wake, blasphemy came to play a more prominent role, reinforcing in their positions as moral guardians associations such as the Society for the Suppression of Vice and, of course, the church.[139] Meanwhile, the government saw prosecutions for blasphemous libel less as punishment for offences against God and more as a tool for the suppression of public disorder. If 'the poor' were 'robbed of the consolations of religion', they would be less willing docilely to accept the immiseration of 'the status quo in return for promised rewards in an afterlife'.[140] When, in 1841, the Royal Commission on the Criminal Law reviewed the law of blasphemous libel, it agreed. This is Levy's account:

> Laws for the punishment of offences against religion, it asserted, were 'justifiable on mere temporal grounds upon two principles'. The first was that religion served Caesar: it prompted obedience to the law, particularly among the 'ignorant and unthinking', because it inspired moral conduct. To weaken its influence on 'the great mass of inhabitants' risked further violations of penal enactments. Second, most people in civilised countries regarded religion as worthy of respect; therefore, 'the criminal law may properly be employed to protect the feelings and opinions of the community on this subject from wanton insult'.[141]

There was no danger to freedom of expression, in the view of the Commissioners. Blasphemy unquestionably deserved punishment because it reflected malice and wanton disregard. Moreover, it was injurious to the community by diminishing the efficacy of religion as the basis for moral conduct.[142]

---

[137] See Gilmour (n 92) 400–05.

[138] Christopher Hilliard, *A Matter of Obscenity: The Politics of Censorship in Modern England* (Princeton, Princeton University Press, 2021) 12.

[139] See Leonard Levy, *Blasphemy: Verbal Offense against the Sacred from Moses to Salman Rushdie* (New York, Knopf, 1993) esp chs 16–17.

[140] ibid 358.

[141] ibid 434.

[142] ibid 434–35. Levy's verdict on the views of the Commissioners was damning: 'an intellectually reprehensible performance, lacking rectitude, consistency, or even a scintilla of argument' (ibid 441).

By the middle of the nineteenth century anti-vice campaigners were arguing that blasphemy alone did not reach far enough, and that fresh legislation was needed. The result was the Obscene Publications Act 1857, which gave magistrates the power to order that offensive publications be destroyed. This Act sat alongside – and did not replace – the common law offence of obscene libel. Obscenity, even more than blasphemy, saw non-state actors in the foreground. We have already met the Society for the Suppression of Vice. Its successor was the National Vigilance Association. In the twentieth century, Mary Whitehouse's National Viewers' and Listeners' Association would take up the cause, using not only more modern obscenity statutes (such as the Obscene Publications Act 1959, which remains in force to this day), but also much older common law offences, including blasphemous libel.[143]

The most powerful essay ever written in English about freedom of speech was fully alive to the new threats to free expression posed by the age of offence. When John Stuart Mill published his great tract *On Liberty* in 1859 his principal target was neither church nor state: what he was most concerned about was what he called 'social tyranny'.[144] 'When society is itself the tyrant', he wrote, 'its means of tyrannising are not restricted to the acts which it may do by the hands of its political functionaries'.[145] Rather, it may practise 'a social tyranny more formidable than many kinds of political oppression, since, though not usually upheld by such extreme penalties, it leaves fewer means of escape, penetrating much more deeply into the details of life, and enslaving the soul itself'.[146] Legal penalties and persecution by the authorities are not to be underestimated. But their true potency was that 'they strengthen the social stigma. It is that stigma which is really effective'.[147] This line of argument rings as true in the twenty-first century as it did in the middle of the nineteenth: 'opinion', Mill knew, 'is as efficacious as law; men might as well be imprisoned, as excluded from the means of earning their bread'.[148]

It is true that 'our merely social intolerance kills no one' but it has effects every bit as devastating for human growth, for it 'induces men to disguise' their opinions, 'or to abstain from any active effort for their diffusion'.[149] Mill did not use the term but nowadays we call this the 'chilling effect', and Mill's recognition that it is a great harm is noteworthy. He continues: 'the price paid for this sort of intellectual pacification is the sacrifice of

---

[143] See, notoriously, *Whitehouse v Lemon* [1979] AC 617.
[144] For a modern edition, see John Stuart Mill, *On Liberty and Other Essays* (John Gray (ed), Oxford, Oxford University Press, 1991). All citations below to *On Liberty* are to this edition.
[145] ibid 8.
[146] ibid 8–9.
[147] ibid 37.
[148] ibid.
[149] ibid.

the entire moral courage of the human mind'.[150] And further: 'the greatest harm is done to those who are not heretic, and whose whole mental development is cramped, and their reason cowed, by the fear of heresy'.[151]

Mill's most famous argument in *On Liberty* is his articulation of the 'harm principle'. This, he says, is the one principle which should 'govern absolutely the dealings of society with the individual in the way of compulsion and control, whether the means used be physical force in the form of legal penalties, or the moral coercion of public opinion'.[152] In his words:

> That principle is, that the sole end for which mankind are warranted, individually or collectively, in interfering with the liberty of action of any of their number, is self-protection. That the only purpose for which power can be rightfully exercised over any member of a civilised community, against his will, is to prevent harm to others. His own good, either physical or moral, is not a sufficient warrant. He cannot rightfully be compelled to do or forbear because it will be better for him to do so, because it will make him happier, because, in the opinion of others, to do so would be wise, or even right. These are good reasons for remonstrating with him, or persuading him, or entreating him, but not for compelling him, or visiting him with any evil in case he do otherwise.[153]

This, in a nutshell, is the view of free speech this book takes. Speech should only ever be interfered with, restricted, censored or censured if it causes demonstrable harm to others. This same rule should apply – as it did for Mill – to church, state and society alike. It should govern both pre-publication licensing and post-publication censure. It should operate not only in the arena of human rights (which individuals may be able to enforce against public authorities) but also in the social and private arenas. This rule, simple though it may be to state, is but a starting point and not a conclusion. It leaves open (for now) the matter of what 'demonstrable harm' may be. But we will see in part II of this book that 'demonstrable harm' does not extend to the right not to be offended, hurt, or upset by someone else's speech. Whilst there is no right to use words to threaten or to abuse other people, if your words are merely 'offensive' to those who disagree with them, what that should trigger (as Mill says in the extract just quoted) is counter-speech ('remonstrance') not silencing. But this is to get ahead of ourselves, and to trespass onto territory explored in depth in later chapters.

The harm principle may be Mill's best-known argument in *On Liberty*, but it was not what he regarded his core contention to be. (And he never

---

[150] ibid 38.
[151] ibid 39.
[152] ibid 14.
[153] ibid.

did the work, as we shall have to do in part II of this book, of figuring out what exactly is – and is not – a 'harm' for the purposes of a law of speaking freely.) The heart of the matter, for Mill, was individual growth, development and autonomy. *On Liberty* was a key part of Mill's working himself loose from the utilitarianism of his father, his upbringing and his education.[154] For the utilitarians, securing the 'greatest happiness for the greatest number' was the gold standard. For Mill, by contrast, the foundational principle was to give 'full freedom to human nature to expand itself in innumerable and conflicting directions'.[155] This is why what Mill called freedom of 'thought and discussion' were so central to his argument in *On Liberty*: because they are a 'vital precondition' for the sort of individual flourishing and self-development he was advocating.[156] Ten years before *On Liberty*, in a lecture delivered in 1848 at the University of St Andrews, Mill had put it as follows:

> Improvement consists in bringing our opinions into nearer agreement with the facts; and we shall not likely to do this while we look at facts only through glasses coloured by those very opinions. But since we cannot divest ourselves of preconceived notions, there is no known means of eliminating their influence but by frequently using the differently coloured glasses of other people.[157]

If we are to develop and flourish as individuals, we simply *need* to read and to hear from others, especially those with whom we disagree or who are telling us things we do not already know. Indeed, in a moment some would consider markedly illiberal, Mill goes so far as to suggest this is no mere right, but a duty: 'there is always hope when people are *forced* to listen to both sides; it is when they attend only to one that errors harden into prejudices'.[158]

From the argument for human flourishing flows another: Mill's argument from truth:

> The peculiar evil of silencing the expression of an opinion is that it is robbing the human race; posterity as well as the existing generation; those who dissent from the opinion, still more than those who hold it. If the opinion is right, they are deprived of the opportunity of exchanging error for truth: if wrong, they lose, what is almost as great a benefit, the clearer perception and livelier expression of truth, produced by its collision with error ...

---

[154] See Richard Reeves, *John Stuart Mill: Victorian Firebrand* (London, Atlantic, 2007) esp ch 11.

[155] ibid 268. In his autobiography, Mill described *On Liberty* as 'a kind of philosophical textbook' of this 'single truth' (ibid).

[156] ibid.

[157] ibid 190.

[158] Mill (n 144) 58 (emphasis added).

> We can never be sure that the opinion we are endeavouring to stifle is a false opinion; and if we were, stifling it would be an evil still … All silencing of discussion is an assumption of infallibility.[159]

As we have seen earlier in this book, Milton and Cato also made claims for free expression based on arguments relating to truth. Mill's argument, however, is not the same as those made in *Areopagitica* or *Cato's Letters*. He is close to Milton where Milton writes that it is the collating of diverse opinions which offers us the speediest route to attaining the truth. But, as we saw, Milton's conception of the truth is grounded in his strong sense of Christian duty: for him, it was man's sinful nature that required him always to strive for (divine) truth. Mill's is not the secular approach to free speech we see in Trenchard and Gordon: Mill's concern goes far wider than Cato's narrow focus on political speech and the nature of government. The focus for Mill is liberal human flourishing. He echoes something of Cato's optimism that 'wrong opinions and practices gradually yield to fact and argument'.[160] But, in contrast with *Cato's Letters*, that is not the core of Mill's argument from truth, for he takes the argument in a new direction, found neither in Cato nor Milton. What he says is that

> facts and arguments, to produce any effect on the mind, must be brought before it. Very few facts are able to tell their own story, without comments to bring out their meaning. The whole strength and value, then, of human judge-ment, depending on the one property, that it can be set right when it is wrong, reliance can be placed on it only when the means of setting it right are kept constantly at hand.[161]

Thus, human judgement is valuable – reliable – *only* when it is liable to develop, grow or change as new facts, new interpretations, or new opin-ions emerge. And for this to be possible, the means of allowing new facts, interpretations and opinions to emerge must be 'constantly at hand'. Those means, of course, are the liberty of thought and discussion. There can be no human flourishing unless people are able to grow – and change – their minds. As this is impossible without the freedom to speak (and hear and read) freely, freedom of speech is essential. It is not just the 'great bulwark of liberty': it is the great bulwark of humanity itself.

There is one final difference between Mill's argument and those of Cato (and Hume) which we surveyed earlier in this chapter. As we noted, it was

---

[159] ibid 21–22.
[160] ibid 25. Mill adds, more persuasively, that 'truth has no chance but in proportion as every side of it, every opinion which embodies any fraction of the truth, not only finds advocates, but is so advocated as to be listened to' (ibid 59). It is not that truth will inevitably *prevail* when there is freedom of discussion, but that we can endeavour to *seek* it only if we have freedom of discussion.
[161] ibid 25.

a hallmark of eighteenth-century claims for free speech that expression had to be conditioned – that is to say, curtailed – by manners and taste. Mill considers and expressly rejects this point of view. 'Before quitting the subject of freedom of opinion' Mill reflects on the contention that speaking freely should be permitted only if the manner of its expression is temperate and does not 'pass the bounds of fair discussion'.[162] This is no good, he says, because 'experience testifies that ... offence is given whenever [an] attack is telling and powerful'.[163] Every opponent who pushes you hard, and whom you find it difficult to answer, may appear to you to be intemperate.[164] To set the bounds of free speech, Mill relies not on the polite/rude distinction of the eighteenth century but on a speech/action distinction reminiscent of British government's change in perception at the opening of the nineteenth century that sedition should be understood less in terms of what people write and more in terms of how people behave. Mill says this:

> No one pretends that actions should be as free as opinions ... An opinion that corn-dealers are starvers of the poor, or that private property is robbery, ought to be unmolested when simply circulated through the press, but may justly incur punishment when delivered orally to an excited mob assembled before the house of a corn-dealer.[165]

This is very modern, and looks forward to twentieth-century legal views about the limits to free speech much more than it looks back to the eighteenth-century Enlightenment views of David Hume. As Richard Reeves glosses the point, 'for Mill, the fact that someone's views gave offence to others could never be a reason for their repression. The only ground for regulating speech was to prevent incitement to illegal actions'.[166] Again, this is precisely the view of free speech this book adopts.

V. Conclusions

Mill was a pioneer and, like most pioneers, he was for the most part a lonely outlier in his time, his influence far greater on later generations than on his own. *On Liberty* came of age a century after it was published, in the social liberalism of the 1960s and 1970s. Until the middle of the twentieth century, Mill's remarkably egalitarian optimism about how far down the social orders liberty of opinion and discussion should be allowed to

---

[162] ibid 59.
[163] ibid 60.
[164] ibid.
[165] ibid 62.
[166] Reeves (n 154) 270.

trickle was too much for the ruling classes to stomach. The eighteenth-century view was that, even if men of rank may entertain (in private) the occasional reforming opinion, they should do their damnedest to ensure such opinions did not find their way 'into the minds of the lower orders of the people'. So instructed the Lord Chief Justice, Lord Eyre, in a treason trial in 1794.[167] And such remained the established view even into the early 1960s.[168] Infamously, when Penguin Books was prosecuted for publishing DH Lawrence's novel, *Lady Chatterley's Lover*, in 1960, Crown counsel asked the jury whether the book was one they would want their 'wife or ... servants to read'.[169] The jury acquitted (as it had done, too, in the 1794 treason trial just mentioned) and Penguin sold more than two million copies of the novel in the weeks leading up to Christmas.[170]

But juries did not always acquit when freedom of speech was in the dock, not even in 'the liberal hour' of the 1960s and 1970s.[171] What led to the not guilty verdicts in both 1794 and 1960 may have been, at least in part, the jury's dislike of the paternalist authoritarianism officials brought into the courtroom. In contrast, when *Oz Magazine* was prosecuted for obscenity in 1970, and when Mary Whitehouse brought a private prosecution against *Gay News* for blasphemy in 1977, juries returned guilty verdicts and the defendants were convicted.[172]

The tide was flowing, though, in a liberal direction, and Mill's influence in Britain can be seen in the key breakthrough moments of the Wolfenden report of 1957 and the Williams report of 1979. The former led to the decriminalisation of homosexuality (by eventual force of the Sexual Offences Act 1967); the latter to a revised model for dealing with obscenity as nuisance (moving it, in other words, from the realm of mere speech to the domain of action)[173] as well as to a reformed approach to film censorship. In both reports – but particularly in the latter – Mill's influence was supreme.[174] The Williams Committee wrote, for example, that 'there is a

---

[167] See Gilmour (n 92) 404.

[168] Such a view is far from being uniquely British. Voltaire, among many others on the Continent, shared it. For all that Voltaire was an enthusiast for the notion that eighteenth-century France should emulate England's approach to the liberty of the press, he never regarded free speech as more than 'a privilege for the enlightened few': see Jacob Mchangama, *Free Speech: A Global History from Socrates to Social Media* (London, Basic Books, 2022) 133.

[169] See Hilliard (n 138) 1. As Hilliard notes (103), Penguin attracted prosecution for its cheap paperback edition of *Lady Chatterley's Lover* whereas, in the same period, Weidenfeld and Nicolson did not when they published Vladimir Nabokov's *Lolita* only in hardcover. The former cost 3/6d; the latter 25/-.

[170] ibid 106.

[171] The phrase is Hilliard's: (ibid) ch 5.

[172] The stories of these trials are told in Hilliard (ibid) chs 6–7.

[173] Thus, obscenity would not be prosecuted just because someone found it offensive: it would be prosecuted only if it was a nuisance to someone who wished to avoid it.

[174] See Hilliard (n 138) ch 8.

right to free expression, a presumption in favour of it, and weighty consid-erations in terms of harms have to be advanced by those who seek to curtail it'.[175] Williams' debt to Mill was enormous.

It matters less that the newly elected Thatcher government chose not to implement the full range of recommendations made by the Williams Committee (which had been appointed by the new administration's Labour predecessors in office). What matters rather more is that the approach taken by Williams set both the tone for and the substance of British law and policy from the 1980s on. It took a long time but Mill, finally, prevailed. Whether his victory will prove short-lived or whether it will endure is a question we turn to in part II of this book.

---

[175] Committee on Obscenity and Film Censorship (Williams Committee), *Final Report*, para 5.24.

3

A Legal Right to Speak Freely?

The argument for free speech was a struggle which spanned centuries and, in each of its phases, was an argument *against* established authority. The forces of the law were not on its side. When Milton strained against licensing he was arguing against the law. When Trenchard and Gordon attacked ideas and practices of seditious libel it was not just the ministry's use of repression they had in their sights: it was the common law itself, which gave the administration all the ammunition it needed. Even when Mill crafted his great plea for toleration and liberty, he knew that both common law and legislation pertaining to blasphemy and obscenity were ranged squarely against him. The law buttressed and empowered those who sought to quash speech, whether on grounds of heresy, sedition or offensiveness.

And yet, by the end of the eighteenth century, revolutionaries in France and the United States had managed to write into their constitutional documents formal legal recognition not merely of the importance of free speech but, in the new Enlightenment constitutions, that freedom of speech was a basic right. Article 11 of the Declaration of the Rights of Man, adopted by the French National Assembly in 1789, proclaimed that 'the free communication of thoughts and opinions is one of the most precious of the rights of man'. Even on paper, though, its commitment to free speech was barely more robust than Blackstone had understood English law's to be, for the Declaration continued: 'Every citizen may therefore speak, write and print freely, if he accepts his own responsibility for any abuse of this liberty in the cases set by the law'. The Declaration may have signalled the law's opposition to pre-publication censorship, but it was hardly the sort of unbridled commitment to free speech that would have satisfied the authors of *Cato's Letters*, never mind the author of *On Liberty*. And in practice, the Declaration manifestly failed to deliver even the 'precious' little it had promised. Revolutionaries attacked and suppressed royalist newspapers every bit as violently as the *ancien régime* had sought to attack and suppress them. As Revolution gave way to Terror, counter-revolutionaries found that the new republic's commitment was not remotely to free speech, but to the brutal repression and execution of everyone who 'by their conduct, associations, comments or writings has shown themselves partisans of tyranny and enemies of liberty'.[1] Free speech was guillotined, for all that the Declaration of the Rights of Man had augured.

In America, the constitutions of several states included commitments to the idea of freedom of speech. Most noteworthy was the Virginia Declaration of Rights (1776), drafted by George Mason with help from James Madison, which provided in section 12 that 'the freedom of the press is one of the great bulwarks of liberty, and can never be restrained but by despotic governments'. That line – the great bulwark of liberty – was lifted directly from *Cato's Letters*. When it came to writing a constitution for the United States, though, no Bill or Declaration of Rights was at first included. The US Constitution was ratified in the summer of 1788. Congress met for the first time the following March. Within three months Madison had introduced his proposed Bill of Rights into the House of Representatives. That Bill of Rights contained 12 amendments, the third of which concerned free speech. Only the last 10 amendments were ratified by the requisite number of states. The first two proposed amendments fell and what, in Madison's draft, had been his third amendment became, in 1791, the First Amendment to the US Constitution.[2]

I. The First Amendment

Nearly two and a half centuries on, the First Amendment has become the world's most powerful, as well as its most iconic, legal commitment to free speech. But this is a strikingly recent development. For the first half of its life, the First Amendment was understood to do no more than to write into US constitutional law what Blackstone had said of English common law: namely, that whilst the government has no power to license (or censor) the press, writers, printers and publishers alike are liable to both civil penalties and to criminal sanction in respect of what is said. The full text of the First Amendment is as follows:

> Congress shall make no law respecting an establishment of religion, or prohib-
> iting the free exercise thereof; or abridging the freedom of speech, or of the

---

[1] The Law of Suspects, 17 September 1793, quoted in Jacob Mchangama, *Free Speech: A Global History from Socrates to Social Media* (London, Basic Books, 2022) 179.

[2] See Akhil Reed Amar, *The Bill of Rights: Creation and Reconstruction* (New Haven, Yale University Press, 1998) ch 1. Madison's first and second amendments had been concerned with the membership and composition of the House of Representatives and with the remuneration of Congressmen. The second of these was finally ratified in 1992, to become the Twenty-Seventh Amendment.

press, or the right of the people peaceably to assemble, and to petition the Government for a redress of grievances.

To a modern lawyer's eyes, a great deal is packed into this single sentence. A twenty-first century draftsman would doubtless separate each of the First Amendment's five topics into its own bespoke provision: there shall be no established church or religion; there shall be freedom of conscience; there shall be freedom of speech; there shall be freedom of peaceful assembly; and there shall be the right of citizens to petition the government for redress of grievances.

As far as speech is concerned, it is worth noting two matters about the structure of the First Amendment. First, there is a close relationship in the drafting between freedom of speech and freedom of thought, conscience and religion. This underscores the point made in chapter one that freedom of speech emerged and grew out of the struggle for freedom of conscience: freedom of speech starts with an argument about conscience. Secondly, there is likewise a close relationship between free speech and petitioning the government about grievances. If we do not like what the government is doing, we have a right to say so, to complain about it, and to seek to get the government to change course – and no legislation may be enacted to 'abridge' that right. Structurally, therefore, the First Amendment nods both to the struggles of the age of heresy and to those of the age of sedition.

A superficial reading of the US Constitution may give the impression that the protection of free speech is accorded pride of place. But this would in fact be triply misleading. First, the original constitution (even if it was in force in its original form for only three and a half years) contained no commitment to free speech at all; secondly, that free speech appears in the First Amendment is a product of accident, not design; and thirdly, the commitment to free speech is in any event only one and – to its authors – hardly the most important pledge made in the Amendment in which it appears. There are those who think freedom of speech is the most important right.[3] Perhaps they are right to do so. But this was certainly not the view of the Founding Fathers. The radicalism of the American revolution lay in its commitment to republican self-government, its desire to separate power, and its invention of federalism, where the atom of sovereignty was split between the states, on the one hand, and the nation, on the other.[4] Even if they thought that freedom of speech was one the great bulwarks, necessary to support a new constitutional order as radical as this, they

---

[3] See, among many examples, Sir John Laws, 'Law and Democracy' [1995] *Public Law* 72, 81 ('freedom of speech may be taken as a paradigm' basic right) and Eric Heinze, *The Most Important Human Right: Why Free Speech is Everything* (Cambridge MA, MIT Press, 2022).

[4] See, eg, Gordon Wood, *The Radicalism of the American Revolution* (New York, Knopf, 1992).

thought that meant only that the press had to be unlicensed and the people free to petition for the redress of grievances.[5] The rhetoric may have owed a debt to *Cato* but, beyond that, there was no sense that what the Founders were seeking to achieve was the realisation in law of what the *Letters* had argued for in terms of free speech.

This remained the position even into the twentieth century. It was not until well into that century – in 1919, to be exact – that the power and reach of the First Amendment began to be awakened. Even then, the awakening was at first a minority position, found mainly in dissenting judgments of the US Supreme Court. The story may be relatively well-known in the United States. But elsewhere it not widely appreciated that the First Amendment has not long meant what it is now held to mean. Its awakening has occurred in three discrete bursts of judicial reinterpretation. The first commenced in 1919 and was led by Oliver Wendell Holmes and Louis Brandeis. The second was in the 1960s, when the Warren Court turned what had been uttered mainly in dissent by Holmes J and Brandeis J into mainstream orthodoxy. The third did not reach its crescendo until 2010, when today's hardline free speech militancy became the majority position on the US Supreme Court, a position it still enjoys.

A. Awakenings (1919–27)

The constitutional orthodoxy of the First Amendment's first 120 years was set out authoritatively in a decision the US Supreme Court handed down in 1907: *Patterson v Colorado*. Ironically, given what was to come, the opinion of the court in *Patterson* was written by Oliver Wendell Holmes. In it, Holmes J explained both the orthodoxy that the First Amendment did not apply to the states[6] – it provides, after all, that *Congress* shall make no law abridging the freedom of speech – and the orthodoxy that its scope outlawed only prior restraints. It was the court's view, just as it

---

[5] See Forrest McDonald, *Novus Ordo Seclorum: The Intellectual Origins of the Constitution* (Lawrence, University Press of Kansas, 1985) 49: 'no public figure in America during the 1780s expressed a view of freedom of the press that differed in any substantial way from the views of Blackstone'. Even Benjamin Franklin, 'one of the most ardent defenders of liberty of the press' (ibid), wrote that newspapers which printed scurrilous or defamatory remarks on government were an 'infamous disgrace' (see ibid). Gordon Wood does not disagree: 'Americans believed in freedom of the press … But they believed in it as Englishmen did … [to mean] no prior restraint or censorship of what was published': see Gordon Wood, *Revolutionary Characters: What Made the Founders Different* (New York, Penguin, 2006) 269.

[6] The Bill of Rights did not apply to the states until after the post Civil War ('reconstruction') Fourteenth Amendment. The First Amendment was first held by the US Supreme Court to apply to the states in *Gitlow v New York* 268 US 652 (1925), albeit in a case in which the court *upheld* the constitutionality of New York legislation criminalising the promotion of anarchist views.

had been Blackstone's and indeed Lord Mansfield's, that 'whenever a man publishes, he publishes at his peril'.[7] As Holmes J put it: the purpose of the First Amendment was simply to prevent such prior restraints upon publications 'as had been practised by other governments', not to prevent 'the subsequent punishment of such as may be deemed contrary to the public welfare'.[8] If you write or publish something libellous, or something in contempt of court, you can and should be punished for it, if necessary by the criminal law. Holmes J saw nothing wrong with that and, moreover, he could find nothing in the First Amendment to make him think otherwise.

Holmes J came to champion a deeper conception of free speech only late in his life. He was born in Boston in 1841. He fought in the Civil War, was seriously injured three times and, each time, returned to the front to fight again. He served as a judge in Massachusetts for 20 years before being appointed to the US Supreme Court in 1902 (aged 61) and remained on the court until his retirement 30 years later. He was nearly 80 years old when he penned his celebrated defences of free speech in the wartime cases of *Schenck* and *Abrams*[9] and nearly 90 years old when he joined his friend Louis Brandeis' concurring opinion in *Whitney v California*,[10] probably the most brilliant defence of free speech ever presented from the bench. In part, Holmes' coming round to the importance of free speech was a late flowering of a sentiment which had animated him all his adult life, ever since the end of the Civil War. In another respect, though, it was a more immediate reaction to what a group of his friends had been telling him in the years leading up to 1919, and to what was happening to some of those friends as a result of their views.

If Holmes' thought about law, life, politics and economics could be reduced to a single sentence, it would be: 'we might be wrong'. The lesson, for him, of the Civil War was that the forces of the Confederacy were as sure they were right as the forces of the Union had been. He knew which side he was on, and he put his very life on the line to fight for it. This taught him courage, a theme of his First Amendment jurisprudence to which we shall return. But it also taught him to be sceptical, not only of others' most heartfelt beliefs, but also of his own. He distrusted and detested 'zealotry and causes of all kinds'.[11] A recent biography notes that Holmes 'never mistook his own views for eternal truth'.[12] In 'The Path of the Law', he wrote

---

[7] *Patterson v Colorado* 205 US 454 (1907); *Peck v Tribune Co* 214 US 185 (1909).

[8] *Patterson v Colorado* (ibid) 462.

[9] *Schenck v United States* 249 US 47 (1919) and *Abrams v United States* 250 US 616 (1919).

[10] *Whitney v California* 274 US 357 (1927).

[11] See Stephen Budiansky, *Oliver Wendell Holmes: A Life in War, Law and Ideas* (New York, Norton, 2019) 130.

[12] ibid 223.

that 'certainty generally is an illusion'.[13] We might be wrong, he thought, and the only way to find out is through experiment. This was an approach, both to life and to the law, which shaped Holmes' judgments in a variety of legal fields, including, after 1919, in the field of free speech.

But he had to be pushed to see it, and among those who pushed hardest were his friends Learned Hand, Harold Laski, Louis Brandeis and Felix Frankfurter. Learned Hand and Holmes first met (on a train) in 1918. The younger man was, at the time, a District Court judge in New York (he later rose to become Chief Judge of the US Court of Appeals for the Second Circuit). Learned Hand was troubled by how limited the law was when it came to the protection of free speech, and he shared his anxieties with Holmes, both in conversation and in a long series of correspondence. Harold Laski was an academic at Harvard (where Holmes had also taught, before his elevation to the Supreme Court). He first met Holmes in 1916 and their friendship blossomed instantly. Louis Brandeis was a fabulously successful Boston lawyer, whom Holmes had known since the late 1870s and who joined Holmes as a Justice of the US Supreme Court in 1916. And Felix Frankfurter was one of a circle of much younger friends Holmes made in Washington DC – he was only 28 years old when he first met Holmes in 1911; by the time of the First World War he was teaching at Harvard Law School; after Holmes' death he would also serve as a Justice of the US Supreme Court.

All four of these extraordinary men were close with Holmes in the years leading up to 1919. All four shared with him their views about the importance of a more liberal freedom of speech. And at least two of them were hounded for their political views. Both Laski and Frankfurter were outspoken in their public criticism of the government's (often illegal) raids on and arrests and searches of suspected Communist Party members and Bolshevik leaders in the years of the 'Red Scare'.[14] Harvard's donors were outraged at Laski's and Frankfurter's outspokenness, placing intense pressure on the Dean of the Law School (Roscoe Pound) and, when he would not budge, on the president of the university at least to discipline if not to dismiss the pair of them. Holmes was appalled at the treatment to which his friends were subjected, not least by the vicious anti-Semitism which all too often coloured it (both Laski and Frankfurter were Jewish, as was Brandeis).[15] Harvard stood by Frankfurter, whose career prospered. He helped found the American Civil Liberties Union and went on to serve as an advisor to FDR.[16] But Laski was attacked both within the university

---

[13] Oliver Wendell Holmes, 'The Path of the Law' (1897) 10 *Harvard Law Review* 457; see Budiansky (n 11) 243.

[14] For an account, see Budiansky (n 11) ch 14.

[15] Brandeis J was the first Jewish Justice of the US Supreme Court.

[16] It was President Franklin D Roosevelt who nominated Frankfurter to serve on the US Supreme Court in 1939.

as well as without. In 1920 he quit and moved to the London School of Economics, where he spent the rest of his life.

This was the climate in which Holmes approached the first of the great free speech cases for which he is renowned and remembered. This case – *Schenck v United States* – arose out of proceedings taken against socialists under the Espionage Act 1917.[17] Under this legislation, passed by the US Congress during the First World War, it was an offence of conspiracy to obstruct the recruitment and enlisting service. The offices of the Socialist Party were raided and pamphlets were seized which urged servicemen (and those recruited) to obstruct the draft, offering advice as to how to do so. Schenck was indicted (he was the general secretary of the Socialist Party) and, in a unanimous judgment written by Holmes J, the US Supreme Court upheld the constitutionality of his indictment. However, in the course of his opinion, Holmes J laid the foundations for a new US law of free speech, and for a new approach to the First Amendment which was a radical departure from the established orthodoxy. First, he conceded that 'it may well be that the prohibition of laws abridging the freedom of speech is not confined to previous restraints', even if the prevention of prior restraints may have been 'the main purpose'.[18] He continued: 'we admit that in many places and in ordinary times' Schenck and his comrades 'saying all that was said' in the pamphlets 'would have been within their constitutional rights'.[19] This, as we have seen, had been regarded as recently as *Patterson v Colorado* in 1907 as anathema. It was a stunning turnaround. For the first time, it was intimated, the First Amendment would outlaw not only the prior restraints of licensing and pre-publication censorship, but could also come to the protection of those who were being punished because of what they had said or written.

But that was not all: Holmes J was not done. Not only did he cast doubt on the old law, that the First Amendment guarded only against prior restraints, he also sketched what a new approach would look like. When there is 'a clear and present danger', said Holmes J – but only when there is a clear and present danger – may Congress enact a law abridging the freedom of speech.[20] Here, that test was readily satisfied, in the court's view: the nation was at war, after all, and it was critical to its national security that men could be found to fight. Holmes, the old soldier, could never have thought otherwise.[21] Whether in other circumstances the test is satisfied,

---

[17] *Schenck* (n 9).
[18] ibid 51–52.
[19] ibid 52.
[20] ibid.
[21] *Schenck* was not a one-off. It was one of a string of Espionage Act cases to reach the US Supreme Court in 1919, in which Holmes J ruled, along with his colleagues, that similar convictions should be upheld. See, to like effect, *Frohwerk v United States* 249 US 204 (1919) and *Debs v United States* 249 US 211 (1919).

however, is 'a question of proximity and degree'.[22] 'The character of every act depends upon the circumstances in which it is done', said Holmes J, illustrating his point with what has become a world-famous example: even 'the most stringent protection of free speech would not protect a man in falsely shouting fire in a theatre and causing a panic'.[23] The implication was clear: you may not use words to cause others immediate harm. You may not shout fire in a crowded theatre (unless you believe there really is a fire), and you may not seek to persuade your comrades to put down their arms and refuse to fight when the nation requires them to serve. But if your words cause no 'clear and present danger', then you may well be 'within your constitutional rights' to use them, and the US Congress 'shall make no law … abridging' that right.

Later that same year – 1919 – in another Espionage Act case to reach the Supreme Court, Holmes J ruled that on the facts of the case, no clear and present danger had been shown and that, consequently, criminal proceedings taken against the individuals concerned were a breach of their constitutional right to free speech under the First Amendment. But, in this case, Holmes J was dissenting. The majority of the Supreme Court upheld the constitutionality of the individuals' convictions. Only Brandeis J joined Holmes J in dissent. But it was that dissent which, as we shall see, went on to form the basis of the Supreme Court's twentieth-century case law on the First Amendment. The case was *Abrams v United States*.[24] The defendants, Russian emigrés resident in New York City, had written and printed a number of pamphlets which were critical of US government policy as regards – and war efforts in – Russia. Some were printed in English, others in Yiddish. They were distributed in New York by the inexact means of throwing them out of an apartment window. The defendants were convicted under the Espionage Act of offences which outlawed, whilst the United States was at war, 'disloyal, scurrilous and abusive language' about the US government, intended to bring the government into 'contempt, scorn, contumely and disrepute'. The defendants were sentenced to 20 years' imprisonment. By majority, the Supreme Court upheld the convictions, ruling that the 'plain purpose' of the 'propaganda was to excite, at the supreme crisis of the war, disaffection, sedition, riots and, as [the defendants] hoped, revolution'.[25]

Holmes J dissented, not because he had changed his mind about anything since *Schenck, Frohwerk* and *Debs* but because, applying the 'clear and present danger' test he had adopted in those cases, no such danger

---

[22] *Schenck* (n 9) 52.
[23] ibid.
[24] *Abrams* (n 9).
[25] ibid 623.

was posed by the defendants in *Abrams*. For that reason, their convictions could not be upheld. In Holmes J's judgment, the pamphlets Abrams and his comrades had written were no more than 'poor and puny anonymities', espousing a 'creed of ignorance and immaturity'.[26] Clearly, Holmes J had no sympathy whatever with the content of the emigrés' anarchism. He was contemptuous of their position. But people have the right to be wrong, he thought, and people have the right to express themselves even when they are wrong and even when, in doing so, they voice criticisms of the government. Holmes J was sure that the *Abrams* defendants were wrong – poor, puny, ignorant and immature – but, as we noted above, he rarely lost sight of the fact that he also might be wrong. All of us might be wrong. Even the President of the United States might be wrong. Given this, the expression of opinion should not be punished unless it poses a real and imminent risk: a clear and present danger. Holmes J set out his reasoning in the following terms:

> Persecution for the expression of opinions seems to me perfectly logical. If you have no doubt of your premises or your power and want a certain result with all your heart you naturally express your wishes in law and sweep away all opposition ... But when men have realised that time has upset many fighting faiths, they may come to believe even more than they believe the very foundations of their own conduct that the ultimate good desired is better reached by free trade in ideas – that the best test of truth is the power of the thought to get itself accepted in the competition of the market ... That at any rate is the theory of our Constitution. It is an experiment, as all life is an experiment.[27]

It follows, said Holmes J, that 'we should be eternally vigilant against attempts to check the expression of opinions that we loathe'. Only where they 'so imminently threaten immediate interference' with safety and security that 'an immediate check is required to save the country' can a law abridging freedom of speech be upheld.

In this justly famous passage, Holmes J is channelling not only John Stuart Mill, but Thomas Jefferson. There is a clear echo of Mill's argument from truth,[28] albeit that Holmes J frames it in the context of his scepticism (and his consequent commitment to pluralism) rather than, as Mill did, as part of the liberal argument for human flourishing. The echo of Jefferson – author of the Declaration of Independence – is of the line often attributed to him, that 'the price of liberty is eternal vigilance'. We must be eternally vigilant, says Holmes J, not to reach for the power and sanction

---

[26] ibid 629.

[27] ibid 630.

[28] As we saw in ch 2, Mill wrote in *On Liberty* that 'we can never be sure that the opinion we are endeavouring to stifle is a false opinion; and if we were, stifling it would be an evil still ... All silencing of discussion is an assumption of infallibility'.

of the criminal law in order to silence opinion just because we loathe what is being said. To these well-known sources Holmes J adds a twist of his own: the introduction of the notion of the 'marketplace of ideas'. There is a far better solution to the problem of 'opinions we loathe' than to censor them: it is to expose them. If the ideas are wrong (poor, puny, ignorant or immature) they will struggle for air time, they will suffocate under the inescapable weight of the truth, and they will die. It is a very American way of putting it, to speak of a 'marketplace' of ideas: it appeals directly to its capitalist aspirations, just as John Locke, grounding his argument against licensing in invective about restraint of trade, had so appealed to the English parliamentarians of the 1690s looking to build a commercial society.

This approach to free speech was taken further in an opinion which Brandeis and Holmes JJ co-signed, concurring in the judgment of the Supreme Court in *Whitney v California* in 1927.[29] Whitney had been convicted of a felony ('criminal syndicalism') for assisting in organising the California Communist Party. The US Supreme Court upheld the consti-tutionality of her conviction, ruling that it was not in breach of her First Amendment right to free speech. Brandeis and Holmes JJ concurred in this judgment. They took the opportunity to restate the 'clear and present danger' test, to clarify it, and to develop the reasoning that underpins it. The judgment, one of the clearest and most impassioned defences of free speech ever handed down in a court, repays close examination. And yet it cannot be overlooked that the judgment in the end supported Whitney's conviction. We will notice several times in this chapter that the strongest judicial dicta in favour of free speech are often to be found in judgments in which the speech interest is ultimately held not to prevail; this is true not only of the famous Brandeis and Holmes opinion in *Whitney*, but also of key judgments in the development of the law of free expression in the United Kingdom and in the European Court of Human Rights (ECtHR).

In *Whitney*, Brandeis and Holmes JJ restated the view that the right to free speech, whilst not absolute, may be subject only to such restrictions as are 'required' in order to protect the government from 'destruction or other serious injury, political, economic or moral'.[30] Amplifying this, and seeking to clarify what the by now familiar test means in practice, Brandeis and Holmes JJ continued as follows:

Fear of serious injury alone cannot justify suppression of free speech and assembly. Men feared witches and burnt women. It is the function of speech

---

[29] *Whitney* (n 10).

[30] ibid 373: 'a valid restriction does not exist unless speech would produce, or is intended to produce, a clear and imminent danger of some substantive evil', they added (ibid).

to free men from the bondage of irrational fears. To justify suppression of free speech there must be reasonable ground to fear that serious evil will result if free speech is practised. There must be reasonable ground to believe that the danger apprehended is imminent.[31]

Thus, restrictions on speech will be lawful only where they are *required* (rather than merely where they are expedient). This can be demonstrated only where there are *reasonable* grounds (rather than spurious grounds) to believe that *serious* harm (rather than non-serious harm) *will* ensue (rather than may be suspected) and that the harm is *imminent*. This might be called a quadruple lock, requiring evidence of (1) reasonable grounds to believe that (2) serious harm (3) will ensue (4) imminently.

Having set out the test to be applied, Brandeis and Holmes JJ explained what would be required in order to satisfy it in the context of 'criminal syndicalism' (or speech advocating the breaking of the law). Even advocating law-breaking, 'however reprehensible morally, is not a justification for denying free speech where the advocacy falls short of incitement and there is nothing to indicate that the advocacy would be immediately acted on', they ruled.[32] Rather, to support a finding of clear and present danger, 'it must be shown either that immediate serious violence was to be expected or was advocated, or that ... past conduct furnished reason to believe that such advocacy was then contemplated'.[33] Not all advocacy of law-breaking is incitement, just as not all preparatory acts are criminal attempts, and not all assemblies are unlawful conspiracies. All this is important, but none of it is why *Whitney v California* is remembered today, nor why the Brandeis and Holmes opinion is so revered. The reasons for this lie, rather, in what the opinion said about *why* free speech should be protected via the quadruple lock. The reasoning built on the foundations that Holmes J had laid in *Schenck* and *Abrams*. It is worth quoting at length:

> Those who won our independence believed that the final end of the State was to make men free to develop their faculties; and that in its government the deliberative forces should prevail over the arbitrary. They valued liberty both as an end and as a means. They believed liberty to be the secret of happiness and courage to be the secret of liberty. They believed that freedom to think as you will and to speak as you think are means indispensable to the discovery and spread of political truth; that without free speech and assembly discussion would be futile; that with them, discussion affords ordinarily adequate protection against the dissemination of noxious doctrine ... They recognised the risks to which all human institutions are subject. But they knew that order cannot be secured merely through fear of punishment for its infraction; that

---

[31] ibid 376.
[32] ibid.
[33] ibid.

it is hazardous to discourage thought, hope and imagination; that fear breeds repression; that repression breeds hate; that hate menaces stable government; that the path of safety lies in the opportunity to discuss freely supposed grievances and proposed remedies; and that the fitting remedy for evil counsels is good ones ...

Those who won our independence by revolution were not cowards. They did not fear political change. They did not exalt order at the cost of liberty. To courageous, self-reliant men, with confidence in the power of free and fearless reasoning applied through the processes of popular government, no danger flowing from speech can be deemed clear and present, unless the incidence of the evil apprehended is so imminent that it may befall before there is opportunity for full discussion. If there be time to expose through discussion the falsehood and fallacies, to avert the evil by the processes of education, the remedy to be applied is more speech, not enforced silence. Only an emergency can justify repression.[34]

Again, the debt to Mill is obvious: men (and women) must be 'free to develop their faculties' and the freedom to speak freely is an essential component not only of human flourishing but of happiness itself. And once again, the nod to Jefferson is there, who had linked 'liberty' and 'the pursuit of happiness' so tightly to one another in the Declaration of Independence. We see, in this passage, not only a reprise of the argument from truth but also its coupling to an argument from order and public security. Repression, warn Brandeis and Holmes JJ, breeds instability. Stable government is government that allows and accommodates dissent, not government that seeks to silence it.[35] We see recognition that not all speech is good – that speech can be false, noxious or evil – but that, unless there is an emergency, the remedy is to defeat it in argument, not to silence it in censorship. In free discussion the good, the wise and the true will prevail over the wicked, the ignorant and the false. So Brandeis and Holmes JJ believed. Finally, and coming full circle, we see in this opinion the importance of courage. It appears twice in the passage just quoted ('courage is the secret of liberty' and 'to courageous and self-reliant men'). There is no doubt that Oliver Wendell Holmes and Louis Brandeis were both courageous and self-reliant men. Holmes, as was noted above, more than once proved his courage on the battlefields of the US Civil War. Brandeis required a different sort of courage to progress to and thrive at the top of the American legal system in the face of what, at times, was a sustained campaign of anti-Semitism against him. They were fiercely intelligent, well-educated and highly successful. For the great bulk

---

[34] ibid 375, 377.
[35] This echoes Trenchard and Gordon's point in *Cato's Letters* that free speech is 'the symptom, as well as the effect, of good government' (see ch 2).

of their adult lives they occupied positions of privilege and, by the end of their lives, power. They had plenty of resources upon which they could rely.

But not everyone is so blessed. Some are more vulnerable, less robust, less fortunate. Not everyone is a courageous and self-reliant man and, even if we de-gender it, not everyone can be. I do not suggest for one moment that life was always easy for either Holmes or Brandeis. It was not. But it is nonetheless far easier to build up one's courage and self-reliance if one has the fierce intelligence, the world-class education and the early-career success that Holmes and Brandeis enjoyed. In neither their era nor ours can courage and self-reliance be said to be wholly divorced from wealth, privilege and status. Many underprivileged and politically powerless people are, of course, hugely courageous; there is no necessary link between courage and privilege. But, for all its brilliance and bravery, there is a dimension to the Brandeis and Holmes account of free speech which is missing. It is the dimension of power and, specifically, of the great inequalities of power which both existed in their society and continue to exist in ours.

This is a theme to which we shall return several times in part II of this book, when we consider how our modern laws of free speech navigate a range of different power imbalances (between the media and the privacy of the individual, between the perpetrator and the target of hate speech, between a social media platform and a self-harming teenager). It is a theme, also, which goes back right to the beginning of the struggle for free speech. John Milton, in *Areopagitica*, placed the worthy and virtuous reader at the heart of his argument against censorship. Readers, he claimed, need no state protection from rotten words, contrasting them with the consumers who may well need legal protection from rotten food.[36] As we shall see, it is one of the major fault-lines in today's free speech law, between the US model which adheres to the Milton/Holmes/Brandeis model of the courageous and self-reliant man, and the European (and Canadian) model which has moved away from it, offering more protections to those perceived to need it, and offering weaker protection to freedom of speech as a result.

B. The Liberal Hour (1964–71)

We saw in the previous chapter that it was during 'the liberal hour' of the 1960s and 1970s that Mill's arguments for tolerance enjoyed their greatest influence in Britain. The same era saw a similar moment of liberal flowering in the United States: it was the second phase of the First Amendment's twentieth-century 'awakening'. What happened in this era was twofold.

---

[36] See ch 1.

First, what Holmes and Brandeis JJ had developed in the 1919–27 period became mainstream judicial orthodoxy, rather than dicta to be found only in dissent or in concurring opinions which no other Justice joined. Secondly, the free speech interests at stake in the cases started to prevail. For all the jurisprudential development of the Holmes and Brandeis era, in none of the cases examined from that period did the free speech interest actually win out in the Supreme Court: Schenck's, Frohwerk's, Debs', Abrams' and Whitney's indictments, convictions and criminal sentences were *upheld* by the court in those cases.

New York Times v Sullivan[37] did not arise out of criminal proceedings: it concerned neither the Espionage Act nor allegations of criminal syndicalism. Rather, it concerned a civil action for defamation. Defamatory speech had never been regarded as falling within the protections of the First Amendment; whatever the scope of the right to free speech no one considered that it should extend to the right to besmirch or undermine somebody else's reputation. Just as the English common law had always sought to protect people's reputations, so too the First Amendment. *Sullivan* changed all this, and did so in dramatic terms.

The case concerned an advertisement placed in the *New York Times* in March 1960 by the Committee to Defend Martin Luther King. It was signed by more than 60 celebrities, including leading names from Hollywood and from the music business (among them Marlon Brando, Nat King Cole, Sammy Davis Jr and Sidney Poitier). Under the heading 'Heed Their Rising Voices' it detailed a number of cases in which thousands of Black southern students had been engaged in peaceful demonstrations for their equal rights, only to be met with systemic violence from 'official state apparatus and police power'. The advertisement claimed that 'again and again', officials had answered Martin Luther King's call for peaceful protests with 'intimidation and violence'. One of the instances cited in the advertisement had taken place in Montgomery, Alabama. Sullivan was the locally elected police commissioner for Montgomery and, despite the fact that he was not named in the advertisement, he sued the *New York Times* for libel. A jury in the local state court awarded him $500,000 in damages, an award which was upheld by the Supreme Court of Alabama.

This was, therefore, a case of libel brought by a public official against critics of his official conduct. The US Supreme Court, overturning the award of $500,000 in damages, ruled that no such action could be brought consistently with the First Amendment unless the official could show that the statement published against him was made with 'actual malice',

---

[37] *New York Times v Sullivan* 376 US 254 (1964).

ie, 'with knowledge that it was false or with reckless disregard of whether it was false or not'.[38] Here, the court ruled, there was no such malice, notwithstanding that not everything claimed in the advertisement was true. That the advertisement contained a number of factual inaccuracies, the court ruled, did not mean that it met the high threshold of having been written with actual malice. Such mistakes as there were in the advertisement had been honestly made, and were not malicious. The Supreme Court was unanimous as to the result.[39]

The court's reasoning is instructive. It was based on what was described as 'a profound national commitment to the principle that debate on public issues should be uninhibited, robust, and wide-open, and that it may well include vehement, caustic, and sometimes unpleasantly sharp attacks on government and public officials'.[40] This commitment the court drew from a number of sources, not least the Brandeis and Holmes JJ concurrence in *Whitney v California*, particularly the passage (quoted above) that 'order cannot be secured merely through fear of punishment' and that 'stable government ... lies in the opportunity to discuss freely supposed grievances'. The First Amendment, the court had said in an obscenity case in 1957, 'was fashioned to assure unfettered interchange of ideas for the bringing about of political and social changes desired by the people'.[41] That some of these ideas would be false, and that expression would on occasion extend not only to the well-mannered but also to the caustic and unpleasant, was simply a price which had to be paid. The court quoted Madison's statement that 'some degree of abuse is inseparable from the proper use of everything' and that this was as much the case for the freedom of the press as it was for anything else. Speech will not be free if it is confined only to that which the speaker knows to be true; mistakes are inevitable in a free debate and these too 'must be protected' if freedom of expression is to have the 'breathing space' it needs to survive.[42]

The Supreme Court approved dicta from a lower court in another case, where it had been ruled that the old doctrine, that the governed must not criticise their governors, is 'obsolete'.[43] Again Madison was cited. In 1794 in the House of Representatives he argued that, in the republican form of government enjoyed in the United States, 'the censorial power is in the

---

[38] ibid 280.

[39] Three Justices (Black, Douglas and Goldberg JJ) concurred in the result, but would have gone further: they would have outlawed altogether actions in defamation brought by a public official against his or her critics, even where it could be shown that the author (or publisher) of the statement knew it to be false (ibid 293, 298).

[40] ibid 270.

[41] *Roth v United States* 354 US 476, 484 (1957), cited by the Court in *Sullivan* (n 37) 269.

[42] *Sullivan* (ibid) 271–72, quoting in part from *NAACP v Button* 371 US 415, 433 (1963).

[43] *Sullivan* (ibid) 272.

people over the government, and not in the government over the people'.[44] Repression of criticism of the government can be justified, 'if at all, only by a clear and present danger', the court concluded.[45] If speech were to obstruct the course of justice, for example, repression may be justified – to speak in contempt of court may not be protected under the First Amendment. But the outspoken criticism of elected officials, even if the criticism contained factual errors or attacked their reputation, was protected. If the officials concerned did not like it, their remedy lay not in seeking to silence their critics, but in seeking to defeat them in argument.

Five years later, *Brandenburg v Ohio* underscored just how far the Supreme Court's First Amendment jurisprudence had evolved from the foundations laid a generation earlier by Holmes and Brandeis JJ.[46] It contrasts sharply with *Whitney v California*. Whilst the facts of the two cases were quite different, the underlying state laws under which Whitney and Brandenburg were charged were similar. Both were 'criminal syndicalism' statutes making it an offence to advocate violence as a means of accomplishing political reform. In *Brandenburg v Ohio* a unanimous Supreme Court ruled that such provisions were unconstitutional as being in violation of the First and Fourteenth Amendments. In the process *Whitney v California* was overruled.

Brandenburg v Ohio concerned the Ku Klux Klan. A Klan rally was filmed and a number of racist and anti-Semitic remarks were recorded. Claims were made at the rally that the federal government suppresses 'the white, Caucasian race' and that, if this continues, 'there might have to be some revengeance taken'. Proceedings were commenced against the leader of the group and he was convicted under the Ohio criminal syndicalism statute of advocating violence as a means of accomplishing political reform, and of assembling with others to teach or advocate such means. The US Supreme Court, overturning *Whitney*, ruled that

> the constitutional guarantees of free speech and free press do not permit a State to forbid or proscribe advocacy of the use of force or of law violation except where such advocacy is directed to inciting or producing imminent lawless action and is likely to incite or produce such action.[47]

This ruling, like the judgment in *New York Times v Sullivan*, marks a significant expansion of the protections afforded by the First Amendment. Just as state officials will not be able to sue in defamation unless criticism is

---

[44] Indeed, this line was so good, in the view of the court, that the judgment cites it twice: ibid 275 and 282.

[45] ibid 273.

[46] *Brandenburg v Ohio* 395 US 444 (1969).

[47] ibid 447.

made with 'actual malice', states will not be able to take action against agita-
tors for political reform unless violence is directly incited. Short of this,
people must be free to criticise their rulers, to condemn their government,
even to advocate revolution and to argue for a different system of government altogether. Moreover, they must be free to do so even if they choose
to employ the most aggressively racist or anti-Semitic language.

The *per curiam* decision of the court in *Brandenburg v Ohio* did not
mention Holmes J's 'clear and present danger' test, but the concurring
opinions of Black and Douglas JJ did. They suggested that it should have
no place in the court's First Amendment jurisprudence, not least because
of the 'great misgivings [that] are aroused' when one examines how the test
has been applied.[48] After all, even in the hands of Holmes and Brandeis JJ,
that test led to the constitutionality of criminal proceedings taken against
Schenck, Frohwerk, Debs and Whitney being upheld. Yet, said Douglas J,
'the threats were often loud but always puny and made serious only by
judges so wedded to the status quo that critical analysis made them
nervous'.[49] Douglas J gave concurring judgments in both *Sullivan* and
Brandenburg. In the former, he suggested that public officials should not
be able to sue in defamation even where actual malice could be shown.
In the latter, he suggested that the 'clear and present danger' test may not
be robust enough to give the First Amendment full effect. This hardline
approach is noteworthy, not least because it heralds the direction in which
the court's free speech case law would travel in the third phase of its development (to which we shall shortly turn). But before we come to that phase
there is one further case from the 'liberal hour' of the 1960s and 1970s to
consider.

That case is *New York Times v United States*, also known as the
'Pentagon Papers' case.[50] The 'Pentagon Papers', formally a 'History of
US Decision-making Process on Vietnam Policy' was a highly classified
set of documents which examined in great detail the history of America's
involvement in Vietnam, from the mid-1950s down to 1968.[51] It was
leaked, in redacted form, to the *New York Times*. Journalists at the paper
spent three months reading through it and decided, in the summer of 1971,
to publish a ten-part serialisation. Despite the fact that the core revelations concerned the preceding Kennedy and Johnson administrations, the
incumbent Nixon administration decided to seek an injunction constraining the *Times* from publishing. The case reached the US Supreme Court in

---

[48] ibid 454.
[49] ibid.
[50] *New York Times v United States* 403 US 713 (1971).
[51] See Geoffrey Stone, *Perilous Times: Free Speech in Wartime* (New York, Norton, 2004)
500–16.

an expedited manner and, four days after hearing argument on the matter, the court ruled by six votes to three that the press could not be prevented from printing what they knew. It made no difference, in the opinion of the justices in the majority, that the material had been leaked to the press unlawfully. Applying what Holmes J had said in *Schenck*, the court ruled that it is only when the country is at war that the First Amendment's 'ban on prior judicial restraint may be overridden'.[52] Brennan J noted that 'the entire thrust of the Government's claim' in the case was that publication 'could' or 'might' or 'may' prejudice national security.[53] That was never enough: 'only government allegation and proof that publication must inevitably, directly and immediately cause the occurrence of an event' imperilling the safety of the country could justify the imposition of a prior restraint such as the one sought here.[54]

Following the judgment, publication went ahead. Shortly thereafter the man who had leaked the Pentagon Papers to the press, Daniel Ellsberg, turned himself in. He was charged with and tried for offences contrary to the Espionage Act but his trial collapsed – and he walked free – when it emerged that the offices of Ellsberg's psychiatrist had been burgled on the orders of the White House in order to dig up dirt on Ellsberg's character. President Nixon was reported to say: 'the sonofabitching thief is made a national hero and is going to get off on a mistrial. And the *New York Times* gets a Pulitzer for stealing documents … What in the name of God have we come to?'[55] Not everyone was enthused that the liberal hour had struck.

C. Modern Militancy (the Present Day)

The modern law of the First Amendment is really quite extraordinary. Not only is 'speech' broadly interpreted (to include a number of matters which, in Britain and Europe, would be classified as action or behaviour, rather than as expression). But the legal protection given to 'speech' is remarkably strong, admitting of few exceptions and, perhaps more strikingly from a European perspective, allowing for little balancing of free speech against other compelling public interests. It is not quite an absolutist approach to free speech – even in modern America there are limits to free speech – but it is certainly an approach to free speech marked by a strident militancy.

An early example can be seen in *RAV v City of St Paul*.[56] RAV was a teenager who, with several of his young friends, constructed a wooden

---

[52] *New York Times v United States* (n 50) 726 (Brennan J).
[53] ibid 725.
[54] ibid 726–27.
[55] See Stone (n 51) 515.
[56] *RAV v City of St Paul* 505 US 377 (1992).

cross which they planted on the lawn of a Black neighbour and set light to. The burning cross is an unambiguous sign of racist hatred designed to threaten and intimidate. RAV was prosecuted under a local ordinance which made it an offence to place a symbol 'including, but not limited to, a burning cross or a Nazi swastika, which one knows' or has reasonable grounds to know arouses anger, alarm or resentment in others on the basis of race, color, creed, religion or gender'.[57] The US Supreme Court ruled that the ordinance was contrary to the First Amendment. The court confirmed that the First Amendment does not protect all speech: speech which is 'of such slight social value' that it is 'clearly outweighed by the social interest in order and morality' is not protected by the First Amendment.[58] There are three categories of such (unprotected) speech: obscenity, defamation and 'fighting words'. Each category has been narrowed as the Supreme Court's First Amendment jurisprudence has developed, meaning that less and less speech is excluded from the First Amendment's protection.[59] 'Fighting words' are speech tending to incite an immediate breach of the peace.[60] They are excluded from the scope of the First Amendment's protection not because of their offensive *content* but because of the *mode* of their delivery. It does not matter what is being said: if you express yourself in a such a *manner* as to incite immediate violence, your words may not be protected. This, ruled the Supreme Court in *RAV*, was the problem with the City of St Paul's ordinance: it sought to prohibit speech not on the basis of its aggressive mode of communication, but on the basis that certain substantive things should not be said. It was the singling out of expression targeted at 'race, color, creed, religion or gender' which made the ordinance unconstitutional. By indicating that such speech was disapproved of whereas, for example, homophobic speech was not, the City of St Paul was privileging some messages whilst condemning others. This the First Amendment forbade: 'St Paul has no such authority to license one side of a debate to fight freestyle while requiring the other to follow Marquis of Queensberry rules'.[61]

This did not remotely mean that local law enforcement officers had no grounds on which they could proceed against RAV and his friends. What the teenagers had done could be charged as arson, as criminal damage, or as racially motivated assault. The ruling in *RAV* also did not mean that

[57] ibid 380.

[58] ibid 383, citing *Chaplinsky v New Hampshire* 315 US 568 (1942).

[59] Thus, the test of obscenity was narrowed in *Miller v California* 413 US 15 (1973); the law of defamation was narrowed, as we saw above, in *New York Times v Sullivan* (n 37); and *RAV v City of St Paul* (n 56) itself confirms how narrow the 'fighting words' exception is. See further on 'fighting words' and on offensive and hate speech, ch 5.

[60] See *Chaplinsky* (n 58).

[61] *RAV* (n 56) 392.

states could not ban cross-burning, if they wanted to. This was clarified in the later case of *Virginia v Black*, in which the Supreme Court upheld the constitutionality of a Virginia statute which outlawed cross-burning 'with intent of intimidating any person or group'.[62] The difference between the Virginia statute and the St Paul ordinance was twofold. First, the Virginia statute applied only to cross-burning, singling out that one act as deserving to be criminalised because of its unique status as a threatening gesture celebrating or warning of impending violence. Secondly, the Virginia statute applied to all cross-burning with intent to intimidate *any* person or group whereas, as we have seen, the St Paul ordinance identified particular – but limited – grounds on which 'anger, alarm or resentment' was not to be aroused.

Nonetheless, one of the noteworthy aspects of *RAV* is the lack of deference shown by the court to the judgement of the local legislature as to what it is necessary to criminalise in the name of 'order and morality'. This contrasts sharply with the Supreme Court's First Amendment jurisprudence from earlier eras, and has become one of the hallmarks of its more modern, more militant, approach. Recall for example the deference shown to the judgement of the California legislature by all of the Justices – including Brandeis and Holmes JJ – in *Whitney v California*. The court was content to leave it to the state legislature to determine what sorts of 'syndicalism' (public associations or secret meetings) needed, in the public interest, to be criminalised. That tradition – of deferring to the judgement of the local legislature – was carried on later into the twentieth century by Justices such as Felix Frankfurter (whose friendship with Oliver Wendell Holmes was noted above).

Consider *Beauharnais v Illinois*, for example.[63] Beauharnais was convicted of an offence for handing out racist and white supremacist literature on the streets of Chicago. Frankfurter J, giving the opinion of the court, upheld the conviction as being compatible with the First Amendment on the basis that the history of race riots gave the Illinois legislature all the reason it needed to judge that distributing such literature 'promote[d] strife and tend[ed] powerfully to obstruct ... free, ordered life in a metropolitan, polyglot community'.[64] The local legislature, not the Supreme Court, should be the judge of what was necessary to be done to combat inter-racial violence, Frankfurter J ruled.[65] Forty years later, when *RAV* was

---

[62] *Virginia v Black* 538 US 343 (2003).

[63] *Beauharnais v Illinois* 343 US 250 (1952).

[64] ibid 259.

[65] Four Justices dissented: Black, Reed, Douglas and Jackson JJ. *Beauharnais* can be seen as one of the last blasts of judicial deference to the legislature that Frankfurter J had inherited from his one-time mentor Holmes J. As we have seen, by the following decade, the more

decided, no sense remained that it was the role of the court to give any weight to the judgement of the legislature as to what kinds of restriction on expressive conduct were necessary in the public interest.

A similar approach to that taken in *RAV* can be seen in *Republican Party of Minnesota v White*.[66] In this case the Supreme Court held that a Minnesota rule banning candidates for judicial office from announcing their views on disputed political issues was contrary to the First Amendment. The rule was intended to protect both the impartiality of the judiciary and the public's confidence in the independence of the judiciary. These are undoubtedly matters of public importance and, even in a jurisdiction (such as Minnesota) where judges are elected to office, they may be seen as justifications for limiting speech; if you choose to be a candidate for public office (still more if you choose to take up public office) you may well find that your speech is constrained in all sorts of ways. The court applied its 'strict scrutiny' test to the rule in question. This requires that any restriction on speech is '(1) narrowly tailored, to serve (2) a compelling state interest'.[67] By a five-to-four majority, the court held that the rule failed to meet this test. Judicial impartiality, in the opinion of the court, meant at its core that judges must not exhibit any bias for or against a party in proceedings before them. As the rule was not 'narrowly tailored' to meet this concern, but was considerably broader than that, it was contrary to the First Amendment. If, in the alternative, judicial impartiality meant that judges should keep an open mind about legal *issues*, rather than only that they must not be biased for or against any *party*, this, in the opinion of the court, was a legitimate state interest but not one so 'compelling' as to meet the onerous requirements of the strict scrutiny test. However judicial impartiality is construed, and notwithstanding its undoubted importance, the Minnesota rule banning candidates for judicial office from announcing their views on disputed political issues was unconstitutional. So ruled the Supreme Court.

Characteristic of *Republican Party of Minnesota v White* is that it split the Supreme Court five-to-four. The modern era of free speech militancy is far from the only period of the court's First Amendment case law to feature divisions among the justices. *Beauharnais* was a five-to-four decision and *New York Times v United States* was a six-to-three decision. But in the modern era it is not just the frequency with which the court divides,

---

uncompromising approach taken by the dissenting Justices in *Beauharnais* started to prevail. Frankfurter's influence waned (and, with it, Holmes') as Justices such as Hugo Black and William Douglas shaped the altogether more robust and self-confident First Amendment jurisprudence of the Warren Court. Holmes' cautionary approach – 'we might be wrong' – which Frankfurter echoed, faded away.

[66] *Republican Party of Minnesota v White* 536 US 765 (2002).
[67] ibid 775.

it is the partisan nature of the divisions which is so notable. For nearly a decade the Rehnquist Court comprised five more conservative justices (Rehnquist CJ and O'Connor, Scalia, Kennedy and Thomas JJ) and four more liberal justices (Stevens, Souter, Ginsburg and Breyer JJ).[68] Its successor Roberts Court was similarly divided (with the more conservative justices being Roberts CJ and Scalia, Kennedy, Thomas and Alito JJ and the more liberal justices being first Stevens, Ginsburg, Breyer and Sotomayor JJ and then later, Ginsburg, Breyer, Sotomayor and Kagan JJ).[69] When President Trump was able to nominate three justices to the court, its balance of power swung further towards the conservative bloc. These groups of judges do not always vote as blocs[70] and nor do they always diverge from one another,[71] but it is nonetheless notable that many of the key constitutional law decisions of the last 30 years have been five-to-four or six-to-three decisions split along the ideological lines outlined here.[72] The court's First Amendment case law has not been immune to this. *Republican Party of Minnesota v White* was decided by Scalia J, with whom Rehnquist CJ and O'Connor, Kennedy and Thomas JJ agreed. Stevens, Souter, Ginsburg and Breyer JJ dissented. A similar split marked what is probably the most famous of the First Amendment decisions of the modern era: *Citizens United v Federal Election Commission*.[73]

Citizens United is representative of the Supreme Court's modern approach to the First Amendment. If *Schenck*, *Abrams* and *Whitney v California* are the emblematic cases of the era of the awakening, and if *New York Times v Sullivan* is emblematic of the case law of the liberal hour,

---

[68] All of the more conservative justices were nominated by Republican presidents; of the more liberal justices, two were nominated by Republican presidents and two by Democratic presidents.

[69] Roberts CJ and Scalia, Kennedy, Thomas and Alito JJ were all nominated by Republican presidents; Ginsburg, Breyer, Sotomayor and Kagan JJ were all nominated by Democratic presidents.

[70] *US v Alvarez* 567 US 709 (2012) is interesting in this regard. It is an example of the hard line taken by the modern trend of free speech militancy, but it split the conservative bloc. Two of the more conservative justices combined with the more liberal justices to form the majority, whilst three of the more conservative justices dissented. Such a split is very much the exception, though, rather than the norm. See further on *Alvarez*, ch 6.

[71] *Snyder v Phelps* 562 US 443 (2011) is a notable First Amendment case in which almost all of the justices – from both blocs – joined (with just Alito J dissenting).

[72] Consider, for example, *US v Lopez* 514 US 549 (1995) (on federalism and the Commerce Clause); *District of Columbia v Heller* 554 US 570 (2008) (on gun control and the Second Amendment); and *Dobbs v Jackson Women's Health Org* 597 US 215 (2022) (on abortion). There are, of course, exceptions, of which a well-known example is *Obergefell v Hodges* 576 US 644 (2015) (in which Kennedy J sided with the more liberal Justices to rule that the Fourteenth Amendment prohibits states from refusing to recognise same-sex marriages).

[73] *Citizens United v Federal Election Commission* 558 US 310 (2010). This case was decided by Kennedy J, with whom Roberts CJ and Scalia, Thomas and Alito JJ agreed. Stevens, Ginsburg, Breyer and Sotomayor JJ dissented.

Citizens United is equally emblematic of the stridency of the modern era's militancy.

Citizens United is a conservative non-profit organisation and political action group which, among other things, campaigns for conservative candidates and against liberal candidates in the United States. In 2008 it paid for a lengthy television documentary and associated attack ads targeted at Hillary Clinton who, at the time, was the front-runner to obtain the Democratic Party's nomination to run for President of the United States. (In the event, she was beaten to the nomination by Barack Obama, who won the presidential election later that year.) Citizens United wanted to pay for the broadcasts from their general treasury funds. This brought the organisation into conflict with provisions of the Bipartisan Campaign Reform Act, passed by the US Congress in 2002. In relevant part, these provisions required that (1) broadcast, cable or satellite communications, (2) capable of reaching at least 50,000 persons, (3) made within 30 days of a primary or 60 days of a general election, (4) designed as an appeal to vote for or against a particular candidate, could not be paid for by a corporation out of its general treasury funds. A broadcast meeting these criteria could be paid for out of corporate funds only via a PAC – a political action committee. PACs are more heavily regulated under US electoral law than are a corporation's general treasury funds. Citizens United ran a PAC[74] but it did not want to use the resources in its PAC to pay for the broadcasts: it wanted to use its general treasury funds instead.

Citizens United argued that the relevant provisions of the Bipartisan Campaign Reform Act were an unconstitutional violation of its First Amendment rights. By five votes to four this argument prevailed in the Supreme Court, and the relevant provisions of the legislation were struck down. Two things are immediately striking about the facts of this case, even before we get into the argument as to how or why the legislation was held to be in breach of the First Amendment. First, the case does not concern 'speaking' at all. It concerns spending. The relevant provisions of the legislation did not prevent Citizens United from *saying* anything. They regulated how the organisation would be required to *pay* for its speech, given that its medium of choice was paid-for advertising on cable television. Secondly, the case concerns *corporate* spending. Corporations may be able to spend money on political messaging in election campaigns, but they cannot vote. Of course, their directors, employees and shareholders may be eligible to vote. But corporations as such are not. Thus, to hold that the relevant provisions of the legislation were an interference with Citizens United's freedom of political speech may strike one as odd when

---

[74] Indeed, its PAC was described by Stevens J (dissenting) as 'wealthy', with 'millions of dollars in assets': ibid 393.

there is surely a far greater impediment to the organisation's ability to take part in the electoral process (because the organisation, being a corporation, may not vote). From a British or European perspective, then, *Citizens United* may seem not to be a case about free speech at all but, rather, a case about corporate spending. However, this is not the perspective adopted in the United States. As noted at the beginning of this section, 'speech' in America has come to acquire an expansive meaning. It includes such forms of 'expressive conduct' as placing a burning cross on a Black family's lawn – and it includes how corporations may spend money on political advertising.

As it did in *Republican Party of Minnesota v White*, so too here the Supreme Court applied the strict scrutiny test, meaning that in order to comply with the First Amendment the legislative provisions would have to be shown to be narrowly tailored to further a compelling interest. Two such interests were cited to the court: an anti-corruption interest and an anti-distortion interest. The former is relatively well-established in US electoral law. As long ago as in *Buckley v Valeo* in 1976 it was recognised to be sufficiently compelling to be capable of restricting campaign *contributions*.[75] But case law has ruled it insufficiently compelling to be capable of restricting campaign *expenditure*. Thus it could not be relied upon to justify the legislative provisions about which Citizens United had complained. The second interest – the anti-distortion interest – was developed in more recent case law,[76] partly in order to get around the problem that the anti-corruption interest could justify limiting donations but not expenditure. The anti-distortion rationale was said to create a public interest allowing law-makers to prevent 'the corrosive and distorting effects of immense aggregations of wealth' in corporations.[77] However, in *Citizens United* the Supreme Court was scathing about this so-called interest and overruled the case law in which it had been identified. Giving the opinion of the court, Kennedy J said that the anti-distortion rationale could be used to justify more or less any censorship of corporations.[78]

Kennedy J's opinion for the court in *Citizens United* was outspoken in its condemnation of the relevant provisions of the Bipartisan Campaign Reform Act. Its provisions were 'an outright ban' on speech, 'backed by criminal sanctions', he said.[79] And further: 'the censorship we now confront is vast in its reach'.[80] Hyperbole such as this is hard to take seriously.

---

[75] *Buckley v Valeo* 424 US 1 (1976).
[76] Namely, *Austin v Michigan Chamber of Commerce* 494 US 652 (1990).
[77] *Citizens United* (n 73) 348.
[78] ibid 349.
[79] ibid 337.
[80] ibid 354.

As Stevens J patiently pointed out in his dissent, the issue in the case was never *whether* Citizens United could engage in its intended electioneering: the question was only ever *how* Citizens United should be required to finance it. Citizens United could have used its PAC to televise and promote its *Hillary* documentary wherever and whenever it wanted and it could have spent unrestricted sums to broadcast it at any time other than the 30 days before the primary. Further, the Bipartisan Campaign Reform Act had no application to political campaigning online, on the telephone, or via print media. As Stevens J put it: 'neither Citizens United's nor any other corporation's speech has been "banned".[81] In Stevens J's judgment, the legislation should have been upheld as a valid exercise of Congress' 'legitimate interest in preventing the money that is spent on elections from exerting an undue influence'.[82] Not only did Stevens J see this as a matter in respect of which the court should defer to Congressional judgement:[83] he also saw it as consistent with numerous precedents in which the court had, for example, upheld the exclusion of independent candidates from television debates, upheld a prohibition on the display of campaign materials near a polling place, upheld restrictions on campaign spending by foreign nationals, and upheld restrictions on government employees from contributing to or participating in political activities.[84] In all of these instances the court had ruled that restrictions on political speech were compatible with the First Amendment, given the undoubted public importance of preserving the integrity of the electoral process.

To every rule there is an exception. Whilst, in general, the majority conservative bloc of the Rehnquist and Roberts courts has fashioned a strident, militant line on the importance of free speech, there are, even in the modern era, exceptions which go the other way. One such is *Holder v Humanitarian Law Project*.[85] Congress enacted legislation which made it an offence knowingly to provide 'material support' for a foreign terrorist organisation. By a six-to-three majority, the Supreme Court ruled not only that this criminalised certain forms of speech but that this was compatible with (and not in violation of) the First Amendment. Whilst independent advocacy for an outlawed group was not caught by the material support provisions, support that had been coordinated with such a group was unlawful even if the support amounted only to speech. So ruled Roberts CJ, with whom Stevens, Scalia, Kennedy, Thomas and Alito JJ joined.

---

[81] ibid 393.
[82] ibid 447.
[83] ibid 460.
[84] ibid 422–23.
[85] *Holder v Humanitarian Law Project* 561 US 1 (2010).

Three of the more liberal justices dissented (Breyer, Ginsburg and Sotomayor JJ): these Justices would have read the legislation as excluding teaching or advocacy from the scope of 'material support'. In order to prove material support, they argued, the government would need to show that the defendants provided support 'they knew was significantly likely to help the organisation pursue its unlawful terrorist aims'.[86]

Holder is atypical, however. The general pattern, even if it is subject to exceptions, is that 'speech' has an expansive meaning in US law and that its freedom is militantly safeguarded. This is not what the First Amendment has always been held to mean but, thanks to the interpretation given to it by the US Supreme Court, it is what it means now.

II. The Law in the United Kingdom

Judges in the United Kingdom have been far slower – and more reluctant – to uphold freedom of expression than have their counterparts in the United States. The common law courts were more concerned to provide remedies for the manifold harms which judges thought speech could cause than they were to fashion any sort of right to free speech. Obscenity was a common law offence long before it was legislated for.[87] Blasphemy was a common law offence.[88] Libel was a common law offence. Sedition was a common law offence.[89] Publication in breach of confidence would be punished by the courts, as would publication in contempt of court.[90]

Yet there is much myth-making about this. Even now, British judges like to announce themselves as guardians of free expression and British politicians are similarly wont to proclaim the United Kingdom as the home of free speech. One of the most prominent free speech lawyers of his generation, Geoffrey Robertson KC, rather brilliantly punctured such bombast in his recent short book, *Lawfare*, whose dust jacket states simply – and quite correctly – that 'the British tradition of free speech is a myth'.[91] Robertson quotes Dominic Raab who, as Secretary of State for Justice in Boris Johnson's government, introduced into Parliament a Bill of Rights Bill (in 2022) which would have made new provision for free

---

[86] ibid 56 (Breyer J, dissenting).
[87] Indeed, even after the Obscene Publications Acts of 1959 and 1964 the common law offences of conspiracy to corrupt public morals or to outrage public decency continued: see, notoriously, *Shaw v DPP* [1962] AC 220 and *Knuller v DPP* [1973] AC 435.
[88] See eg *Whitehouse v Lemon* [1979] AC 617.
[89] See ch 2.
[90] Breach of confidence and contempt of court are discussed below.
[91] Geoffrey Robertson, *Lawfare* (London, TLS Books, 2023).

speech.[92] Raab is quoted as claiming that free speech is a 'quintessentially UK right ... a unique and precious liberty on which the UK has historically placed great emphasis in our traditions'. Robertson dispatches this without ceremony: 'This is nonsense', he says.[93] It was likewise nonsense when Lord Goff claimed in a House of Lords case in 1988 that 'we may pride ourselves on the fact that freedom of speech has existed in this country perhaps as long as, if not longer than, it has existed in any other country in the world'.[94] Judges in the United Kingdom like to pretend that there is no difference between the common law's commitment to free speech and the right to freedom of expression in Article 10 of the European Convention on Human Rights (ECHR).[95] But again – no matter how frequently and fervently this is repeated – it is, very regrettably, nonsense.

In the very first case in which the United Kingdom was found by the ECtHR to have breached Article 10, it was the common law judgment of the court that was found to violate free speech, not provisions of legislation.[96] In *Attorney General v Times Newspapers* the House of Lords had upheld an injunction preventing the *Sunday Times* from running a story about what the pharmaceutical company Distillers had known about the risks associated with their drug, thalidomide, before that drug had become available to patients.[97] At the time, actions against Distillers were pending but, because negotiations were under way to seek to settle them, the legal actions were not active. The House of Lords nonetheless held that the *Sunday Times* should be constrained from publishing. Trial by newspaper was at all costs to be avoided, their Lordships said. As Lord Reid put it, 'anything' which may have the 'possible effect' of prejudicing either a particular case or the authority of judicial proceedings in general may justify an injunction preventing publication.[98] This went far too far for the ECtHR. Such an injunction, in its view, could be upheld 'only if it appeared absolutely certain' that publication would present 'a threat to

---

[92] The Bill was dropped before being debated in either House of Parliament. The differences it might have made to the law of free expression are considered in ch 4.

[93] Robertson (n 91) 32.

[94] *Attorney General v Guardian Newspapers (No 2)* [1990] 1 AC 109, 283.

[95] Article 10 ECHR is set out and discussed below.

[96] This was not a one-off. In the *Spycatcher* cases, too (considered below), Strasbourg ruled that it was court rulings, and not legislation, which brought the UK into conflict with Article 10: see *Observer and Guardian v United Kingdom* (1992) 14 EHRR 153 and *Attorney General v Guardian Newspapers* [1987] 1 WLR 1248, discussed further below. Yet another example is the 'McLibel' judgment, where the ECtHR found that the libel trial of Steel and Morris, in an action brought by McDonald's, was so unfair that it breached not only Article 10 ECHR, but also Article 6 ECHR: see *Steel and Morris v United Kingdom* (2005) 41 EHRR 22.

[97] *Attorney General v Times Newspapers* [1974] AC 273.

[98] ibid 300.

the authority of the judiciary'.[99] The result of Strasbourg's judgment was that Parliament enacted legislation to change the law. Under the Contempt of Court Act 1981 it is now the case that 'substantial risk' of proceedings being 'seriously impeded or prejudiced' must be shown before any media outlet can be censored by the courts.[100]

Even judges with as normally acute a sense of history as Lord Bingham seem to prefer to propagate myth rather than reality when it comes to the common law's relation to free speech. In *Shayler*,[101] for example, Lord Bingham said that 'the fundamental right of free expression has been recognised at common law for very many years' but that, in contrast, it was not until the Human Rights Act 1998 that it was 'underpinned by statute'. This myth-making comes from two sources. First, it is true (as David Hume remarked in 1741) that the decision to allow the Licensing Act to lapse at the end of the seventeenth century meant that, in the eighteenth and nineteenth centuries, the British press was a great deal freer than its European counterpart. This matters; but as we saw in the previous chapter it also matters that the mere absence of pre-publication licensing does not of itself mean that speech is free. Secondly, it is also true that the common law was remarkable in its advancement and protection of several aspects of individual freedom. The right to liberty was protected by the law of habeas corpus. The right to freedom of contract was robustly protected at common law. And the right to private property was likewise protected by the common law courts, even in the face of serious political interference.[102] But even if the press was free from licensing and even if the common law was admirably robust in protecting aspects of liberty, it does not follow from either of these facts that the common law was enthusiastic about protecting free speech. It was not, and Geoffrey Robertson is right to say that it is 'nonsense' to claim otherwise.

This does not mean there are no dicta from common law judges in which the foundational importance of free speech is set out. To make that claim would also be nonsense. Sedley LJ said in *Redmond-Bate v DPP*, a breach of the peace case, that 'free speech includes not only the inoffensive but the irritating, the contentious, the eccentric, the heretical, the unwelcome and the provocative, provided it does not tend to provoke violence. Freedom only to speak inoffensively is not worth having'.[103] Sedley LJ meant what he said, and his dictum is as powerful as it is famous. *Redmond-Bate* is an honourable exception – the appellants' conviction for obstruction was

---

[99] *Sunday Times v United Kingdom* (1979) 2 EHRR 245 [66].
[100] Contempt of Court Act 1981, s 2(2).
[101] *R v Shayler* [2002] UKHL 11, [2003] 1 AC 247 [21]–[22].
[102] See, above all, the great case of *Entick v Carrington* (1765) 19 St Tr 1029.
[103] *Redmond-Bate v DPP* [2000] HRLR 249.

overturned in that case – but, in the main, dicta from judges in the United Kingdom about the importance of free speech are offered in cases where the right to free speech loses out to some countervailing interest, such as security, morality, confidentiality, or the maintenance of the authority of the judiciary.

The truth is that the law in the United Kingdom has come only slowly and reluctantly towards regarding freedom of speech as a right worthy of protection. UK law has been pulled there in large measure under the influence of the ECHR. The ECHR is neither a uniform nor always a very strong protector of free expression (as we shall see in the final section of this chapter) but it has, nonetheless, done more than any other source to help the common law see that freedom of speech merits at least a degree of legal protection. The journey of the common law towards an acknowledgment of freedom of speech can be seen by looking at three cases decided at the end of the twentieth century: *Spycatcher*, *Brind* and *Reynolds*.

Spycatcher was the name of a book written by Peter Wright; it was a memoir of Wright's life and career as a senior officer in Britain's Security Service, MI5. Like all MI5 officers, Wright owed a lifelong obligation of confidentiality to the Crown in respect of everything he had learned during the course of his public service. Margaret Thatcher's government sought injunctions in the English courts preventing the publication in England and Wales of any of the allegations Wright made in *Spycatcher*. Some of those allegations were that MI5 had acted unlawfully in a number of respects; there was considerable press interest in what Mr Wright had to say. The injunctions were sought in the law of breach of confidence and were granted in July 1986 by Millett J. They became known, in later proceedings, as the Millett injunctions. Wright had retired to Australia and he sought to publish *Spycatcher* there. The UK government went to court in Australia to have the publication stopped, and the Millett injunctions extended so far as to prevent the press in England and Wales from running stories about the legal action in Australia, if those stories would have revealed secrets that Wright's book sought to divulge.

Despite the scope and force of the Millett injunctions, by the summer of 1987 the nature of the allegations made by Wright had become widely known. This was not least because of the book's publication in the United States in July 1987 (publication which had attracted considerable press coverage in the United States and elsewhere).[104] At that point the press in England and Wales returned to court to seek to have the Millett injunctions discharged. Their argument was that as the material discussed in

---

[104] As we saw in the previous section, cases such as *New York Times v United States* (n 50) show that any attempt by the UK government to prevent publication of the book in the US would have been bound to fail. No such attempt was made.

Spycatcher was now in the public domain, it was no longer confidential and, that being the case, no injunction in the law of breach of confidence could sensibly be maintained any longer. If the rest of the world's press could discuss *Spycatcher*, why could not the press in the United Kingdom do so? The High Court accepted this argument, but its decision was swiftly overturned by the Court of Appeal, whose decision to maintain the Millett injunctions in force was upheld by a divided House of Lords.[105] The decision of the House of Lords in the case demonstrates perfectly the very limited recognition awarded by the law in the United Kingdom to freedom of expression. Three Law Lords comprised the majority – Lord Brandon, Lord Templeman and Lord Ackner – and two Law Lords dissented – Lord Bridge and Lord Oliver.

Two of the Law Lords in the majority gave freedom of speech the shortest of shrift. For Lord Brandon it was a 'public right' easily displaced by the public interest in protecting the 'maintenance of the secrecy of the British Security Service',[106] not least because the Millett injunctions (which Lord Brandon said should be maintained in force) were temporary only.[107] For Lord Ackner it was not even that. The 'rock' on which he founded his judgment was the courts' power to control the press. To accept, as the press urged, that the injunctions should be discharged just because the book had been published in the United States would replace that rock, said Lord Ackner, with a 'jellyfish'. Were this to be the result, 'English law would have surrendered to the American constitution. There the courts, by virtue of the First Amendment, are, I understand, powerless to control the press. Fortunately, the press in this country is, as yet, not above the law'.[108] The controlling factor, for Lord Ackner, was Wright's lifelong obligation of confidentiality: neither he, nor his publishers, nor the press should be at liberty to profit from the breach of it. Neither Lord Brandon's nor Lord Ackner's approaches are compatible with Article 10 of the European Convention. Article 10 provides that freedom of expression is a fundamental right and that exceptions to it should be permitted only where 'necessary in a democratic society'. The right should be generously interpreted and exceptions to it should be construed narrowly.[109] It is not (contra Lord Brandon) that free speech, confidentiality and national security are equally important

---

[105] The judgments of all three courts are reported together: *AG v Guardian* [1987] (n 96).
[106] ibid 1288.
[107] They were interlocutory (or interim) injunctions, designed to be maintained in force pending the outcome of a trial.
[108] *AG v Guardian* [1987] (n 96) 1306.
[109] As the ECtHR had put it as long ago as 1979: in such situations the courts are 'not faced with a choice between two conflicting principles but with a principle of freedom of expression that is subject to a number of exceptions which must be narrowly interpreted': see *Sunday Times v United Kingdom* (n 99) [65].

public interests and that all the court has to do is to identify that some such public interest is in play in order to conclude that free speech must give way. And it is certainly not (contra Lord Ackner) that free speech is to be regretted. It is, rather, that freedom of speech is the privileged matter – the fundamental right – and that exceptions to it can be permitted only when they clearly outweigh it.

The third Law Lord in the majority in *Attorney General v Guardian Newspapers* – Lord Templeman – did at least get this framing broadly right: he asked himself the right question. It is just that he got the wrong answer. Unlike Lord Brandon and Lord Ackner, Lord Templeman did at least see that 'this appeal involves a conflict between the right of the public to be protected by the Security Service and the right of the public to be supplied with full information by the press'.[110] The question, he said, is therefore 'whether the interference with freedom of expression constituted by the Millett injunctions', were they to be continued in force by the House of Lords, was 'necessary in a democratic society in the interests of national security ... [or] for preventing the disclosure of information received in confidence'.[111] Lord Templeman concluded that it was necessary. He gave three reasons, the most important of which was that, when allegations are made against it, MI5 cannot defend itself. Instead, it 'relies on the Attorney General, acting in the public interest, to seek to prevent the mass circulation of accusations and attributions and insinuations' which would otherwise threaten its reputation.[112] To prevent the Attorney General from doing so – which would be the effect of allowing the Millett injunctions to be discharged – would be contrary to the public interest. Allegations of wrongdoing in the Security Service, Lord Templeman observed, should be made neither in public nor for commercial gain, but should be referred in confidence via the appropriate channels (the police, the prime minister, the Security Commission, etc) which exist to safeguard the lawfulness of the Security Service's operations.

Lord Bridge and Lord Oliver dissented. Both indicated that they considered the Millett injunctions to have been correctly granted in 1986, but both thought it no longer made sense to continue them in force once the nature of Wright's claims in *Spycatcher* had entered the public domain. Lord Oliver said it was neither effective nor appropriate to do so.[113] Lord Bridge was more forthright: he said it was 'nonsensical'.[114] He explained as follows: 'If, as I have always thought, the interest of national security in

---

[110] *AG v Guardian* [1987] (n 96) 1296.
[111] ibid 1297.
[112] ibid 1298.
[113] ibid 1316.
[114] ibid 1284.

protecting sensitive and classified information is to conceal it from those who might make improper use of it, it is manifestly now too late for the Millett injunctions to serve that purpose'.[115] This may be 'deplorable', his Lordship opined, but if a remedy was needed it lay in an action against Wright's publishers for an account of profits, not in what he called 'the massive encroachment on freedom of speech which the continuance of the Millett injunctions … necessarily involves'.[116] Lord Bridge was outspoken in his condemnation (this is not too strong a word) of the majority's position in the case. His 'confidence in the capacity of the common law to safeguard' free speech was 'seriously undermined' by the decision, he said.[117] He continued as follows:

> Freedom of speech is always the first casualty under a totalitarian regime. Such a regime cannot afford to allow the free circulation of information and ideas among its citizens. Censorship is the indispensable tool to regulate what the public may and what they may not know. The present attempt to insulate the public in this country from information which is freely available elsewhere is a significant step down that very dangerous road. The maintenance of the ban, as more and more copies of the book *Spycatcher* enter this country and circulate here, will seem more and more ridiculous. If the Government are determined to fight to maintain the ban to the end, they will face inevitable condemnation and humiliation by the European Court of Human Rights in Strasbourg. Long before that they will have been condemned at the bar of public opinion in the free world.[118]

Lord Bridge was quite right about the ECtHR. *Observer and Guardian v United Kingdom* was heard by a panel of 24 judges.[119] Not one of them agreed with the Brandon/Templeman/Ackner position. The European Court was unanimous that, once *Spycatcher* had been published in the United States, the maintenance in force of the Millett injunctions was a violation of Article 10. Moreover, 10 of the 24 would have ruled that the Millett injunctions were unlawful from the outset. A majority, however – 14 judges – agreed with Lord Bridge and Lord Oliver that, whilst they were lawful to start with, the injunctions should have been discharged from the summer of 1987. In the event, they were finally discharged only the following autumn (in October 1988).[120] For more than two years the British press had been censored: prevented by force of law from reporting to their readers the nature of the scandalous allegations about MI5 which Peter Wright had made in *Spycatcher*, the courts' gagging orders remaining in force

---

[115] ibid.
[116] ibid 1285.
[117] ibid 1286.
[118] ibid.
[119] *Observer and Guardian v United Kingdom* (n 96).
[120] See *AG v Guardian (No 2)* (n 94).

some 15 months even after those allegations had become widely known via the book's publication in the United States. It was a ludicrous situation. But it was not just the Thatcher government which stood condemned at the bar of public opinion for chasing Mr Wright through the world's courts, seeking to shut the door long after the horse had bolted. It was English law itself. English law failed in *Spycatcher*. It failed to protect free speech. Indeed, in the hands of some of its most senior judges, it failed even to recognise that freedom of speech was a value worthy of protection at all.

Matters had improved only marginally by the time of the UK courts' next encounter with the Thatcher government's actions relating to free speech. In 1988 ministers decided that it was no longer acceptable for spokesmen for terrorist organisations, paramilitary organisations and those who support them to have direct access to television and radio in the United Kingdom. The broadcasters were therefore directed by ministers to refrain from broadcasting the 'direct statements' of persons representing, supporting, or inviting support for a proscribed organisation, Sinn Fein or the Ulster Defence Association.[121] Images of such spokesmen could be broadcast, and viewers would be able to see their lips moving (and their gestures), but their words would be dubbed, their voices silenced and replaced by an actor's. The broadcasters accepted the government's directives, but they were challenged in court by members of the National Union of Journalists. The claimants argued that, in issuing the directives, the secretary of state had exceeded his powers. The case is *R v Secretary of State for the Home Department, ex parte Brind*.[122]

Given that English administrative law was still in a state of development at the time the case was heard, the challenge was ambitious. As the law stood, ministerial discretion such as that exercised by the secretary of state in this case could be challenged by way of judicial review on only three grounds: that it was unlawful (because it had been exercised for an improper purpose); that it was irrational (in the sense of being so unreasonable as to be perverse); and that it was procedurally unfair (because it was biased or because no fair hearing had been held). None of these grounds assisted the claimants in this case. Brind's lawyers, though, tried to fashion two further arguments. First, they contended that the secretary of state's decision was disproportionate. Secondly, they contended that his decision was contrary to Article 10 of the European Convention. These arguments related closely to one another. Both were rejected by the House of Lords.

---

[121] The directives were issued by the Secretary of State for the Home Department, under the authority of the Broadcasting Act 1981, s 29 and under the authority of the BBC licence and agreement. On the law relating to broadcasting regulation, see ch 4.

[122] *R v Secretary of State for the Home Department, ex p Brind* [1991] 1 AC 696.

There was in the 1990s much argument that the European test of proportionality should either supplement or replace the old English test of irrationality (or *Wednesbury* unreasonableness). Irrationality was either too variable and vague a standard or it was a bar set too low, said its critics.[123] This criticism the judges of the time rejected. As Lord Lowry put it, the argument for proportionality was intended 'to move the focus of discussion away from the hitherto accepted criteria for deciding whether the decision-maker has abused his power ... into an area in which the court will feel more at liberty to interfere'.[124] The *Brind* case was part of this campaign. In the event, it was not until the Human Rights Act 1998 was about to come into force that the judges started to change their minds. Only at that point was it conceded that proportionality should be admitted as a separate ground of judicial review and, even then, it is an argument available to claimants only in cases concerning fundamental rights.[125] Lord Lowry's warning in *Brind* was correct: the advent of proportionality has indeed resulted in a public law regime in which the courts 'feel more at liberty to interfere'.[126] Whether this means the law now offers more effective protection to freedom of expression, however, remains to be seen.

As for Brind's argument that the secretary of state's directives could be challenged on the basis that they were in breach of Article 10, this also was rejected. Whilst the United Kingdom had ratified the ECHR and was bound by it as a matter of international law, the ECHR could have only a limited role in domestic legal proceedings (such as the *Brind* case) unless and until Parliament legislated to give it a greater one. Its role was limited to cases in which courts were required to interpret ambiguous legislation. If statute was ambiguous, courts would interpret it in the light of the UK's international treaty obligations, so as to read it to be compatible and not in conflict with them. But that was the only role a treaty such as the ECHR could play: it could not be used as the basis of a claim in judicial review that ministerial or official discretion had been unlawfully exercised. That was the law as it stood at the time of *Brind* and the Law Lords in that case were unanimous that it was not for them to change it. Since then, the Human Rights Act 1998 has transformed the landscape. Were the facts of *Brind* to recur today, the case would be argued on the basis of section 6 of that Act, which provides that 'it is unlawful for a public authority to act in a way

---

[123] See Jeffrey Jowell and Anthony Lester, 'Beyond *Wednesbury*: Substantive Principles of Administrative Law' [1987] *Public Law* 368. Lord Lester, who co-wrote this article with Professor Jowell, was leading counsel for Brind.

[124] *Brind* (n 122) 766.

[125] *R (Daly) v Secretary of State for the Home Department* [2001] UKHL 26, [2001] 2 AC 532; *Bank Mellat v HM Treasury (No 2)* [2013] UKSC 39, [2014] AC 700.

[126] For discussion, see *R (Carlile) v Secretary of State for the Home Department* [2014] UKSC 60, [2015] 1 AC 945.

which is incompatible with a Convention right' such as the right to freedom of expression in Article 10. A post-Human Rights Act *Brind* would be all about Article 10 and all about proportionality.[127] The House of Lords was unanimous in the actual *Brind*, however, that such a step-change in UK public law could be engineered only by Parliament and not by the common law's incremental development of the law of judicial review.

This explains why the House of Lords had so much more to say in *Brind* about proportionality and about the role in domestic legal proceedings which the ECHR could play than it had to say about freedom of speech. Whilst the outright hostility to free speech exhibited by some of their Lordships in *Spycatcher* was absent in *Brind*, there was little forensic attention paid in *Brind* to the importance or even to the proper scope of freedom of expression. Free speech was in the background of the judges' minds, whilst they were focused on what they thought the case was really about. And what it was really about, as we have seen, was the campaign to transform the grounds of judicial review in English administrative law. Thus, whilst Lord Ackner said that 'in a field which concerns a fundamental human right – namely that of free speech – close scrutiny must be given to the reasons provided as justification for interference with that right', he also insisted that such 'close scrutiny' could amount to the courts doing no more than ensuring the secretary of state had not acted perversely.[128] No higher, greater or deeper standard of judicial review was available. Their Lordships were at pains to stress that the secretary of state had explained the government's broadcasting directives in Parliament, where he had given reasons for them, taken questions on them, and obtained widespread parliamentary support for them. That was more than sufficient for the Law Lords to find it 'quite impossible to hold' that the minister's 'political judgment that the appearance of terrorists on programmes increases their standing and lends them political legitimacy is one that no reasonable Home Secretary could hold'.[129] In short, if there was to be 'close scrutiny' of the free speech implications of the broadcasting directives, it was to be pursued in parliamentary questioning rather than in a court of law.

This was the constitutional orthodoxy of the day and the Law Lords in *Brind* saw no reason to disturb it, not least in a case in which the interference with free speech was, on the facts, only marginal. Broadcasters were not being directed not to air the views of terrorist or paramilitary

---

[127] This does not mean that the result would necessarily be any different. Indeed, when Brind took his case to Strasbourg, he lost, the claim being dismissed as manifestly ill-founded: see *Brind v United Kingdom* (1994) 77-A DR 42.

[128] *Brind* (n 122) 757.

[129] ibid 759.

sympathisers: they were simply being told that, when airing such views, they had to do so indirectly. Terrorists and their supporters could be quoted verbatim, but their words had to be dubbed. As Lord Templeman put it, 'the interference with freedom of expression is minimal'.[130] Lord Bridge, who had been so vocal about freedom of speech in *Spycatcher*, firmly agreed. He started, he said, 'from the premise that any restriction of the right to freedom of expression requires to be justified and that nothing less than an important competing public interest will be sufficient'.[131] He immediately maintained, however, that 'in any civilised and law-abiding country the defeat of the terrorist is a public interest of the first importance'. Seeking to limit terrorists' and their sympathisers' supply of the oxygen of publicity could not, in such a country, be categorised as unreasonable. Indeed, 'what is perhaps surprising is that the restriction imposed is of such limited scope. There is no restriction at all on the matter which may be broadcast, only on the manner of its presentation'.[132]

The turn of the millennium was a time of considerable flux in British constitutional law. The years from 1998 to 2000 saw not only the advent of devolution, but also the coming into force of the Human Rights Act 1998. This legislation gave fresh provision to a legal right to freedom of expression: indeed, it sought to give particular weight to that right.[133] As noted above, the United Kingdom was bound *in international law* by the terms of the ECHR from the moment that treaty entered into force. But its role in *domestic legal proceedings* was severely limited. The Human Rights Act changed all that, and it did so in three main ways. First, it must now be certified whether any bill introduced into Parliament is compatible with Convention rights.[134] This forces both those who propose legislation (including ministers) and those who enact it to consider the rights implications of proposed legislation. Secondly, the courts are now required, so far as it is possible to do so, to read and give effect to all legislation (whenever passed) compatibly with Convention rights.[135] If they cannot do so, they may issue a 'declaration of incompatibility'.[136] Thirdly, it is now unlawful for a public authority – including a court or tribunal – to act incompatibly

---

[130] ibid 751.

[131] ibid 748–49.

[132] ibid 749.

[133] The Human Rights Act 1998, s 12 provides that, in cases concerning freedom of expression, courts 'must have particular regard to the importance' of that right. It is doubtful this provision has had any material effect – see further ch 4.

[134] ibid s 19. Similar provision is made in the law of devolution as regards bills introduced into one of the devolved legislatures.

[135] ibid s 3.

[136] ibid s 4. A declaration of incompatibility does not affect the validity, continuing operation or enforcement of the provision(s) in respect of which it is given: s 4(6).

with a Convention right.[137] Freedom of expression is one of the Convention rights. It is provided for in Article 10 ECHR as follows:

(1)   Everyone has the right to freedom of expression. This right shall include freedom to hold opinions and to receive and impart information and ideas without interference by public authority and regardless of frontiers. This Article shall not prevent States from requiring the licensing of broadcasting, television or cinema enterprises.

(2)   The exercise of these freedoms, since it carries with it duties and responsibilities, may be subject to such formalities, conditions, restrictions or penalties as are prescribed by law and are necessary in a democratic society, in the interests of national security, territorial integrity or public safety, for the prevention of disorder or crime, for the protection of health or morals, for the protection of the reputation or rights of others, for preventing the disclosure of information received in confidence, or for maintaining the authority and impartiality of the judiciary.

The structure of this right is typical of the ECHR. The first paragraph sets out the scope of the right and the second provides for the tests which must be met for an interference with the right to be lawful. Free speech, like most rights in the ECHR, is not absolute. It is qualified. In order for an interference with free expression to be lawful under Article 10, three tests must be satisfied. First, the interference must be 'prescribed by law'. Secondly, it must be for one of the legitimate aims listed in the article, ie, the interference with free speech must be for the sake of protecting national security, health or morals, the rights of others, etc. And thirdly, the interference must be 'necessary in a democratic society'. This phrase, which appears repeatedly in the ECHR, has been interpreted by the ECtHR to mean that an interference must be 'proportionate'. This means, in essence, three things. There must be a *rational connection* between the interference (the means) and the reason why the interference has occurred (the legitimate aim). The interference must be the *least restrictive available means*: a test of *minimal impairment*. And a *fair balance* must be struck between the rights of the individual and the needs of society.

The Human Rights Act was passed in 1998 but did not come fully into force until October 2000. In that period, and in the years immediately following, many important changes were made in order to smooth the Act's absorption into the UK's constitutional fabric. For example, the common law's understanding of the relationship of legislation to fundamental rights was authoritatively restated.[138] And the common law's traditional hostility

---

[137] ibid s 6.
[138] See *R v Secretary of State for the Home Department, ex p Simms* [2000] 2 AC 115.

to notions that proportionality should become a ground of judicial review was softened – in that respect, the authority of *Brind* did not last long.[139] The law of free speech was not immune in this era of restatement and refashioning, its moment coming in *Reynolds v Times Newspapers*.[140]

Albert Reynolds was a former Taoiseach (prime minister) of Ireland. He was forced to resign in 1994 in political scandal. The *Sunday Times* ran a story which, in Reynolds' view, claimed that he had deliberately misled the Dáil (the Irish Parliament) in the run-up to his resignation. Reynolds sued the *Sunday Times* for libel. By the time the case reached the House of Lords (in 1999) the issue for their Lordships was whether, and if so, how what Lord Nicholls called 'the interaction between two fundamental rights: freedom of expression and protection of reputation' needed to be restated or refashioned.[141] The context is reminiscent of the great US Supreme Court case, *New York Times v Sullivan*, considered above. Like *Sullivan*, *Reynolds* concerned the law of libel in a political context: ie, in the context where the claimant is an elected office-holder. *Reynolds* concerned what we can, for convenience, call 'responsible journalism'. At the heart of both cases lay the freedom of the press responsibly to carry reports about what it honestly believed to be true in relation to a major political story of the day.

We saw that in *Sullivan* the US Supreme Court effectively ruled out the possibility of a libel action being brought in such circumstances. Only where the press acted with 'actual malice' – ie, where the journalists knew that what they were writing was false – could such an action lie. In *Reynolds*, counsel for the *Sunday Times* did not contend that English law should copy and paste from this American authority. But they did argue that the English law of libel should develop a new 'qualified privilege' shielding the press from liability in defamation in the context of 'the discussion of political matters concerning the conduct of government in a democratic society'.[142] This the House of Lords refused to do. Such a step, reasoned their Lordships, would tilt the balance between protection of free speech and protection of reputation too far in favour of the former. The judgment in *Reynolds* had the effect, however, of achieving the result sought by the *Sunday Times*, albeit via different means. Rather than create a new 'qualified privilege' their Lordships were of the view that the existing law of libel should be allowed to continue to develop incrementally, emphasising, though, that in the context of cases concerning 'responsible journalism', all 'appropriate weight' should be given to 'the importance of freedom of expression by the media on all matters of public concern'.[143]

---

[139] See *R (Daly) v Secretary of State for the Home Department* (n 125).
[140] *Reynolds v Times Newspapers* [2001] 2 AC 127.
[141] ibid 190.
[142] ibid 180.
[143] ibid 204 (Lord Nicholls). The English law of defamation was later amended by Act of Parliament: s 4 of the Defamation Act 2013 now provides for a defence of 'publication on a

What is most noteworthy about the judgment in *Reynolds* is the framing of the issue: it is the framing, rather than the technical ruling on the detailed points of 'qualified privilege', which has come to matter. Consider the following, for example, from the leading speech of Lord Nicholls:

> My starting point is freedom of expression ... Freedom to disseminate and receive information on political matters is essential to the proper system of parliamentary government ... To be justified, any curtailment of freedom of expression must be convincingly established by a compelling countervailing consideration, and the means employed must be proportionate to the end sought to be achieved.[144]

'Above all', said Lord Nicholls,

> the court should have particular regard to the importance of freedom of expression. The press discharges vital functions as a bloodhound as well as a watchdog. The court should be slow to conclude that a publication was not in the public interest ... especially when the information is in the field of political discussion. Any lingering doubts should be resolved in favour of publication.[145]

Lord Steyn was even more explicit: 'there is a constitutional right to freedom of expression in England', he proclaimed.[146] By categorising it as such, 'its higher normative force is emphasised'.[147] This, he said, was about to be 'reinforced' by the imminent coming into force of the Human Rights Act.[148] He continued as follows:

> The new landscape is of great importance inasmuch as it provides the taxonomy against which the question before the House must be considered. The starting point is now the right of freedom of expression, a right based on a constitutional or higher legal order foundation. Exceptions to freedom of expression must be justified as being necessary in a democracy. In other words, freedom of expression is the rule and regulation of speech is the exception requiring justification. The existence and width of any exception can only be justified if it is underpinned by a pressing social need.[149]

This is all very different from the framing adopted by the House of Lords in *Spycatcher* or even *Brind*. Freedom of speech is no longer one public interest among many. Still less is it a mere inconvenience to be dispensed with whenever the interests of government require. Now, it is the 'starting point', the rule to which exceptions will be admitted only where 'convincingly

matter of public interest'. Thereafter, Scots law was likewise amended: see the Defamation and Malicious Publication (Scotland) Act 2021, s 6.

[144] ibid 200.

[145] ibid 205.

[146] ibid 207.

[147] ibid.

[148] ibid. *Reynolds* was decided by the House of Lords after the Human Rights Act had been passed by Parliament but before it had come fully into force.

[149] ibid 208.

established' by a 'compelling' consideration. Now, freedom of expression is elevated: it is a right. Its 'normative force' is 'higher' than that of other, countervailing considerations (such as protection of reputation). This is indeed, as Lord Steyn put it, a 'new landscape'. English law has changed. For all that the judges may wish to dress up decisions such as *Reynolds* as if they were more about continuity than change, and for all that they may want to pretend that there was never any difference between the old common law and Article 10 of the European Convention, this is a disguise. Until the dawn of the Human Rights Act era, the old common law was never very enthusiastic about protecting free speech. Under the 'new landscape', by contrast, more substantial enthusiasm has to be exhibited.

This does not mean, however, that the *results* of cases will necessarily be different.[150] How you frame an argument might lead to a different outcome but, equally, it might not: there is a difference between acknowledging a right to free speech and enforcing it. A good example is *Shayler*.[151] Section 1 of the Official Secrets Act 1989 makes it an offence for a member or former member of the security and secret intelligence services, without authority, to disclose 'any information, document or other article' which he or she obtained by virtue of his or her position or in the course of his or her work for the services. The Act allows for no public interest defence: thus, the offence is committed even if the defendant made a disclosure in the public interest. Shayler, a former MI5 officer, was charged with an offence contrary to section 1. He argued, such was the breadth of the offence, that it was a disproportionate interference with the right to freedom of expression (which, as we have seen, expressly includes in Article 10(1) the right to receive or impart information). The total absence of any sort of public interest defence was emphasised. *R v Shayler* was argued and decided after the Human Rights Act had come into force. When the case reached the House of Lords, their Lordships decided unanimously that section 1 of the Official Secrets Act was compatible with Article 10 of the European Convention. Such interference with free expression as it posed was 'necessary in a democratic society', the Law Lords ruled.

The reason given was that members or former members of the security and secret intelligence services did not need to make matters public if, for example, they wished to draw attention to what they considered to be wrongdoing in the services. They had a number of channels for reporting such concerns, whether to the Attorney General, Director of Public Prosecutions, Commissioner of the Metropolitan Police, Joint Intelligence Committee, or the secretariat of Parliament's Intelligence and Security Committee. Section 1 was therefore seen not as a 'sweeping, blanket ban,

---

[150] We will see this clearly in ch 4.
[151] *Shayler* (n 101).

permitting of no exceptions', but as a prohibition only on making unauthorised disclosures in public.[152] That none of the safeguards available are independent of government did not seem to perturb their Lordships. The Law Commission, reporting in 2020, opined that *Shayler* may well have been wrongly decided and may well be decided differently today.[153] Their recommendation that the Official Secrets Act be amended to write into it a limited public interest defence was not taken up, however.[154]

III. Strasbourg's Contribution

The terms and structure of Article 10 of the ECHR were set out and explained in the previous section. Article 10 is one of four closely connected rights in the ECHR, each of which has the same structure. Articles 8, 9, 10 and 11 can be read together. Each is designed with the others in mind. Article 8 protects privacy (the right to respect for private and family life, for home and for correspondence). Article 9 protects freedom of thought, conscience and religion. Article 10 protects freedom of expression. And Article 11 protects freedom of peaceful assembly and freedom of association. Each article comprises two paragraphs: in each case, the first paragraph outlines the scope of the right and the second provides for the tests which must be met for an interference with the right to be lawful. In each case the tests are the same: the interference must be prescribed by law;[155] it must be for the sake of one of the legitimate aims listed in the article;[156] and it must be necessary in a democratic society. Thus, none of these rights is absolute: all are qualified and all are qualified in the same basic way.

The four articles progress out of one other. Freedom of conscience grows out of privacy, just as freedom of speech grows out of freedom of conscience. And freedom of action (assembly and association) is treated separately from freedom of expression. We can conceive of the four provisions as being concerned, respectively, with 'being', 'thinking', 'speaking' and 'acting'. This echoes the story told in chapters one and two, of how the struggle for free speech emerged out of the struggle for freedom of conscience and of how, by the beginning of the nineteenth century, assembly and association had come to be seen by the state as separate (and more

---

[152] ibid [36] (Lord Bingham).

[153] Law Commission, *Protection of Official Data*, Law Com 395 (2020) ch 9.

[154] The National Security Act 2023 updated other aspects of the UK's national security and official secrets legislation, but left s 1 of the Official Secrets Act 1989 unamended.

[155] Article 8 actually uses the term 'in accordance with the law' rather than 'prescribed by law' but there is no material difference between the two terms.

[156] The legitimate aims listed in each article overlap, but they are not identical. More are listed in Article 10 than in any of Articles 8, 9 or 11.

pressing) threats than seditious words were. There is a logic to the progression of privacy to conscience to expression to assembly, just as there is a historical story to tell about how these values emerged during the course of the centuries of Reformation, Enlightenment and liberty to crystallise into the basic rights we know today.

The story of how the ECtHR has contributed to a jurisprudence of free speech is a tale of two halves. The first half is impressive and the second disappointing and frustrating. Reading Strasbourg's free speech case law, one cannot help feeling that the European Court's best days may be behind it. The first period was categorised by the court setting out clearly the framework by which freedom of expression needed to be understood and by the court then applying that framework robustly in a series of cases in which a range of European powers were found to have breached the standards of Article 10. In the second period, whilst the basic framework set out in earlier case law has endured, the court's track record in applying the framework to the illiberal laws and practices of various European states has grown ever patchier. Some of the court's more recent rulings on Article 10 are so weak they take your breath away.

A. Establishing the Framework

It was in *Handyside v United Kingdom* that the ECtHR first set out its approach to freedom of speech.[157] In an echo of the story told above about the US Supreme Court's early twentieth-century case law on the First Amendment, *Handyside* is more memorable for what the court said than for what it actually decided. The outcome, in *Handyside*, was dismal from a free speech perspective. But the dicta within the court's judgment as to how free expression should be understood are genuinely impressive: and they have endured to this day. They form the bedrock of how European human rights law approaches the idea of speaking freely. The case concerned the publication of the English edition of a Danish book, known as *The Little Red Schoolbook*. Aimed at teenagers, the book included information and advice about a range of matters pertaining to sex, sexual health and sexual practices. It was avowedly 'progressive'. It sought to liberate teenagers from the strictures of what church leaders – and even teachers – might tell them (about such matters as masturbation, for example). The book's publication attracted considerable press comment and was a matter of controversy. The Director of Public Prosecutions asked to the Metropolitan Police to investigate. A warrant was issued under the Obscene Publications Acts of 1959

---

[157] *Handyside v United Kingdom* (1976) 1 EHRR 737.

and 1964, and more than one thousand copies of the *Little Red Schoolbook* were seized. Handyside, who had prepared and published the English edition, was prosecuted; he was convicted of two offences contrary to the Obscene Publications Acts. Similar charges were brought in Scotland against a Glasgow bookseller, but the prosecution there failed, the judge ruling that the material in the *Little Red Schoolbook* was neither indecent nor obscene.

Handyside argued that the proceedings taken against him, including the seizure of his unsold copies of the book, were contrary to Article 10 ECHR. By thirteen votes to one the ECtHR ruled against him, concluding that the United Kingdom had not acted in breach of his right to freedom of expression. The interference with his right to free speech was necessary in a democratic society, the court ruled, for the protection of morals. This is a conclusion which, on its facts, would surely not be reached today, attitudes to teenage sexual awareness having matured somewhat over the 50 years since the decision was handed down. As noted above, however, what has endured in this case is not its illiberal verdict, but the dicta in the court's judgment about the scope of free speech as it is understood in European law. The court stated as follows:

> Freedom of expression constitutes one of the essential foundations of [a democratic] society, one of the basic conditions for its progress and for the development of every [person] … It is applicable not only to 'information' or 'ideas' that are favourably received or regarded as inoffensive or as a matter of indifference, but also to those that offend, shock or disturb the State or any sector of the population. Such are the demands of that pluralism, tolerance and broadmindedness without which there is no 'democratic society'.[158]

This could not be more important. Two points are underscored in these dicta. First, that free speech is rooted in the demands of 'pluralism, tolerance and broadmindedness' which are the hallmark of modern European society. And secondly, that free speech extends to and includes that which others might find 'offensive, shocking or disturbing'. If the first point echoes Oliver Wendell Holmes (we might be wrong, and in order to test our information and our ideas, we have an obligation to hear the other side of the argument), the second anticipates Sedley LJ (freedom to speak only inoffensively is not worth having). Both are fundamental to modern European human rights law. The right to speak freely reflects and is an embodiment of our commitment to a plural, tolerant and broadminded society. And it extends to the offensive, the shocking and the disturbing. That others may be offended, shocked or disturbed by what we say is no reason for censorship. We might try not to offend each other but, when that fails,

---

[158] ibid [49]. The internal quotations are taken from the text of Article 10.

the solution is not to censor the speaker but to speak back, countering the offensive speech with better speech, showing why or how it was wrong.

B. Applying the Framework: The Early Years

This analysis sits alongside – and reinforces – the doctrine of proportionality which lies at the core of so much modern European human rights law. We saw in the previous section that the notion of 'necessity' in a 'democratic society' has been interpreted by the ECtHR to be a test of proportionality. To satisfy this test an interference with rights must be rationally connected to its objective, it must be the least intrusive means available, and it must balance fairly the rights of the individual with the needs of society. We saw in the previous section how the court applied this in two free speech cases concerning the United Kingdom. In the *Sunday Times* (thalidomide) case the Strasbourg court ruled that the public interest in maintaining the authority of the judiciary could justify censoring the press only when there was a real risk of substantial prejudice to legal proceedings, and that the House of Lords' willingness to impose an injunction constraining the *Sunday Times* in lesser circumstances could not be supported consistently with the requirements of Article 10. And in the *Observer and Guardian (Spycatcher)* case the court ruled that, once Peter Wright's book had been published in the United States, the British press could no longer be censored from running stories about what Wright had alleged. As the matters were no longer confidential, no injunction in the law of breach of confidence could be regarded as necessary in a democratic society. That the House of Lords was 'disturbed' by the prospect of potential actions against Distillers being compromised by the *Sunday Times* coverage, and that the British government was 'shocked' by Wright's treachery – by the betrayal of his lifelong obligation of confidentiality – were insufficient, in the court's judgments, to justify interfering with press freedom under Article 10.

These were sound and robust decisions, even if there is a case for arguing that the court might have gone further in *Spycatcher*, and might have ruled that the Millett injunctions were unlawful not only from the point at which the book was published in the United States, but from the outset. Leaving that contention to one side, however, these were important decisions, which were of a piece with a series of similarly robust rulings on Article 10 handed down by the court in cases from Austria, Spain and Denmark. *Lingens v Austria* arose out of a journalist's reporting of the historic involvement of leading 1970s Austrian politicians in Nazi atrocities during the Second World War.[159] The politicians brought private prosecutions

---

[159] *Lingens v Austria* (1986) 8 EHRR 103.

against Mr Lingens for criminal defamation. Lingens complained that the Austrian courts' judgments against him were in breach of Article 10 ECHR and in Strasbourg he prevailed: 18 judges of the European Court ruling unanimously in his favour. *Castells v Spain* concerned an elected representative who was a Basque separatist.[160] He had written an article strongly critical of the Spanish authorities' failure to identify and punish the killers of a long series of named Basque separatists. The article resulted in Mr Castells being prosecuted for insulting the government (an offence in the Spanish Criminal Code akin to sedition). He was convicted, sentenced to a term of imprisonment, and barred from holding public office. The ECtHR was again unanimous that Article 10 ECHR had been breached. *Jersild v Denmark* concerned a Danish journalist, who had broadcast the racist views of a group of disaffected (and violent) young Danish men, known as the Greenjackets.[161] The young men were prosecuted, and Jersild was prosecuted alongside them for aiding and abetting their making of a statement which threatened, insulted or degraded a group of persons on account of their race, contrary to the Danish Penal Code. Jersild was convicted, his conviction was upheld on appeal, and he took his case to the ECtHR. The Strasbourg court ruled by twelve votes to seven that there had been a breach of Article 10. Jersild's broadcast had sought not to sympathise with the Greenjackets' racist views, but to expose them. The Greenjackets' speech could not be protected by Article 10 – it was hate speech, which took their expression outside the scope of Article 10's protection – but Jersild as a journalist was seeking not to indulge in hate speech, but to draw attention to it.[162] To punish him for doing so was a breach of Article 10.

C. Strasbourg Loses its Touch

Lingens, *Castells* and *Jersild* are powerful, robust decisions, in which the ECtHR rightly ruled that decisions of (high-level) national courts and actions taken by (equally high-level) politicians and prosecuting authorities were disproportionate interferences with free speech. Unfortunately, in the years since these decisions were made the Strasbourg court has failed to maintain this standard. Its protection of Article 10 has not been so robust in the years since the mid-1990s as it was in earlier years. There are exceptions – *Perinçek*,[163] discussed in chapter five, is one of the more important – but, in the main, greater deference has been shown by the Strasbourg court to the illiberal, censorious and intolerant decisions taken by judicial and

---

[160] *Castells v Spain* (1992) 14 EHRR 445.
[161] *Jersild v Denmark* (1995) 19 EHRR 1.
[162] Hate speech is examined in detail in ch 5.
[163] *Perinçek v Switzerland* (2016) 63 EHRR 6.

political actors at national level. Free speech is no longer so impressively defended in European human rights law as, for a period, it once was. Five examples of the European Court's case law will suffice to illustrate this point. The first is *Otto Preminger Institut v Austria*.[164] This decision, handed down in fact just three days before the judgment in *Jersild*, was perhaps the first Strasbourg case to show that, despite the rhetoric of *Handyside* and despite the verdicts in *Sunday Times*, *Lingens*, *Castells* and *Jersild*, the ECtHR could not be relied on to fashion a truly robust law of free speech for Europe.

The Otto Preminger Institut in Innsbruck was an arts centre, dedicated to the promotion of the creative arts. It wanted to show a film version of the controversial play, written in 1894 by Oskar Panizza, *Das Liebeskonzil*. The play and the film portray God as old, infirm and ineffective, Jesus as a young boy of low intelligence, and the Virgin Mary as an unprincipled wanton. They collude with the Devil to punish humanity, agreeing that humans will infect one another with a sexually transmitted disease: syphilis.[165] On the application of the local Catholic church, a judge ordered the film to be seized, meaning it could not be shown. Despite the fact that the film's proposed screenings had been widely advertised, only those who paid to attend could view the film: there was no danger, therefore, of anyone being exposed to objectionable material against their wishes.[166] Nonetheless, Innsbruck is in an area of Austria – the Tyrol – which is overwhelmingly Catholic (as high as 87 per cent of the population) and the Austrian authorities considered there to be a 'pressing social need' to preserve 'religious peace'.[167] By a majority of six votes to three, the ECtHR agreed. Neither the seizure nor the subsequent forfeiture of the film were held to contravene Article 10. Quite where the 'pluralism, tolerance and broadmindedness' of which the court had so eloquently spoken in *Handyside* had gone, the court in *Otto Preminger Institut* did not say. And quite why it was now apparently 'necessary in a democratic society' to prevent fee-paying cinema-goers watching a film they wanted to see, on the basis solely that others might find its content 'offensive, shocking or disturbing', the court did not explain.

Religious sensibility was also at the heart of the matter in *Wingrove v United Kingdom*.[168] The claimant had made an 18-minute film, which he wished to release on video. The film, *Visions of Ecstasy*, was an erotic depiction of a nun who, at one point, could be seen 'astride the recumbent body of the crucified Christ engaged in an act of an overtly sexual nature'

---

[164] *Otto Preminger Institut v Austria* (1995) 19 EHRR 34.
[165] ibid [21].
[166] ibid [53], [54].
[167] ibid [52].
[168] *Wingrove v United Kingdom* (1997) 24 EHRR 1.

(as the European Court put it).[169] The British Board of Film Classification (BBFC) refused to license the film, on the ground that it was blasphemous. Wingrove's appeal to the Video Appeals Committee was unsuccessful. He took his case to Strasbourg, but the ECtHR found the BBFC's decision to be compatible with Article 10, notwithstanding that 'the measures taken by the authorities amounted to a complete ban on the film's distribution.'[170] Declining to grant the film a licence for distribution was held to be a proportionate means of ensuring that the rights of others were protected. The European Court noted that the application of blasphemy laws had become increasingly rare (not only in the United Kingdom but throughout Europe) and that several European countries had repealed them altogether. But Strasbourg elected to follow rather than to lead this debate, leaving individual European states to decide for themselves the extent to which they wanted to maintain blasphemy laws in force. In the event, the common law offences of blasphemy and blasphemous libel were abolished by Act of Parliament in 2008 (for England and Wales) and 2021 (for Scotland).[171] The decision to do so was a political one made by national legislatures, not a judicial one made under the force of human rights law.

A third example of the Strasbourg court's weak Article 10 jurisprudence is *Sürek v Turkey (No 1).*[172] Two readers' letters were published a newspaper which Sürek owned. He was neither the editor of the paper nor the author of the letters. The letters made allegations about Turkish brutality against Kurds and vowed revenge. Sürek was prosecuted. He was acquitted of incitement to violence but convicted of disseminating separatist propaganda. The ECtHR found that his trial had been unfair (and that Turkey had breached Article 6 ECHR) but, by eleven votes to six, that the criminal proceedings taken against Sürek were not in breach of Article 10 ECHR. The court found that the letters amounted 'to an appeal to bloody revenge ... and ... deadly violence'.[173] This, it is submitted, is a difficult claim to sustain in the light of Sürek's acquittal of charges of incitement, but the European Court saw matters differently, opining that 'what is in issue ... is hate speech and the glorification of violence'.[174] What was in issue in Sürek's conviction, however, was not the glorification of violence but the crime of having published 'separatist propaganda'. The verdict of the Strasbourg court in this case was a serious misstep. The reasoning of the short dissenting judgments is far more persuasive both in principle and

---

[169] ibid [61].
[170] ibid [64].
[171] Criminal Justice and Immigration Act 2008, s 79 and Hate Crime and Public Order (Scotland) Act 2021, s 16.
[172] *Sürek v Turkey (No 1)*, judgment of 8 July 1999.
[173] ibid [62].
[174] ibid.

in the light of Strasbourg's earlier case law on Article 10. Judge Palm, for example, noted that the 'general accusatory tone' of the letters 'undoubtedly … shock and disturb the reader' but that even such 'fighting words' are protected by Article 10 unless the language 'intended to inflame or incite violence' or unless there was a 'real and genuine risk' that the language used might do so.[175] That is how high the bar should be set; and that is how high the bar had been set in the court's earlier case law. The letters in Sürek's newspaper did not clear that bar and, for that reason, the court should have ruled that the criminal proceedings taken against him were a violation of Article 10.

Similarly dispiriting is the court's decision in *Stoll v Switzerland*.[176] Stoll was a journalist who received a diplomatic memorandum leaked illegally to him (by a person unknown) in contravention of Swiss official secrets law. The memorandum, written by the Swiss Ambassador to the United States, reflected the Ambassador's views about negotiations which were at the time ongoing between the Swiss authorities and the World Jewish Congress concerning 'compensation due to Holocaust victims for unclaimed assets deposited in Swiss bank accounts'.[177] The Ambassador's views were so undiplomatic, describing the Jewish claims for compensation as a 'campaign against Switzerland' that, when Stoll's newspaper made them public, the Ambassador had to resign. Criminal proceedings were taken against Stoll, and he was convicted of an offence contrary to Swiss official secrets law. He took his case to Strasbourg, but the European Court ruled that his conviction was not in breach of Article 10. This was despite the fact that the court found that the publication contributed to an important matter of public debate and despite the fact that, contrary to the Swiss government's contentions, the publication did not mean that no settlement could be reached in the negotiations with the World Jewish Congress.[178] It was enough, for the court, that the partial disclosure of the Ambassador's memo 'was capable of undermining the climate of discretion necessary to the successful conduct of diplomatic relations' even if it in fact did not so undermine the success of the negotiations.[179] That Stoll had reported the matter in an apparently 'sensationalist style', exaggerating the extent to which it could be thought that the Ambassador was motived by anti-Semitism, and misleading the reader about the Ambassador's 'personality and abilities', also counted against him, in the court's judgment.[180]

---

[175] ibid, dissenting opinion of Judge Palm. The dissenting opinion of Judge Bonello was in similar terms.
[176] *Stoll v Switzerland* (2008) 47 EHRR 59.
[177] ibid [14].
[178] ibid [124] and [130].
[179] ibid [136].
[180] ibid [148]–[152].

It is hard, however, to see why any of these considerations is relevant. The legitimate interest in respect of which Stoll's right to freedom of expression had been interfered with was 'preventing the disclosure of information received in confidence'. The question for the court, therefore, was whether Stoll's criminal conviction was necessary in a democratic society in order to satisfy the demands of confidentiality. The answer should surely have been 'no'. No damage to diplomatic negotiations was caused by Stoll's reporting of the leaked memo; the negotiations were concluded despite the leak and despite the newspaper reports about it. If Stoll's reporting was so one-sided that it unfairly impugned the Ambassador's reputation, the solution would lie in an action for defamation, not in Stoll being prosecuted.

A final example of the weakness of Article 10 is *Palomo Sánchez v Spain*.[181] Six employees were sacked from the delivery company they worked for when they published in a trade union magazine an offensive cartoon of the company's human relations manager. At the time of the publication of the cartoon, the employees were in dispute with their employer. The employees argued before the Spanish courts that their dismissal was unfair, its sole basis being that they had published the cartoon. The Spanish courts dismissed the employees' claim, and the case was taken to Strasbourg. The ECtHR, by a majority of twelve votes to five, ruled that there had been no breach of Article 10. The court insisted that 'a clear distinction must be made between criticism and insult and that the latter may, in principle, justify sanctions'.[182] The court saw the cartoon as 'an attack on the respectability of individuals' by using 'offensive expressions in the professional environment'.[183] The 'disruptive effects' of such action was, in the court's verdict, 'a particularly serious form of misconduct capable of justifying severe sanctions'.[184] This abject finding turns the dicta of *Handyside* on their head. If an employee draws a cartoonish caricature of his manager he may be sacked, losing his job and his livelihood, and this is somehow a proportionate outcome – necessary in a democratic society – notwithstanding all the claims the Strasbourg court once made about protecting speech which others may find offensive, shocking or disturbing.

As we will see in part II of this book, these poor and problematic decisions have become all too typical of Strasbourg's approach to freedom of expression. As the US Supreme Court has become ever more uncompromising in its protection of free speech and as the UK courts have belatedly begun to acknowledge the importance of free speech (if not always to give effect to it), the ECtHR has moved in the opposite direction, retreating

---

[181] *Palomo Sánchez v Spain* (2012) 54 EHRR 24.
[182] ibid [67].
[183] ibid [76].
[184] ibid.

from its earlier case law and, in the process, diminishing itself as an effective force for the protection of free speech in Europe.

IV. Conclusions

We have come a long way in this chapter, from revolutionary America, through the various stages of the First Amendment's development, via the common law's hostility – now lessened – to free speech, to the changing fortunes of Article 10 ECHR. We have seen that neither the First Amendment, nor the common law, nor Article 10 has been able to offer consistent protection to free speech. Many cases have failed to offer anything like adequate protection. A handful have gone too far the other way, insisting on a near absolutist position when a more nuanced approach would have been wiser. Along the way there have been numerous memorable and remarkable dicta, from judges in all the courts surveyed here, out of which a compelling law of speaking freely could yet be fashioned. But the lesson of this chapter is that the legal roots of a right to free speech are both shallow and insecure.

Part II of this book examines three current controversies in the law of free speech: media freedom, offensive and hate speech, and online safety. It examines them in the light of what we have found so far: that the legal foundations of a right to speak freely are weak. None of this means they could not yet be made more secure but that work, if it is to be done, still lies ahead of us.

PART II

Free Speech Today

4

Media Freedom

The struggle for a free press was a major strand of the long battle for free speech in the seventeenth and eighteenth centuries. Cases involving the press have been core to the realisation of a law of speaking freely on both sides of the Atlantic. *New York Times v Sullivan*, the *Spycatcher* cases, *Brind*, *Sunday Times v United Kingdom*, *Lingens v Austria* and *Jersild v Denmark*, among many others, were all concerned with aspects of media freedom. Despite this, Article 10 of the European Convention on Human Rights (ECHR) explicitly provides, in the third sentence of its first paragraph, that 'this Article shall not prevent States from requiring the licensing of broadcasting, television or cinema enterprises'. State licensing of books, newspapers and magazines may now be unlawful, but the same plainly does not apply to other forms of media. This chapter asks why that is, and whether the explanations for it which were set out when television broadcasting commenced in the twentieth century remain valid now, amid a much changed (and still evolving) media landscape.

In doing so, the chapter examines four contemporary aspects of media freedom: more accurately, four aspects of media regulation – four ways in which the media are not free to say, write, print, or broadcast whatever they want. We start where Article 10 invites us to start, with the licensing of the broadcast media. We examine that matter both in the United States and in Britain. We then move to one of the areas in which the severest prohibitions remain in force – at least in the United Kingdom – as regards broadcasting: namely, the blanket ban on political advertising. We then consider the press, focusing on the changing dynamics of the legal regulation of the relation between press freedom and the right to privacy, an area of the law of free speech much changed in the United Kingdom since the Human Rights Act 1998 came into force. And we close with a brief examination of press regulation.[1]

---

[1] Online and social media are considered separately in ch 6.

I. The Licensing of Broadcast

We saw in part I of this book that law must respond to technology and that, oftentimes, law's response to technology is slow. Law lags behind. First came the introduction of the printing press; then came the legal regulation of printing; thereafter came the growth and spread of the technology; and only much later came the eventual abolition of press licensing. In the modern age, communications have evolved faster than perhaps any other aspect of human activity. Radio, television, the telephone, electronic communications, the internet and social media have transformed how we may speak with one another. Among the most striking features of the law's regulatory responses to these waves of communication revolution are its variety, its scale and its struggle to keep up.

No two elements of the media are regulated in law in the same way: there are huge differences, in particular, between the press, broadcasting and online communications (to say nothing of film distribution, commercial advertising, or video streaming). As for scope, when we consider broadcasting, in particular, the scale of legal regulation is vast. To take the United Kingdom as an example, the principal enactment is the Communications Act 2003, which as currently in force runs to more than one thousand printed pages, were you to download it from legislation.gov.uk. Yet this Act of Parliament is far from a complete code of broadcasting regulation. It sits on top of the Broadcasting Acts 1990 and 1996 and alongside the Digital Economy Acts 2010 and 2017, the Wireless Telegraphy Act 2006, and the Online Safety Act 2023. And that is to list only the main instruments of primary legislation. Under the statutes sit not only an array of delegated instruments, but also regulatory codes such as Ofcom's Broadcasting Code.[2] Such instruments are amplified, applied and interpreted not only by regulatory decision-making (summaries of which can be viewed in an extensive range of now more than 500 bulletins issued by Ofcom) but also, of course, in case law.

A. The Position in the United States

This is unique neither to the United Kingdom nor to Europe. Even in the United States, broadcasting was subject to extensive federal regulation, at least in its earlier years. It certainly was not the case that Congress could

---

[2] Ofcom – the Office of Communications – is the UK's telecoms, broadcast, electronic and online communications regulator. It is a mega-regulator. In 2023 its operating expenditure was £175 million and it employed more than 1,350 people. To give just one comparator: this is 10 times the annual budget of the Equality and Human Rights Commission.

make no law abridging the freedom of broadcast speech. In large measure this was driven by necessity, as the US Supreme Court's broadcasting
case law makes clear. In its early years, radio and television were broadcast
over an electromagnetic spectrum which is limited in range. If two or more
channels sought to broadcast on the same wavelength, they would interfere with one another, with the result that neither could be heard. At the
same time, parts of the spectrum needed to be off limits to broadcasters,
so that the police and the emergency services could communicate with one
another without interference, or so that distress, safety, or search and rescue
signals could be received. Even now, it remains the case that the spectrum
is used for multiple purposes, ranging from baby monitors and Bluetooth
to mobile phones, and from shortwave radio to satellite communications.
The spectrum is a limited resource and, as the US Supreme Court has put
it, 'the scarcity of broadcast frequencies ... required the establishment of
some regulatory mechanism to divide the electromagnetic spectrum and
to assign specific frequencies to particular broadcasters'.[3] In the United
States, this is a job for the Federal Communications Commission (FCC),
established by Congress in 1934. In the United Kingdom, it has since the
Communications Act 2003 been one of Ofcom's tasks.[4]

But it is not just that broadcast is licensed. It is that the licences come
with conditions. Several such conditions limit freedom of expression
directly, and moreover, in ways which find no equivalent in any other
medium. The matter was considered by the US Supreme Court in *Red Lion
Broadcasting v FCC*.[5] The case concerned what was known as the FCC's
'fairness doctrine', which imposed two requirements on licensed radio and
television broadcasters: that they include discussions of public issues in
their programming and that, in such discussions, they give fair coverage
to both sides of a debate. Red Lion was licensed to operate a Pennsylvania
radio station. The station broadcast a discussion by the Reverend Billy
James Hargis in which a book written by Fred J Cook was attacked. Mr
Cook demanded a right of reply, but this was refused. The FCC ruled
that the radio station had breached the fairness doctrine and that it must
make broadcast time available for Mr Cook to air his side of the story.
The Supreme Court upheld the fairness doctrine and ruled that it was

---

[3] *Turner Broadcasting System v FCC* 512 US 622, 637–38 (1994).

[4] See: www.ofcom.org.uk/spectrum/. Ofcom inherited this task from a series of earlier
regulators. When it was created in 2003 it took over the work of five pre-existing regulators (including the Radio Authority, the Independent Television Commission and the
Broadcasting Standards Commission). Since 2003 it has acquired numerous further powers
and responsibilities, not least under the Online Safety Act 2023. See further ch 6.

[5] *Red Lion Broadcasting v FCC* 395 US 367 (1969). This is a decision which hails from the
height of the liberal hour – 1969 is the same year as *Brandenburg v Ohio* and five years after
New York Times v Sullivan.

compatible with the First Amendment. The fairness doctrine, in the view of the court, was both authorised by Congress and was such as to 'enhance rather than abridge' free speech.[6]

It was the FCC's statutory responsibility to allocate broadcast frequencies in the public interest. From its very earliest days, the Commission took the view that the 'public interest requires ample play for the free and fair competition of opposing views'.[7] The court founded its conclusion that this regulatory stance was constitutional on two propositions. First, that 'differences in the characteristics of new media justify difference in the First Amendment standards applied to them'.[8] And secondly, that 'it is the right of the viewers and listeners, not the right of the broadcasters, which is paramount'.[9] Both propositions followed from the court's finding that 'it is the purpose of the First Amendment to preserve an uninhibited marketplace of ideas in which truth will ultimately prevail, rather than to countenance monopolisation of that market, whether it be by the Government itself or a private licensee'.[10] Radio frequencies are a scarce resource. Those who are privileged to broadcast on them must ensure that opinion is broad and diverse, and not monopolised by a particular voice (or point of view). And the government has every right – indeed, arguably a duty – to design and implement a regulatory regime in order to secure exactly this, which is the very 'purpose of the First Amendment'. That regime will necessarily be different depending on the particular characteristics of each new form of media. In the words of the court,

> it does not violate the First Amendment to treat licensees given the privilege of using scarce radio frequencies as proxies for the entire community, obligated to give suitable time and attention to matters of great public concern. To condition the granting or renewal of licenses on a willingness to present representative community views on controversial issues is consistent with the ends and purposes of the those constitutional provisions forbidding the abridgement of freedom of speech.[11]

The court acknowledged, though, that this ruling was for the time being. If radio technology developed in the future in such a way as to mean that the scarcity of the spectrum became less of an issue, then the constitutional judgment may likewise have to evolve.

---

[6] ibid 375.
[7] ibid 377. The quotation is from a ruling of the Federal Radio Commission in 1929. The FCC replaced the Radio Commission in 1934.
[8] ibid 386.
[9] ibid 390.
[10] ibid.
[11] ibid 394.

Neither the reasoning nor the outcome of *Red Lion Broadcasting* was to apply to the press. This is starkly illustrated by *Miami Herald v Tornillo*, decided only five years after *Red Lion Broadcasting*.[12] When the *Miami Herald* newspaper printed articles which were critical of Mr Tornillo (who was a candidate for election to the Florida House of Representatives), Tornillo demanded that the paper offer him a right of reply, as was required by Florida legislation in force at the time. The paper refused to print his reply. The Florida Supreme Court ruled for Tornillo, but the US Supreme Court reversed, holding that the Florida statute was in breach of the First Amendment. What is fascinating about the case is the way the argument was put for Tornillo, for it had all sorts of echoes of the argument which had found favour in *Red Lion Broadcasting* – yet the results in the two cases could hardly have been more different.

The argument for Tornillo was as follows. When the First Amendment was ratified the marketplace of ideas existed in the press because 'entry into publishing was inexpensive', pamphlets and books providing 'meaningful alternatives to the organised press'.[13] Further, even if 'many of the newspapers were intensely partisan and narrow in their views, the press collectively presented a broad range of opinions to readers'.[14] By the late twentieth century, by contrast, none of this remained the case. Entry into media publishing had become prohibitively expensive, newspapers having become big business. Further, there were far fewer of them: 'chains of newspapers, national newspapers, national wire and news services, and one-newspaper towns, are the dominant features of a press that has become non-competitive and enormously powerful and influential in its capacity to manipulate popular opinion'.[15] Media ownership had become so concentrated and, moreover, the press printed the same homogeneous and nationally 'syndicated' copy that it resembled the 'scarce resource' and near 'monopoly' the court had talked about in the context of radio in *Red Lion Broadcasting*. Given the realities of the market, the only way to safeguard the purpose of the First Amendment in preserving an uninhibited marketplace of ideas in the press was for the government to take positive action regulating the press, requiring it – as the Florida statute did, for example – to confer, where appropriate, a right of reply.

This argument the Supreme Court unanimously dismissed. At no point in its judgment in *Miami Herald v Tornillo* is *Red Lion Broadcasting* even referred to. For the court in *Tornillo*, it was axiomatic and core to the First Amendment that 'no government agency – local, state, or federal – can tell

---

[12] *Miami Herald v Tornillo* 418 US 241 (1974).
[13] ibid 248.
[14] ibid.
[15] ibid 249.

a newspaper in advance what it can print and what it cannot'.[16] A responsible and balanced press may well be a desirable goal, the court opined, but it is neither a constitutional requirement nor a virtue which can be legislated for.[17] No analogy from the sphere of broadcasting could be read across into the sphere of the press, no matter how much in common their respective markets may appear to share. As far as the legal regulation of the press was concerned, broadcasting was an alien world, of no relevance whatever to how the First Amendment was to be applied to newspapers.

In the decades since these seminal cases, the worlds of broadcasting and of the press have indeed come closer together but, in the United States, it is the legal regulation of broadcasting that has given way to the logic of the First Amendment as it applies to the press, and not the other way around. (We will see later in this section that the like move has not yet been made in Britain and Europe.) That broadcasting regulation would soften in the United States was hinted at in *FCC v Pacifica Foundation*.[18] The comedian George Carlin recorded a 12-minute monologue called 'Filthy Words' before an audience in California. The monologue was a satire on how 'words you couldn't say in public' were, in fact, said all the time in ordinary American conversation. A New York radio station broadcast the monologue as part of a programme exploring contemporary use of language. A listener, who had heard the programme whilst driving in his car with his young son, complained. The FCC upheld the complaint but did not impose a sanction, other than keeping a record of the complaint on its file (which it would refer to in the event that the radio station applied in the future to renew its licence).

It was accepted that the Carlin monologue was not obscene. As such, it therefore fell within the scope of the First Amendment's protections.[19] A majority of the Supreme Court ruled, however, that the FCC would be acting within its powers – and constitutionally – were it to sanction a radio station for broadcasting 'indecent' speech which was not obscene and which did fall within the scope of the First Amendment's protections. Two reasons were offered in support of this judgment. The first related to the 'pervasiveness' of broadcasting and the second concerned the protection of children. The court accepted that broadcasters were subject to rules limiting their First Amendment rights to which no one else is subject. Such rules had been established in order to 'serve the public interest' because the broadcast media have 'a uniquely pervasive presence in the lives of all

---

[16] ibid 255–56.

[17] ibid 256.

[18] *FCC v Pacifica Foundation* 438 US 726 (1978).

[19] We saw in the previous chapter that some categories of speech fall outside the scope of the First Amendment's protection. These categories include obscene speech, defamatory speech and fighting words.

Americans', even 'in the privacy of the home'.[20] Moreover, 'broadcasting is uniquely accessible to children, even those too young to read'.[21] Brennan and Marshall JJ dissented. Their dissent did nothing to disturb the well-established doctrine that the First Amendment does not protect obscene speech, but argued that speech which fails to meet this threshold and is understood to be merely indecent or offensive cannot be abridged. If listeners encounter speech on the radio they find indecent, the solution is to turn off the radio (or tune it to a different station). To empower the FCC to sanction radio stations for broadcasting material even when it is not obscene is to ignore the constitutional rights both of those who wish to transmit the material and of those who wish to hear it.

Pacifica was not a deregulatory decision – the US Supreme Court upheld the FCC's powers – but it nonetheless indicated that deregulation was to come for two reasons. First, and most obviously, the court in *Pacifica* is divided, and the Brennan/Marshall dissent is powerful. Secondly, though, the reasoning offered by the majority has changed from the much more convincing reasoning of the court in *Red Lion Broadcasting*. There, the reason for needing broadcast speech to be regulated was the scarcity of available frequencies on the spectrum. Now, by contrast, it has morphed into a sense that because broadcasting pervades deep inside the privacy of the home, people need to be protected from it. The *Red Lion* reasoning is consistent with – and was avowedly based on – the purpose and goal of the First Amendment (to secure a marketplace of ideas where a plurality of opinion could be heard). The *Pacifica* reasoning, by contrast, is not, and it was robustly attacked by Brennan and Marshall JJ in their dissent. They complained that it revealed

> a depressing inability to appreciate that in our land of cultural pluralism, there are many who think, act, and talk differently from Members of this Court, and who do not share their fragile sensibilities [of what is 'indecent']. It is only an acute ethnocentric myopia that enables the Court to approve the censorship of communications solely because of the words they contain.[22]

The FCC's approach to its 'fairness doctrine', and the Supreme Court's support for that doctrine in *Red Lion Broadcasting*, was firmly rooted in the fact that, at least in its earlier years, broadcasting was of necessity a scarce physical resource. We noted above that in *Red Lion* itself, the court accepted that changes in broadcasting technology may lead in due course to changes in broadcasting regulation. And so it transpired. By the mid-1980s the FCC had come to the view, such was the growth in the number

---

[20] *Pacifica* (n 18) 748.
[21] ibid 749.
[22] ibid 775.

of broadcasting outlets in the United States, that the fairness doctrine was no longer required in the public interest. The FCC continued to enforce it, however, believing that to do so was required by statute. The federal courts clarified in 1989 that the FCC was mistaken in this belief, and that Congress had not legislated to require the FCC to impose the fairness doctrine on broadcasters.[23] From that point on, it was dropped.

By the 1990s cable TV had started to dominate the US market, offering dramatically greater viewing choice than the earlier, over-the-air, channels had been able to achieve. The Supreme Court made it clear that the approach it (and the FCC) had taken in earlier cases such as *Red Lion* would not apply to cable TV. The rationale for that approach – 'the dual problems of spectrum scarcity and signal interference' – simply did not apply in the context of cable, the court ruled.[24] This does not mean that cable TV is unregulated in the United States. Statutory and regulatory requirements that cable operators must carry certain numbers of local broadcast TV stations, for example, were upheld by the Supreme Court.[25] But it does mean that more onerous and editorially far more limiting requirements such as the 'fairness doctrine' have long since ceased to apply to the broadcasting sector in the United States. First came the technology; then came the legal regulation; and thereafter came its relaxation as the technology developed and the need for regulation faded.

B. The Position in Britain and Europe

This stands in marked contrast to the position in the United Kingdom. Both statute and Ofcom impose onerous restrictions on the editorial freedom of the UK's broadcasters, both as regards radio and, even more so, television. Unlike the position in the United States, there is little sign as yet of these restrictions being lessened or liberalised as consumer choice expands, viewing (or listening) habits evolve, and technology develops. Courts in the United Kingdom, supported by key decisions of the European Court of Human Rights (ECtHR), have to date upheld the continuing legislative and regulatory disciplining of the broadcast sector.

It is an offence in the United Kingdom to provide television services without a licence.[26] Broadcasting licences are issued by Ofcom to such persons deemed 'fit and proper'.[27] Licences come with conditions attached,

---

[23] *Syracuse Peace Council v FCC* 867 F.2d 654 (DC Cir 1989).

[24] *Turner Broadcasting System v FCC* (n 3).

[25] ibid; see also *Turner Broadcasting System v FCC* 520 US 180 (1997).

[26] Broadcasting Act 1990, s 13. On the licensing of radio (and connected offences), see the Wireless Telegraphy Act 2006.

[27] Broadcasting Act 1990, s 3. On the 'fit and proper' test and its application in certain cases, see further below.

a number of which are required by Act of Parliament. It is Ofcom's responsibility to ensure that such conditions are complied with.[28] The most wide-ranging legislative conditions apply to 'public service television'. This includes all TV services provided by the BBC, ITV (Channel 3), Channel 4 and Channel 5.[29] Public service television is required by law to satisfy the following: that it deals with a wide range of subject-matters; that it is likely to meet the needs and satisfy the interests of as many different audiences as practicable; that it is properly balanced; and that it maintains high general standards as regards content, quality, professional skill and editorial integrity.[30] In addition to these legislative stipulations, Ofcom is required by law to establish a Broadcasting Code for all television and radio services.[31] Statute provides that the Code must, among other matters, ensure that children and young people are protected, that news is presented with 'due impartiality' and that 'generally accepted standards are applied' so as to protect the public from 'offensive and harmful material'.[32]

The argument in this section will focus, in the main, on 'due impartiality'. First, however, a short word is needed to note two cases on 'offensiveness' and 'harm'. The leading case on the Broadcasting Code's rules as to offensiveness is *R (Gaunt) v Ofcom*.[33] Jon Gaunt was a radio talk-show host who interviewed live on air a local authority councillor about the local authority's controversial policy to ban smokers from becoming foster parents. Gaunt became animated during the interview, calling the councillor a 'health Nazi' and an 'ignorant pig'. Within 10 minutes of the broadcast Gaunt apologised on air for having 'lost his rag'. His radio station suspended him later that day and thereafter terminated his contract. After receiving complaints from listeners, Ofcom investigated. It found that the broadcast contravened the Code, although it imposed no sanction. Gaunt sought judicial review of Ofcom's finding, contending that it interfered with his right to freedom of expression. The Court of Appeal ruled that Ofcom had not acted unlawfully: 'when one combines the extremely aggressive tone of the interview, the constant interruptions, the insults, the ranting, the consequent lack of any substantive content, and the time which the interview was allowed to run on', it was clear in the court's judgment that Ofcom had been correct to find the interview in breach of the Code.[34] Two matters were critical in the court's judgment: that the show's producers

---

[28] Communications Act 2003, s 263.

[29] ibid s 264(11).

[30] ibid s 264(4). Additional statutory requirements as to innovation, creativity, diversity and educational programming are imposed on Channel 4: ibid s 265(3).

[31] ibid s 319.

[32] ibid.

[33] *R (Gaunt) v Ofcom* [2011] EWCA Civ 692, [2011] 1 WLR 2355.

[34] ibid [46]. A subsequent complaint to Strasbourg was dismissed as 'manifestly ill-founded': *Gaunt v United Kingdom*, decision of 29 September 2016.

could (and should) have cut the interview short once it had become clear that Gaunt had lost control of it (but that they chose not to); and that this was not the first time that the particular radio station had allowed such an interview to degenerate on air. Given that no sanction was imposed, it is hard to argue that Ofcom's action was a disproportionate interference with free speech.

A recent case on the Broadcasting Code's rules as to harm is *R (Steyn) v Ofcom*.[35] Mark Steyn presented a show on the TV station GB News. Ofcom determined that two of his shows broadcast in 2022 breached the Code's stipulations that viewers must be protected from 'harmful material' and that news and current affairs items must not 'materially mislead the audience'.[36] Both episodes concerned Covid vaccines. In the first, Steyn alleged that statistics had shown that receiving a booster vaccine increased chances of hospitalisation and death; in the second Steyn interviewed a guest who alleged that the vaccine roll-out amounted to pre-meditated mass murder. Whilst Ofcom found that both broadcasts breached the Code, no sanction was imposed. When GB News did not support Steyn, he left the station in 2023, moving his show to his own website. Steyn sought judicial review of Ofcom's decisions that the Code had been breached, but was unsuccessful. The High Court ruled that the right to 'journalistic freedom' is so important that 'it covers possible recourse to a degree of exaggeration or even provocation', but that even if 'the right to provoke will be protected by the courts ..., it does not found any right to mislead'.[37] Steyn had crossed the line from challenging government policy and public information as to Covid vaccines to misleading the public about the dangers of the vaccines; and in its determinations on the matter, Ofcom had gone to considerable lengths to explain how Steyn's right to freedom of expression needed to be balanced against the public interest in obtaining accurate and reliable information about public health. Like the *Gaunt* case, this seems a reasonable judgment.

Decision-making as regards 'due impartiality', by contrast, may be more questionable. Alongside the Broadcasting Code, Ofcom has also published extensive 'guidance notes' on its provisions.[38] The current edition of the guidance note on due impartiality runs to 22 pages and includes links to dozens of regulatory decisions in which Ofcom has determined that the

---

[35] *R (Steyn) v Ofcom* [2024] EWHC 2028 (Admin).

[36] Broadcasting Code, Rules 2.1 and 2.2. The full text of the Broadcasting Code is available via Ofcom's webpages: www.ofcom.org.uk/tv-radio-and-on-demand/broadcast-standards/broadcast-code/.

[37] *Steyn* (n 35) [100]–[101].

[38] See: www.ofcom.org.uk/tv-radio-and-on-demand/broadcast-standards/broadcast-code/.

Code has or (as the case may be) has not been breached.[39] The notion of 'due impartiality' is explained as follows:

> 'Due' is an important qualification to the concept of impartiality. Impartiality itself means not favouring one side over another. 'Due' means adequate or appropriate to the subject and nature of the programme. So 'due impartiality' does not mean an equal division of time has to be given to every view, or that every argument and every facet of every argument has to be represented. The approach to due impartiality may vary according to the nature of the subject, the type of programme and the channel, the likely expectation of the audience as to content, and the extent to which the content and approach is signalled to the audience.

Clearly, this is a variable standard which invests considerable discretion not only in editors, but in the regulator also. Section 5 of the Broadcasting Code contains several rules which bring greater clarity to the matter. Among these are the following:

- News, in whatever form, must be reported with due accuracy and presented with due impartiality.
- Significant mistakes in news should normally be acknowledged and corrected on air quickly.
- No politician may be used as a newsreader, interviewer or reporter in any news programmes unless, exceptionally, it is editorially justified.
- Programmes ... must exclude all expressions of the views and opinions of the person providing the service on matters of political and industrial controversy and matters relating to current public policy.
- In dealing with matters of major political and industrial controversy and major matters relating to current public policy an appropriately wide range of significant views must be included and given due weight.
- Broadcasters should not give undue prominence to the views and opinions of particular persons or bodies on matters of political or industrial controversy and matters relating to current public policy.

The application of these rules has been challenged in a number of recent cases. To date, no legal challenge to Ofcom's determinations as to 'due impartiality' has been successful, and the rules themselves have not been found by a court to be in breach of Article 10's guarantee of freedom of expression. We can consider a number of cases by way of illustration. The first concerns elections. The second is a set of cases connected, in one way or another, with Russia. The third concerns GB News.

---

[39] See: www.ofcom.org.uk/siteassets/resources/documents/tv-radio-and-on-demand/broadcast-codes/politicians-research/broadcast-code-guidance-section-5.pdf.

Televised leadership debates have become a feature of recent election and referendum campaigns in the United Kingdom. This is a relatively new aspect of election campaigns in Britain: before the 2010 general election no such debates took place. There is no established pattern. The leaders of the three largest parties took part in TV debates in 2010; a different pattern was used in 2015; in 2017 there was no debate featuring the leaders of all the larger parties (as Theresa May, the leader of the Conservative Party, declined to take part). In 2019 ITV agreed to broadcast the following: a live debate between the leaders of the two main parties (Boris Johnson for the Conservatives and Jeremy Corbyn for Labour); a live interview-based programme, to be broadcast the same evening, for other party leaders; and a further debate for all party leaders. The Liberal Democrats objected, arguing that it was wrong for their leader to be excluded from the first of the leaders' debates. The Scottish National Party also objected. The Liberal Democrats sought judicial review of ITV's broadcast proposals, but the claim was refused on the basis that ITV, as an independent broadcasting corporation, was not amenable to judicial review.[40] An alternative remedy existed, whereby the parties could complain to Ofcom if they considered ITV to be in breach of its duties to exercise 'due impartiality'. The High Court opined, however, that there was 'no arguable case' that ITV had breached the Broadcasting Code.[41] The court noted that due impartiality may be achieved over a period, by a series of linked programmes, which is exactly what ITV was proposing: 'the whole statutory scheme ... is predicated on the basis that broadcasters exercise editorial judgment and ascribe due weight to relevant factors as they think fit. That is what ITV here did, acting conscientiously and carefully'.[42]

The case is an example of how light-touch judicial review is likely to be in the event that there is no intervention by the regulator. Judicial review, though, might be no less light-touch when the regulator has intervened. The leading case relates to RT, formerly known as Russia Today.[43] Ofcom found that seven of RT's programmes broadcast in March and April 2018 breached due impartiality rules ('the breach decisions'). Two concerned the Salisbury poisonings of Sergei Skripal and his daughter (these programmes had been presented by George Galloway); four concerned Syria; and one concerned Ukraine. Ofcom imposed a financial penalty of £200,000 on RT

---

[40] *R (Liberal Democrats) v ITV Broadcasting* [2019] EWHC 3282 (Admin), [2020] 4 WLR 4.
[41] ibid [111].
[42] ibid.
[43] *R (TV Novosti) v Ofcom* [2020] EWHC 689 (Admin), [2020] 1 WLR 3130 (High Court) and [2021] EWCA Civ 1534, [2022] 1 WLR 481 (Court of Appeal). A further case concerned the China Global Network Service, but the ruling in that case raised no new point of law, the court following and applying the approach taken by the High Court and Court of Appeal in *TV Novosti*: see *R (Star China Media) v Ofcom* [2023] EWCA Civ 843, [2024] 1 WLR 248.

for these breaches. It is important to note that Ofcom did not challenge the accuracy of what was reported in these broadcasts.

RT went to court to challenge both the breach decisions and the financial penalty on the ground that they were disproportionate interferences with RT's right to freedom of expression under Article 10 ECHR. The legal action did not seek to challenge any obligation (whether arising under statute or by virtue of the Broadcasting Code) that RT was required to act with due impartiality: the challenge was solely that Ofcom's application of the rules as to due impartiality was unlawful. RT's challenge failed in both the High Court and the Court of Appeal.[44] The High Court commenced by analysing the due impartiality rules as 'part of a carefully designed tripartite series of measures'[45] which had to be understood alongside the prohibition on political advertising in the UK's broadcast media and the requirement that broadcast time must be made freely available to political parties in the form of party political broadcasts and party election broadcasts.[46] All three have been features of broadcasting law in the United Kingdom since at least the mid-1950s: they were carried over into the Communications Act 2003 from earlier enactments dating back to the Television Act 1954. Having set this out, the High Court stated that it did not

> accept that the passage of time and the technological developments which have occurred since the due impartiality requirements were introduced in 1954 into the regime for regulating the broadcast media, mandates a different interpretative approach or affects the underlying policy considerations.[47]

This was stated to be because 'the broadcast media maintains a reach and immediacy that remains unrivalled by other media'.[48]

This approach, as we have seen, is fundamentally at odds with that taken in the United States, where regulators and courts alike have seen that the radical liberalisation of broadcasting technology – we no longer have only a handful of channels to choose from – has necessitated a similar liberalisation of broadcasting regulation. What may have been a 'pressing social need' in the 1950s is no longer anything like as pressing, given the vastness of the choice now available to listeners and viewers. What may have been 'necessary' in the 'democratic society' of the 1950s may well be quite unnecessary in the altogether different broadcast landscape of the 2020s.

---

[44] Senior judges presided at both levels. The High Court was comprised of Dame Victora Sharp, President of (what was then) the Queen's Bench Division, and Dingemans LJ. The Court of Appeal was comprised of Sir Geoffrey Vos MR and Baker and Warby LJJ.

[45] *R (TV Novosti) v Ofcom* [2020] EWHC 689 (Admin), [2020] 1 WLR 3130 [21].

[46] See, respectively, Communications Act 2003, ss 321(2) and 333. Political advertising is considered in the next section of this chapter.

[47] *R (TV Novosti)* (n 45) [21].

[48] ibid.

Yet neither the High Court nor (as we shall see) the Court of Appeal chose to see it this way. Their reasons for not doing so are unpersuasive.

It is not only the proportionality analysis which is weak in these judgments, it is also the analysis of the 'legitimate aim' for the sake of which the interference with freedom of expression was said to be made. It will be recalled that Article 10 ECHR permits public authorities to interfere with freedom of expression only in order to safeguard one or more of the following 'legitimate aims': national security, territorial integrity or public safety, the prevention of disorder or crime, the protection of health or morals, the protection of the reputation or rights of others, preventing breach of confidence, or maintaining the authority and impartiality of the judiciary. None of these was relevant to RT's case save 'protecting the rights of others'. Thus, in order to be lawful under Article 10 ECHR, Ofcom's breach decisions and financial penalty had to be shown to be necessary (ie, proportionate) in order to protect the rights of others. The relevant 'right of others' is the right of viewers to receive a range of opinions, information and ideas. As the High Court put it, the legitimate aim is 'to ensure that other viewpoints are received by viewers who may then participate on an informed basis in the democratic processes including those of debate and voting'.[49]

RT is a state broadcaster. It is funded directly by the Russian government from its annual state budget, as well as by commercial advertising. Its broadcasts put Russia's point of view. On the matters in respect of which Ofcom found RT to be in breach of due impartiality, Russia's point of view was avowedly and starkly different from that of the British government, the European Union and the UK's NATO allies. RT's viewers in the United Kingdom know this full well. Specifically, they are likely to be fully aware of the West's narrative on the Salisbury poisonings, on the Kremlin's involvement in Syria, and on Moscow's hostility towards Ukraine. Indeed, they are likely to be watching RT to inform themselves precisely of the differences between Russia's take on these matters and mainstream opinion (of governments and commentators alike) in the West. In other words, they are using and taking advantage of their right to receive multiple viewpoints so as better to inform themselves, not having that right abused.

This, of course, was RT's argument. But it was rejected by Ofcom and the courts alike. Due impartiality had to be demonstrated within programmes and within channels, not by comparing RT's programming with what RT called the 'dominant narrative' available to viewers elsewhere. The Court of Appeal noted that 'Ofcom's breach decisions did not analyse the harm that might be caused to [RT's] viewers by [RT's] failure to present opposing views'.[50] The Court of Appeal further noted that the High Court did not

---

[49] ibid [64].
[50] *R (TV Novosti) v Ofcom* [2021] EWCA Civ 1534, [2022] 1 WLR 481 [62].

undertake a 'close and penetrating examination of the factual justification' for Ofcom's decisions.[51] Yet, despite all this – despite the fact that no actual harm to viewers was demonstrated either by Ofcom or by the High Court – the Court of Appeal ruled that the breach decisions and the £200,000 financial penalty were lawful. They were lawful because they were held to be necessary interferences with freedom of expression.

Perhaps this outcome is justified when it is remembered that RT was not actually *prevented* from broadcasting its pro-Russian views about the Salisbury poisonings, the war in Syria, or events in Ukraine. RT was required merely to broadcast such views in a balanced way, alongside other views which opposed the Russian authorities' narrative. Perhaps it is justified also when it is remembered that if RT had wanted to convey its views online, rather than via broadcast, it would not have been subject to 'due impartiality' rules at all, as these rules apply in the United Kingdom only to broadcast and not to other communications media.

RT has not broadcast at all in the United Kingdom since 2022. The events described in the preceding paragraphs predate Russia's military invasion of Ukraine. That invasion prompted widespread imposition of sanctions on Russia throughout the West, sanctions which made it impossible for RT to continue to broadcast. Within a month of RT going off air in the UK, Ofcom decided to revoke its broadcasting licence altogether. Ofcom noted that it had not found RT to be in breach of any provision of the Broadcasting Code since the seven breach decisions which had led to the court case narrated above. But, following the invasion of Ukraine, Russia had made it an offence in its law (punishable by up to 15 years' imprisonment) for anyone to describe the invasion of Ukraine as a war. As such, RT's 'position as a state broadcaster, financed by a state which has recently invaded a sovereign state and effectively criminalised independent journalism' means that it is no longer a 'fit and proper' person to hold a broadcasting licence. So Ofcom ruled.[52]

It is unlikely that the ECtHR would find any of these decisions to be contrary to Article 10. Its leading case on the licensing of broadcasting is *NIT v Moldova*, a decision of the Grand Chamber handed down in April 2022.[53] In the same vein as the more recent Strasbourg authorities considered at the end of the previous chapter, *NIT v Moldova* is a case which fails to offer free speech the protection it needs. At the time when the facts of the case took place, in 2012, NIT was one of five national television

---

[51] ibid [67].
[52] Ofcom's revocation notice is available via its website: www.ofcom.org.uk/siteassets/resources/documents/about-ofcom/bulletins/content-sanctions-and-adjudications/revocation-notice-ano-tv-novosti.pdf.
[53] *NIT v Moldova*, judgment of 5 April 2022.

broadcasters in Moldova. Its editorial line was hostile to the government of the day (a coalition known as the Alliance for European Integration) and supportive of the party which had formerly been in power but which in 2012 was Moldova's only opposition party (a party which had emerged out of the Communist Party, which had ruled Moldova when it was part of the Soviet Union). In 2012 the Moldovan broadcasting regulator withdrew NIT's licence to broadcast. This followed a series of instances in which NIT had been found to be in breach of the Moldovan Broadcasting Code, breaches in respect of which the regulator had imposed an escalating series of sanctions (from fines, to a requirement that NIT may not broadcast advertisements for a period, to a suspension of its licence for a period). NIT's breaches concerned its news broadcasts being politically one-sided; this, then, is a case about fairness and balance, even-handedness, and due impartiality.

The European Court of Human Rights ruled by fourteen votes to three that there had been no breach of Article 10 ECHR. The judgment is as unpersuasive as it is troubling. As the short dissenting opinion of Judge Lemmens, Judge Jelić and Judge Pavli points out, the court effectively endorsed the cancellation of Moldova's only national television broadcaster whose channel gave prominence to the country's only opposition party.[54] Delicensing, in the view of the dissenting judgment, could be compatible with Article 10 only in extremis. Here, by contrast, whilst NIT news broadcasts used outspoken and intemperate language to describe government ministers (that they were dictators, usurpers, criminals or traitors, for example), the court found that there was no risk to national security or territorial integrity, and no incitement to violence or hatred. It found, nevertheless, that 'the news reporting at issue could hardly be said to have been of a kind calling for the enhanced protection afforded to press freedom under Article 10'.[55] In the court's verdict, NIT had not 'contributed to political pluralism in the media in any meaningful way'.[56] It is hard to avoid the conclusion that the European Court was driven by its distaste for NIT's anti-European and pro-Russian editorial line. It is even harder to believe that the court would have been so sanguine had the facts been reversed. Suppose it was a pro-Russian coalition in government and a pro-European party in opposition, and suppose that alone of Moldova's television stations, NIT had supported the opposition and been critical of the government. Would the ECtHR in such circumstances have ruled that it was within the national authorities' margin of appreciation to remove the broadcaster from the airwaves?

---

[54] ibid, joint dissenting opinion [3].
[55] ibid, judgment of the court [215].
[56] ibid [216].

As it stands, *NIT v Moldova* is as damaging for the protection of editorial freedom as it is for the principle of media pluralism. Even if one accepts that regulators and government still have a legitimate role in controlling the broadcast media, so that a multiplicity of voices is able to be heard, and that the market cannot be relied on to achieve this result without regulatory intervention, it is far from clear how sanctioning NIT's removal from the airwaves achieves this result. Surely, the decision has the opposite effect: a *narrower* range of opinion is now available on Moldova's four remaining nationwide broadcast channels. In an attempt to justify its decision, the European Court of Human Rights talked loosely about how states need to guarantee what it calls 'true effective pluralism' without explaining how either 'true' or 'effective' condition the pluralism the court is after.[57] Again, the suspicion lurks that what the court really means is 'pluralism we approve of' rather than 'pluralism that includes dangerously pro-Russian views, unwelcome on European airwaves'. NIT's voice added pluralism to the Moldovan broadcast media, but it was somehow not true and somehow not effective. NIT contributed to pluralism, but not in a 'meaningful way' (meaning: not in the way 'we' want).[58]

Even if British and European case law is for the time being unpromising, it appears that the courts in the United Kingdom may soon have the opportunity to rule once again on the matter – or, at least, on aspects of the matter – and the opportunity should be taken for a fresh start. GB News started television broadcasting in 2021. By July 2024 Ofcom had determined that GB News had breached the Broadcasting Code in 12 instances, with an additional six pending further investigation. GB News has announced it is challenging at least two sets of Ofcom's determinations against it in court. All are concerned with various rules concerning due impartiality. One set of determinations concerns the channel's use of serving MPs as presenters. Jacob Rees-Mogg, Esther McVey and Philip Davies presented current affairs programmes on GB News whilst serving as Conservative MPs. Among Ofcom's rules on due impartiality (as we saw above) is the instruction that 'no politician may be used as a newsreader'. The Broadcasting Code does not define 'news' and its distinction from 'current affairs' is blurred. The Rees-Mogg and McVey/Davies programmes distinguished news bulletins from the current affairs interviews and discussions which the politicians presented but Ofcom ruled that in five instances the two had not been kept sufficiently separate, and that a number of the items presented by the politicians were 'news'.[59] A separate determination concerned a February 2024 broadcast in which the incumbent prime minister, Rishi Sunak, was given a platform to answer audience questions for one hour. GB News claimed that the then leader of the opposition, Sir Keir Starmer, would be afforded a like opportunity but, in the event, no such broadcast was made. Ofcom found that the Sunak show breached the Code's requirements as to due impartiality[60] and, in October 2024, announced it was imposing a fine of £100,000 on GB News.[61]

At the time of writing it seems that GB News' challenges are likely to focus on whether Ofcom has directed itself properly as to the law and on whether Ofcom's decisions were reasonable, proportionate and fair.[62] Thus, the challenge at least to start with is to Ofcom's interpretation and implementation of the rules rather than to the lawfulness of the rules themselves. Whether the GB News cases develop into a full-frontal dispute about the proportionality of the UK's onerous restrictions on broadcast speech remains to be seen. Certainly, the argument is there to be made, should the parties wish to pursue it.

C. A Footnote on Russia: And a Conclusion

To be critical of the regulatory regimes for broadcasting, operating in Britain and Europe, and to criticise how judicial decisions in both Britain and Europe have upheld regulatory decisions which interfere – in some cases profoundly – with freedom of expression, does not mean that democratic states should be powerless to counter what appears to be a concerted and wide-ranging Russian propaganda effort. It would seem that Russian agents have been active in the West, since long before the invasion of Ukraine, spreading fake news and disinformation in all forms of media. It is clear that Russia's 'established threat' to the West, as the UK's Intelligence and Security Committee (ISC) put it in 2020, is far from confined to online (cyber) interference, even if that has been one of its focal points.[63] The findings of the ISC's *Russia Report* are one of the reasons why the UK Parliament legislated in 2023 for new offences relating to 'foreign interference'. Among other matters, it is now an offence in the UK to post false or misleading information on behalf of a foreign power if doing so affects participation in political processes (such as elections or referendums).[64] There can be no credible argument that such offences are contrary to Article 10 ECHR.

---

[60] Ofcom, *Broadcast and On Demand Bulletin*, No 498 (20 May 2024).
[61] Ofcom, Sanction 167(64) GB News, decision of 28 October 2024.
[62] *R (GB News) v Ofcom* [2024] EWHC 2658 (Admin).
[63] Intelligence and Security Committee, *Russia Report*, HC 632, July 2020 [1].
[64] National Security Act 2023, ss 13–16; see further ch 6.

The Sanctions and Anti-Money Laundering Act 2018 empowers the secretary of state to make sanctions regulations where he considers it appropriate in the interests of international peace and security or for the furtherance of foreign policy objectives. Such regulations were made in 2019 in response to Russia's annexation of Crimea and its campaign to destabilise Ukraine, and they were amended and expanded following Russia's invasion of Ukraine in 2022. Under the regulations a person 'involved in destabilising Ukraine' may be sanctioned, the result being that the person's bank accounts and financial arrangements are frozen. In the summer of 2022 Graham Phillips was sanctioned under these regulations. He claimed he was a journalist, reporting from an avowedly pro-Russian point of view Moscow's policies and actions relating to Ukraine, both before the invasion and during the war (reporting from behind Russian lines). The British government saw him not as a journalist but as a Russian agent acting under the cover of being a journalist. Phillips challenged his designation under the sanctions regulations as being a disproportionate interference with his Article 10 right to freedom of expression.[65] The High Court dismissed his claim: had Phillips been an 'objective, independent and fair-minded journalist who had happened to say some things that did not align with [British] foreign policy objectives', it would have been difficult to justify the measures taken against him, the court said.[66] But he was none of these things: 'he is, to all intents and purposes, a Russian asset who has signed up to Russia's propaganda war', the court ruled.[67] As such, the measures taken against him were lawful.

The High Court was quite right in *Phillips* to rule that there had been no breach of Article 10. There is a significant difference, however, between sanctioning a 'journalist' who (for example) praised the fall of Mariupol as 'a huge victory' returning the city to 'the will of the people', on the one hand, and taking a TV channel off the air because its reporters are outspoken in their criticism of government ministers. There is a similar difference between having a regime which allows a democracy to respond in a targeted manner to the specific threats of a propaganda machine – which is consistent with the idea of speaking freely – and having a regime which imposes blanket requirements of balance and due impartiality on one sector of the media irrespective of the market conditions in which that sector operates.

There will be many millions of viewers (and listeners) not only in the United Kingdom but across Europe who do not want to consume news on the broadcast media that is unduly partial. Even readers of the most partisan newspapers might want a different colour of news on television or

---

[65] *Phillips v Foreign Secretary* [2024] EWHC 32 (Admin), [2024] 1 WLR 2227.
[66] ibid [148].
[67] ibid.

radio. But there will also be viewers and listeners who, for whatever reason, want something different. They might want to know what 'the right' are thinking – and they might think that GB News offers that in a way the BBC never could. Or they might want to know how the geopolitics of, say, Eastern Europe looks from an avowedly non-Western point of view. Why should they be denied this? When the limitations of the spectrum allowed there to be only a handful of broadcast channels, it made sense for governmental regulation to ensure even-handedness, balance and 'due impartiality'. But those days are long gone. Nowadays viewers (at least in the West) have hundreds, if not thousands, of platforms and channels to choose from. Moreover, the devices on which we may view our chosen channels do not have to be old-fashioned television sets. They might be laptops, tablets or smart phones. On a single half-hour train journey into work I might watch three videos of the same news item on my phone, one embedded in a newspaper subscription I pay for, one on a magazine's YouTube channel, and one, a recording from the previous evening's TV news, on the BBC website. What sense does it make for one of these to be subject to 'due impartiality' rules when the other two are not?

Abandoning due impartiality rules for the broadcasting sector does not mean that viewers or listeners will no longer be able to access impartial news coverage. For as long as there is consumer demand for it, the market will surely provide it. And, if the market is providing it, what is the justification for thinking that legislation and regulation are required to secure it? This was understood in the United States as long as 40 years ago. Is it not time for it also to be understood in Britain and Europe? Milton and Locke challenged print licensing in similar terms more than three centuries ago. Ultimately their arguments prevailed, not just for print but, eventually, also for the stage. The purported justifications for treating broadcasting differently have long since worn thin.

II. Political Advertising

A particularly severe restriction on broadcasting concerns political advertising. In the United Kingdom there is a complete ban on all forms of political advertising on broadcast media. The ban is long-standing: it has been a feature of the UK's broadcasting law ever since the launch of commercial television in Britain.[68] The ban can without exaggeration be described as a blanket ban. It applies not only during election and referendum campaigns, but all of the time. And it applies not only to political parties, but to anybody seeking to pay to broadcast a political message.

---

[68] See the Television Act 1954.

The prohibition can be found in section 321(2) of the Communications Act 2003. This bans an advert which 'is inserted by or on behalf of a body whose objects are wholly or mainly of a political nature', 'is directed towards a political end', or 'has a connection with an industrial dispute'. The phrases 'objects of a political nature' and 'political ends' are expansively defined in section 321(3) to include: influencing the outcome of a referendum or election; advocating for a change in the law; influencing policy; influencing public opinion on a matter of public controversy; or promoting the interests of a party or other group organised for political ends.

Notwithstanding its longevity and, at least until recently, its strong cross-party support, the extent of the ban on political advertising in the UK's broadcast media has long been controversial. Professor Barendt, the UK's leading free speech lawyer of the period – and a scholar whose work is characterised much more by moderation than outspokenness – argued in 2002 that the ban was so widely drawn it could amount in certain cases to a 'monstrous and unjustifiable infringement of freedom of expression'.[69] He noted, for example, that car manufacturers could pay to advertise their cars for sale, whereas those concerned that ever growing volumes of road traffic contribute to climate change could not. I share Professor Barendt's view of this matter, but we are in the minority, at least in the United Kingdom (at least for the time being).

The Communications Act 2003 was passed with extensive cross-party support, after years of careful policy consideration and public consultation. The Committee on Standards in Public Life considered the matter of whether the UK's ban on broadcast political advertising should be continued in a report published in 1998. The Committee concluded unanimously that it should be continued.[70] The government agreed. Its proposals were thereafter published in a White Paper, which was open to public consultation.[71] There followed a draft bill, which was likewise subject to public consultation as well as to pre-legislative scrutiny in Parliament.[72] Only after all this was a bill finally introduced which, after lengthy, detailed and careful legislative consideration, was passed into law as the Communications Act 2003.[73] Since its enactment, the House of Lords has ruled unanimously

---

[69] Eric Barendt, evidence to the Joint Committee on Human Rights, June 2002, cited by the European Court of Human Rights in *Animal Defenders International v United Kingdom* (2013) 57 EHRR 21 [43].

[70] Committee on Standards in Public Life, *The Funding of Political Parties*, Cm 4057 (October 1998) 176.

[71] HM Government, *A New Future for Communications*, Cm 5010 (December 2000).

[72] See Joint Committee on the Draft Communications Bill, *Final Report*, HC 876, 2001–02.

[73] For further accounts of the legislative passage of the bill into law, see the judgments of the House of Lords and the ECtHR in *R (Animal Defenders International) v Secretary of State for Culture, Media and Sport* [2008] UKHL 15, [2008] 1 AC 1312 (*ADI*) and *Animal Defenders International v United Kingdom* (n 69).

that section 321(2) is compatible with Article 10 ECHR[74] and, albeit by the narrowest of margins, the Grand Chamber of the ECtHR has agreed.[75]

With respect, these judgments are mistaken. To set them in context, let us start by considering the following well-known dicta. In *Simms*, Lord Steyn said that:

> [F]reedom of speech is the lifeblood of democracy. The free flow of information and ideas informs political debate. It is a safety valve: people are more ready to accept decisions that go against them if they can in principle seek to influence them. It acts as a brake on the abuse of power by public officials. It facilitates the exposure of errors in the governance and administration of justice of the country.[76]

In *Reynolds*, Lord Nicholls said that:

> [F]reedom to disseminate and receive information on political matters is essential to the proper functioning of the system of parliamentary democracy cherished in this country. This freedom enables those who elect representatives to Parliament to make an informed choice, regarding individuals as well as policies, and those elected to make informed decisions ... To be justified, any curtailment of freedom of expression must be convincingly established by a compelling countervailing consideration, and the means employed must be proportionate to the end sought to be achieved.[77]

In *Shayler*, Lord Bingham said that:

> Modern democratic government means government of the people by the people for the people. But there can be no government by the people if they are ignorant of the issues to be resolved, the arguments for and against different solutions and the facts underlying those arguments ... [and] there can be no assurance that government is carried out for the people unless the facts are made known, the issues publicly ventilated.[78]

In *Campbell v Mirror Group Newspapers*, Lady Hale said that:

> There are undoubtedly different types of speech ... Top of the list is political speech. The free exchange of information and ideas on matters relevant to the organisation of the economic, social and political life of the country is crucial in any democracy. Without this, it can scarcely be called a democracy at all.[79]

These are not old dicta. They were all uttered in cases decided in the first few years after the Human Rights Act 1998 was passed. Nor are they

---

[74] *ADI* (n 73).
[75] *Animal Defenders International v United Kingdom* (n 69). The ECtHR reached this conclusion by nine votes to eight.
[76] *R v Secretary of State for the Home Department, ex p Simms* [2000] 2 AC 115, 126.
[77] *Reynolds v Times Newspapers* [2001] 2 AC 127, 200.
[78] *R v Shayler* [2002] UKHL 11, [2003] 1 AC 247 [21].
[79] *Campbell v MGN* [2004] UKHL 22, [2004] 2 AC 457 [148].

minority or dissenting views. Nor are they controversial. Every one of these dicta comes from the judgment of a senior judge in the UK's highest court. None of these dicta was contradicted or doubted by any other judge who heard or decided the cases from which they are drawn. These dicta are as authoritative a set of statements of modern British free speech law as it would be possible to assemble. They tell us that there is no speech more worthy of protection than political speech. They tell us that the protection of political speech is 'essential'. That it is the very 'lifeblood of democracy'. That 'there can be no government by the people' without it. And they tell us that 'any curtailment' of the freedom of political speech must be 'convincingly established' by a 'compelling countervailing consideration'. Any such curtailment, we are told, 'must be proportionate'. This is setting the bar deliberately and admirably high. These are good dicta, making sound points, rooted in a welcome commitment to protect free speech.

Animal Defenders International (ADI) is a non-profit company which campaigns against cruelty to animals, for the alleviation of their suffering, and for the protection and conservation of their natural environment. In particular, 'it campaigns against the use of animals in commerce, science and leisure, seeking to achieve changes in law and public policy and to influence public and parliamentary opinion towards that end'.[80] In 2005 ADI launched a campaign called 'My mate's a primate', drawing attention to the abuse of primates by humans. The campaign was to comprise newspaper adverts, direct mailshots and a television advert. The latter, however, the broadcasters declined to air, on the basis that to do so would breach section 321(2) of the Communications Act 2003. ADI went to court, seeking a declaration under the Human Rights Act that section 321(2) is incompatible with the right to freedom of expression under Article 10.

ADI should have won this case, but they failed in the High Court and, as we have seen, in the House of Lords and at Strasbourg. ADI would have won its case in the domestic courts had those courts applied the dicta cited above from Lord Steyn in *Simms*, Lord Nicholls in *Reynolds*, Lord Bingham in *Shayler* and Lady Hale in *Campbell v MGN*. But, for reasons we shall explore, the domestic courts ruled otherwise. ADI would have won its case in Strasbourg had the ECtHR applied its own precedents to the case. But, again for reasons we shall explore, that court chose not to. The *ADI* saga is hardly Strasbourg's finest hour. Indeed, the European Court has made a real mess of this area of law. Twice it has ruled that legislative prohibitions on broadcast advertising comparable to the UK's ban in section 321(2) are in breach of Article 10. In 2001 the court ruled that Swiss rules very similar to those at issue in *ADI* were a violation of Article 10.[81] And again in 2009

---

[80] See *ADI* (n 73) [2] (Lord Bingham).
[81] *VgT v Switzerland* (2001) 23 EHRR 159.

the same verdict was reached in a case from Norway.[82] When the House of Lords took a different view in its ruling in ADI's case in 2008 (ie, after the Swiss case had been decided at Strasbourg but before the Norwegian case), expectations were high that their Lordships' verdict would be over-ruled in Strasbourg. Such expectations were not merely frustrated but were confounded when in 2013 the Grand Chamber handed down its extraordi-nary majority judgment, upholding by nine votes to eight what the House of Lords had decided. The law is not only a mess: it fails to protect the very form of speech – political speech – which, the courts like to tell us, is most worthy of protection. What is the explanation?

We can start with the good news. The explanation is not that the courts simply lost their enthusiasm for uttering dicta proclaiming the importance of political speech. Indeed, we are treated to a liberal dose of such dicta in Lord Bingham's leading judgment in *ADI*. He says the following:

> Freedom of thought and expression is an essential condition of an intellectu-ally healthy society. The free communication of information, opinions and argument about the laws which a state should enact and the policies its govern-ment at all levels should pursue is an essential condition of truly democratic government.[83]

That not being enough, he goes on to explain that:

> The fundamental rationale of the democratic process is that if competing views, opinions and policies are publicly debated and exposed to public scrutiny the good will over time drive out the bad and the true prevail over the false. It must be assumed that, given time, the public will make a sound choice when, in the course of the democratic process, it has the right to choose.[84]

But if this is the case, how is it necessary to deprive the public of ADI's views, at least as they wish to broadcast them on TV? Lord Bingham offers the following answer. Political debate, he says, must take place on the broad-cast media on a level playing field: it must be balanced. This is achieved, he says, by the obligations of due impartiality which are imposed on broad-casters. It is not achieved, he goes on to say, 'if political parties can, in proportion to their resources, buy unlimited opportunities to advertise …, so that elections become little more than an auction. Nor is it achieved if well-endowed interests which are not political parties are able to use the power of the purse to give enhanced prominence' to their views.[85] Lord Bingham identifies a risk that matters which are 'essentially political' may 'come to be accepted by the public' not because they are shown to be right

---

[82] *TV Vest v Norway* (2009) 48 EHRR 51.
[83] *ADI* (n 73) [27].
[84] ibid [28].
[85] ibid.

in debate but 'because, by dint of constant repetition, the public has been conditioned to accept them'.[86]

With all respect to Lord Bingham, this is hard to take seriously. ADI wished to run an advertisement drawing the public's attention to what they perceive to be the abuse of primates in scientific research, by certain commercial interests, and in the leisure and tourism industries. The public are hardly prone to 'come to accept' ADI's views about primates just because they happen to view a TV commercial. Plenty of well-resourced voices are available to put a counterview, should they wish to do so, not least the voices of the commercial organisations that use animals in their laboratory experiments. But even if I am wrong about that, and even if Lord Bingham's argument has more weight than I would give it, does it have sufficient weight to meet the deliberately high threshold which (we were told in all those dicta) must be met before 'any curtailment' of political speech may be justified? Is this a 'compelling countervailing consideration'? Has it been 'convincingly established'? And, even if it has, has it been applied proportionately: is this the least intrusive available means, and has a fair balance been struck between the rights of the individual and the interests of the public? My answer to all these questions would be 'No'.

Lady Hale, giving a concurring judgment in *ADI*, was clear as to what the 'countervailing consideration' is. She described it as 'the elephant in the room' and identified it as the 'enormous sums' which are spent on television advertising, and therefore 'have to be raised, at election times' in the United States.[87] So the reason why we ban political advertising on the UK's broadcast media is because we do not want our election and referendum campaigns to become awash with the need to raise and spend vast sums of money as happens in the United States. I have no problem with that. Money can both distort and even corrupt the electoral process (as the advocates of Congress' Bipartisan Campaign Reform Act knew).[88] But if that is the countervailing consideration why does the UK's ban on political advertising extend not only to political parties but to campaign groups such as Animal Defenders International as well? ADI were not standing for election. There was no electoral process for them to distort or corrupt. Likewise, if safeguarding the integrity of elections is the 'countervailing interest', why does the ban in section 321(2) apply all of the time, and not just during the 'regulated period' of an election or referendum campaign? Proportionality, let us recall, requires that the means used are rationally connected to the end desired. A blanket ban such as that found in

---

[86] ibid.

[87] ibid [47].

[88] See the discussion in ch 3 of *Citizens United v Federal Election Commission* 558 US 310 (2010).

section 321(2) fails this test because it prohibits far more speech than it needs to in order to achieve its goal. Proportionality also requires that the means used are the least intrusive available method. Again, section 321(2) fails this test because other, lesser, means are available. By all means limit the ability of parties and candidates to broadcast advertisements during election or referendum periods. There are compelling reasons for doing so. But to extend the reach of such a ban to all other groups as well as to parties, and to other times as well as to election periods, is disproportionate, and the House of Lords was wrong in *ADI* to rule otherwise.

There is a further point to consider. Suppose I am wrong, and that it really is necessary in a democratic society to censor ADI's ability to broadcast its speech. If it is necessary to keep ADI away from our television screens, why would it not also be necessary to keep their dangerously one-sided views out of the newspapers, away from bookshops and libraries, and off our billboards? If ADI may not broadcast an advertisement, how come they can make a YouTube video? How come they may advertise on social media? There was, of course, no restriction on ADI's access to the print media; there is no suggestion that ADI's advertisement was in any way offensive or indecent. It is only the broadcast media that are off limits. Why? Lord Bingham's answer is the same as that offered in support of the ongoing imposition of due impartiality requirements on broadcasters: that TV and radio possess a greater 'immediacy and impact' than other forms of media.[89] But, as in cases such as *TV Novosti*, considered in the previous section of this chapter, this point is merely asserted. Nowhere is it actually evidenced. It was true, once upon a time, that broadcasting had an immediacy and an impact that no other medium could even dream of. Whether that era extended as late as 2008 (when the House of Lords decided *ADI*) or 2013 (when Strasbourg decided the case) may be doubted. Technology had already started to move on, and viewing habits had already started to change. But even if the unique 'immediacy and impact' of broadcasting was arguable then, it has long since ceased to be so now.

The judgments in *ADI* are characterised by a great deal of deference. Lord Bingham was impressed by how carefully Parliament had considered the matter when it enacted the Communications Act 2003.[90] Moreover, he said, 'the judgment of Parliament on such an issue [as how to safeguard the integrity of our democracy] should not be lightly overridden'.[91] When the case reached Strasbourg similar deference was shown to the

---

[89] *ADI* (n 73) [30].

[90] The European Court of Human Rights was similarly impressed: s 321(2), the ECtHR noted, was 'the culmination of an exceptional examination by parliamentary bodies of the cultural, political and legal aspects of the prohibition'. See *Animal Defenders International v United Kingdom* (n 69) [114].

[91] *ADI* (n 73) [33].

verdict of the House of Lords. Despite its earlier rulings in *VgT* and *TV Vest*, the European Court preferred to lean more heavily on the House of Lords reasoning in *ADI* than on its own precedents. This is for two reasons. First, the European Court felt hamstrung by the fact that there was no pan-European consensus on whether the integrity of democracy requires a complete ban on political advertising in the broadcast media. Several countries, particularly in Western Europe, have bans similar to that in the United Kingdom. But not all do: Austria, Finland, Greece and the Netherlands do not, and neither do several countries in Central and Eastern Europe.[92] Even though the margin of appreciation to be given to national authorities is normally narrow in the context of interferences with freedom of political expression,[93] the lack of a European consensus meant the court felt it had little choice but to widen it.[94]

The second reason, hidden from the text of the judgment, is political. *Animal Defenders International* was decided by the ECtHR at a time when British scepticism about the European Convention and the Strasbourg Court was in danger of reaching fever pitch. In 2006 the court had controversially decided that the UK's blanket ban excluding prisoners from the franchise was unlawful.[95] Just like section 321(2) that was a legislative prohibition, which was both long-standing in the UK's political culture and recently re-enacted by Parliament with strong cross-party support. The incumbent prime minister said in the House of Commons that it made him 'sick to the stomach' to contemplate giving prisoners the vote and commentators from across the political spectrum felt that Strasbourg had overstepped the mark in ruling the ban unlawful. Had Strasbourg made the same move again in relation to section 321(2) there was real fear that the United Kingdom would simply withdraw from the court's jurisdiction (and, indeed, from the Convention altogether). On this view, the court faced an unenviable choice: depart from its own precedents and hold that the UK's blanket ban on political advertising was somehow compatible with Article 10; or follow its precedents and run the risk that the United Kingdom would revoke the Convention altogether. Whether wisely or not, the court blinked, and opted (albeit by the narrowest of margins) that the former was the lesser evil.

The overbreadth of the UK's ban on political advertising can be seen in the case of *London Christian Radio*.[96] A publisher of Christian magazines wished to advertise on the radio station Premier Christian Radio (which is

---

[92] See *Animal Defenders International v United Kingdom* (n 69) [66].
[93] ibid [104].
[94] ibid [123].
[95] *Hirst v United Kingdom (No 2)* (2006) 42 EHRR 41.
[96] *R (London Christian Radio) v Radio Advertising Clearance Centre* [2013] EWCA Civ 1495, [2014] 1 WLR 307.

run by London Christian Radio). The publisher's advertisement was in the following terms:

> Surveys have shown that over 60% of active Christians consider that Christians are being increasingly marginalised in the workplace. We are concerned to get the most accurate data to inform public debate. We will then use this data to help make a fairer society.

The advertisement then directed listeners to the publisher's website, where they could take part in a survey. The radio station wanted to run the advertisement but clearance was refused by the regulator (the Radio Advertising Clearance Centre) on the ground that the advert was 'directed towards a political end' and fell within the scope of the ban on political advertising in section 321(2) of the Communications Act. The publishers and radio station sought judicial review of this decision, but the Court of Appeal ruled by a majority of two-to-one against them. Lord Dyson MR and Richards LJ upheld the lawfulness of the decision to prohibit the advertisement; Elias LJ dissented.

The case hinged on whether the terms of the advertisement really were 'directed towards a political end'. For the majority, that the publisher wished in the future to use data obtained from the survey to 'help make a fairer society' was sufficient. Elias LJ would have preferred a narrower reading. For him, section 321(2) was aimed at ensuring that advertisements did not seek to influence the outcome of a referendum or election, did not advocate for a change in the law, and did not seek to influence policy or public opinion. Here, the advertisement itself did none of those things (even if the publishers might have used survey data in the future to attempt to do a number of these things). For Elias LJ the justification for reading section 321(2) more narrowly was 'reinforced' by the fact that the ban 'interfere[s] with freedom of speech'.[97] As he noted, 'there is nothing in this advertisement ... which is seeking to influence others'.[98] Yet it was nonetheless deemed too political to broadcast, and was banned.

It is sometimes claimed that the ban on political advertising is compensated for by the fact that the broadcasters are under a legal duty to make airtime freely available to political parties to broadcast party political broadcasts (PPBs) or party election broadcasts (PEBs). This did not help in the *ADI* or *London Christian Radio* cases, of course. None of the claimants in those cases was a political party, and PPBs and PEBs are available only to parties who field candidates, and not to other groups whose messages are deemed 'political'. The leading UK case on PPBs and

---

[97] ibid [52].
[98] ibid [56].

PEBs is *R (ProLife Alliance) v BBC*.[99] It is every bit as disturbing, from a free speech point of view, as are the leading cases on political advertising.

ProLife Alliance, a political party opposed to abortion, fielded a sufficient number of candidates in Wales in the 2001 general election to entitle it to a PEB to be broadcast in Wales. It duly made its broadcast and submitted a tape to the broadcasters. The video was graphic: it depicted the mutilation of the foetus which an abortion may entail. It was graphic, but it was accurate and it was not sensationalised. It was designed to put, as forcefully as possible, ProLife's political message. The broadcasters declined to air the PEB, on the ground that it would offend against taste and decency. ProLife Alliance duly edited it, making its images fuzzier. Still the broadcasters declined to air it. Finally a version of the PEB was submitted with a voiceover and an entirely blank screen. This version was broadcast. ProLife sought judicial review of the broadcasters' decision not to air the first (unedited) version of the PEB, arguing that the broadcasters had disproportionately (and therefore unlawfully) interfered with ProLife's freedom of political expression. The Court of Appeal agreed unanimously with ProLife, but a divided House of Lords overruled the Court of Appeal, ruling four-to-one that the broadcasters had not acted unlawfully.

The leading judgment in the Court of Appeal was given by Laws LJ. He framed the issue as follows: 'the court has to decide whether ... considerations of taste and offensiveness ... constituted a legal justification for the act of censorship involved in banning' the proposed PEB.[100] This is the correct framing and Laws LJ, along with his Court of Appeal colleagues Jonathan Parker and Simon Brown LJJ, gave the right answer. On the facts, they ruled, it was clear that the broadcasters had 'failed altogether to give sufficient weight to the pressing imperative of free political expression'.[101] Considerations of taste and decency could prevail over free speech by a political party at election time only 'wholly exceptionally' (such as when a PEB was deceitful or misleading, which it was not in ProLife's case).[102] On appeal to the House of Lords, only one of the Law Lords hearing the case agreed with the Court of Appeal: Lord Scott. He noted that the material in ProLife's PEB might well be justifiably excluded from other broadcasts – its content might reasonably be thought inappropriate in light entertainment, for example – but the fact that this was a party election broadcast directed at the electorate shifted the balance, in Lord Scott's view. The broadcasters' refusal to air the PEB revealed 'a significant and fatal undervaluing' of the importance of free political speech, in Lord Scott's judgment.[103]

---

[99] *R (ProLife Alliance) v BBC* [2002] EWCA Civ 297, [2003] UKHL 23, [2004] 1 AC 185.
[100] ibid [22] (Laws LJ).
[101] ibid [44] (Laws LJ).
[102] ibid.
[103] ibid [96] (Lord Scott).

The majority of the House of Lords disagreed. For the majority, it was enough that the broadcasters had shown they had 'taken into account' ProLife's right to freedom of expression.[104] That the broadcasters had failed to attach any great weight to that consideration and had found it so easily displaced by considerations of taste and decency did not mean, ruled the House of Lords, that the broadcasters had acted unlawfully.

These twin decisions – *ADI* and *ProLife* – show how limited freedom of political speech is in the UK's broadcast media. Laws LJ was right in *ProLife* to characterise the case as being 'about the censorship of political speech'.[105] That word – censorship – is often used loosely and inadvisedly and is often deployed in order to turn up the heat on a question of controversy rather than to shine light on a matter of analysis. But in this instance it was right word to use. Both cases are examples of political censorship. Both were wrongly decided. And both illustrate that freedom of political speech in the United Kingdom falls a long way short in reality of what we would be entitled to expect were the dicta of Lord Steyn, Lord Nicholls and Lord Bingham and Lady Hale in *Simms*, *Reynolds*, *Shayler* and *Campbell v MGN* taken seriously. For now, the gap between what the judges say and what they all too frequently decide remains.

III. Privacy and the Press

In 1990 Gordon Kaye was a household name in the United Kingdom and one of the most recognisable faces in British popular culture. Throughout the 1980s he had starred in the hit BBC television primetime sitcom, *'Allo 'Allo!* In January 1990 he suffered a terrible car accident, which he was fortunate to survive. He was severely injured, spent several days on life support and was in intensive care in hospital. During this period a photographer and a journalist from the *Sunday Sport*, a salacious British tabloid newspaper, entered Mr Kaye's hospital room, photographed him and talked with him. Mr Kaye was at the time in no condition to consent to this, and within 15 minutes of the photographer and journalist being removed from his room by nursing staff, he had no recollection of it having happened. It was a disgraceful breach of Mr Kaye's privacy. On his behalf, Mr Kaye's agent sued the editor of the *Sunday Sport* for an injunction to restrain the newspaper from publishing 'anything which could be reasonably understood or convey to any person' that Mr Kaye had 'voluntarily permitted'

---

[104] ibid [13] (Lord Nicholls). The majority comprised Lord Nicholls, Lord Hoffmann, Lord Millett and Lord Walker.
[105] ibid [1] (Laws LJ).

any photographs to be taken or interview to be conducted.[106] In the Court of Appeal Glidewell LJ said the following:

> It is well known that in English law there is no right to privacy, and accordingly there is no right of action for breach of a person's privacy. The facts of the present case are a graphic illustration of the desirability of Parliament considering whether and in what circumstances statutory provision can be made to protect the privacy of individuals.[107]

This is a classic privacy case. What the *Sunday Sport* had done was invade Gordon Kaye's privacy. Yet English law knew no right to privacy. The common law had never developed a remedy for breach of privacy, and Parliament had never legislated for the creation of such a right. So Kaye's lawyers had to shoehorn his claim into a pre-existing legal wrong, otherwise they would be denied the injunction they sought. They tried four such causes of action: libel, malicious falsehood, trespass to the person and passing off. They were fortunate that one of these four just about fitted the facts of the case: malicious falsehood. Libel did not (libel protects reputation, not privacy). Trespass to the person did not (there was no assault and no battery committed). Passing off did not (Mr Kaye was not a trader whose products needed legal protection). The ingredients of the tort of malicious falsehood were, at the time, that a *false* publication has been procured *maliciously* and that *special damage* has followed as a direct result. The Court of Appeal found that an injunction could be granted on the basis of this tort. Bingham LJ, agreeing with Glidewell LJ, put his finger on what the case was really about (and why it matters). He said the following:

> Any reasonable and fair-minded person hearing the facts ... would in my judgment conclude that these defendants had wronged the plaintiff ... This case nonetheless highlights, yet again, the failure of both the common law of England and of statute to protect in an effective way the personal privacy of individual citizens ... The defendants' conduct towards the plaintiff here was 'a monstrous invasion of his privacy' ... If ever a person has a right to be let alone by strangers with no public interest to pursue, it must surely be when he lies in hospital recovering from brain surgery ... It is this invasion of his privacy which underlies the plaintiff's complaint. Yet it alone, however gross, does not entitle him to relief in English law.[108]

Kaye v Robertson was far from a one-off: it is but one example, albeit a particularly stark one, of a significant gap in English (and Scots) law. The failure of the legal system to provide for a remedy in the face even of the most grotesque invasions of privacy was a cause of widespread concern in

---

[106] *Kaye v Robertson* [1990] EWCA Civ 21, [1991] FSR 62.
[107] ibid 6.
[108] ibid 14–15. The internal quotation comes from the judgment of Griffiths J in *Bernstein v Skyviews Ltd* [1978] QB 479, 489.

Britain. The matter was under official review at the time *Kaye v Robertson* was decided: a desire to wait upon the outcome of the review is one reason for the Court of Appeal's reluctance to develop the common law in that case such that it could offer a remedy for breach of privacy. The review in question was conducted by the Calcutt Committee on Privacy. Its report,[109] published in 1990, led to no change in the *law* relating to privacy but did result in changes to press self-regulation (a topic we consider in the final section of this chapter).

Thus, even after *Kaye v Robertson* and even after the Calcutt Report it was still the case that Parliament failed to legislate for a right to privacy and that the common law failed to fashion a remedy for breach of privacy. The legal position was not to change until the Human Rights Act 1998. The Convention rights to which the Human Rights Act gives domestic legal effect include not only freedom of expression, but the right to respect for private and family life in Article 8 ECHR. During the passage of the legislation through Parliament, the press voiced concerns that the Human Rights Act would herald a new law of privacy via the back door. The press lobbied for the Human Rights Act to be amended accordingly. The result was the Human Rights Act section 12. This section applies 'if a court is considering whether to grant any relief which, if granted, might affect the exercise of the Convention right to freedom of expression'.[110] In such a case, section 12(4) provides that the court 'must have particular regard to the importance of the Convention right to freedom of expression'. In addition, section 12(3) provides that 'no relief is to be granted so as to restrain publication before trial unless the court is satisfied that the applicant is likely to establish that publication should not be allowed'. The aim of these provisions is clear: they were intended to soften any blow to press freedom which the incorporation of Article 8 ECHR into domestic law might otherwise land. As we shall see, section 12 has not had this effect in practice.[111]

There are three leading cases: *Campbell v MGN Ltd*,[112] *PJS v News Group Newspapers*,[113] and *Bloomberg v ZXC*.[114] The first concerned the

---

[109] *Calcutt Committee on Privacy* Cm 1102 (1990). For a useful survey, see Cheryl Reid, 'Press Censorship in the 1990s: the Calcutt Report and the Protection of Individual Privacy' (1992) 43 *Northern Ireland Legal Quarterly* 99.

[110] Human Rights Act 1998, s 12(1).

[111] The Bill of Rights Bill (2022), cl 4 would have required courts to give 'great weight to the importance of protecting' the right to freedom of speech. (Or at least it would have done in certain cases: the rule would not have applied to criminal cases, to cases concerning breach of confidence, to immigration cases, or to cases concerning national security: cl 4(3).) Whether substituting a test of giving 'great weight' for one of having 'particular regard' to free speech would have made any material difference to the legal relation of privacy to the press, is a matter of speculation – the Bill of Rights Bill was dropped before it could be debated in either House of Parliament.

[112] *Campbell* (n 79).

[113] *PJS v News Group Newspapers* [2016] UKSC 26, [2016] AC 1081.

[114] *Bloomberg v ZXC* [2022] UKSC 5, [2022] AC 1158.

world-famous supermodel, Naomi Campbell, so renowned 'even the judges know who [she] is'.[115] Campbell had been photographed in the street leaving a Narcotics Anonymous meeting. The *Mirror* newspaper published the pictures and ran a story highlighting the fact that Campbell was in treatment for drug use. Campbell had a history of claiming that, 'unlike many fashion models, she did not take drugs'.[116] This was a carefully curated part of her public image, but it was evidently a lie.[117] Campbell sued the *Mirror* for damages. She conceded that the paper was entitled to publish the facts that she had been an addict and was in treatment for her addiction. But the pictures and the accompanying details were in breach of confidence, she claimed. By a three-to-two majority the House of Lords agreed with her. The disagreement amongst their Lordships was not as to the law, but as to the application of the law to the facts.[118] The House of Lords were agreed that the law of breach of confidence needed to be interpreted – ie, freshly reinterpreted – to accommodate claims such as Naomi Campbell's.

We encountered the law of breach of confidence in the previous chapter (when we considered the *Spycatcher* cases). We saw that it is rooted in equitable doctrine which protects notions of good conscience. If you are in a confidential relationship with someone and you receive information from that person in confidence, it would be unconscionable and inequitable for you to breach that confidence: you would be acting in bad faith. Thus, doctors may not reveal to the public what they know about their patients, just as Crown servants such as Peter Wright may not reveal to the world what they know by virtue of their work in the security and secret intelligence services. Understood in this light, there was nothing confidential about the pictures and accompanying story the *Mirror* ran about Campbell. She was a public figure photographed in a public place, albeit that she had been photographed covertly. But the House of Lords saw that the old law of breach of confidence needed to be allowed to develop, so that it would protect what Lord Nicholls called 'a reasonable expectation of privacy'[119] howsoever that expectation had been created (specifically, whether it had been created by virtue of a confidential relationship or not). Reinterpreted thus, breach of confidence had less to do with conscience, equity and good faith, and more to do with protecting 'individual autonomy and dignity', as Lord Hoffmann put it.[120] Or, as Lord Nicholls explained it, breach of confidence, newly reconceived, became concerned with the 'wrongful

---

[115] *Campbell* (n 79) [127] (Lady Hale).
[116] See, eg, ibid [24].
[117] ibid [36], [54].
[118] Lord Hope, Lady Hale and Lord Carswell ruled that the *Mirror* had acted unlawfully; Lord Nicholls and Lord Hoffmann dissented.
[119] ibid [21]. Lady Hale used the same term [137].
[120] ibid [51].

disclosure of information', irrespective of whether the wrong was 'akin to a breach of trust'.[121]

There are several reasons why the House of Lords felt able to make this move in *Campbell v MGN* whereas the Court of Appeal had felt constrained from doing so in *Kaye v Robertson* (not least, how the cases came to court and how the arguments were presented by counsel). But the single most important reason is unquestionably the Human Rights Act. As Lady Hale put it, whilst the Human Rights Act created no 'new cause of action between private persons', it requires courts as public authorities to act compatibly with Convention rights.[122] This means, at the least, that courts must fashion (and, if necessary, refashion) existing remedies so as to give effect to Convention rights, including to the right to respect for private and family life. The advent of the Human Rights Act, in short, required the courts authoritatively to recalibrate the balance between the freedom of the press to publish and the right of individuals to have their privacy respected.

Therein lies the key term for the House of Lords in *Campbell v MGN*: balance. Their Lordships were at pains to stress that their judgment did not mean media freedom now had always to give way to a public person's claims to his or her privacy. In every case, a balance requires to be struck and, moreover, this is a balance between two values of equal weight. Both privacy and free speech are 'vitally important rights', said Lord Nicholls: 'Neither has precedence over the other'.[123] Likewise for Lord Hoffmann: there is 'no question' that either right has 'automatic priority' over the other and 'nor is there a presumption in favour of one rather than the other'.[124] Lord Hope agreed.[125] So too did Lady Hale.[126]

The restatement of the law in *Campbell v MGN* is a clear improvement on the unjust legal position represented by *Kaye v Robertson*. Where there is a reasonable expectation of privacy it would indeed be wrongful, as the House of Lords found in *Campbell*, for the press to publish regardless. There is nothing in this sensible, prudent recalibration of the law inconsistent with anything Parliament enacted in the Human Rights Act. Specifically, there is nothing in *Campbell* to suggest that the Law Lords were failing to have 'particular regard' to the importance of free speech.[127]

At the same time as the House of Lords was rebalancing the law in the United Kingdom, the ECtHR was acting likewise in Strasbourg. Later in the

---

[121] ibid [12]–[13].
[122] See ibid [132] and Human Rights Act 1998, s 6(3).
[123] ibid [12].
[124] ibid [55].
[125] ibid [113].
[126] ibid [138].
[127] Human Rights Act 1998, s 12(4). This provision was cited several times in the judgments in *Campbell* (n 79).

same year as the judgment in *Campbell* was handed down, the European Court decided the case of *Von Hannover v Germany*.[128] Like the *Campbell* case, *Von Hannover* concerned the publication of pictures of a public person in a public place (in this instance, the person was a member of the Monaco royal family). The German courts had ruled that the press had not breached the claimant's privacy by publishing the pictures but, in a unanimous judgment, Strasbourg disagreed. There was no public interest story relating to the pictures: they had been published merely for readers' entertainment. As such, the free speech interests in the case were weak and were outweighed, on the facts, by the claimant's right to privacy. In the later case of *Mosley v United Kingdom* the Strasbourg court explained that 'there is a distinction to be drawn between reporting facts – even if controversial – capable of contributing to a debate of general public interest in a democratic society, and making tawdry allegations about an individual's private life'. Sensational, even 'lurid news, intended to titillate and entertain' does not attract robust protection under Article 10.[129]

The balance between privacy and press freedom has not always been so carefully struck in subsequent case law, however. Consider *PJS v News Group Newspapers*, for example.[130] PJS is a public figure, married to another public figure (who is globally famous). Together, they had two children. PJS's marriage with his partner was known to be committed, but not monogamous (there was no secret about any of that). PJS had an affair with another couple. That couple took the story to the *Sun* newspaper (owned by News Group Newspapers), who wanted to publish it. PJS obtained an injunction in the English courts to prevent publication. The story of PJS's sexual relations with the couple was then published in various media outlets in other jurisdictions, notably in the United States, Canada and Scotland, and was widely discussed on social media. Given this change of circumstance News Group Newspapers returned to court to have the injunction lifted.

The Court of Appeal ruled for News Group Newspapers but by a four-to-one majority the UK Supreme Court allowed PJS's appeal. The Supreme Court offered two principal reasons for requiring the injunction to remain in place. The first was to safeguard not PJS's own, but PJS's *children's* right to privacy. The second was that the story was simply a 'kiss and tell'. The press could not rely on any public interest to justify printing the story: the story would not be correcting a falsehood (as in *Campbell v MGN*) and the press would not be performing any sort of 'public watchdog' function in running

---

[128] *Von Hannover v Germany* (2005) 40 EHRR 1.
[129] *Mosley v United Kingdom* (2011) 53 EHRR 30 [114]; compare *Axel Springer v Germany* (2012) 55 EHRR 5.
[130] Above (n 113).

the story. The result – just as in the *Spycatcher* case considered in the previous chapter – was that the press in England and Wales was prevented by force of law from running a story which the rest of the world knew all about. There are two problems with this, as Lord Toulson pointed out in his dissent in the Supreme Court: not only does it fail to strike a sensible balance between the competing privacy and free speech interests at stake, but it also flies in the face of what Parliament plainly intended in enacting section 12 of the Human Rights Act. To insist that newspapers in England and Wales may not write about a matter which the rest of the world's press (and social media) may freely write about cannot be 'necessary in a democratic society'. Such an interference with free speech is disproportionate. That was true in the *Spycatcher* saga; it should also have been how the courts resolved the *PJS* case. As it is, the result in *PJS* is a sorry example of the UK's highest court failing to do what Parliament directed the UK's courts and tribunals to do: to have 'particular regard to the importance' of freedom of expression.

The judgment of the UK Supreme Court in *PJS* is a poor statement of the law but, on the facts of the case, does it really matter? Celebrity tittle-tattle about who sleeps with whom is hard to get worked up about. It is low-level speech. Judgments of the Supreme Court, however, can rarely be confined to particular facts of individual cases: they set the approach and direction which courts may be expected generally to follow. What the Supreme Court says about the relation of privacy to press freedom matters even when the speech in a particular case is as low-level as it was in *PJS*. The speech at issue in *Bloomberg v ZXC* was of an altogether different nature.[131] Bloomberg runs media channels which are among the world's leading sources for financial and corporate news. Its journalism and reporting is relied upon and respected globally. *Kaye v Robertson*, *Campbell v MGN* and *PJS v News Group Newspapers* each arose out of the tabloid press wanting to run stories about celebrities (about the private lives of public people). That is not at all what *Bloomberg v ZXC* is about: it is much graver than that.

Bloomberg was seeking to report on what appears to be serious criminal wrongdoing. ZXC is the anonymised name of a person working in the United Kingdom for X Ltd, an anonymised company trading internationally. We know that ZXC was working at a senior executive level but we do not know anything else about him. We do know that an unnamed UK law enforcement agency was investigating both X Ltd and ZXC (we might guess that the law enforcement agency is the Serious Fraud Office).[132] We know that the criminal investigation was focused on allegations of fraud, bribery

---

[131] Above (n 114).
[132] This is Geoffrey Robertson's assumption: see his *Lawfare* (London, TLS Books, 2023) 18.

and corruption. We know also that the criminal wrongdoing was thought to be so serious that MPs had asked parliamentary questions about it.[133] At the time of the Supreme Court's decision in *Bloomberg v ZXC*, however, none of X Ltd's personnel had been charged with a criminal offence.

Bloomberg ran an article about the criminal investigation into X Ltd and ZXC. It appears that almost all the information in the article was leaked to Bloomberg and emanated from a 'letter of request' which the (unnamed) UK law enforcement body had sent to its counterpart in another jurisdiction to seek its assistance in investigating what would appear to be transnational criminal wrongdoing. Such 'letters of request' are, of course, sent in confidence. ZXC brought an action against Bloomberg seeking both damages and an injunction constraining Bloomberg from further disseminating the article. ZXC was successful in the High Court, which awarded him £25,000 in damages and granted the injunction. Bloomberg's appeals to the Court of Appeal and thereafter to the Supreme Court were dismissed. The legal basis of ZXC's claim was that he had 'a reasonable expectation of privacy' in the information contained in the article, and that its publication was 'a misuse of private information'.[134]

The Supreme Court ruled that, in general, individuals under suspicion of, or under investigation for, criminal wrongdoing have a legally enforceable expectation of privacy up to the point at which they are charged with an offence. Such an expectation is not absolute: it is capable of being displaced. A number of factors need to be applied to decide whether it is displaced (or outweighed), including: how well-known the individual is; his or her prior conduct; the method of obtaining the information and its veracity; and the nature of the publication.[135] In ZXC's case what seems to have been decisive is that the information Bloomberg published was leaked to it. Moreover, in the Supreme Court's view, a responsible journalist should be imputed to have known that it was leaked in breach of confidence. For these reasons, ZXC's privacy was held not to have been outweighed by Bloomberg's right to freedom of expression.

Geoffrey Robertson KC, one of the UK's leading media lawyers, is damning of this ruling. A highly respected news agency, with globally recognised expertise in financial journalism, was barred from reporting what Robertson calls 'a highly significant development in tackling corruption'.[136] Complaints had apparently been raised for years about aspects of X Ltd's business and 'a law-enforcement agency was finally doing something about them'.[137] Not only was this 'of obvious public interest', in

[133] *Bloomberg* (n 114) [8]–[9].
[134] ibid [4]–[5].
[135] ibid [62].
[136] Robertson (n 132) 18.
[137] ibid 19.

Robertson's view, but it would also have served as the basis for further investigation into whether the UK law enforcement agency's request to its foreign counterpart for assistance was being followed up and complied with.[138] In Robertson's view, privacy law was being used by ZXC and X Ltd to help cover up corruption. 'Judges are not much good these days as protectors of free speech', he concludes.[139] His book *Lawfare* is an argument 'to change the law in favour of investigative journalism'.[140]

Robertson's argument is compelling. Getting the balance right between privacy and the press is not easy. English law used to get it badly wrong, by radically under-valuing and under-protecting privacy. A recalibration was needed, and the House of Lords was right in *Campbell v MGN* to set out how that should be done. But in the years since, the pendulum has swung too far in favour of the protection of privacy at the expense of free speech. *PJS* and *ZXC*, in very different contexts, are both examples. The solution is unlikely to come from legislation.[141] Parliament has already set out its view as to how the relation of privacy to press freedom should be managed. Yet no weight at all was attached by the Supreme Court in *Bloomberg v ZXC* to section 12 of the Human Rights Act. The provision was cited, but only in passing, and the case was decided as if section 12 had never been enacted. It is not clear that Parliament can easily fix this problem: if the judges choose to overlook section 12 what would there be to stop them likewise choosing to overlook any legislative attempt to buttress it? The fault, as exposed in both *PJS* and *ZXC*, lies with the judges, and it is for the judges to fix it.

IV. Conclusion: Regulating the Press

That said, the press has not exactly made it easy for itself and has hardly covered itself in glory. All too often we have been reminded that the unethical behaviour of the *Sunday Sport* journalists which led to *Kaye v Robertson* is far from a one-off, but is part of a pattern. All too often we have seen the responsibilities that come with press freedom being abused: responsibilities 'to respect the truth, to obey the law, and to uphold the rights' of others.[142] All too often this has caused 'real hardship' and, on occasion, 'wreaked havoc with the lives of innocent people' whose rights have been 'disdained'.[143] It was just such a pattern of disreputable

---

[138] ibid.

[139] ibid 21.

[140] ibid 29.

[141] Here, I refer back to cl 4 of the Bill of Rights Bill: above (n 111).

[142] *Leveson Report on the Culture, Practices and Ethics of the Press*, HC 779 (2012), executive summary [6]. See further on Leveson below.

[143] ibid [7].

behaviour which led to the appointment of Sir David Calcutt to review the matter around the time *Kaye v Robertson* was decided.[144] A string of press abuses, concerning the Yorkshire Ripper Peter Sutcliffe, the singer Elton John and the TV presenter Russell Harty, amongst others, resulted in growing concern that the press was abusing its freedom. In the event, Calcutt's recommendations were modest. The cliché of the time was that the press was 'drinking in the last-chance saloon' but that a reformed system of self-regulation would be given one final shot before any move to statutory regulation – or any move to legislate for a new right to privacy – would be undertaken. Thus the old Press Council was wound up and replaced with a new Press Complaints Commission (PCC) and a new Editors' Code.

It did not work. Only a few years later Princess Diana was chased to her death by a pack of paparazzi and, in the following years, it slowly emerged that the culture, practices and ethics of the press were even darker. The long-range camera lenses that had so hounded Diana (and Naomi Campbell and Princess Caroline of Monaco) were the least of it. The tabloid press was trading extensively in illicitly obtained private and confidential information. Hundreds of thousands of pounds were being spent obtaining information that had been procured in 'wholesale criminal breaches of data protection legislation'.[145] This emerged first in the context of the Royal Household, whose phones were hacked, leading to the high-profile criminal conviction in 2006 of a *News of the World* journalist (Clive Goodman) and of a private detective he had worked with (Glenn Mulcaire). In the same year the Information Commissioner placed two reports before Parliament, *What Price Privacy?*[146] and *What Price Privacy Now?*,[147] drawing attention to how widespread such malpractice had become, both at the *News of the World* and at other titles. Yet nothing changed: none of the 2006 revelations led to any British newspaper conducting an investigation into its practices.[148]

More revelations followed. In 2008 to 2009 it was reported that the *News of the World* paid £700,000 in costs and damages to Gordon Taylor, chief executive of the Professional Footballers' Association, after his phone messages had allegedly been hacked. In 2011 the actress Sienna Miller was awarded £100,000 in damages after the same paper admitted to hacking her phone. Again, these were far from isolated cases. If the press was drinking in the last-chance saloon, it was a long old session.

---

[144] Above (n 109).

[145] *Leveson Report*, executive summary [20].

[146] Information Commissioner's Office, *What Price Privacy?*, HC 1056 (2006).

[147] Information Commissioner's Office, *What Price Privacy Now?*, HC 36 (2006).

[148] *Leveson Report*, executive summary [21].

At last, time was called. In the summer of 2011 it emerged that Milly Dowler's phone had been hacked. Milly Dowler was a teenager who had disappeared in 2002 and whose body was found six months later. Not only had her voicemail been hacked at the time of her disappearance, but messages from it had apparently been deleted, leading to a false impression of what had happened to her. Public revulsion at the appalling behaviour of the press finally boiled over. Rupert Murdoch closed down the *News of the World*, and the prime minister David Cameron appointed Lord Justice Leveson to conduct a statutory inquiry into the culture, practices and ethics of the British press.

After an inquiry costing more than £5 million, Leveson reported a year and a half later. His report ran to more than 1,900 pages and was published in four volumes. It was, he noted grimly, the seventh such report into the press in Britain in the last 70 years.[149] Leveson's principal findings were fourfold. First, he noted that 'the press, operating properly and in the public interest is one of the true safeguards of our democracy'.[150] The British press, he insisted, 'serves the country very well for the vast majority of the time'.[151] Secondly, however, and as an exception to his first finding, the culture, practices and ethics of the press had suffered from serious wrongdoing: wrongdoing so serious that it was criminal. There had been a 'recklessness in prioritising sensational stories'.[152] Parts of the press had taken the view that public figures were 'fair game': 'public property with little, if any, entitlement to any sort of private life'.[153] Further, there had been 'a willingness to deploy covert surveillance, blagging and deception in circumstances where it is extremely difficult to see any public interest justification'.[154] And the 'virtue of persistence has sometimes been pursued ... to the point of vice', where it had become a form of harassment.[155]

Leveson's third finding was that the PCC, set up in the wake of the Calcutt Report, had manifestly failed to ensure high standards in the press, and needed to be replaced. The PCC was 'not actually a regulator at all', Leveson observed: it was a complaints handling body.[156] It lacked independence, it had too tight a budget, it lacked resources, its powers were inadequate and were, in any event, under-utilised, and it failed to monitor press compliance with the Editors' Code.[157] In practice, it proved itself to be altogether too closely 'aligned with the interests of the press'.[158]

---

[149] For an account of the previous six, see *Leveson Report*, vol 1, 195–214.
[150] ibid, executive summary [5].
[151] ibid [8].
[152] ibid [32].
[153] ibid [33].
[154] ibid [34].
[155] ibid [35].
[156] ibid [42].
[157] ibid [42]–[44] and [46].
[158] ibid [45].

None of these findings was controversial, but Leveson's final finding was heavily contested. He was not of the view that the press should be subject to statutory regulation, at least, not directly. He concluded that what was needed was 'genuinely independent and effective' self-regulation[159] and that legislation was required to underpin in. This last step, he argued, was 'essential'.[160] The legislation would achieve three things: it would enshrine a legal duty to protect the freedom of the press; it would provide for a process to reassure the public that the new regulatory scheme – unlike all previous such schemes – was genuinely independent and effective; and it would validate a new standards code and a system for arbitrating on claims it had breached. He recommended that these roles (of reassurance and validation) should be undertaken by Ofcom.[161]

The legislation Leveson envisaged has never been passed. Instead, a Royal Charter on Press Regulation was granted in 2013. This allowed for an independent self-regulatory body to be recognised and overseen by a new Press Regulation Panel (rather than by Ofcom, as Leveson recommended). Such a self-regulatory body now exists – IMPRESS – but most British press titles have chosen not to opt into it. Instead, most are self-regulated by IPSO (the Independent Press Standards Organisation), which has no intention of seeking recognition from the Press Regulation Panel. Other titles (such as the *Guardian*) have elected to be regulated neither by IMPRESS nor by IPSO: that title has appointed its own ombudsman instead. Thus the current position is that the UK's press has a mishmash of self-regulatory schemes, one of which is formally underpinned by Royal Charter, but none of which has the statutory backing of an Act of Parliament that Leveson thought essential.[162] The result reflects not only the deep aversion to statutory regulation felt by the press, but also the reluctance of the UK's political parties to use legislation, even indirectly, to regulate the press.[163] The insistence that the press must remain unlicensed in the United Kingdom is profound. As we have seen, it has a long heritage, going all the way back to John Milton in 1644 (via Locke, Hume and Blackstone, to name just three).

Less has changed on the regulatory front than Leveson would have wanted. But the culture, practices and ethics of the press have nonetheless evolved considerably since 2011. More than anything else, this is due to the

---

[159] ibid [51].

[160] ibid [70].

[161] ibid [72].

[162] For an insightful discussion examining this in comparative perspective, see Lara Fielden, 'A Royal Charter for the Press: Lessons from Overseas' (2013) 5 *Journal of Media Law* 172.

[163] The arguments are patiently (and sometimes critically) dissected in Eric Barendt, 'Statutory Underpinning: A Threat to Press Freedom?' (2013) 5 *Journal of Media Law* 189. Barendt sees some of the arguments as 'neurotic rather than philosophical', suggesting they sometimes overlook differences between mere statutory underpinning and direct legislative regulation.

consumers of the press: readers and members of the public. The grotesque Milly Dowler revelations, which led directly to Leveson being set up and to the *News of the World* being wound down, appear to have triggered such public revulsion that the press has had no option but to change its ways. It is public opinion, rather than statutory regulation, that has brought about the change; and the modern press, whatever its flaws, has always been acutely sensitive to the opinions of its readers. In the court of public opinion, the case against the press had been building for years. Diana's tragic death began to shift the dial. The criminal convictions of those who had been involved in hacking the phones of members of the Royal Household shifted it further. And the Milly Dowler revelations brought matters to a head.

Newspapers have to compete for readers. Their market has been shrinking for decades. And public opinion about the importance of privacy has matured, similarly to the way in which the House of Lords in *Campbell* and the European Court in *Von Hannover* recalibrated the relationship between privacy and press freedom. Margins are ever tighter for newspaper owners. Reputation matters more than ever: potential advertisers think hard before placing advertisements in papers known to adopt corrupt or illicit methods. Celebrity tittle-tattle does not sell in the way it once did; most of us have come to accept that public figures, even politicians, have private lives into which we have no general right to intrude, unless there is a clear public interest in doing so (such as when ministers were breaching Covid lockdown regulations in private, whilst saying something very different in public).

This is all to the good, and long may it last. But it does once again invite us to pose the question this chapter opened with. If public opinion is the most effective regulator of the press, why would it not also be the most effective regulator of the broadcast media? Since Leveson the British press has changed its product, to bring it into line with a more mature and wiser set of public expectations as to what newspapers should – and should not – print. Is it not time to learn the lesson of that, and to apply it also to other sectors of the modern mass media?

5

Offensive and Hate Speech

'Sticks and stones may break my bones, but words can never hurt me' is a well-worn children's adage, dating back to at least the nineteenth century, chanted even now against the playground bully to fend off spiteful name-calling. We can admire its tone of defiance. But it is not true. Name-calling is not merely unpleasant: it can indeed be hurtful. Its wounds can take longer to heal than a bruise.

To inflict a bruise, whether with a fist or with sticks and stones, may be a criminal offence. One of the most contentious areas of free speech is whether the law should similarly criminalise injurious words. Should the law ape the defiance of the playground rhyme, insisting that the answer to insulting speech is 'courage and self-reliance'?[1] Or should the law offer more support for victims, knowing that those who are on the receiving end of threats and abuse are not always in a position to fight back, even with words? Is the better response to speech we may hate – to hateful or offensive speech – that we should ban it through the censorship, or at least through the censure, of the criminal law? Or, in a tolerant society, should we seek to defeat the hateful and the offensive with speech of our own? In short, is the answer to hate speech that we need *less* speech (via censorship) or *more* speech (by talking back)?

I. Criminal Law: Canada and the United States

Precisely this question came before – and divided – the Supreme Court of Canada in one of the leading cases on hate speech, *R v Keegstra*.[2] Keegstra was a high-school teacher who had been dismissed. He was an anti-Semite, who brought his anti-Semitism into the classroom. He had taught his students that Jews were 'treacherous', 'subversive', 'sadistic', 'money-loving',

---

[1] An echo of Brandeis and Holmes JJ in *Whitney v California* 274 US 357, 377 (1927): see ch 3 and see further below.
[2] *R v Keegstra* [1990] 3 SCR 697.

'power hungry' and 'child-killers'. He had told them that the Holocaust had been invented by Jews 'to gain sympathy'. Not only was Keegstra dismissed from employment: he was also charged with a criminal offence contrary to section 319(2) of the Canadian Criminal Code. This provided that a person who, 'by communicating statements, other than in private conversation, wilfully promotes hatred against any identifiable group' may be guilty of an offence. 'Identifiable group' was defined as 'any section of the public distinguished by colour, race, religion or ethnic origin'. The offence was subject to a number of defences, as set out in section 319(3). It was a defence, for example, to establish that the statements were true or, if relating to religion, that they were made in good faith, or that they were relevant to a subject of public interest and were reasonable in the circumstances.

Keegstra was tried and convicted. He appealed, arguing that section 319(2) was contrary to his Charter right to free speech. The Canadian Charter of Rights and Freedoms had been adopted in 1982. It was a new bill of rights for Canada and became part of Canada's constitutional law. The Charter was very different from the eighteenth-century Bill of Rights adopted in 1791 by Canada's southern neighbour. It owed a greater debt to twentieth-century instruments such as the European Convention on Human Rights (ECHR) than it did to the constitutional traditions of the United States. (And, in turn, other more recent bills of rights have owed a considerable debt to the Canadian Charter, not least the New Zealand Bill of Rights Act 1990 and the UK's Human Rights Act 1998.[3]) The Charter right to free speech is included in section 2(b) of the Charter, which provides that 'everyone has the following fundamental freedoms: ... freedom of thought, belief, opinion and expression'. This right needs to be read in the light of section 1 of the Charter, which provides that the rights and freedoms it sets out are 'subject only to such reasonable limits prescribed by law as can be demonstrably justified in a free and democratic society'. The language here is a deliberate echo of the ECHR which, as we saw in earlier chapters, talks of limits to rights needing to be 'prescribed by law' and 'necessary in a democratic society'. To cement the link, the Supreme Court of Canada ruled in *R v Oakes* in 1986 that section 1 of the Charter imposed a proportionality test.[4] In order to be lawful under the Charter a restriction on one of its rights and freedoms must satisfy three tests of proportionality: there must be a *rational connection* between the restriction and what it is aiming to achieve; the restriction must be the least intrusive means available (a test of *minimal impairment*);

---

[3] See, in general, Stephen Gardbaum, *The New Commonwealth Model of Constitutionalism* (Cambridge, Cambridge University Press, 2013).

[4] *R v Oakes* [1986] 1 SCR 103.

and a *fair balance* must be struck between the rights of the individual and the interests of the community.[5]

The question for the Supreme Court in *Keegstra*, therefore, was whether the offence in section 319(2) was a proportionate interference with freedom of expression. Could it be 'demonstrably justified'? Did it satisfy the tests of rational connection, minimal impairment and fair balance? The question divided the Supreme Court of Canada almost down the middle. Four justices ruled that section 319(2) was lawful; three dissented. There was one judgment for the majority, delivered by Dickson CJ. There was likewise one judgment for the dissent, delivered by a judge who would herself go on to become Chief Justice, McLachlin J. Each of these judgments is a finely crafted essay in how the law might approach hate speech. McLachlin J contends that the defiance of the old schoolground adage is right. Dickson CJ makes the opposite argument. *Keegstra* illustrates how the answer we reach may depend on how we frame the question.

Dickson CJ's framing is Millian. John Stuart Mill, as we saw in chapter two, argued in *On Liberty* (1859) that the 'sole end for which mankind are warranted ... in interfering with liberty' is 'to prevent harm'. The first step of Dickson CJ's analysis is accordingly to identify whether hate speech is harmful. He judges that it is: not only does it humiliate and degrade those at whom it is targeted, but it also harms society at large by sowing seeds of discord and division. It does not follow, from this alone, that hate speech should be outlawed, because freedom of speech is valuable. It is valuable for particular reasons, though, and Dickson CJ's next step is to remind us of *why* we protect free speech. He identifies three main reasons (all familiar from the preceding chapters of this book): the argument from truth; the argument from individual self-fulfilment; and the argument from democracy. (Again, Dickson CJ's debt to Mill is evident.) None of these reasons for protecting speech applies with much force in the context of hate speech, contends Dickson CJ. There was no 'truth' to Keegstra's anti-Semitic remarks and nor is the truth more likely to emerge and to defeat falsehood by allowing such lies as the blood libel to be repeated, least of all in a classroom. The argument from self-fulfilment, in Dickson CJ's analysis, does not mean that any one individual should be permitted to say anything with impunity. The argument is designed to protect *everyone* in society: it is our collective 'human flourishing' that is important. As such, an individual's expression must be 'tempered' in so far as it advocates 'intolerance and prejudice' with 'inordinate vitriol'.[6] As for the argument from democracy,

---

[5] We have encountered this formulation of proportionality in previous chapters. It has been widely copied and pasted, including in the UK: see *Bank Mellat v HM Treasury (No 2)* [2013] UKSC 39, [2014] AC 700.

[6] *Keegstra* (n 2) 763.

in Dickson CJ's view this seeks to safeguard all citizens' need 'to be treated with equal respect and dignity so as to make participation in the political process meaningful'.[7] Keegstra's speech, by contrast, sought to undermine that equality, not to serve it.

Dickson CJ's third and final step is to attend to proportionality, reaching the matter only after he has judged both that hate speech is harmful and that Keegstra's speech is low value. Section 319(2), he rules, is not a disproportionate interference with freedom of expression. It is neither over-broad nor impermissibly vague: it does not criminalise private conversation; it criminalises only the wilful promotion of hatred; and, as we have seen, it is subject to a number of defences.

McLachlin J's judgment relies more on the jurisprudence of Oliver Wendell Holmes and Louis Brandeis than it does on the political theory of JS Mill. Dickson CJ, by contrast, said that whilst he found the American case law 'tremendously helpful', he was 'dubious' as to its applicability in Canada, not least because there is no equivalent in the First Amendment of section 1 of the Canadian Charter.[8] He was keen to stress the differences between the categorical approach of the US Supreme Court and the proportionality-based approach which the Charter laid down for Canada. McLachlin J saw matters differently. Her analysis opens not only with a citation to Holmes J's 'clear and present danger' test in *Schenck*[9] but also with the famous dictum from the Brandeis and Holmes concurrence in *Whitney*: 'to courageous and self-reliant men, with confidence in the powers of free and fearless reasoning ..., no danger flowing from speech can be deemed clear and present, unless the incidence of the evil apprehended is so imminent that it may befall before there is opportunity for full discussion'.[10] Violence is harmful, and speech which is akin to violence – a direct and immediate threat, for example – may be treated by the criminal law similarly to the way in which it treats violence. But hate, in and of itself, is not harmful in the same way that violence is. Hatred may well be hurtful, but that does not necessarily make it harmful, in McLachlin J's judgment. McLachlin J therefore disagrees with the first step of Dickson CJ's analysis: in his judgment hatred as such is a harm which may warrant interference with liberty, whereas in her judgment it is not, unless it expresses a violence so imminent there is no opportunity to speak back. To McLachlin J, then, the answer to hate speech is always counter-speech, unless there is simply no time for that, so pressing is the threat.

---

[7] ibid 765.
[8] ibid 741–43.
[9] *Schenck v United States* 249 US 47, 52 (1919). See ch 3.
[10] *Whitney* (n 1).

This framing means that McLachlin J approaches the proportionality analysis very differently from how Dickson CJ approached it. In her view, section 319(2) failed the minimal impairment test and may also have failed the rational connection test. Her concerns as to the latter are twofold. First, the provision may have 'a chilling effect on defensible expression by law-abiding citizens' and, secondly, 'it is far from clear that it provides an effective way of curbing hate-mongers'.[11] Fears of the chilling effect are well known: people may self-censor even perfectly lawful speech out of concerns that, by speaking, they would open themselves to the risk of criminal investigation. Such self-censorship may impede truth. More likely it may impede effective political participation. Most definitely it impedes self-fulfilment and human flourishing. Dickson CJ was surely correct when he ruled that Keegstra's speech was of low value (whatever argument for free speech we rely on); but McLachlin J cast the issue more broadly, and considered not only Keegstra's words, but also other expression – including perfectly lawful expression – liable to become caught in section 319's net. At the same time, she also considered that section 319(2) has unintended consequences. Prosecutions under it attract attention, giving racists and anti-Semites a more prominent platform and a louder megaphone than they would otherwise command. As such, it certainly amplifies racism. It may even encourage racist speech, goading an anti-Semite to become a so-called 'free speech martyr', leading someone to say something solely because the person knows that the ensuing criminal proceedings will serve to spread his message. McLachlin J is far from the first to make this point. Samuel Johnson made it more than two hundred years earlier (as we saw in chapter two). And, in a different context, Margaret Thatcher's Government learned the hard way that prosecuting *Spycatcher* through the world's courts had little effect besides handing to Peter Wright sales his publishers could otherwise only have dreamt of. It is not always rational to turn to the law to seek to curb speech you hate (and given that rationality is a core component of proportionality, it is not always proportionate, either).

McLachlin J was clear that section 319(2) failed the minimal impairment test. Because it was based on the subjective emotion of hatred, which may be proved by mere inference, rather than an objective test of violence or injury, the offence was over-broad and vague. Criminal liability could attach, she noted, even if no person was actually moved to any emotion by the speaker's words: the offence could be committed even if no 'actual harm' was caused.[12] Such vagueness only compounds fears of the chilling effect. The over-breadth of the provision was neither fanciful nor hypothetical, in McLachlin's view. Rather, it was borne out by the facts, for example,

[11] *Keegstra* (n 2) 852.
[12] ibid 857.

that a pro-Zionist novel had faced calls for banning in Canada, that copies of Salman Rushdie's *The Satanic Verses* had been stopped at the Canadian border, and that arrests had been made for distributing pamphlets containing the words 'Yankee Go Home'.[13]

It is sometimes said that Dickson CJ's view represents the approach taken by the law in Europe and that McLachlin J's view represents that taken in the United States. But the reality is more complex. It is true, as we saw in chapter three, that the First Amendment offers fuller protection for free speech than we find in Britain or Europe (or Canada or New Zealand). It is also true that this applies to hate speech as much as it applies to other forms of expression. But it would be an error to think that hate speech is not criminalised at all in the United States, just as it would be an error to think that it is uniformly unlawful in Britain, Europe and Commonwealth jurisdictions such as Canada and New Zealand.

The relevant American case law was surveyed in chapter three. Very briefly to recap: 'fighting words' are not protected by the First Amendment.[14] But this exception to free speech is narrowly construed: it applies only to speech tending to incite an immediate breach of the peace. Even within its narrow application, the fighting words exception to free speech has not always been consistently interpreted and applied. Two pairs of cases can be taken as illustrations. In *Beauharnais v Illinois* in 1952 the US Supreme Court upheld the lawfulness of Beauharnais' conviction for handing out racist and white supremacist literature on the streets of Chicago.[15] But in *Brandenburg v Ohio* in 1969 the conviction of a Ku Klux Klan leader was ruled unconstitutional because the advocacy of violence may be criminalised only where 'such advocacy is directed to inciting or producing imminent lawless action and is likely to incite or produce such action'.[16] Whilst *Beauharnais v Illinois* has never (yet) been formally overruled, it is unlikely to have survived the hardening of the court's First Amendment jurisprudence seen over the last half century.

A further contrast can be drawn between *RAV v City of St Paul* and *Virginia v Black*.[17] In the former, the court struck down a city ordinance which made it an offence to place a symbol such as a burning cross, 'which one knows or has reasonable grounds to know arouses anger, alarm or resentment in others on the basis of race, color, creed, religion or gender'. In the latter, the court upheld a Virginia statute which outlawed cross-burning 'with intent of intimidating any person or group'. We explored the contrast between these two cases in chapter three.

---

[13] ibid 859.
[14] *Chaplinsky v New Hampshire* 315 US 568 (1942).
[15] *Beauharnais v Illinois* 343 US 250 (1952).
[16] *Brandenburg v Ohio* 395 US 444, 447 (1969).
[17] *RAV v City of St Paul* 505 US 377 (1992) and *Virginia v Black* 538 US 343 (2003).

What they show is that, even in the United States, there are cases in which the Supreme Court has upheld convictions for (or legislative restrictions on) offensive or hate speech.[18] What they also show, though, is that there are some criminal laws which are held to be unconstitutional in the United States, which would have been upheld as reasonable and proportionate interferences with free speech elsewhere. The convictions in *Brandenburg v Ohio* and in *RAV v City of St Paul* – and the laws under which those convictions were secured – would have been ruled as being lawful had the cases arisen in the United Kingdom, for example.

II. Hate Speech: *Strossen v Waldron*

The literature on offensive and hate speech is vast. It includes several first-class book-length studies. Among the leading works are Hare and Weinstein's wide-ranging collection, *Extreme Speech and Democracy*,[19] and Eric Heinze's ambitious *Hate Speech and Democratic Citizenship*, which tries to move beyond the 'counter-speech v criminal censure' framing of the debate by seeking to tie the issues more closely to questions of democratic stability and security.[20] Despite Heinze's hopes, however (and, to be fair, as he recognises), we are still stuck in a 'counter-speech v criminal censure' framing. Three and a half decades on from *Keegstra*, the issues are still presented, by advocates and activists, by judges and by law-makers, just as they were by Dickson CJ and McLachlin J, and just as they were in the introductory paragraphs of this chapter. Whatever one thinks about whether we *should* move beyond a 'counter-speech v criminal censure' framing (as Heinze has urged), the fact is we have not done so and, for the time being, we are stuck with it.

The most compelling book-length argument that hate speech should be met not with censorship but with counter-speech is Nadine Strossen's *Hate: Why We Should Resist It with Free Speech, not Censorship*.[21] Likewise, the most compelling book-length counter-argument is Jeremy Waldron's *The Harm in Hate Speech*.[22] Before moving on to the law relating to hate speech in the United Kingdom, I want to pause to consider aspects of their

---

[18] This was the case in *Chaplinsky, Beauharnais* and *Virginia v Black*.

[19] Ivan Hare and James Weinstein (eds), *Extreme Speech and Democracy* (Oxford, Oxford University Press, 2009).

[20] Eric Heinze, *Hate Speech and Democratic Citizenship* (Oxford, Oxford University Press, 2016).

[21] Nadine Strossen, *Hate: Why We Should Resist It with Free Speech, Not Censorship* (New York, Oxford University Press, 2018).

[22] Jeremy Waldron, *The Harm in Hate Speech* (Cambridge MA, Harvard University Press, 2012).

arguments, as it will be helpful to present the recent and ongoing British debates in their light.

Nadine Strossen is a US law professor who served for many years as president of the ACLU, the American Civil Liberties Union. She happens to be Jewish which, as we shall see, is not irrelevant. Her book is a powerful articulation of the argument McLachlin J made in *Keegstra*. Like McLachlin, Strossen worries about the chilling effect of hate crime legislation. And like her, she considers that such laws suffer from two fatal flaws: they are over-broad and they are impermissibly vague. Like Holmes and Brandeis JJ, she contends that the answer to speech we hate is not to silence it, but to speak back. And she offers, as one of her prime examples, a story from 1970s America which may be well known in the United States, but deserves to be better known beyond its shores. It is the story of Skokie, Illinois.

Skokie, Illinois, is a suburban village, just north of Chicago. After the Second World War it became home to a large number of Jewish families, including several Holocaust survivors. In the 1970s an American neo-Nazi group, the National Socialist Party of America, held a series of rallies in Chicago. In 1977 they wanted to move their rally to Skokie. The authorities sought to stop them. For a Holocaust survivor, just seeing the swastika being waved at such a rally is horrific, never mind hearing the venom accompanying it through the megaphone. At this point, up stood the ACLU, an avowedly liberal, progressive and activist lobby group that works to defend and advance US constitutional rights, including the First Amendment right to free speech. Up stood the ACLU, that is, to *defend* the constitutional right of the Nazis to hold their demonstration in Skokie if that is what they wanted to do. Yes, the swastika is offensive – horrific, even. But if you take free speech as seriously as Nadine Strossen and the ACLU take it, not even Nazis have to ask the government's permission before speaking.

This is an extreme case, sorely testing anyone's commitment to free speech. But its conclusion shows how, in the end, we might be right to adhere to that principle even on facts as stark as these, and that we would be wrong to give in to the impulse to censor or ban what we find so profoundly offensive. For the conclusion was this: the Jewish community of Skokie, Illinois, founded and opened a new Holocaust Museum and Education Centre. Many of Skokie's Holocaust survivors had wanted to leave the past behind – they had wanted to bury it, and to forget all about it – but they found they could not remain silent. The Holocaust Museum and Education Centre is dedicated to combating the Nazi hatred that led to the Holocaust not by censoring it, but by educating people about the preju-dice, ignorance and cold indifference that led to it. For campaigners such as Nadine Strossen, what a monument to the power of counter-speech that museum is. Censorship could never have achieved anything like it.

We saw above McLachlin J's citation of the famous Brandeis and Holmes dictum about 'courageous and self-reliant' people.[23] Strossen has courage in abundance, and no doubt self-reliance too. She admires others who have the same character: men such as Martin Luther King, whom she cites several times in her book. And women such Ruth Simmons, Brown University's president from 2001 to 2012 and the first African-American president of an Ivy League university. Strossen quotes Simmons' inaugural convocation address:

> You know something that I hate? When people say, 'That doesn't make me feel good about myself'. I say, 'That's not what you're here for' … I believe that learning at its best is the antithesis of comfort. If you come to this campus for comfort, I would urge you to walk through yon iron gate. But if you seek betterment for yourself, for your community and posterity, stay and fight.[24]

Strossen's own view is as follows:

> To be sure, campuses and other arenas in our society must strive to be inclusive, to make everyone welcome, especially those who traditionally have been excluded or marginalised. But that inclusivity must also extend to those who voice unpopular ideas, especially on campus, where ideas should be most freely aired, discussed and debated. Encountering 'unwelcome' ideas, including those that are hateful and discriminatory, is essential for honing our abilities to analyse, criticise, and refute them.[25]

Is this robust, forthright, point of view an admirably uncompromising statement of principle – or is it cavalier? What if you are not courageous and self-reliant? And what if the reason for that is not some character defect – not something you can fix within yourself – but the product of the fact that the speaker has power over you, and you are in no position to speak back? Think of the school pupils in Keegstra's classroom, for example. Should they be expected to summon the courage and to conjure the self-reliance to counter their teacher's anti-Semitism? Few are possessed of the extraordinary courage and conviction of a Martin Luther King. Is it fair, just and reasonable for the law to assume that we should be? Or would it not be more realistic for the law to recognise that there are grave power imbalances in our society, and for the law take on the responsibility of seeking to protect the relatively powerless from the over-mighty?

Jeremy Waldron, a New Zealander who has studied and taught in the United Kingdom, but who has spent most of his illustrious career in the United States, sees these questions in a more comparative light than is

---

[23] Brandeis and Holmes JJ did not write 'people'. They wrote 'men'. I return to this point below.

[24] Strossen (n 21) 2.

[25] ibid.

evident in much of the US literature. His jurisprudence is avowedly liberal; his commitments both to freedom and to democracy run deep. But he is worried that American theorists and commentators have taken their zeal for free speech too far, that they have fetishised it, and that the mantra that the answer to hate speech must always be counter-speech leads to unjust and unreasonable results. In *The Harm in Hate Speech*, he seeks to defend laws such as that which was (narrowly) upheld in *R v Keegstra* (and which, as we shall see, have also been enacted in the United Kingdom) from the sorts of arguments preferred by lawyers like Nadine Strossen.[26] However, and this is critical to Waldron's account – it is what makes it so important – he does not think that such laws can be defended on the ground that the speech they prohibit is offensive. Quite the contrary: he is clear that 'offence is not something the law should seek to protect people against'.[27] And again: 'offence, however deeply felt, is not a proper object of legislative concern'.[28]

Instead, he founds his argument on dignity and public order. First, he notes that laws such as section 319(2) of the Canadian Criminal Code – and indeed, laws such as that upheld by the US Supreme Court in *Chaplinsky v New Hampshire* – are concerned more with public order than they are with speech as such. Section 319(2) targets statements which 'wilfully promote hatred against an identifiable group'. The offence of which *Chaplinsky* was convicted was breach of the peace. As we shall see in the next section, the UK's equivalent offences to Canada's section 319(2) make it a crime to 'stir up hatred'. It is no accident that the UK offences are found in the Public Order Act 1986 (for England and Wales) and in the Hate Crime and Public Order (Scotland) Act 2021 (for Scotland). Breach of the peace is a public order offence, and so are the stirring-up offences in the United Kingdom. They are, says Waldron,

> set up to vindicate public order, not just by pre-empting violence, but by uphold-ing against attack a shared sense of the basic elements of each person's status, dignity, and reputation as a citizen or member of society in good standing.[29]

The key word, here, is 'dignity'. Waldron argues that hate speech is harm-ful because and insofar as it undermines dignity. The protection of dignity is part of our public order, on his account. He draws an analogy with libel. If the law of defamation protects one facet of dignity – individual reputation – laws against the stirring-up or wilful promotion of 'hatred against an identifiable group' protect another.[30] Statements such as 'Muslims

---

[26] Waldron (n 22).

[27] ibid 15.

[28] ibid 105.

[29] ibid 47.

[30] As Waldron notes (39–40), in some countries, Germany being an example, hate speech is referred to and understood explicitly as a form of 'group libel'.

Out', 'Jews Go Home', or 'No Blacks Allowed' are, in Waldron's analysis, 'reputational attacks' which 'amount to assaults upon the dignity of the persons affected – 'dignity' in the sense of their basic social standing, the basis of their recognition as social equals and as bearers of human rights'.[31] Such statements are an attack on dignity and public order because they are degrading. This is a word, as Waldron notes, used in Article 3 ECHR, which outlaws torture and 'inhuman or degrading treatment'. It is also a word which Dickson CJ used in *Keegstra* to identify what he considered to be the harm of hate speech: that persons are 'humiliated and degraded'.[32]

Waldron, importantly, is careful to distinguish degradation from offensiveness. Degradation, he says, 'is not about wounded feelings'.[33] It is something much more profound than that, as its place alongside torture in Article 3 ECHR suggests. He recognises that there will be occasions when 'it will not be easy to differentiate' the merely offensive or wounding or spiteful from the genuinely degrading.[34] He cites the well-known Danish cartoons affair of 2005 as an example: were the cartoons published in a Danish newspaper portraying the prophet Muhammed as a bomb-throwing terrorist merely offensive, or were they a degrading assault on the dignity of Muslims, a group libel? Where there are 'fine lines to be drawn', says Waldron, 'the law should generally stay on the liberal side of them'. He cautiously concludes that it was 'probably appropriate' for the Danish authorities not to prosecute, even if the newspaper's actions in publishing the cartoons were hardly 'admirable'.[35]

Waldron is conscious of the twin critiques that laws criminalising hate speech inevitably run into problems of over-breadth and vagueness. He pushes his argument as hard as he can to ensure that 'dignity' (unlike 'offensiveness') can withstand these critiques. Plainly, he finds religious hatred a more troublesome case than racial hatred: he is far more confident that racial slurs are degrading assaults on dignity than he is that religious insults are. In the United Kingdom, as we will see in the next section, the first stirring-up offences concerned racial hatred. Likewise in the United States, most of the key cases are concerned with racism (*Beauharnais, Brandenburg v Ohio, RAV v City of St Paul* and *Virginia v Black*). In England and Wales, stirring-up offences had already been extended to cover religious hatred (as well as racial hatred) by the time Waldron came to write *The Harm in Hate Speech*. This troubles him, because the all-important line

---

[31] ibid 59.
[32] *Keegstra* (n 2) 746.
[33] Waldron (n 22) 110.
[34] ibid 113.
[35] ibid 126. A more robustly pro-publication (indeed, pro-republication) argument about the cartoons is put by Timothy Garton Ash, *Free Speech: Ten Principles for a Connected World* (London, Atlantic Books, 2017) 143–48.

between dignity and degradation on the one hand, and mere offensiveness on the other, seems harder to define in the context of religion than it is for race (meaning that the critiques of over-breadth and vagueness have more purchase in the context of religious hate speech than they do in the context of racist hate speech). In the end, Waldron concludes that his argument still holds, even for religious hatred,[36] but in so arguing he fires a number of warning shots, whose resonance has only grown in the years since his book was published.

First, he reiterates that his position 'combines sensitivity to assaults on people's dignity with an insistence that people should not seek social [or legal] protection' against offensiveness.[37] Secondly, he notes that, somehow or other, 'religion is an area where offence is *always* in the air'.[38] To give just one example, what Jews and Muslims believe about Jesus causes offence to Christians, and *vice versa*. As Waldron puts it, 'religious freedom means nothing if it is not freedom to offend'.[39] That is an arresting way of putting it, but he is surely right. There are echoes here of where this book started, with the struggles for freedom of conscience in the age of heresy: that we have the right to think and to say heretical things is *always* and *inevitably* going to offend someone, somewhere. This is why protecting against offensiveness can never be compatible with free speech.

Finally, Waldron warns that claiming too much for 'dignity' and 'degradation' is, as he puts it, 'irresponsible'.[40] Claiming, for example, that insulting my working-class identity is such a degrading assault on my dignity that it should be criminalised, would be irresponsible. Likewise, claiming that my liberal opinions or my gender identity can never be challenged – for to challenge them would be an affront to my dignity – is irresponsible. Why? Because, such 'identity politics' attempts 'to claim more by way of influence and protection for … interests and opinions than they are entitled to'.[41] Waldron is explicit about this:

> When I say that I *identify* with some opinion I hold, when I say it is part of my identity, then I purport to elevate that opinion above the scrum of ordinary politics, into the realm in which protection is accorded to fundamental interests.[42]

---

[36] In so concluding, Waldron has in mind the fact that, as we shall see in the next section, stirring up religious hatred is a much narrower and more tightly defined offence in English law than stirring up racial hatred is.

[37] ibid 126.

[38] ibid 127 (emphasis added).

[39] ibid 130.

[40] ibid 131.

[41] ibid.

[42] ibid 133 (emphasis in the original).

This is wrong and irresponsible because, in a plural, tolerant and broad-minded society, 'everyone has to be willing from time to time to accept' political defeat.[43] Identity politics, whether fuelled by religious zealotry, political intolerance, or gender ideology, 'recklessly present[s] claims about offence as though they were non-negotiable … If I identify my *self* with my beliefs, then criticisms of them will seem like an assault on me.'[44] And, if that move is made, Waldron's argument in defence of hate speech laws collapses entirely into the pitfalls of over-breadth and vagueness.

There is truth in both Strossen's and Waldron's arguments. We do not have to choose between them but can combine elements of both. Strossen is right to point to the outcome of the Skokie case – the founding of the Holocaust Museum and Education Centre – as being, quite literally, a monument to the superior power of counter-speech over censorship. But Waldron is right to object that even if counter-speech should where possible be our preferred response to hate speech, that response is not always possible. He is also right to insist absolutely that just because speech is offensive to someone can never be a sufficient reason for censoring or criminalising it: something much more than mere offensiveness is required. In short, I am with Strossen that the general principle should be that hate speech should be met with counter-speech rather than with censorship or criminal sanction. But I am with Waldron that, as with many general principles, there are exceptions, albeit that the exceptions must be extremely carefully crafted so as not to fall into the traps of vagueness and over-breadth. At the least, relying on subjective notions of identity can never hope to avoid such traps; hate crime laws which seek to protect subjective notions of identity can never be compatible with the right to speak freely.

III. Criminal Law: The United Kingdom

In 1965 the UK Parliament enacted its first Race Relations Act. It contained no general right to non-discrimination – and it made no specific provision for tackling discrimination in the workplace – but it made it an offence for hotels or restaurants, theatres or cinemas and buses or trains to refuse to serve people on the basis of their 'colour, race, or ethnic or national origins.'[45] It was but the beginning of a long legislative journey towards enshrining notions of equality and non-discrimination into UK law, a field in which the principal enactment is now the Equality Act 2010. Section 6

---

[43] ibid 131.
[44] ibid 135 (emphasis in the original).
[45] Race Relations Act 1965, s 1.

of the Race Relations Act 1965 created a new offence against public order, supplementing the Public Order Act 1936. It provided that it is an offence for a person, 'with intent to stir up hatred against any section of the public ... distinguished by colour, race, or ethnic or national origins', either to publish or distribute written matter, or to use words in a public place or at a public meeting, which are 'threatening, abusive or insulting', if the matter or words were 'likely' to stir up such hatred.[46] Thus the offence of stirring up racial hatred was born.

A. The Stirring-Up Offences in England and Wales

Twenty years later, the Thatcher Government sought to update and codify the UK's public order law. The resulting Public Order Act 1986 abolished the old common law offences of riot, unlawful assembly and the like, replacing them with new statutory offences; it repealed a host of earlier public order provisions, dating all the way back to the Tumultuous Petitioning Act 1661 and the Seditious Meetings Act 1817; it provided for a suite of police powers to control and to impose conditions on public assemblies and processions; and it refreshed and revised the law of stirring up racial hatred. The Public Order Act 1986 (as amended) remains the primary source of law on the stirring-up offences in England and Wales.[47] It defines 'racial hatred' to mean 'hatred against a group of persons defined by reference to colour, race, nationality (including citizenship) or ethnic or national origins'.[48] Section 18 of the Act, in relevant part, provides as follows:

(1)   A person who uses threatening, abusive or insulting words or behaviour, or displays any written material which is threatening, abusive or insulting, is guilty of an offence if (a) he intends thereby to stir up racial hatred or (b) having regard to all the circumstances racial hatred is likely to be stirred up thereby.

(2)   An offence under this section may be committed in a public or a private place, except that no offence is committed where the words or behaviour are used, or the written material is displayed, by a person inside a dwelling and are not heard or seen except by other persons in that or another dwelling.

   ...

(5)   A person who is not shown to have intended to stir up racial hatred is not guilty of an offence under this section if he did not intend his words or behaviour, or the written material, to be, and was not aware that it might be, threatening, abusive or insulting.

---

[46] ibid s 6(1).

[47] The primary source in Scotland is now the Hate Crime and Public Order (Scotland) Act 2021, which is examined below.

[48] Public Order Act 1986, s 17(1).

Section 18 is concerned with 'words or behaviour'. Section 19 makes similar provision for 'publishing or distributing written material'; section 20 for the public performance of a play; section 21 for 'distributing, showing or playing a recording'; and section 22 for broadcasting. In addition, section 23 makes it an offence to have in one's possession material which is 'racially inflammatory' (ie, threatening, abusive or insulting on grounds of race) with a view to displaying, publishing, distributing or otherwise showing or playing the material.

When they were enacted in 1986 these provisions applied to England and Wales and to Scotland. Since then, however, the law has developed differently in the two jurisdictions. The stirring-up provisions were extended for England and Wales (but not for Scotland) in 2006 and 2008. Subsequently, the Hate Crime and Public Order (Scotland) Act 2021 carried the stirring-up offences into new – and more contested – territory (but only in Scotland). It is instructive to consider the English amendments of 2006 and 2008 before turning to the Scottish legislation. The Racial and Religious Hatred Act 2006 created an offence of stirring up religious hatred. The Criminal Justice and Immigration Act 2008 created an offence of stirring up hatred on grounds of sexual orientation. Both enactments did so by amending the Public Order Act 1986, section 29B(1) of which now provides as follows:

> A person who uses threatening words or behaviour, or displays any written material which is threatening, is guilty of an offence if he intends thereby to stir up religious hatred or hatred on the grounds of sexual orientation.

Section 29B(2) makes the same provision for public and private places and dwellings as is made in section 18(2).[49] Section 29J provides as follows:

> Nothing in [the provisions relating to the stirring up of religious hatred] shall be read or given effect in a way which prohibits or restricts discussion, criticism or expressions of antipathy, dislike, ridicule, insult or abuse of particular religions or the beliefs or practices of their adherents, or of any other belief system or the beliefs or practices of its adherents, or proselytising or urging adherents of a different religion or belief system to cease practising their religion or belief system.

Section 29JA provides that, 'for the avoidance of doubt, the discussion or criticism of sexual conduct or practices or the urging of persons to refrain from or modify such conduct or practices shall not be taken of itself to be threatening or intended to stir up hatred'. Likewise, discussion or criticism

---

[49] s 29C–29G covers 'publishing or distributing written material', the public performance of a play, 'distributing, showing or playing a recording', broadcasting, and possession of inflammatory material, and may be compared accordingly with ss 19–23.

of same-sex marriage is not, of itself, to be taken as threatening or intended to stir up hatred.[50]

There are three principal differences between the racial hatred offences, on the one hand, and the religious and sexual orientation offences, on the other. All of these differences narrow the scope of the criminalisation of speech in the latter contexts when compared with race. First, only 'threatening' words or behaviour are criminalised in the context of religion and sexual orientation, whereas 'threatening, abusive or insulting' words or behaviour may fall within the scope of the criminal law regarding race. Secondly, the offences of stirring up hatred on religious grounds or on grounds of sexual orientation can be committed only where such hatred is intended, whereas in the context of race the offence can also be committed where such hatred is likely to be stirred up. Finally, sections 29J and 29JA explicitly protect certain kinds of speech about religious matters and about sexual orientation, whereas there is no equivalent provision in the context of racist speech. These are not merely cosmetic differences. Hate speech is much more narrowly defined in English law in the contexts of religion and sexual orientation than it is in the context of race.

B. The Hate Crime and Public Order (Scotland) Act 2021

The 2006 and 2008 amendments did not extend to Scotland, where the recent history of legislating on hate crimes has been quite different. When the Scottish Parliament first turned its attention to the public disorder that could be caused by the stirring up of hatred, its focus was sectarianism and, in particular, its well-known flashpoint: Old Firm football matches between Celtic and Rangers. Sectarian disorder was particularly problematic in the 2011 football season. The outcry that 'something must be done' was near universal and the outcome was the Offensive Behaviour at Football and Threatening Communications (Scotland) Act 2012. Enacted in haste, this was a woeful piece of legislation. It did nothing to tackle the underlying causes of sectarian violence. It overlapped messily with pre-existing offences in Scots law, recriminalising matters which were crimes already. It had indefensible consequences (such that singing a certain song in a pub might be an offence if there was a football match being screened in the pub at the time, but not if a rugby match was being screened). And a number of its provisions were so catch-all that the legislation was

---

[50] Thus, 'discussion or criticism' is protected in the contexts of both religion and sexual orientation; but 'expressions of antipathy, dislike, ridicule, insult or abuse' are protected only in the context of religion.

condemned as illiberal: 'behaviour that a reasonable person would be likely to consider offensive' was an offence under section 1(2)(e) of the Act, for example. In 2018 the Scottish Parliament repealed the Offensive Behaviour at Football Act.[51]

The Scottish Government (which had opposed the repeal of the 2012 Act) was concerned that too large a gap had reopened in the criminal law.[52] Ministers commissioned Lord Bracadale to review the law relating to hate crimes in Scotland, and to make recommendations.[53] Bracadale reported in 2018,[54] concluding that the Offensive Behaviour at Football Act did not need to be replaced, that relying on statutory aggravators should 'continue to be the core method of prosecuting hate crimes in Scotland',[55] and that stirring-up offences should be introduced for a range of 'protected characteristics'. Lord Bracadale recommended that age and gender should be protected characteristics, alongside race, religion, sexual orientation and disability, but that otherwise exploiting people because of 'perceived vulnerabilities' (such as homelessness, for example) should not be.[56] His review concluded that 'all Scottish hate crime legislation should be consolidated'.[57]

The Scottish Government accepted Lord Bracadale's recommendations, and brought forward a bill to implement them: the Hate Crime and Public Order (Scotland) Bill. The minister responsible for the bill was Humza Yousaf MSP, who subsequently served as First Minister of Scotland (2023–24). As introduced, the bill would have consolidated the existing offence of stirring up racial hatred and, in addition, would have created a new offence of stirring up hatred on grounds of age, disability, religion, sexual orientation, transgender identity, or variations in sex characteristics. This new offence would apply where someone behaved in a 'threatening or abusive manner' or communicated 'threatening or abusive material', and it would apply either where the person intended to stir up hatred, or where it was

[51] I was a Member of the Scottish Parliament in 2018; I voted for the legislation to repeal the 2012 Act.

[52] When the 2012 Act was enacted the governing party (the Scottish National Party) enjoyed an overall majority in the Scottish Parliament; when the legislation was repealed in 2018 the SNP was still the governing party, but it constituted a minority government. In the 2016–21 session, when all four opposition parties united, they could outvote the SNP in Holyrood by two votes.

[53] Lord Bracadale was a Senator of the College of Justice (ie, a Court of Session judge) with extensive experience of Scots criminal law.

[54] *Independent Review of Hate Crime Legislation in Scotland* (2018); available at: www.gov. scot/publications/independent-review-hate-crime-legislation-scotland-final-report/.

[55] ibid, recommendation 1. If the commission of an offence is 'aggravated by prejudice', whereby 'the offender demonstrates malice and ill-will towards the victim' on the basis of a protected characteristic, such aggravation must be taken into account in sentencing and must be stated on the offender's criminal record. See now, Hate Crime and Public Order (Scotland) Act 2021, ss 1–2.

[56] ibid, recommendation 3.

[57] ibid, recommendation 20.

likely that hatred would be stirred up.[58] The new offence could be committed in public or in private.

The Hate Crime Bill, then, would have extended Scots criminal law significantly beyond its scope south of the border. The 2006 and 2008 extensions of criminal liability in England and Wales applied only to religious hatred and to hatred on grounds of sexual orientation (they did not apply also to hatred on grounds of age, disability, transgender identity, or variations in sex characteristics); they applied only to 'threatening' words or behaviour (not to 'threatening or abusive' words or behaviour); they were offences which could be committed only if the offender intended to stir up hatred (and not merely because it was likely that hatred would be stirred up); and they were offences which could be committed only in public. Moreover, there was no equivalent in the Hate Crime Bill of section 18(5) of the Public Order Act: the defence of neither intending nor being aware that the words or behaviour were threatening or abusive. Instead, the bill proposed an undefined defence of reasonableness. Finally, whilst the bill echoed the Public Order Act in carving out protections for free speech as regards religion and sexual orientation, there were no similar carve-outs protecting the expression of views about age, disability, transgender identity, or variations in sex characteristics.

For all these reasons, the bill attracted widespread criticism. Indeed, the volume of objections was unprecedented: opposition to the bill generated more submissions of evidence than had ever previously been received by the Scottish Parliament in respect of proposed legislation (some 2,000 separate written submissions). But it was not just the volume of evidence: it was its outspokenness that was remarkable. The Law Society of Scotland said that the bill as drafted 'present[ed] a significant threat to free speech'. The Faculty of Advocates agreed, urging that the bill was so damaging it needed to be withdrawn entirely.[59] Key among the authorities cited by bodies such as the Law Society and the Faculty of Advocates were Sedley LJ's dictum in *Redmond-Bate* and the European Court of Human Rights (ECtHR) ruling in *Handyside*. Sedley LJ, it will be recalled, said in *Redmond-Bate* that 'free speech includes not only the inoffensive but the irritating, the contentious, the eccentric, the heretical, the unwelcome and the provocative ... Freedom only to speak inoffensively is not worth having'.[60] The European Court in *Handyside* explained that freedom of expression protects not only

---

[58] The bill would have maintained the position (as under the Public Order Act) that 'threatening, abusive or insulting' words or behaviour could fall within the offence of stirring up racial hatred.

[59] See Scottish Parliament Justice Committee, *Stage 1 Report on the Hate Crime and Public Order (Scotland) Bill*, SP Paper 878 (session 5), 2010 (available via the Scottish Parliament website; archived on the National Records of Scotland website). The Law Society's and the Faculty of Advocates' evidence is referred to in the Justice Committee's report.

[60] *Redmond-Bate v DPP* [2000] HRLR 249: see further ch 3.

that which is 'favourably received or regarded as inoffensive' but also words which 'offend, shock or disturb'. Such are the 'demands', according to the court, 'of that pluralism, tolerance and broadmindedness without which there is no democratic society'.[61]

To his credit, Humza Yousaf realised he would need to make concessions in order to improve his bill. Some amendments were thereafter suggested by ministers themselves; some were agreed to after having been proposed by others.[62] But, as always in the law-making process, there was a limit: some amendments which (in my view) would have improved the bill further were resisted, and were not accepted. The result is a complex piece of legislation which, as enacted, poses much less of a threat to free speech than the original bill but which, as an MSP, I could still not support.[63] The Hate Crime and Public Order (Scotland) Act goes too far in its criminalisation of hate speech. Let me explain why – and how I think hate crime legislation should be crafted.

Four sets of amendments improved the bill. The first was to remove the idea that the stirring-up offences, other than for race, could be committed either intentionally or where hatred was likely to be stirred up. As enacted, the stirring-up offences, other than for race, can be committed only intentionally.[64] Secondly, the stirring-up offences can be committed only where *a reasonable person* would consider the words or behaviour to be threatening or abusive, making the notion of 'threatening or abusive' objective, not subjective.[65] Thirdly, the reasonableness defence which was left open-ended and undefined in the bill as introduced was amended with *Handyside* expressly in mind, so that the legislation as enacted explicitly provides that words which 'offend, shock or disturb' are to be protected, not condemned.[66] It is only that which *a reasonable person* would consider to be *threatening or abusive* which might attract criminal liability, not that which *an individual* may find *offensive*. Fourthly, the 'carve-out' provision, protecting 'discussion or criticism', modelled on section 29JA of the Public Order Act, was extended to cover discussion or criticism not only relating to sexual orientation, but also relating to age, disability, transgender identity and variations in sex characteristics.[67]

---

[61] *Handyside v United Kingdom* (1976) 1 EHRR 737 [49]; see further ch 3.

[62] I played a role in this process. I was an MSP when the bill was being debated and I was convener of the Scottish Parliament's Justice Committee, which worked on a cross-party basis to improve the bill.

[63] The bill was passed by the Scottish Parliament on 11 March 2021 by 82 votes to 32.

[64] Hate Crime and Public Order (Scotland) Act 2021, s 4(2)(b) (compare s 4(1)(b)(ii)).

[65] ibid s 4(2)(a)(i). Stirring up racial hatred can be committed only where a reasonable person would consider the words or behaviour to be threatening, abusive or insulting: s 4(1).

[66] ibid s 4(5).

[67] ibid s 9(a). As under the Public Order Act, there is a larger carve-out for protected speech regarding religion: in that context it is not only 'discussion or criticism' which is protected, but also 'expressions of antipathy, dislike, ridicule or insult': s 9(b).

Three further sets of amendments were resisted, however. First, the stipulation that there needed to be a public element to the stirring-up offences was resisted. As enacted, the stirring-up offences in the Hate Crime Act can be committed either in public or in private, even wholly in private. There is no equivalent in the Scottish legislation of section 18(2) or section 29B(2) of the Public Order Act 1986. Secondly, an attempt to restrict the stirring-up offences (other than for race) to 'threatening' words or behaviour, rather than 'threatening or abusive' words or behaviour, as they are under the changes made to English law in 2006 and 2008, was also unsuccessful. Whether this failure will mean that the offences have been too broadly crafted will depend in practice on the success or otherwise of the Parliament's turning of the 'threatening or abusive' test from a subjective to an objective one. If the police investigate complaints of hate crime only where they are satisfied that a reasonable person would consider the words used to be abusive, that ought to pose no threat to freedom of speech. But, if the police open investigations into people's speech even where a reasonable person would view the words as merely offensive, rather than as abusive, the law will be far more problematic. This matter is explored further, below.

Finally, an attempt to add 'sex' as a protected characteristic was also unsuccessful. Whatever one's view of the Hate Crime Bill it was not exactly born under a lucky star. It emerged out of the poison of sectarianism and controversies about offensive behaviour at football. It then found itself embroiled in heartfelt debates about free speech. And it heralded the start of the next controversy of Scottish politics: the clash between those who insist sex is biologically immutable and those who believe gender to be a potentially fluid matter of mere self-identity.[68] Transgender identity is a protected characteristic under the Hate Crime Act, but sex is not. As such, it is an offence to stir up hatred on grounds of transgender identity, but not on grounds of sex. Some MSPs voiced fears that this was unfair and risked criminalising gender-critical feminists opposed to the notion that any (biological) man who identifies as a woman should necessarily be recognised and treated as a woman. Whatever view is taken about that dispute, it is certainly a striking omission to exclude 'sex' from the list of characteristics protected by the Hate Crime Act. Ministers resisted attempts to include it on the basis that they had commissioned a review of whether crimes of

---

[68] This clash came to a head with the passing of the Gender Recognition Reform (Scotland) Bill in 2022, legislation which was then prevented from coming into force by the Secretary of State for Scotland, using a power under the Scotland Act 1998, s 35. The Secretary of State's action was upheld as lawful by the Court of Session in *Petition of Scottish Ministers re Gender Recognition Reform (Scotland) Bill (Prohibition) Order* [2023] CSOH 89. I had left the Scottish Parliament before any of these events; I took no part in parliamentary debates and deliberations on them.

misogyny needed bespoke legislation in Scots law.[69] It is possible that sex may yet be added as a protected characteristic under the Hate Crime Act but, to date, that has not occurred.[70]

The result of all this is that the Hate Crime and Public Order (Scotland) Act provides for three different sorts of hate crime. The first category concerns hatred on grounds of age, disability, sexual orientation, transgender identity and variations in sex characteristics. The second category concerns race. The third concerns religion. Race is more heavily protected than the other two categories; religion is the least protected (or, put another way, speech is most curtailed as regards race and least curtailed as regards religion). Thus, in the first category, it is an offence to use words or behaviour which (1) a *reasonable person* would regard as (2) *threatening or abusive*, where the words or behaviour are (3) *intended* to stir up hatred and (4) are *not reasonable* in the circumstances (having regard to the principle that freedom of expression may protect that which others may find offensive, shocking or disturbing), noting that (5) *discussion or criticism* of age, disability, sexual orientation, transgender identity, or variations in sex characteristics is not to be taken as threatening or abusive.

For race,[71] the law in Scotland is different as regards points (1) and (2), and there is no equivalent of point (5). Thus, it is an offence to use words or behaviour which (1) a reasonable person would regard as (2) threatening, abusive *or insulting*, where the words or behaviour are (3) *either* intended *or likely* to stir up hatred and (4) are not reasonable in the circumstances (having regard to the principle that freedom of expression may protect that which others may find offensive, shocking or disturbing). For religion, the law in Scotland is the same as it is for age, disability, sexual orientation, transgender identity and variations in sex characteristics, save that in point (5), in addition to discussion or criticism being protected, *expressions of antipathy, dislike, ridicule or insult* are also protected.

These differences – for race and religion alike – were written into the law not for reasons of principle. Their explanation lies in what might be called the vicissitudes (or accidents) of legislative history. The Hate Crime Act is in part a consolidating measure. It consolidated the existing law on stirring up racial hatred (without altering its scope) and it copied and pasted protections for religious (or irreligious) speech from provisions that had been enacted for England and Wales in 2006. There is no legal principle which requires the offence of stirring up racial hatred being more

---

[69] The review's report was published in 2022 and is available at: www.gov.scot/publications/misogyny-human-rights-issue/documents/.

[70] See Hate Crime and Public Order (Scotland) Act 2021, s 12.

[71] Race, for the purposes of the Act, includes colour, nationality, citizenship and ethnic or national origins: ibid s 4(1)(b)(i).

widely drawn than the other stirring-up offences. On the other hand, there is nothing wrong in principle with affording different characteristics different levels of protection. It may well be thought that racial slurs *should* be criminalised, even while insulting someone's religion is protected. As we noted above, the Public Order Act 1986 shares with the Hate Crime Act the fact that different characteristics are treated differently.

This has been a long discussion, ranging widely from *Keegstra*, to a number of US Supreme Court cases, to the competing arguments of Nadine Strossen and Jeremy Waldron, to English public order law, and to Scotland's Hate Crime Act. It is time to come to a conclusion. My view, in the light of all the sources and contentions considered above, is that hate speech should be criminalised when, but only when, it meets all of the following requirements. The words must be such that (1) a *reasonable person* would regard them as (2) *threatening or abusive*, where they are (3) expressed *in public* and (4) *intended* to stir up hatred on grounds of race, religion, sex, sexual orientation, or disability and (5) are *unreasonable* in the circumstances (having regard to the principle that freedom of expression may protect that which others may find offensive, shocking or disturbing), noting that (6) *discussion or criticism* of questions of race, sex, sexual orientation, or disability is not to be taken as threatening or abusive and (7) that neither discussion or criticism, nor *expressions of antipathy, dislike or ridicule* as regards religion, are to be taken as threatening or abusive.

This, if you will, may be taken as a sort of model law of hate speech. Applying it to the sources considered in this chapter, it would justify the conclusion McLachlin J came to in dissent in *Keegstra*, rather than Dickson CJ's judgment (as section 319(2) of the Canadian Criminal Code was cast in terms rather broader than this model would prescribe).[72] The decision of the US Supreme Court in *RAV v City of St Paul* would appear hard to justify on this model, but its decisions in the other cases considered in this chapter would seem to be defensible.[73] My model borrows both from Nadine Strossen and from Jeremy Waldron. It recognises that mere offensiveness can never be a sufficient justification for criminalising speech. It sides with Strossen in that counter-speech, not criminalisation, will almost always be the appropriate reaction to hate speech. But it sides with Waldron that this cannot always be the case, and that there are some extreme situations where it is appropriate to criminalise hate speech. Fully alive to the twin perils of vagueness and over-breadth, however, my model defines such

---

[72] It would justify her conclusion, but not all of her reasoning. There is nothing in my model law to suggest that Dickson CJ was wrong to see that there is harm in hate speech.

[73] That is to say: the court was right to find that the Ohio law in *Brandenburg* had been drafted too broadly, and right to find that the New Hampshire law at issue in *Chaplinsky*, the Illinois law in *Beauharnais* and the Virginia law in *Virginia v Black* were compatible with freedom of speech.

situations narrowly, with laborious (but necessary) precision, in objective terms, avoiding references to subjective notions of identity.

There is one final aspect of this area of law which must be examined before we move on: the recording (by the police) of non-crime hate incidents. This has been an issue of controversy both in England and Wales and in Scotland. The leading case is *R (Miller) v College of Policing.*[74] Harry Miller, a retired police officer, posted a series of tweets expressing his gender-critical views. A complainant, who was offended by the tweets, complained to Humberside Police. In accordance with the College of Policing's Hate Crime Operational Guidance, Humberside Police recorded the incident as a non-crime hate incident. They compiled a Crime Report describing Mr Miller as a 'suspect' (and the complainant as a 'victim') and a police officer visited Mr Miller, warning him that, whilst he had not committed a crime, if his behaviour escalated it may become criminal, and advising him to cease tweeting gender-critical messages.[75]

Miller sought judicial review both of Humberside Police's actions and of the Guidance under which its officers had been operating. At first instance he succeeded as regards the former but not the latter. The judge found that the police's actions had led Mr Miller 'reasonably to believe that he was being warned not to exercise his right to freedom of expression about transgender issues on pain of potential criminal prosecution' without the police ever explaining to Mr Miller the basis on which they thought his tweets could 'escalate' into a criminal offence. The judge also found that 'there was not a shred of evidence that Mr Miller was at risk of committing a criminal offence'.[76] As such, the judge ruled, Humberside Police unlawfully interfered with Mr Miller's freedom of expression. By contrast, the judge dismissed Miller's claim against the College of Policing in respect of the lawfulness of the Guidance.

Miller successfully appealed to the Court of Appeal, which ruled that the relevant provisions of the Guidance were a disproportionate interference with Article 10 ECHR.[77] These provisions required any complaint of a hate incident to be recorded, irrespective of whether the complaint was irrational and even where there was no evidence of actual hostility. There was nothing in the Guidance to address either the chilling effect such a regime would have on freedom of expression or the stigmatising effect which the formal police recording of a hate incident would generate.[78] For these reasons, ruled the Court of Appeal, the Guidance was disproportionate.

---

[74] *R (Miller) v College of Policing* [2021] EWCA Civ 1926, [2022] 1 WLR 4987.
[75] ibid [42]–[43].
[76] See ibid [46].
[77] The Court of Appeal was unanimous; its judgment was delivered by Dame Victoria Sharp, President of the Queen's Bench Division.
[78] ibid [117].

After *Miller* the Guidance was revised to bring it into line with the right to free speech. The Guidance does not apply in Scotland, however, and when the Hate Crime and Public Order (Scotland) Act came into force in 2024 it emerged that Police Scotland were recording non-crime hate incidents in ways alarmingly similar to the unlawful manner in which Humberside Police had acted in Mr Miller's case.[79] After the 2024 general election it was reported that the newly elected Labour government was seeking to revisit the (English and Welsh) Guidance once more – not to reduce the police recording of non-criminal hate incidents – but once again to increase such reporting.[80] Notwithstanding the clarity of the Court of Appeal's welcome ruling in *Miller*, the matter remains one of significant concern. No element of the criminal justice system should have any interest in recording hate speech unless the speech in question meets all seven stipulations of the model definition offered above.

C. Grossly Offensive Communications

The argument in the previous section was that as bright a line as possible needs to be drawn between 'threatening or abusive' expression and expression which is merely 'offensive'. There are circumstances in which the former may legitimately attract the attention of the criminal law: but the latter should not. Unfortunately, the law in the United Kingdom does not adhere to this distinction. We have seen that, even within the context of the stirring-up offences, it does not do so: the stirring-up of racial hatred may be a crime where the speech is threatening, abusive *or insulting*. Were the argument of the previous section to be adopted, this offence would be amended so that, like the other stirring-up offences, it could be committed only where speech is threatening or abusive. The law's blurring of the line between 'threatening or abusive' and 'offensive' is made worse when we consider the communications offences. These are now found in three enactments: the Malicious Communications Act 1988; the Communications Act 2003; and the Online Safety Act 2023. The most troubling is section 127(1) of the Communications Act 2003, which makes it an offence, among other matters, to send 'by means of a public electronic communications network' a message that is 'grossly offensive'.[81] In this section, I argue that this offence should be repealed.

---

[79] See the *Times*, 12 March 2024 and see further: murrayblackburnmackenzie.org/2024/04/27/what-police-scotland-data-on-hate-crime-reveals-about-non-crime-hate-incidents/.

[80] As reported in the *Times*, 29 August 2024.

[81] See Jacob Rowbottom, 'To Rant, Vent and Converse: Protecting Low Level Digital Speech' (2012) 71 *Cambridge Law Journal* 355.

First, we need to understand the relationship between the different communications offences provided for in each of the enactments just mentioned. The Malicious Communications Act 1988, as amended by the Online Safety Act 2023, makes it an offence for a person to send to another person a 'letter, electronic communication or article of any description' which 'conveys a message which is indecent or grossly offensive' (or which is itself 'indecent or grossly offensive') if the purpose of the person sending the communication was that 'it should … cause distress or anxiety to the recipient'. This offence was designed to criminalise 'poison pen' letters and such behaviour as posting excrement through someone's letterbox. It can be committed either online, over the telephone, or by sending a package in the mail (but it cannot be committed in face-to-face conversation). It can be committed only where one person sends a message (or a letter or package) to another person: this offence does not therefore capture messages posted on social media. It can be committed only where the sender's purpose is to cause distress or anxiety to the recipient. It was enacted pursuant to a recommendation of the Law Commission in the 1980s; in 2021 the Law Commission recommended that the offence be repealed and replaced.[82] In the event, the offence was amended but was not repealed by the Online Safety Act.

Two leading cases, which illustrate the scope of the offence, are *Connelly v DPP*[83] and *R v Casserly*.[84] In the former, a woman who for religious reasons opposed abortion sent to a number of pharmacies (which stocked the morning-after pill) graphic images of an aborted foetus. She sent the images with the purpose of shocking the pharmacists. Her conviction under the Malicious Communications Act was upheld as compatible with the right to freedom of expression. The pharmacies had been targeted notwithstanding that they were in no position to alter public policy on abortion. Given this, the distress and anxiety Connelly had caused them could not be justified. In *Casserly*, a constituent with a long-standing concern about his council's poor maintenance of a local cemetery, wrote to his councillor (who was profoundly deaf and visually impaired) that her reading ability was so deficient she was incapable of making a difference and acting effectively as his representative. He was convicted under the Malicious Communications Act but the Court of Appeal quashed the conviction. Elected members and others in public life are expected to have thicker skins, the Court of Appeal noted. Mr Casserly had been extremely rude, and his remarks were offensive and shocking, but a prosecution could be brought only where the

---

[82] Law Commission, *Modernising Communications Offences: Final Report*, Law Com 399 (2021).
[83] *Connelly v DPP* [2007] EWHC 237 (Admin), [2008] 1 WLR 276.
[84] *R v Casserly* [2024] EWCA Crim 25, [2024] 1 WLR 2760.

interference with freedom of expression is necessary and proportionate. The Court of Appeal did not rule that Casserly should not have been prosecuted, but quashed his conviction nonetheless because it was not satisfied that the jury had been properly directed on the matter of the importance of the defendant's right to freedom of political speech.

The Communications Act 2003 provides for a number of communications offences in section 127. Like the Malicious Communications Act, section 127 has been amended – but not repealed – by the Online Safety Act 2023. Section 127(1) provides for the offence of sending by means of a public electronic communications network a 'grossly offensive' message, and also of sending by such means a message of 'an indecent, obscene or menacing character'. Section 127(2) made it an offence, 'for the purpose of causing annoyance, inconvenience or needless anxiety', either to send by means of a public electronic communications network a message known to be 'false', or 'persistently' to use such a network. These offences can be distinguished from the Malicious Communications Act in a number of ways: the section 127 offences can be committed only via a public electronic communications network; they can be committed by posting on social media (they do not require a message to be sent to a particular person); and they can be committed where the sender did not intend to cause offence; unlike under the Malicious Communications Act, it is the effect of the message, as well as its purpose, which may attract criminal liability under section 127.

The Law Commission recommended in 2021 that the offences in both section 127(1) and section 127(2) be repealed and replaced.[85] In the event, the Online Safety Act neither repealed nor replaced the offences in section 127(1).[86] That Act did, however, repeal and replace the offences in section 127(2) for England and Wales.[87] In place of section 127(2) the Online Safety Act created new criminal offences of false communications, threatening communications, and encouraging or assisting serious self-harm.[88] These offences – and the Online Safety Act generally – are considered in the next chapter. In the remainder of this section we shall focus only on section 127(1).

The Communications Act 2003 did not create the offence of grossly offensive communications afresh. Rather, it was a re-enactment of an

---

[85] Law Commission, *Modernising Communications Offences* (n 82).

[86] As introduced, the Online Safety Bill (2022) would have repealed the Malicious Communications Act 1988 entirely and would have repealed both s 127(1) and s 127(2)(a) and (b) for England and Wales, replacing all these provisions with new offences: see clauses 150–58 of the bill as introduced. The story of what happened to the bill is explained below and is further analysed in ch 6.

[87] s 127(2) remains in force in Scotland, unamended by the Online Safety Act.

[88] Online Safety Act 2023, ss 179, 181, 184.

offence which can be traced back to the Post Office (Amendment) Act 1935 (which made it an offence to send a message by telephone which was grossly offensive or of an indecent, obscene or menacing character). That offence was re-enacted in the Post Office Acts of 1953 and 1969, and extended in the Telecommunications Act 1984 (to cover all public telecommunications systems) before appearing in its present form in section 127(1) of the Communications Act. At least part of the purpose of the original offence (as enacted in 1935) was to safeguard telephone operators from abuse.[89] Plainly, that justification has long since ceased to be of any relevance, switchboard operators having been replaced by auto-mated systems from the 1960s on. In the leading House of Lords case, *R v Collins*, Lord Bingham said that the purpose of the section 127(1) offences was 'to prohibit the use of a service provided and funded by the public for the benefit of the public for the transmission of communications which contravene the basic standards of our society'.[90] *Collins* is a troubling case. The defendant telephoned his MP and either spoke with members of the MP's staff or left messages on the MP's answering machine in terms which included a number of offensively racist epithets. Collins was tried for the offence of sending grossly offensive communications but was acquitted, the justices finding that whilst the terms he had used were offensive, they were not grossly so. The Director of Public Prosecutions appealed and whilst his appeal was dismissed by the Divisional Court[91] it was unanimously allowed by the House of Lords.

There are two problems with *Collins*' reading of section 127(1). The first is the elasticity of 'grossly offensive', an elasticity which raises, once again, the twin perils of over-breadth and vagueness. The second is that electronic communication networks are no longer funded by the public. They are provided for the public by private corporations (such as Twitter/X and Meta/Facebook/WhatsApp). If Lord Bingham is right that the justi-fication for the offence is that people should not be permitted to abuse a communications network provided and funded by the taxpayer, this is a justification as irrelevant in the modern world as the safeguarding of switchboard operators.

The latter problem is illustrated by *Cobban v DPP*.[92] Seven Metropolitan Police officers were in a WhatsApp group which included Wayne Couzens,

---

[89] See Law Commission, *Abusive and Offensive Online Communications: A Scoping Report*, Law Com 381 (2018) [4.61].

[90] *R v Collins* [2006] UKHL 40, [2006] 1 WLR 2223 [7].

[91] The Divisional Court comprised Sedley LJ and Mitting J. The former's well-known remarks in *Redmond-Bate v DPP* about offensive speech were quoted earlier in this chapter.

[92] *Cobban v DPP* [2024] EWHC 1908 (Admin). Other cases applying *Collins* on grossly offensive communications include *DPP v Kingsley Smith* [2017] EWHC 359 (Admin) and *Chabloz v CPS* [2019] EWHC 3094 (Admin), [2020] 1 Cr App R 17.

who was convicted of the kidnapping, rape and murder of Sarah Everard in 2021. A number of messages sent within the group were abhorrent in their racism, misogyny, sexism and homophobia. It was through Couzens' arrest in the Sarah Everard case (and via the inspection of his mobile phone) that the messages were discovered. The messages were horrific. But they were also consensual, sent to a closed group, and did not offend anyone in that group. All the officers in the group had either resigned from the Metropolitan Police or been dismissed. There is no dispute but that the messages violated the rules of professional police conduct. In addition, two of the group were prosecuted and convicted under section 127(1) for messages they had sent to the group. They appealed their convictions as being a disproportionate breach of their right to freedom of expression. The Divisional Court (comprising Lady Carr CJ and Saini J) dismissed their appeal. The court opined that 'private messages consensually exchanged on a medium such as WhatsApp between purely private persons (not public officials, such as police officers, discussing police matters)' might be protected, on the ground that the senders of such messages may have a reasonable expectation of privacy in the matter.[93] But the court found that, because the defendants were public officials – police officers – and because the messages at issue discussed policing matters, 'the convictions pursued the legitimate aims of public safety and the prevention of disorder or crime' and were proportionate under Article 10 ECHR.[94]

The messages were 'gratuitously offensive', contributed to no form of 'public debate capable of furthering progress in human affairs', and accordingly fell 'right at the bottom of the hierarchy of speech'.[95] No one could reasonably disagree with any of that. But given that the officers had already rightly been dismissed (or had resigned) from service in the police force, was it really necessary in a democratic society also to prosecute and convict them? There was no public element to their speech. They were not stirring-up hatred, merely expressing to one another, in a private, closed group, their hateful views. Their views were despicable: these men were plainly not fit to serve as public officials or police officers. Had they written letters to each other or spoken with one another in the terms in which they had written their WhatsApp messages, they would have committed no crime. It was only because their messages were sent via an electronic communications network that they had crossed the criminal threshold. What is the justification for that, when there are no switchboard operators to protect and when the defendants were using a service *available to* the public, for sure, but neither *provided nor funded by* the public?

---

[93] *Cobban v DPP* (ibid) [110].
[94] ibid [103].
[95] ibid [105]–[106].

The courts' rulings on other aspects of section 127(1) have not been as problematic, from a free speech perspective, as its rulings in *Collins* and *Cobban* on grossly offensive communications. *Chambers* is the leading case on menacing communications.[96] Nine days before Chambers was due to fly from Doncaster Robin Hood Airport, he learnt it was closed due to adverse weather conditions. He tweeted that the airport had a week to get its 'shit together, otherwise I am blowing [it] sky high'. He was convicted of sending a menacing communication, but his conviction was overturned by the Divisional Court. Lord Judge CJ ruled that, in the circumstances, the tweet could not reasonably have created fear or apprehension in those to whom it was communicated and, for this reason, was not 'menacing'. This is a sensible decision: it was a stupid thing to tweet, but it should not have been regarded as a criminal matter.

A similarly sensible outcome was reached in *Scottow v CPS*, on the offence of persistently using a public electronic communications network for the purpose of causing annoyance, inconvenience, or needless anxiety.[97] Scottow had been involved in several unpleasant 'twitter spats' with Stephanie Hayden, a well-known activist and advocate on transgender rights. Hayden complained of both harassment and malicious communication. Yet Scottow was charged under neither the Protection from Harassment Act 1997 nor the Malicious Communications Act 1988. She was charged instead under the section 127(1) offence relating to persistent use of an electronic communications network. The Divisional Court ruled her prosecution to be a disproportionate interference with her right to free speech and her conviction was quashed. The section 127(1) offence could not be used, the court ruled, as a 'harassment-lite' offence. Much more than mere annoyance or inconvenience is required before such an interference with free speech would be justified. There was no evidence that Scottow had tweeted *for the purpose* of annoying or causing needless anxiety. Rather, she was taking part in a debate on an important matter of public policy and the annoyance to others was caused because other people disagreed with her.

The Law Commission of England and Wales spent three years examining the communications offences. A scoping report was published in 2018, followed by a consultation document in 2020 and a final report in 2021. The Law Commission's conclusion was clear: the combination of the Malicious Communications Act and section 127(1) of the Communications Act is doubly unfit for purpose. The provisions both over-criminalise and under-criminalise. They over-criminalise not least because they rely on terms which are too vague and imprecise, such as 'indecency' and 'gross

---

[96] *Chambers v DPP* [2012] EWHC 2157 (Admin), [2013] 1 WLR 1833.
[97] *Scottow v CPS* [2020] EWHC 3421 (Admin), [2021] 1 WLR 1828.

offensiveness'. And yet gaps remain. Because some provisions target particular *modes* of communication whilst others target particular *purposes*,
the communications offences are an incoherent patchwork: incomplete as
well as being over-broad. The Law Commission recommended the repeal
both of the Malicious Communications Act and of section 127(1) of the
Communications Act. They should be replaced, in the Law Commission's
view, with a new, harm-based offence, which would have the following
elements:

- the defendant sent or posted a communication that was likely to cause
  harm to a likely audience;
- in so doing the defendant intended to cause harm to a likely audience;
  and
- the defendant behaved without reasonable excuse.

Communication, for this purpose, would include any letter, article or
electronic communication and harm would mean 'psychological harm,
amounting to at least serious distress'.[98] The government accepted this
recommendation and included in its Online Safety Bill a provision designed
to implement it.[99] This provision – clause 150 of the bill as introduced –
was withdrawn, however, as the bill inched its way through the House of
Commons. Various aspects of the bill were controversial (the full story is
told in the next chapter). At the centre of the controversy were provisions –
unrelated to the communications offences – which would have required
the regulation and possible removal of certain 'lawful but harmful' content
online. Concerns were raised as to how the bill would have defined such
content: the bill's notion of 'harmful' was dangerously under-defined, its
critics warned. As a result, the 'lawful but harmful' provisions of the bill
were removed and, at the same time, other provisions in the bill which
referred to notions of harm in an insufficiently precise manner were also
excised, including clause 150. (What was 'at least serious distress' supposed
to mean, for example?)

The result, as we have seen, is that the Malicious Communications Act
is amended (but not repealed); section 127(1) of the Communications
Act remains in force (including its provision about gross offensiveness);
section 127(2) of the Communications Act is repealed and replaced for
England and Wales, but remains in force in Scotland; and several additional offences have been created. The patchwork is even messier now than
it was before the Law Commission started work on it in 2018, and the
Law Commission's objections to this area of the law are, if anything, even

---

[98] Law Commission, *Modernising Communications Offences* (n 82) recommendation 1.
[99] Online Safety Bill (2022) cl 150.

more valid now than they were then. The UK's communications offences are not fit for purpose. They are a clear threat to freedom of expression. They are over-inclusive, vague and over-broad. It is no surprise the case law is inconsistent. Some cases protect free speech relatively well (*Casserly*, *Chambers*, *Scottow*) whilst others leave it alarmingly exposed (including the leading case of *Collins*). As for the stirring-up offences, so too for the communications offences: the 'harm' the offences are targeting needs to be pinned down with clarity of intent and precision of language. Terms such as 'gross offensiveness', 'indecency' and 'at least serious distress' fail to fulfil this purpose. They do not explain what the harm is which the law is seeking to target and they are so vague as to fall foul of the familiar vice of over-breadth.

IV. Strasbourg's Case Law on Hate Speech

The case law of the ECtHR has played only a background role in shaping criminal offences in the United Kingdom touching upon offensive or hate speech. Neither the UK's stirring-up offences nor its communications offences have generated Strasbourg case law, to date.[100] The European Court's most influential dictum in this field, as far as the United Kingdom is concerned, has been its statement in *Handyside* that freedom of expression extends to and includes protection for words which 'offend, shock or disturb'.[101] *Handyside* was a case concerned with obscenity, however, rather than with hate speech; and it is a case, we must remember, in which the Strasbourg court upheld as lawful the repressive actions of the UK's law enforcement agencies. The free speech interest in that case did not prevail, notwithstanding the importance of the European Court's famous dictum.

One of the leading Strasbourg authorities on hate speech is *Perinçek v Switzerland*, a Grand Chamber decision of 2015 in which the court summarised and reviewed its case law on the matter.[102] Perinçek was a Turkish politician who, in a series of public speeches in Switzerland, denied the Armenian genocide of 1915 had taken place. He was convicted in the Swiss courts and fined. It is an offence in Switzerland for a person, on

---

[100] The nearest is *Norwood v United Kingdom*, discussed below. In 2022 Joseph Kelly was convicted by the Sheriff Court at Lanark of grossly offensive communications, contrary to s 127(1) of the Communications Act. Kelly had tweeted, after Captain Tom Moore had died, that 'the only good Brit soldier is a dead one' and was sentenced to a community payback order. It was reported that Kelly would take his case to Strasbourg as a breach of his Article 10 right to freedom of expression but, at the time of writing, no such case is listed on the ECtHR's webpages.

[101] Above (n 61).

[102] *Perinçek v Switzerland* (2016) 63 EHRR 6.

grounds of race, ethnic origin or religion, to deny, grossly trivialise, or seek to justify a genocide or other crime against humanity.[103] Holocaust denial is an offence also in Germany, Austria and Belgium (in these countries the offence relates specifically to the Holocaust committed by the Nazis). A broader offence of denial of crimes against humanity, including denial of genocide, has been legislated for in other European countries, including Spain and France, as well as Switzerland.

Perinçek argued that his conviction was a disproportionate interference with his Article 10 right to freedom of expression. By a ten-to-seven margin, Strasbourg's Grand Chamber agreed. The court ruled that the interference was prescribed by law and that it was for the legitimate aim of protecting the rights of others, but that it was not necessary in a democratic society. Whether it is proportionate to convict someone of hate speech will, in the court's analysis, depend on the interplay of three factors, each drawn from a long string of the court's case law. They are as follows. First, whether the statement was made against a tense political or social background: 'the presence of such a background has generally led the court to accept that some form of interference with such statements was justified'.[104] Secondly, whether the statement, fairly construed, could be seen as a direct or indirect call for violence or as a justification for violence, hatred or intolerance. In assessing this point, the court noted that it had been 'particularly sensitive towards sweeping statements attacking or casting in a negative light entire ethnic, religious or other groups'.[105] The final factor is the manner in which the statement was made and its capacity to lead to harmful consequences. In one case, for example, comments made on electoral leaflets 'had enhanced the effect of the discriminatory and hateful message that they were conveying'.[106] It is the interplay of the three factors, not any one of them in isolation, that determines the question of proportionality: it is, therefore, 'highly context-specific'.[107] Applying the three factors to the particular facts of the case, the court noted that Perinçek's comments were not made against the background of a tense situation on the ground in Switzerland, and that they were neither a call to violence nor made in a manner likely to stir up violence. For these reasons, the court ruled that his conviction was not necessary in a democratic society.

In the course of its judgment the court noted that numerous cases about Holocaust denial had been brought to Strasbourg in the past.[108] All had been dismissed, most at the admissibility stage as being 'manifestly

---

[103] ibid [32].
[104] ibid [205].
[105] ibid [206].
[106] ibid [207].
[107] ibid [208].
[108] ibid [209]–[212].

ill-founded'. Some had been dismissed because it was found that the interference with the applicant's right to freedom of expression was necessary in
a democratic society (proscription of Holocaust denial being necessary to
protect the rights of others). Others had been dismissed not on Article 10
grounds, but on the basis of Article 17 ECHR. This provides that 'Nothing
in [the] Convention may be interpreted as implying for any ... group or
person any right to engage in any activity ... aimed at the destruction of
any of the rights and freedoms set forth herein'. Article 17 means, in the
context of speech, that no one has the right to express themselves such as
to aim at the destruction of the rights of others. If your speech is so intolerant as to destroy the rights of others, it will not be protected. As the court
noted in *Perinçek*, however, this rule is 'only applicable on an exceptional
basis and in extreme cases'.[109] It was held not to apply to Perinçek's speech.

   Perinçek and the cases it discusses are concerned with speech so hateful
it is violent, speech so intolerant it aims to destroy the rights of others. This is
some distance removed from speech which is merely insulting or offensive.
On such forms of speech, Strasbourg case law is growing. The trend –
as in other aspects of its Article 10 jurisprudence – is moving in favour of
upholding more restrictions on speech. An early case is *Norwood v United
Kingdom*.[110] Norwood was a member of the British National Party who, in
late 2001, displayed in the window of his home a photograph of the Twin
Towers in flame, with the words 'Islam out of Britain – Protect the British
People'. He was prosecuted under section 5 of the Public Order Act 1986
for displaying a sign that is threatening or abusive, within the sight of a
person likely to be caused 'harassment, alarm or distress' thereby. He
was convicted and fined £300. His complaint that the proceedings taken
against him were a violation of his Article 10 right to freedom of expression was declared inadmissible by the ECtHR. The court said it agreed with
the verdict of the English courts, that 'the words and images on the poster
amounted to a public expression of attack on all Muslims in the United
Kingdom'. The court added that 'such a general, vehement attack against
a religious group, linking the group as a whole with a grave act of terrorism, is incompatible with the values proclaimed and guaranteed by the
Convention, notably tolerance, social peace and non-discrimination'.[111]
For these reasons, Norwood's actions fell within the scope of Article 17
ECHR and could not be protected by the right to freedom of expression
in Article 10.

---

[109] ibid [114]. On Article 17, see further *Paksas v Lithuania*, judgment of 6 January 2011, and
Hizb ut-Tahrir v Germany (2012) 55 EHRR SE12.
[110] *Norwood v United Kingdom* (2005) 40 EHRR SE11.
[111] ibid.

Norwood may be contrasted with *Fáber v Hungary*.[112] The Hungarian Socialist Party held a demonstration in Budapest to protest against racism and hatred. A right-wing party staged a counter-demonstration. Fáber was next to them, standing at a spot where during the Second World War a large number of Jewish people had been slaughtered. He was holding a banner which had a long association with the far-right in Hungarian politics. He was told either to take it down or to leave, but he refused, arguing that he was doing nothing unlawful. He was arrested for refusing to comply with police instructions, and fined. He took his case to Strasbourg, contending that his rights under Articles 10 and 11 ECHR had been breached. By six votes to one, the European Court agreed with him. The court reasoned that, even if the flag he was holding was offensive and shocking to some of the people who will have seen it, 'its mere display was not capable of disturbing public order' and nor was it an incitement to violence.[113] The court stressed that 'ill feelings or even outrage, in the absence of intimidation' cannot constitute a 'pressing social need' justifying an interference with freedom of expression.[114] The display of a symbol which was ubiquitous during the times of fascist rule may create 'uneasiness'. It may be 'disrespectful'. But such sentiments cannot limit freedom of expression, the court ruled.[115] Unless or until the expression is 'abusive', it would be disproportionate for the police to take action against it.[116]

Fáber, like the Skokie case in the United States, is a case with unsavoury facts. But the point of principle upon which the European Court founds its judgment is surely correct. Speech which induces a sense of moral outrage, speech which makes us feel queasy with nausea, speech which is even grossly disrespectful or is unpleasant, foul, and horrid – such speech, in a tolerant society, must be tolerated. If it crosses the line so that it is not merely offensive, but abusive or threatening, that may well engage criminal liability, and such liability will in those circumstances not of itself breach the right to free expression. That, however, is where the line must be drawn. Hate speech may be unlawful only where it is threatening or abusive. Otherwise, it must be tolerated. Not tolerated in silence, but permitted to be uttered so that we may defeat its hate in reasoned, indeed in impassioned, counter-speech.

Regrettably, this is a line to which the European Court has not always adhered in its more recent rulings on insulting and offensive speech. Indeed, some of the court's decisions on this aspect of Article 10 have

---

[112] *Fáber v Hungary*, judgment of 24 July 2012.
[113] ibid [56].
[114] ibid.
[115] ibid [57].
[116] ibid [58].

become as concerning as those, considered in chapters three and four, in which we have seen Strasbourg losing its way in other areas of free speech. In *Beizaras and Levickas v Lithuania* the applicants were young men in a same-sex relationship.[117] They posted to their Facebook page a picture of them kissing. The post was public, went viral and attracted a large number of comments, including several that were violently homophobic. (The comments in question clearly crossed the threshold from 'merely offensive' to 'threatening and abusive', as can be seen from the court's judgment.) Despite being pressured to do so by organisations representing the rights and interests of the LGBT community, the Lithuanian authorities opted not to open criminal proceedings against those who had posted the homophobic remarks. The applicants complained to Strasbourg that the failure of the national authorities to act was in breach of Articles 8, 13 and 14 ECHR (the right to privacy, the right to an effective remedy, and freedom from discrimination). The court agreed with the applicants.

On the facts, this poses no problem from a free speech perspective (the comments in question were clearly violent, threatening and abusive). There is a problem, however, with the court's reasoning. The court said the following: 'attacks on persons committed by *insulting*, holding up to *ridicule* or slandering specific groups of the population can be sufficient for the authorities to favour combating ... speech' where freedom of expression is 'exercised in an *irresponsible* manner'.[118] The assessment the national authorities had made in this case, the court ruled, was 'not in conformity with the fundamental principles of a democratic state governed by the rule of law'.[119] The terms used in this reasoning – notably, those I have italicised here – are remarkably loose.[120] The problem with the comments on Beizaras' and Levickas' Facebook page was not that they were 'insulting' or 'irresponsible' examples of 'ridicule', but that they were violent, threatening and abusive.

This reasoning – these loose terms – were applied in *Lilliendahl v Iceland*.[121] The applicant had phoned in to a local radio talk-show which was discussing a local authority's policy to offer increased support and counselling to LGBT pupils in secondary school. The applicant disapproved of the policy. He expressed himself in strong terms, describing LGBT people as 'deviants'. He was indicted contrary to the Icelandic penal code. He was acquitted but his acquittal was overturned by a two-to-one majority of the

---

[117] *Beizaras and Levickas v Lithuania*, judgment of 14 January 2020.
[118] ibid [125] (emphasis added).
[119] ibid.
[120] *Beizaras and Levickas* is not a one-off. The same terms are used in several other Strasbourg decisions. Examples include *Féret v Belgium*, judgment of 16 July 2009 and *Vejdeland v Sweden*, judgment of 9 February 2012.
[121] *Lilliendahl v Iceland*, decision of 12 May 2020.

Supreme Court; he was fined €800. In the Supreme Court, the dissenting judgment noted that whilst the applicant's comments were derogatory, they fell a long way short of calling for violence and they had been offered as part of a public discussion on a matter of public importance. The ECtHR agreed, however, with the majority of the Supreme Court, ruling Lilliendahl's complaint that his conviction breached Article 10 ECHR to be 'manifestly ill-founded'. Strasbourg's decision in *Lilliendahl* cannot be supported. Again, as in *Fáber v Hungary* and the Skokie case, we are dealing with obnoxious facts, but *Lilliendahl* is a clear example of insults which are neither violent nor threatening. Such speech, no matter how unpleasant, should not be regarded as criminal.

Similarly concerning is *Sanchez v France*.[122] In this case, an elected National Front politician in France was held criminally liable for comments constituents of his had written on his Facebook 'wall' to the effect that a rival politician (from a different party) had allowed his neighbouring town of Nîmes, in the south of France, to resemble Algiers, governed by Sharia law, overrun with kebab shops and mosques, with drug dealers and prostitutes. Some of the comments were removed; others remained visible. Clearly they were Islamophobic, and the French courts held them to be unlawful (on grounds of incitement to hatred). The authors of the comments were prosecuted but so was the politician, who was fined €4,000 for allowing the comments to appear and remain on his Facebook wall. By thirteen votes to four, the ECtHR's Grand Chamber upheld his conviction and sentence. It was necessary in a democratic society, the court reasoned, for such comments not to be permitted (not even during an election campaign). The court comforted itself that the applicant had only been fined (rather than imprisoned) and that his being sanctioned in this way had not prevented him from being re-elected as mayor of his town. Once again, we have receded a long way from the high-water mark of *Handyside's* dictum. The comments – quite clearly – were offensive, shocking and disturbing. But the politician did not make them and – no matter how much we may disapprove of them – he should not have been criminalised for their appearance.

V. Employment Law

When, in the mid-nineteenth century, the age of sedition moved into the age of offence, liberal opinion was alive to the fact that what John Stuart Mill called 'social tyranny' was at least as grave a threat to free speech as

---

[122] *Sanchez v France*, judgment of 15 May 2023.

the authoritarianism of the state.[123] When Chimamanda Ngoze Adichie delivered her BBC Reith Lecture on freedom of speech in November 2022, she cited what she called 'social censure' – the 'vicious retaliation' of one's fellow citizens who disagree with your views – as the principal cause of the 'epidemic of self-censorship' which, in the lecture, she described and decried. This chapter has so far been concerned with criminal law: with the power of the state. Adichie is right, though, as was Mill: it is social censure we must worry about, at least as much as criminal legislation. It is to this aspect of offensive and hate speech that we turn in this final section.

The pattern typically runs along the following lines. An individual (E) says something, often on a social media platform such as Twitter/X or Facebook, which someone else (C) finds offensive. C then complains to E's employers, suggesting perhaps that E's tweets or Facebook posts are bringing her place of employment into disrepute. E is placed under investigation by her employers. Disciplinary measures may be taken, in some cases leading to dismissal. How is E's free speech protected amid a pattern such as this?

One problem with the right to freedom of expression as it is enshrined in human rights law is that it is a right we have against the state. Section 6 of the Human Rights Act provides that 'it is unlawful for *a public authority* to act' incompatibly with Convention rights (including freedom of expression). If your employer is not a public authority, are they free to discipline or even to dismiss you because they – or their clients – disapprove of something you have written on your social media account?[124] This question has arisen in a series of recent Employment Tribunal cases, in which two strategies have come to the fore in arguments designed to protect the right of employees to speak freely. The first relies on the Equality Act 2010; the second on Article 9 ECHR – the right to freedom of thought, conscience and religion – and the doctrine of proportionality.[125] The leading case on the first strategy is *Forstater v CGD Europe and Center for Global Development*.[126]

Maya Forstater was contracted to the respondent think tank (CGD), where she worked as a consultant. In 2018 she tweeted about proposed reforms to the Gender Recognition Act, proposals on which the UK

---

[123] See ch 2.

[124] This is not a new question, even if the cases surveyed below are starting to address it afresh. For an excellent overview, see Paul Wragg, 'Free Speech Rights at Work: Resolving the Differences between Practice and Liberal Principle' (2015) 44 *Industrial Law Journal* 1.

[125] The two 'strategies' may overlap. Exactly how they should be understood and applied in relation to one another is a matter which, at the time of writing, is in front of the Court of Appeal, in the appeal from *Higgs v Farmor's School* [2023] EAT 89. On *Higgs*, see further below.

[126] *Forstater v CGD Europe and Center for Global Development* [2022] 1 ICR 1, [2021] IRLR 706.

government were then consulting. Staff at CGD raised concerns about a number of Forstater's tweets, alleging they were 'transphobic', 'exclusionary or offensive', and were making them feel 'uncomfortable'.[127] An investigation followed, which resulted in CGD deciding not to offer Forstater further consultancy work: her visiting fellowship at the think tank was not renewed. She brought proceedings against CGD alleging discrimination because of her gender-critical views. The Employment Tribunal ruled that Forstater's views did not constitute a philosophical belief under the Equality Act.[128] She appealed to the Employment Appeal Tribunal (EAT), which allowed her appeal. Thereafter a differently constituted Employment Tribunal upheld Forstater's core complaints of direct discrimination and victimisation.[129]

Forstater's position is that sex is biologically immutable, that there are only two sexes (male and female), that this is a material reality, and that it is impossible to change sex. It follows that, in her view, there are no circumstances in which a trans woman is in reality a woman or that a trans man is a man.[130] It was no part of her position that trans people should not generally be treated in accordance with their wishes, still less that trans people should not be respected or protected from discrimination, or that they should be abused, disparaged or harassed.[131] For Forstater, the statements that 'woman means adult human female' and 'trans women are men' are statements of neutral fact, not expressions of antipathy towards trans people.[132] Forstater's views are known as 'gender-critical beliefs', and the EAT referred to them as such.

The Equality Act 2010 makes it unlawful to discriminate against someone on the basis of a number of protected characteristics. These include race, sex, sexual orientation and, in section 10, 'religious or philosophical belief'. Section 10 defines neither religion nor belief, other than to provide that reference to either term 'includes a reference to a lack of' religion or belief. Clearly, the major religions are protected, as are atheism, secularism, humanism and paganism. So too are sects within religions, such as Jehovah's Witnesses or Orthodox Jews. For a philosophical belief to fall within the scope of section 10, it is not necessary for that belief to entail any faith in or worship of a god (or gods). The leading case on whether a belief is a 'philosophical belief' for the purposes of section 10 is the decision of the EAT in *Grainger plc v Nicholson*,[133] in which the following five criteria

---

[127] ibid [10].

[128] Judgment of 18 December 2019, [2019] 12 WLUK 516.

[129] Judgment of 6 July 2022, [2022] 7 WLUK 106.

[130] Above (n 126) [46].

[131] ibid [47].

[132] ibid [1].

[133] *Grainger plc v Nicholson* [2010] ICR 360, [2010] 2 All ER 253.

were set out: the belief must be genuinely held; it must be a belief and not an opinion or viewpoint based on current information; it must be a belief as to a weighty and substantial aspect of human life and behaviour; it must attain a certain level of cogency, seriousness, cohesion and importance; and it must be worthy of respect in a democratic society, not be incompatible with human dignity, and not conflict with the fundamental rights of others.

Recent years have witnessed ever more beliefs being held to fall within the scope of section 10. Thus, a belief 'in the moral imperative to avoid catastrophic climate change',[134] a belief that 'public service broadcasting has the higher purpose of promoting cultural interchange and social cohesion',[135] 'ethical veganism',[136] a belief in 'left-wing democratic socialism',[137] and a belief in Scottish independence[138] have each been held capable of being a philosophical belief for the purposes of the Equality Act. Support for a particular political party,[139] wearing a poppy,[140] vegetarianism,[141] and support for Rangers Football Club,[142] by contrast, have each been held not to amount to a philosophical belief. The latter two were held to be 'lifestyle choices', rather than philosophical beliefs. In adding gender-critical beliefs to the long and varied list of beliefs found by the courts to attract the protections of the Equality Act, then, the EAT in *Forstater* was not exactly striking out alone.

The EAT's focus in *Forstater* was on the fifth and final of the *Grainger* criteria. This is because the Employment Tribunal had found that gender-critical beliefs failed that criterion, on the basis that they undermine the rights of others. The EAT disagreed. It did so by taking its lead from ECtHR's jurisprudence on Article 17 ECHR.[143] In its case law on the scope of Article 9 ECHR (the right to freedom of thought, conscience and religion), the Strasbourg court has ruled that all such philosophical convictions as are 'worthy of respect in a democratic society and are not incompatible with human dignity' are protected.[144] It is only a conviction that, for example, 'challenges the very notion of democracy' which under Article 17 ECHR would fall outwith the scope of freedom of thought.[145] As the EAT put it: 'to maintain the plurality that is the hallmark of a functioning democracy,

---

[134] ibid.

[135] See *Maistry v BBC* [2014] EWCA Civ 1116.

[136] *Casamitjana Costa v League Against Cruel Sports* ET/3331129/2018.

[137] See *Henderson v GMB Union* [2016] EWCA Civ 1049.

[138] *McEleny v MOD* ET/4105347/2017.

[139] ibid.

[140] *Lisk v Shield Guardian Co Ltd* ET/3300873/2011.

[141] *Conisbee v Crossley Farms Ltd* ET/3335357/2018.

[142] *McClung v Doosan Babcock Ltd* ET/4110538/2019.

[143] See above, discussed in relation to *Perinçek* and *Norwood v United Kingdom*.

[144] *Campbell and Cosans v United Kingdom* (1982) 4 EHRR 293 [36].

[145] *Forstater* (n 126) [59].

the range of beliefs and convictions that must be tolerated is very broad.[146] In particular, and echoing a familiar line of Strasbourg authority, 'it is not enough that a belief or a statement has the potential to "offend, shock or disturb".[147] That is, even beliefs which society (or a section of it) may find offensive and shocking require, in a democracy, to be legally protected. Only those beliefs which are so extreme they would be 'knocked out' by Article 17 ECHR fail to qualify for protection.

Relying on Article 17 ECHR as the threshold measure to control the scope of protected beliefs under the Equality Act is to set the bar high, as the EAT recognised. As we have seen, Strasbourg case law makes it clear that democratic society demands 'pluralism, tolerance and broadmindedness.[148] Just because society at large – or one section of it – disagrees with or is offended by your belief is no reason to seek to curb your expression or manifestation of that belief, not unless it is a belief in something so extreme that it would undermine democracy itself. Only something akin to Nazism or totalitarianism would meet the threshold. Forstater's gender-critical beliefs, whilst undoubtedly controversial and contested, fell a long way short of this threshold and, for this reason, should not have been excluded from the protection of the Equality Act. The EAT was eager to emphasise that this does not mean people are free to abuse the rights of transgender people. Mischaracterising someone's gender could amount to harassment or victimisation, for example.[149] But holding gender-critical views – and, indeed, manifesting such beliefs by expressing them – even if considered 'offensive and abhorrent to some' is not something that 'seeks to destroy the rights of trans persons.[150]

The EAT's holdings in *Forstater* were taken further in the Employment Tribunal's subsequent ruling in Allison Bailey's case: *Bailey v Stonewall and Garden Court Chambers*.[151] Bailey was a criminal defence barrister at Garden Court Chambers. Garden Court signed up to Stonewall's diversity champions scheme in 2018. Bailey objected, arguing that 'Stonewall has been complicit in supporting a campaign of harassment, intimidation and threats made to anyone who questions its trans self-ID ideology especially lesbians and feminists.[152] The following year, Bailey helped to establish a new campaigning group, LGB Alliance. She tweeted, celebrating its launch,

---

[146] ibid.

[147] ibid, echoing *Handyside* (n 61).

[148] *Handyside* (ibid).

[149] *Forstater* (n 126) [90] and [103]–[104].

[150] ibid [111].

[151] Case No 2202172/2020; judgment of 25 July 2022. There was an appeal to the EAT, but the EAT's judgment did not affect any of the points from the ET's decision discussed here: see *Bailey v Stonewall and Garden Court Chambers* [2024] EAT 119.

[152] ibid [63].

that 'gender extremism is about to meet its match'.[153] This was one of a number of tweets Bailey posted in support of her gender-critical beliefs, criticising the actions, statements and policies of those, such as Stonewall, who promote the view that trans women are women. Both her tweets and the launch of LGB Alliance attracted attention and generated publicity, some of it supportive, some of it very much not.

Complaints were made and an investigation was undertaken, which found that, whilst a number of Bailey's tweets were 'deliberatively provocative', they 'did not express transphobic views' and were not in breach of the Bar's social media policy.[154] This was not Stonewall's view, which wrote to Garden Court complaining about Chambers' continued association with 'a barrister who is actively campaigning for a reduction in trans rights and equality, while also specifically targeting our staff with transphobic abuse on a public platform'.[155] Bailey sued her Chambers and Stonewall. She won aspects of her claim against Garden Court: her Chambers had both discriminated against and victimised her, the Tribunal found, and she was awarded damages. But her claim against Stonewall was dismissed. The Tribunal found no evidence that Stonewall had instructed, induced or caused (or had attempted to instruct, induce or cause) Bailey to suffer detriment in Chambers as a result of her gender-critical views.

On the basis of the EAT's ruling in *Forstater*, the parties in *Bailey* had no option but to accept that Bailey's view that sex is 'real and observable' whereas gender is 'a subjective identity: immeasurable, unobservable and with no objective basis' was a philosophical belief, protected under the Equality Act.[156] Bailey contended, however, that the following were likewise aspects of her protected belief: that Stonewall had 'reclassified' sex as gender identity; that Stonewall's campaigning on the matter had been 'binary, absolutist and evangelical', condemning as bigoted any view critical of Stonewall's stance; that this 'absolutist tone' had resulted in threats against women, including threats of violence and sexual violence, becoming commonplace; that gender theory as 'proselytised' by Stonewall was 'severely detrimental to women for numerous reasons, including that it denies women the ability to have female-only spaces'; and that it was likewise 'severely detrimental to lesbians' because heterosexual men who identify as trans women and are sexually attracted to women are to be treated as lesbians.[157] Both Stonewall and Garden Court Chambers sought to resist the contention that all these views and opinions could be classified

---

[153] ibid [130].
[154] ibid [186].
[155] ibid [190].
[156] ibid [279].
[157] ibid.

as a philosophical belief, but the Tribunal ruled in Bailey's favour on the point, holding that 'all the claimant's pleaded beliefs, not just the belief that woman is sex not gender, are protected'.[158]

The rulings in *Forstater* and *Bailey* were based on the Equality Act. The argument in *Higgs v Farmor's School*, by contrast, added to the mix a further argument based on Article 9 ECHR and the doctrine of proportionality.[159] Kristie Higgs worked as a pastoral administrator and work experience manager at the respondent school, a secondary school in Gloucestershire. She posted on her Facebook page a post highly critical of trends in sex and relationships education in primary schools, which she considered to amount to 'brainwashing' children on the subject of same-sex and transgender relationships, making it a 'forbidden' act to teach children about traditional Christian beliefs as to marriage and other relationships.[160] A parent of pupils at the school where Higgs worked complained to the headteacher, sending to him screenshots of Higgs' Facebook posts. Higgs was suspended pending an investigation and later dismissed, on the basis that the views expressed in her posts were 'inflammatory and quite extreme' and that they were 'clear evidence of discrimination ... in the form of harassment' against LGBT pupils.[161] It is to be noted that Higgs' posts were about her son's primary schooling, not about sex and relationships education in the secondary school in which she worked. As the EAT noted, 'no concerns had been raised relating to the claimant's conduct within the school'.[162]

Higgs raised an action in the Employment Tribunal, arguing that her treatment amounted to discrimination and harassment relating to her religion and belief. The Employment Tribunal dismissed the claim, holding that the school had acted out of 'a concern ... that, by reason of her posts, the claimant would be perceived as holding unacceptable views in relation to gay and trans people', making it impossible for her to do her job (of offering pastoral and work experience support to all pupils, including LGBT pupils).[163] Higgs appealed to the EAT, where she was successful. The EAT ruled that the Employment Tribunal had erred by failing to balance the school's reasons for acting as it did against Higgs' Convention right to freedom of thought, conscience and religion. Interference with that right would be lawful only when it was necessary in a democratic society – proportionate – in accordance with the well-established tests set out in *Bank Mellat* (rational connection, least intrusive available means, and fair balance).[164]

---

[158] ibid [293].
[159] *Higgs* (n 125).
[160] ibid [5].
[161] ibid [15].
[162] ibid.
[163] ibid [80].
[164] *Bank Mellat* (n 5): see ch 3.

Courts and tribunals are public authorities for the purposes of section 6 of the Human Rights Act: it is therefore unlawful for a court or tribunal to act incompatibly with a Convention right. Moreover, the Equality Act must be 'read and given effect' compatibly with Convention rights.[165] It follows, ruled the EAT, that in cases concerning religion or belief employment tribunals must 'always' ask whether treatment such as that Mrs Higgs was subjected to is compatible with Convention rights.[166] This will be so, it should be noted, regardless of whether the employer in a particular case is itself a public authority or a private-sector employer. 'Recognising the claimant's right to manifest her beliefs, even when expressed in terms that may disturb or offend, does not mean ... that no restriction or limitation could be placed upon that right', stated the EAT.[167] It does mean, however, that to be lawful, such a restriction or limitation must be proportionate.

A like approach was taken in *Sutcliffe v Secretary of State for Education*.[168] Sutcliffe was a teacher and an evangelical Christian. He believes that sex is immutable, that homosexuality is a sin and that Islam is evil.[169] He expressed a number of these views both in the classroom and on television. A professional conduct panel, established under the Teachers' Disciplinary (England) Regulations 2012, determined that Sutcliffe had acted in breach of professional standards and recommended that he be prohibited from teaching. The secretary of state accepted this recommendation and made the prohibition order (under powers conferred by the Education Act 2002). Sutcliffe appealed to the Divisional Court, arguing that the decision to prohibit him from teaching was a disproportionate interference with his Article 9 right to freedom of thought, conscience and religion. The court accepted that the decision would be lawful only if it was proportionate but ruled that, in this case, it was proportionate. The panel had properly applied the law 'and took into account the seriousness of the conduct, the public interest, the available mitigation, and whether a prohibition order was necessary and proportionate'.[170] Its decision and its recommendation to the secretary of state were lawful.

None of these cases was framed on the basis either of common law or Article 10 protections of free speech, but all are concerned nonetheless with ways in which speech should be protected. All are concerned with the manifestation of beliefs safeguarded by Article 9 ECHR and/or by the protected characteristic of 'philosophical belief' under the Equality Act. Whilst that may limit the range of speech which can be protected via

---

[165] Human Rights Act 1998, s 3(1).
[166] *Higgs* (n 125) [94].
[167] ibid [86].
[168] *Sutcliffe v Secretary of State for Education* [2024] EWHC 1878 (Admin).
[169] ibid [3].
[170] ibid [91].

these routes, such limits may be more apparent than real. This is for two reasons. First, 'belief' as a protected characteristic under the Equality Act has been stretched to include the protection of opinions which are quite some remove from anything resembling religion. Allison Bailey's views about Stonewall and about the consequences of Stonewall's policy position were held by the Employment Tribunal all to fall within the scope of the protected characteristic. This extends the category of protected speech, as a broad range of opinions is protected. Secondly, what is stated in cases such as *Higgs* and *Sutcliffe* about proportionality in the Article 9 context must also apply to proportionality in the Article 10 context. Even if an employee's expression is not a manifestation of their belief, on the logic of *Higgs* and *Sutcliffe* it would be disproportionate for an employer to take action against the employee just because someone claims to be offended by what has been said. If speech is so harmful that it breaches professional standards or brings the profession or the employer into disrepute, the employer may have every right to take action against the employee. But the harm will have to be evidenced and proven, not merely asserted, in order for a court or tribunal to rule that the employer has acted lawfully. And it will have to be shown that the harm to the employer's interests outweighs the interference with the employee's rights, whether under Article 9 or Article 10.

We can give the last word to the Employment Tribunal in another case: *Adams v Edinburgh Rape Crisis Centre*.[171] Roz Adams worked for the Edinburgh Rape Crisis Centre. She brought a claim in the Employment Tribunal that she had been discriminated against, harassed and constructively dismissed by her employer because of her views about sex and gender. She won. It is clear from the Tribunal's judgment that there had been a long-standing climate of deep intolerance at the Rape Crisis Centre for gender-critical views, which were stigmatised as transphobic. The Employment Tribunal ruled as follows: the law imposes a duty, it stated,

> to tolerate each other in the workplace. Tolerance means not just accepting views which one may not be terribly bothered about but means accepting that others hold views which may cut to the core of one's being.[172]

As in the criminal law, so too in the law relating to the workplace, that someone is offended by what you say can never be sufficient grounds for taking legal action against that person, even if you are offended to your core, and even if you feel your very identity has been challenged. Offensiveness by itself is never a harm sufficiently compelling to justify interfering with the right to speak freely, whether that interference comes via the criminal justice system, in the workplace, or through social censure.

---

[171] *Adams v Edinburgh Rape Crisis Centre* 2024 SLT (Tr) 89.
[172] ibid [195].

6

Online Safety

Does expression online require to be regulated differently from expression offline and, if so, how?[1] These are the questions addressed in this final chapter. The short answer to the first of them is 'yes'. As for the second question, we are nearer the beginning than the end of the process of discovering its answer. The argument in this chapter will be that we are likely to make fewer mistakes in answering it if we approach it in the light of the free speech struggles of the past. For all the novelties and for all the breathtaking pace of recent technological change in the online ecosystem, the problems its regulation poses for free expression are pregnant with echoes of the past, if only we would attend to hearing them. In this chapter we consider very modern (and highly complex) legislative instruments of regulatory oversight: the UK's Online Safety Act 2023 and the EU's so-called Digital Services Act, adopted in 2022.[2] We shall try to understand them in their own terms and also in the light of the insights into speaking freely we have gleaned in preceding chapters, from John Milton and *Cato's Letters*, from Jonathan Swift and John Stuart Mill.

I. How Speech is Different Online

As we have seen over and again in this book, the fundamental legal and political approach to expression is that it should be free unless it demonstrably causes identifiable harm to others. Online speech is different from – and needs to be regulated differently from – offline speech for two reasons: because the nature of the harms is different and because the magnitude of the risks is greater. Two of the most important examples of the former are the algorithms used online and the prevalence of anonymity

---

[1] An excellent overview is András Koltay, *New Media and Freedom of Expression: Rethinking the Constitutional Foundations of the Public Sphere* (Oxford, Hart Publishing, 2019).

[2] European Parliament and Council Regulation (EU) 2022/2065, adopted on 19 October 2022 (OJ L277/1, 27 October 2022); hereafter referred to as the Digital Services Act or DSA.

online; two of the most important examples of the latter are exposure to inappropriate material and disinformation.

Let us start with 'algorithms'. Anyone with a Facebook or other social media account will recognise this. It is October and the nights are drawing in. Idly one evening you open your laptop to search on Tui or on booking. com for a cheapish, last-minute-ish deal for a few last days of sun before winter, for a city break, or for a quick flit to a Christmas market. It does not come to anything: prices are too steep, flight times too inconvenient, and the better deals were long ago snapped up. The following morning over coffee you open up Facebook on your phone and, as you scroll, every second post seems to be a holiday advertisement. It was not even your phone you were using the previous evening but somehow your phone knows what you were looking for and thinks it knows what you want even if, having slept on it, you know that you are going nowhere this winter. These are what have come to be called 'the algorithms' at work. As you search, you leave a huge digital footprint, which Big Tech reads and sells to advertisers, and the more you visit holiday sites online – the more you click – the more such advertisements you will see. It is the price you pay for using Facebook's ostensibly 'free' services. Such practices raise all manner of privacy concerns, and there is a wealth of data protection law designed to address them. But these are not our concerns: here we are concerned with speech rather than with privacy.[3] In particular, we are concerned with harmful speech.

Imagine that your search was not for winter sun but for something altogether more troubling. Imagine that the person doing the searching is not a privileged middle-class professional, with aspirations of taking his second (or third) overseas holiday of the year, but a vulnerable teenager in despair at how overweight she thinks she is, or how unattractive she thinks she has become. That she is quite mistaken to have these impressions of herself does nothing, alas, to quieten or reassure her. She opens her laptop and searches up 'weight loss' on Google. She looks at a range of radical options; she consults websites about surgery, she reads about unlicensed drugs. It only takes 10 minutes. In a fit of self-disgust she snaps her laptop shut, picks up her phone, puts some music on, and loses herself scrolling through group chats. Before school the following morning (whilst her dad is downstairs with coffee and holiday advertisements) her Instagram feed seems bizarrely full of reels about anorexia. After a few clicks she is reading about self-harm. Cutting. Body shaming. Even suicide. The algorithms are

---

[3] For an attempt to understand these sorts of concerns in the context of free speech, see Richard Sorabji, *Freedom of Speech and Expression* (New York, Oxford University Press, 2021) ch 3. One aspect of privacy as it relates to the online environment is the so-called 'right to be forgotten'. See Case C-131/12 *Google Spain* [2014] 1 QB 1022, now consolidated (as a 'right to erasure') in the EU's General Data Protection Regulation (GDPR), Regulation (EU) 2016/679: see Jacob Rowbottom, *Media Law* (Oxford, Hart Publishing, 2nd edn 2024) 356–58.

taking her down a rabbit hole, and that she is now late for school is the least of her problems.

If, when I was a teenager, I had gone to my local public library to take out a book on eating disorders or a history of famous rockstar suicides, I would not have been greeted on my return two weeks later (to bring the books back) by the librarian standing on the doorstep with an armful of further reading on the same topics, which the nice thoughtful librarian thought I might be interested in given the books I had recently been perusing. The rabbit holes down which the algorithms send vulnerable teenagers today have no equivalent in the offline world. This is a new harm. As Larry Kramer has put it: 'people no longer need to seek out extremist literature: today it seeks them out.'[4] If I look up 'terrorism' in a twenty-volume encyclopaedia I find on a library shelf, the items in that encyclopaedia will not have been rearranged the next time I consult it with all the entries related to terrorism deliberately placed so they catch my eye. My interest in terrorism may have been a one-off. The next time I go to the same source I might be wanting to learn about butterflies. But once you start looking for something online, search engines and social media platforms make assumptions that you are going to carry on being interested in that thing, feeding you more and more of it.[5] Sometimes, of course, that is incredibly helpful – the algorithms are not *designed* to be harmful – but there is no doubt they may have harmful consequences. And as we have seen in previous chapters, when we think about expression, we need to think about its effects as well as its purposes.

This is the first way in which speech may be more harmful online than offline. The second concerns anonymity. In the offline world, one of the key ways in which we filter speech is via the identity of the speaker. The effect of being told by your lover that 'I love you' is quite different, obviously, from hearing the same words uttered by a leery drunkard on the night bus or, worse, by a boss you had long feared may have predatory instincts. These are not only 'time, manner, place' differences: they are also differences that hinge on the identity of the speaker. Being able to know who the speaker is – being able to identify and verify the source – is critical to how we process information, how we 'receive and impart' it (in the words of Article 10 of the European Convention on Human Rights (ECHR)). How we interpret market analysis published in the *Financial Times* might be very different from how we would interpret similar information overheard in a supermarket. What the foreign secretary says about international security from the despatch

---

[4] Larry Kramer, 'A Deliberate Leap in the Opposite Direction: The Need to Rethink Free Speech' in Lee Bollinger and Geoffrey Stone (eds), *Social Media, Freedom of Speech and the Future of our Democracy* (New York, Oxford University Press, 2022) 37.

[5] See further on how search engines can manipulate results depending not only on your search history but on where in the world your computer thinks you are, Timothy Garton Ash, *Free Speech: Ten Principles for a Connected World* (London, Atlantic Books, 2017) 51.

box of the House of Commons might be received very differently from what a random member of the public says on a late-night radio phone-in show. A controversial claim about the science underlying climate change will carry far more weight if published in a peer-reviewed expert journal than if it appears only in the letters page of the *Daily Mail*. And so on.

Identifying who the speaker is can be far harder online. Anyone can easily set up an anonymous account on social media and it is almost as easy to establish a fake account, pretending to be someone you are not, or presenting yourself as having credentials, experience or expertise which are, in reality, fictitious. Anonymity and non-verifiability can be harmful in a number of ways. Anonymity shields abusers and allows for far more abusive speech on social media (and particularly on Twitter/X) than would otherwise be the case. And the inability to verify sources means that both misinformation (errors) and disinformation (deliberate falsehoods) can be spread – and believed – far more quickly. If anonymity is our second 'online harm', disinformation is our third.

There is, of course, plenty of disinformation offline as well as on the internet. American talk-show radio hosts have wallowed for decades in false conspiracy theories, and we saw in chapter four the concerns, shared in Britain, Europe and the United States alike, about the extent of Russian influence in manipulating public opinion in recent election and referendum campaigns. Disinformation is not unique to online speech, but the scale of the problem is far greater online than anywhere else. This is for several reasons, including the *speed* at which disinformation can spread online and its *reach*, being seen by millions of users in a short space of time ('going viral'). The problem is compounded both by algorithms and anonymity. The more you click on the bait the more of it you see, and the filters by which you would normally edit out the credible and the reliable from the background noise and bilge are missing. Social media is incredibly democratising: everyone has a voice. Instead of news being filtered via a small number of more or less authoritative outlets, the weight stories carry is now measured in how many 'likes' and 'retweets' they attract.

The well-known line that 'a lie can be spread half way around the world whilst the truth is still tying up its boot straps' is often attributed to Mark Twain, although there is no evidence he actually said it. A similar line was in fact written in the early eighteenth century by Jonathan Swift. He wrote as follows:

> It often happens that if a lie be believed only for an hour, it hath done its work, and there is no farther occasion for it. Falsehood flies, and truth comes limping after it; so that when men come to be undeceived, it is too late.[6]

---

[6] Jonathan Swift, *The Examiner* No 14 (1710); quoted in Leo Damrosch, *Jonathan Swift: His Life and His World* (New Haven, Yale University Press, 2013) 210.

We saw in chapter two that Swift wrote bitterly of the 'cultural swamp' and the 'bilge' of falsehood and disinformation in which he considered London to be drowning after the lapse of the Licensing Act. All of a sudden, anyone could write anything, or so it seemed. Amid the din, the truth – the few voices of authority and wisdom (like his) – were finding it ever harder to be heard. 'Falsehood flies, and truth comes limping after it' is a magnificent Swiftian phrase, as apt for the coffee- and ale-houses of 1710 as it is for today's equivalent public square, social media. Two further Swiftian phrases also come to mind: that online debate can all too often appear as 'an engagement of porcupines' featuring a mere 'confederacy of dunces', no more refined than were the propaganda and pamphlet wars of the Hanoverian era.[7]

Disinformation, then, is nothing new. Just as the problem has roots in the past, so too does the approach we should take to addressing it. If even the greatest free speech advocates have on occasion been blithe as to exactly how 'the truth will always prevail', they have nonetheless bequeathed to us two invaluable principles. First, that even though (as Trenchard and Gordon argued) free speech may have vices as well as virtues, the cure of censorship can be far worse than the disease of falsehood. Recall those lines, quoted in chapter two, that just because water can drown and fire burn, we would be mad to switch off the flow of the rivers or to block out the sun. So too with speech – even with online speech, with all its potential for harming others. Just because we know that speech may be harmful is no reason to think we have no choice but to censor it. Secondly, recall Milton's understanding, noted in chapter one, that a world free of censorship demands much of its readers. Not only must we read 'promiscuously', as Milton put it, but as readers we must exercise the virtues of sound judgement. This no longer requires the muscular Christianity which Milton associated with the idea of the 'virtuous' reader, but it surely does at least require us not to be overly credulous. A good rule of thumb is never to believe anything you read on social media (or, for that matter, on Wikipedia) until you have corroborated it somewhere else. Neither blue ticks nor bucket-loads of likes and retweets are any guarantee that what you are reading is reliable, accurate or true.

Disinformation is not the only risk facing readers online. Exposure to inappropriate material is another, and this is our fourth harm of online speech. As with disinformation, this is a harm which is greater in, not

---

[7] For the first phrase, see Swift's *Battle of the Books*, cited in ch 2. The second phrase was made famous by the John Kennedy Toole novel, *A Confederacy of Dunces*, first published 11 years after its author's death, in 1980. What Swift actually wrote (in *Thoughts on Various Subjects* (1706)) was: 'when a true genius appears in the world, you may know him by this sign, that the dunces are all in confederacy against him'.

unique to, the online environment. Once online, there are few obstacles in the way of your seeing, viewing or reading more or less anything you want. Let me return to an example used above. If, when I was a teenager, I had returned several times to my local library to search for ever more material on eating disorders or self-harm (or even, for that matter, on bomb-making or terrorism), the chances are that someone would have noticed and had a word with me, or perhaps with my teachers, or even my parents or others in authority. No such gatekeepers or guardians exist online: today's teenage children can access all manner of material online without any teacher, parent or carer having the first idea about it. Whilst apps certainly exist to enable concerned parents to take various steps in policing their children's exposure to material online, most teenagers are more tech-savvy than most parents and a determined, or even a curious, teenager will not long be prevented from accessing what they want to access.

It does not follow that either the internet or the behaviour of teenagers (or indeed the behaviour of others seeking to access material deemed somehow inappropriate) needs to be constrained by law. The purpose of this section has been simply to demonstrate that online speech may carry harms either different from or greater than offline speech. The question of what, if anything, the law has done or should now do about that, is the question to which we turn in the remaining sections of this chapter.

II. Internet Law 1.0

In the early days of the internet, it was widely perceived as a liberalising technology, not as a source of additional harms. It was welcomed and celebrated, not feared and marked down as a new danger needing fresh regulation. At least, this was the view in the West (more authoritarian regimes elsewhere in the world may have taken a different approach). The internet revolutionised our access to information and our ability to communicate – both their speed and their reach being transformed. To the journalists and academics who first adopted the new technology, little is more highly cherished than access to information and rapid communication. It is hardly a surprise, then, that opinion formers quickly adopted an overwhelmingly positive attitude to the new power of the online.

Part of the liberalising mode of the internet was its very absence of regulation. States did not assume that the new technology had to be licensed (as the Crown had assumed in England upon the introduction of the printing press). Nor was the spectrum of the new technology limited, in the way that hampered radio and television broadcasting in its first decades, when regulation was required simply in order to allow anyone to be heard (as we saw in chapter four). The emergence of broadcasting prompted the United States to create a new federal agency – the Federal Communications Commission – to oversee it. No such body exists in the United States in relation to the internet. Rather, at its dawn the internet was regarded as an exhilarating place of freedom and openness, where innovators were celebrated as pioneers, operating in and opening up the frontiers of a new Wild West. Even as late as 2011, the internet was being heralded as a means whereby the oppressed could escape their oppression – the role social media is said to have played in facilitating the Arab Spring of that year, particularly in Tunisia and Egypt, being the prime example. Whether this example owes more to the mythologisation of social media than to its reality may be contested, but what is undoubtedly the case is that it was this 'liberalising mode' of the internet which determined how the first laws to govern it would be crafted.

The most important such law is section 230 of the Communications Decency Act, federal legislation passed by the US Congress in 1996.[8] This has been referred to as the 'Magna Carta of the internet' and as the legal 'cornerstone of internet freedom'.[9] Section 230 has two key provisions. The first provides that 'no provider or user of an interactive computer service shall be treated as the publisher or speaker of any information provided by another information content provider'. This means that online 'intermediaries' (as they have come to be called) are neither publishers nor authors in law. Thus, if a website enables a user to post a comment on its site, that website is to be treated neither as the publisher nor as the author of that comment. If the post is defamatory, for example, the website could not be sued for libel. The second provision is equally important: it shields intermediaries from civil liability with regard to any action 'voluntarily taken in good faith to restrict access to or availability of material ... [they consider] to be obscene, lewd, lascivious, filthy, excessively violent, harassing or otherwise objectionable'. This means that you cannot sue Facebook or Twitter/X (or any other such platform) for removing your posts or tweets from their service. You likewise cannot sue a newspaper website for removing a comment you have posted.

Section 230 does not confer an absolute immunity from liability. Its terms exclude – as well as child pornography and obscenity – breaches of intellectual property rights. Section 230 does not cover content posted by companies or individuals on their own websites, and nor does it cover paid advertising. It is, nonetheless, 'fundamental' to how social media operates online: 'because of its protections, companies [such as Facebook and

---

[8] 47 USC §230.
[9] See Mary Anne Franks, 'The Free Speech Industry' in Bollinger and Stone (n 4) 68.

Twitter/X] do not have to proactively assess the legality of content' posted on their platforms.[10] Yet section 230 was passed when the internet was in its infancy. None of Google, Facebook or Twitter had yet been founded (Google was founded in 1998, Facebook in 2004 and Twitter in 2006). Back in 1996, when section 230 was enacted, the 'big three' information services in the United States were AOL, CompuServe, and Prodigy. None was free to use: each charged a monthly fee to use their services, subscriptions being their primary source of revenue.[11] Today's business model, in which advertising pays for free-to-use search engines and social media platforms, had barely even been conceived.

Section 230 was not an outlier. Across the Atlantic the European Union enacted legislation in 2000 – the E-Commerce Directive – which adopted a similar approach. It provides that where an 'information society service' is a 'mere conduit', a 'caching service', or a 'hosting service' it will not be liable for content online. This is not a blanket immunity. It applies where a service provider plays a neutral, passive role with regard to what is posted on its site. In any event, once a platform becomes aware that content is illegal, steps should be taken to remove or restrict access to it.[12] The principal aim of the E-Commerce Directive was to make it easier to do business, especially cross-border business, online. It was motivated by concerns as to making online business smoother – how to facilitate it – not by anxieties as to online harms.

This does not mean that there can never be liability for content posted online, even when it is service users posting the content rather than the service provider. This is illustrated by the European Court of Human Rights (ECtHR) case of *Delfi AS v Estonia*.[13] Delfi ran one of the largest online news portals in Estonia. It published an article about the provision of ferry services between the Estonian mainland a number of its islands. Very hostile and aggressive messages were posted as comments under the article, including a number which made personal threats to individuals who ran the ferry services. Because of their threatening nature, it was clear that the comments were unlawful. Once Delfi had been notified about the comments, it took them down. It did this within 24 hours of being notified, but this was some six weeks after the comments had been posted. The Estonian courts ruled that Delfi was not immune from liability.

---

[10] Monika Bickert, 'Defining the Boundaries of Free Speech on Social Media' in Lee Bollinger and Geoffrey Stone (eds), *The Free Speech Century* (New York, Oxford University Press, 2019) 255–56.

[11] See Sheldon Whitehouse, 'Section 230 Reforms' in Bollinger and Stone (n 4) 106.

[12] Directive 2000/31/EC, now amended and supplemented by the Digital Services Act (n 2), on which see further below.

[13] *Delfi AS v Estonia* (2016) 62 EHRR 6.

The E-Commerce Directive had been transposed by legislation into Estonian law, but its scope, ruled the courts, did not extend to a news platform where the comment function had been integrated into the reporting of news, where the platform actively called for comments, and where, as here, advertising revenue was tied directly to the number of comments posted. Delfi had an economic interest in securing comments: for this reason it was neither neutral nor passive. It was therefore liable for the comments.

The damages awarded in the case were low, amounting to only €320. Nonetheless, Delfi took its case to Strasbourg, arguing that the finding of liability was a breach of its right to freedom of expression under Article 10 ECHR. The Grand Chamber ruled, by fifteen votes to two, that there had been no such breach. The case demonstrates two points: that immunity from liability under the E-Commerce Directive is not absolute; and that, when liability is found, such a finding may be compatible with the right to freedom of expression in European law. Both points suggest that, even if the E-Commerce Directive and section 230 of the Communications Decency Act have much in common, they may on occasion yield different results.

Delfi was distinguished in *Magyar Tartalomszolgáltatók Egyesülete v Hungary (MTE)*.[14] MTE, a self-regulatory body monitoring the implementation in Hungary of a professional code of ethical content online, published an article on its website about two real estate management companies, criticising their practices. Comments were posted under the article, which the companies considered to be defamatory: the comments accused the companies of being 'sly' and 'rubbish'. The companies sued MTE, whereupon MTE removed the comments from its site. The companies persisted and were successful, the Hungarian courts ruling that MTE was liable in defamation. MTE took its case to Strasbourg where the ECtHR ruled that the finding of liability was, in this instance, incompatible with Article 10. *Delfi* was distinguished on two grounds. First, the European Court found that the Hungarian courts had not sought to balance MTE's Article 10 right against the companies' right not to be defamed: the latter had simply been held to trump the former, without the former being given any weight. Secondly, the European Court relied on the fact that whereas the comments at issue in *Delfi* were directly threatening and clearly unlawful, the comments at issue in *MTE* were not: they were expressions of opinion critical of the companies' practices. For these reasons, it was disproportionate for MTE to be held liable for them.

As *Delfi* and *MTE* help to illustrate, the internet of today no longer resembles the internet of 1996 and 2000, when section 230 and the E-Commerce Directive were enacted. AOL's dial-up and instant

---

[14] *Magyar Tartalomszolgáltatók Egyesülete v Hungary (MTE)*, judgment of 2 February 2016.

messenger services, pioneering as they were at the end of the twentieth century, have long since become relics. Having been purchased in 2016 by the US telecoms giant Verizon, AOL is now a subsidiary of Yahoo! Inc. CompuServe was swallowed up by AOL not long after section 230 was enacted. And Prodigy no longer exists at all, even as a domain name. But it is not just that the household names and market leaders of 30 years ago have been replaced by others; it is that the very way we use the internet has transformed. The biggest transformation is the rise of social media. Facebook, YouTube, Instagram and Twitter/X, and the hundreds of smaller platforms following in their wake, do not post very much of their own content. Rather, they are platforms on which users are free to post, either to their followers or to the online world, more or less whatever they want. At the same time, so vast has the internet become that we cannot hope to navigate it on our own. We require engines to search it for us. The biggest of them, such as Google, have become the gatekeepers to the internet. When we think of Big Tech now, these are the companies we mean, along with the hardware and software designers, such as Apple and Microsoft.

Internet 2.0 – the internet of social media and search engines – is a radically different place from internet 1.0. EU and UK law have started to respond, as we shall see when we turn to the Online Safety Act and the Digital Services Act. But, in the United States, section 230 remains for the time being unamended. Internet 2.0 is not just technologically innovative: it requires us to think differently about free speech. It has revolutionised expression more radically than anything that has happened since the abolition of print licensing. This is because it has *democratised* expression. We saw in chapter two that the end of print licensing, combined with rapid changes in print technology, unleashed a flood of pamphlets and periodicals in early eighteenth-century London. We also saw what critics such as Jonathan Swift and Samuel Johnson thought about that. It was a revolution in communications the like of which, until the dawning of the age of social media, had never been repeated. Broadcasting was of an altogether different character. As we saw in chapter four, broadcasting required to be channelled through what at first was a very small number of outlets, so small that governments felt compelled to legislate to impose on broadcasters requirements of 'due impartiality' which had no equivalent in any other medium. The broadcasters may have been able to reach a huge public, but their audience was passive. Editors and controllers were the ones who decided what would be aired.

This was the pattern throughout the twentieth century, and it applied to the press every bit as much as it applied to broadcasters. A tiny number of hugely powerful people – overwhelmingly, men – decided what would be broadcast or printed in the mass media. For newspapers it was the age of the press barons. In Britain: Northcliffe,[15] Rothermere[16] and Beaverbrook,[17] to be followed later in the century by Rupert Murdoch and Robert Maxwell.[18] They hired editors who quite literally drove the news agenda of the day: they did not report the news as much as create it. Think of Kelvin MacKenzie at the *Sun* (claiming in 1992 that it was his paper which swung the election behind John Major's Conservatives and against Neil Kinnock's Labour Party) or Paul Dacre at the *Daily Mail*.[19] Without the campaigning politics of papers such as the *Mail* (as well as others), would there even have been a referendum in 2016 on the UK's membership of the European Union, let alone a result in that referendum in favour of Brexit? Wars have been fought because of the power of the press.[20] Elections have been, if not determined, then at least heavily influenced by the power of the press. And a country's very future has been shaped by the power of the press. In each instance, this power was in fact wielded by a tiny number of people – in that sense, it was anything but democratic.[21] We may think of this as being a phenomenon which developed only at the close of the twentieth century, but Stanley Baldwin was fulminating against it as early as 1931:

> The papers conducted by Lord Rothermere and Lord Beaverbrook are not newspapers in the ordinary acceptance of the term. They are engines of propaganda for the constantly changing policies, desires, personal wishes, personal likes and dislikes of two men. Their methods are direct falsehoods, misrepresentation, half-truths, the alteration of the speaker's meaning by publishing a sentence apart from context ... What the proprietorship of these papers is aiming at is power, and power without responsibility – the prerogative of the harlot throughout the ages.[22]

---

[15] It was Alfred Harmsworth, Lord Northcliffe, who coined the term 'tabloid' to describe a style of print journalism. He founded the *Daily Mail*, first published in 1896. See Terry Kirby, *The Newsmongers: A History of Tabloid Journalism* (London, Reaktion, 2024) 62–71.

[16] Harold Harmsworth, Viscount Rothermere, was Alfred's brother. The *Mail* group (also known as Associated Newspapers) is still controlled by the Rothermere family.

[17] Max Aitken, Lord Beaverbrook, turned the *Daily Express* into the biggest-selling British newspaper in the mid-twentieth century; for a time it was the biggest selling daily paper in the world.

[18] On Murdoch and Maxwell, see Kirby (n 15) chs 5–7.

[19] ibid chs 8–9.

[20] The example Kirby gives is the Spanish-American War of 1898, which 'neither country really wanted' but was agitated for by America's first press moguls (the precursors of Northcliffe, Rothermere and Beaverbrook), William Randolph Hearst and Joseph Pulitzer: ibid 59 and ch 2 generally.

[21] Editors and press barons alike would say, of course, that they were only following the preferences (or prejudices) of their readers but, even if that were true, it would miss my point. I am using 'democratic' in its classical sense, to mean rule by the many. The mass media of the twentieth century was an oligarchy, not a democracy: it was ruled by the few (even if the few paid scrupulous attention to the preferences of their massed ranks of readers).

[22] Cited by Kirby (n 15) 107. Baldwin was prime minister from 1923 to 1924, 1924 to 1929 and 1935 to 1937. He was fulminating against Rothermere and Beaverbrook because they had turned against him and were seeking to undermine him. The last phrase of this quotation seems to have been suggested to Baldwin by Rudyard Kipling.

Just as the end of print licensing liberalised the early eighteenth-century press from the prior restraints formally imposed by church and state, democratising print, so has social media liberalised news and current affairs from the oligarchic rule of press barons, station controllers and newspaper editors to the new landscape where anyone with a social media account can write about, can edit and can shape the news. There has never been so much information made so widely available from so many sources so quickly. Like any move from oligarchy to democracy, this is liberalis-ing. At the same time, however, it is hardly cost free. Democracy is rightly heralded as a force for progress and freedom. But it also has a dark side. Just as rule by the one (monarchy) can collapse into tyranny and rule by the few (aristocracy) into oligarchy, rule by the many (democracy) can all too easily corrode into populism, mob rule and anarchy. In the eighteenth century it was well understood that, for precisely this reason, democracy needed to be kept in check. It was but one element, Blackstone argued, in a balanced constitution: it should sit alongside rather than replace monar-chy and aristocracy.[23] Jonathan Swift saw that the democratisation of print had lowered, not raised, its quality. The same risks have played out all over again with the rise of social media. The struggle for free speech now is not how to curb the power of the press barons, but how to reverse the Swiftian axiom that falsehood flies whilst the truth comes limping after: the prob-lem is not the vice of oligarchy but the dark side of democracy. Online, we are 'drowning in lies'.[24] As Cass Sunstein has put it, echoing Oliver Wendell Holmes, 'right now a lot of people are falsely shouting fire in a crowded theatre'.[25]

III. Disinformation and 'Fake News'

Section 230 of the Communications Decency Act means there could be no liability in the United States such as the Estonian courts found (and such as the ECtHR upheld) in *Delfi*. Yet there is ample concern in America – so transformed is the online environment now since section 230 was enacted – that it is no longer fit for purpose. Amending or replacing it, so as to extend liability for online speech is fraught with difficulty, however. Not only is there a lack of political consensus (with progressives thinking there is too much harmful speech online and conservatives worrying that Big Tech already censors online speech

---

[23] Sir William Blackstone, *Commentaries on the Laws of England* (1765–69) vol 1.
[24] Emily Bazelon, 'The Disinformation Dilemma' in Bollinger and Stone (n 4) 42.
[25] Cass Sunstein, 'A Framework for Regulating Falsehoods' in Bollinger and Stone (n 4) 54.

unfairly to favour progressives),[26] but there is also the roadblock of the First Amendment. In *Reno v American Civil Liberties Union* the US Supreme Court ruled that two provisions of section 223 of the Communications Decency Act violated the First Amendment.[27] Both provisions had been enacted in order to protect children from harmful material online. The first, section 223(a), criminalised the transmission of 'obscene or indecent' messages to a recipient under 18 years of age. The second, section 223(d), prohibited the sending or displaying of 'patently offensive' messages to a person under 18.

The Supreme Court ruled that Congress could prohibit obscene messages but that it could not prohibit indecent or offensive messages compatibly with the First Amendment. The court recognised that Congress had a legitimate interest in seeking to protect children from harmful materials but ruled nonetheless that the restrictions on indecent and offensive speech enacted in section 223(a) and (d) could not be justified. Neither indecency nor offensiveness were defined: both terms were vague and lacked precision.[28] Moreover, prior case law upholding restrictions on broadcast speech was held not to apply to the regulation of speech online. There was no equivalent online of the scarcity of available frequencies which had justified the regulation of broadcasting, and the 'invasive' nature of broadcasting did not apply to 'cyberspace', the court ruled.[29]

Reno was an early case in terms of the internet – it was decided in 1997 – but in the years since then its approach to online speech has been underpinned rather than challenged. The Supreme Court reiterated it for example in 2017, in *Packingham v North Carolina*, when it stated that

> a fundamental principle of the First Amendment is that all persons have access to places where they can speak and listen ... While in the past there may have been difficulty in identifying the most important [such] places ..., today the answer is clear. It is cyberspace – the 'vast democratic forums of the internet'.[30]

For both political and constitutional reasons, then, attempts to reform section 230 have thus far come to nothing. Yet the pressure for reform grows. The main concerns in the United States focus on disinformation

---

[26] As Erwin and Alex Chemerinsky have written, 'progressives complain that online speech platforms create breeding grounds for bigotry and misinformation [whilst] conservatives bemoan content moderation practices by tech giants such as Facebook ..., which they claim favour left-leaning views at the expense of conservative speech': see 'The Golden Era of Free Speech' in Bollinger and Stone (n 4) 91.

[27] *Reno v American Civil Liberties Union* 521 US 844 (1997).

[28] ibid 871.

[29] ibid 868.

[30] *Packingham v North Carolina* 582 US 98 (2017), quoting from *Reno v American Civil Liberties Union* (ibid) 868.

and fake news, notably as regards the 2016 presidential election, anti-vax campaigning during the Covid-19 pandemic, and President Trump's insistence that the 2020 presidential election was 'stolen' from him and his statements in connection with the riotous attack on the Capitol in Washington DC on 6 January 2021. A feature of the 2016 presidential election was concern about apparent Russian interference in it, including the creation of a large number of social media accounts to share, repost and drive traffic towards fake news stories which favoured Donald Trump over his rival for the presidency, Hillary Clinton. A Special Counsel report into the matter was published in 2019 – the Mueller Report – which concluded that there was 'sweeping and systematic' illegal Russian interference, but that there was no evidence that the Trump campaign had cooperated or colluded in it.[31] Academic research found that, whilst a clear preponderance of the fake campaign news online favoured Trump over Clinton, there is no evidence that Trump won the election as a result of it: pro-Trump fake news was a feature, but not a determining feature, of the election, it would seem.[32]

During the coronavirus pandemic 'anti-vax' conspiracies circulated widely on social media where, particularly in the United States, they hindered public vaccination programmes that were designed to help ease societies out of lockdown. Facebook was especially criticised in the United States for allowing such conspiracy theories to circulate more freely than posts from authoritative sources such as the World Health Organization – yet another example of falsehood flying whilst the truth limps after and, in this instance, one which had serious adverse consequences for public health.[33] Emily Bazelon has called this 'America's information crisis', and since the 2016 election and the pandemic it has only got worse.[34]

When rioters stormed the US Capitol on 6 January 2021 Donald Trump took to Twitter to repeat false claims about the 2020 presidential election result and to profess his 'love' for the rioters. Twitter first shut Trump's account down and then, two days later, after he tweeted again in apparent support of the 'American patriots' who had rioted, Twitter banned Trump altogether (a ban which was lifted only after Elon Musk acquired Twitter in 2022). Trump was also suspended from Facebook. The rioters, let it not be forgotten, bludgeoned a police officer to death with a fire extinguisher and, among other matters, attempted to locate and assassinate Speaker of the House Nancy Pelosi, whilst erecting a gallows on the Capitol's grounds

---

[31] See Chemerinsky and Chemerinsky (n 26) 98.

[32] Hunt Allcott and Matthew Gentzkow, 'Social Media and Fake News in the 2016 Election' (2017) 31 *Journal of Economic Perspectives* 211.

[33] See Bazelon (n 24) 49.

[34] ibid.

and calling for the execution of Trump's Vice-President, Mike Pence. The conspiracy theories – ie, the fake news – challenging the election result had been circulating with particular virulence on what Mary Anne Franks calls a 'right-wing-dominated social media site' called Parler.[35] On 9 January Google and Apple removed Parler from their app stores, and Amazon also removed it from its web hosting services.[36] Yet these conspiracies were very widely believed to be true: a survey conducted in the months after President Biden's inauguration found 'nearly two-thirds of Republicans believed that the 2020 election had been stolen from former president Trump'.[37] This is not only 'mass manipulation' of information: it is 'mass delusion'.[38] And it is terrifying.

If this is what free speech unleashes, would it not be better to muzzle it? Far from the marketplace of ideas ensuring (as we put it in chapter three) that 'the good, the wise and the true will prevail over the wicked, the ignorant and the false', the radical democratisation of speech online has resulted only in a tsunami of lies. Yet this is speech which, in the United States, is constitutionally protected. The First Amendment safeguards the telling of lies and the spreading of falsehoods alongside its protection of 'the good, the wise and the true'. One need look no further than the iconic *New York Times v Sullivan* as authority for that proposition – the advertisement in the *New York Times* of which Sullivan complained contained a number of factual inaccuracies yet, despite this, Sullivan could not sue the paper for libel.[39] In 1964 the Supreme Court ruled that this was merely the inevitable price society would need to pay in order to give free speech the 'breathing space' it needs to thrive.[40]

In more recent times the Supreme Court has doubled down on this. In *US v Alvarez* the court struck down federal legislation – the Stolen Valor Act – that had made it an offence falsely to claim the award of military decorations, medals or honours.[41] In his trenchant majority opinion, Kennedy J ruled that 'the court has never endorsed the categorical rule ... that false statements receive no First Amendment protection'.[42] Content-based restrictions on speech are permitted under the First Amendment only in a few, narrow categories – ie, where the speech incites imminent lawless action, is obscene or defamatory, or constitutes fighting words, child

---

[35] Franks (n 9) 75.

[36] ibid.

[37] See Kate Starbird, 'Strategy and Structure: Understanding Online Disinformation' in Bollinger and Stone (n 4) 219.

[38] ibid 213.

[39] *New York Times v Sullivan* 376 US 254 (1964).

[40] ibid 272: see ch 3.

[41] *US v Alvarez* 567 US 709 (2012).

[42] ibid 719.

pornography or fraud. Restrictions on speech that target 'falsity and nothing more' are impermissible.[43] Such a position, Kennedy J stated, 'comports
with the common understanding that some false statements are inevitable
if there is to be an open and vigorous expression of views in public and
private conversation'.[44]

The question the events of 2016 to 2021 puts on the table is this: is this
a price for free speech which, in the age of social media, a democracy can
still afford to pay? The answer is 'yes'. Or, more accurately, the answer is
'yes, but'. The caveat is now as it always has been, ever since John Milton
first argued that there were better solutions than to reach for the muzzle.
The caveat is that for freedom of speech to work as it should, audiences
require to have the wit, the discipline and the means to check and to verify
their sources. If audiences are too gullible, too easily led, or too credulous,
then freedom of speech can switch from being a virtue to becoming a vice.
Audiences need sources they can trust: they need the means whereby they
can distinguish the authoritative from the noise, the gossip, the swamp and
the bilge. Falsehood flies only when it is believed. If America is 'drowning
in lies', the answer is not to switch off the tap but to teach people how to
swim. To put it another way, if the marketplace of ideas is broken, the solution is not to abandon it but to fix it.

So let us turn to how that might be done and, indeed, to the steps which
are being taken to address the matter. Since 2020 the online environment
(and, in particular, social media) has moved more transparently towards a
model of self-regulation. In the United Kingdom and European Union this
has been accompanied by a degree of legislative oversight but the legislation
has been designed, as we shall see, to accommodate and to support the self-
regulation of social media, rather than to replace it. For reasons of space,
we shall focus mainly on Meta (which owns Facebook and Instagram) and
Twitter/X. Since Elon Musk acquired Twitter/X in 2022 divergence has
grown between Meta's approach to self-regulation and Twitter's, particularly as regards its implications for free speech. Meta's approach is twofold.
First it has amplified its terms of service, its 'community standards', and
the raft of policies it follows and applies. These are set out at length and in
detail on the webpages of Meta's 'transparency centre'.[45]

Meta's community standards for Facebook are based on four values:
authenticity, safety, privacy and dignity. Accounts which violate these
standards may be suspended or disabled and posts which breach them can
be removed, blocked or demoted. This applies in particular, but not only,

---

[43] ibid.
[44] ibid 718.
[45] See: transparency.meta.com/en-gb/.

to posts which are unlawful, misleading, discriminatory or fraudulent. The transparency centre includes extensive policies on a wide range of topics, including: criminal activity, fraud, violence and incitement, intellectual property, adult sexual exploitation, bullying and harassment, child sexual exploitation, suicide, self-harm and eating disorders, nudity, hate speech, graphic content, misinformation, and spam. Some of these topics are given an extensive scope. Hate speech, for example, is given a conspicuously broad definition, to include 'dehumanising speech, harmful stereotypes, statements of inferiority, expressions of contempt, disgust or dismissal, [and] cursing' as well as violent, threatening or abusive speech. Others are notably vague. Meta recognises, for example, that 'misinformation' is problematically vague. Sarcasm can be misinformation, as can exaggeration. Meta says that it focuses on misinformation which risks imminent violence or serious physical harm, which relates to public health, or which seeks to interfere with electoral or other political processes. Meta's policy documents on misinformation recognise that this is a moving feast and that it is impossible to draw lines as sharply in this context as it may be in others.

The second limb of Meta's approach is the establishment in 2020 of an Oversight Board, an arm's length body which is funded by Meta but operationally independent of it. It now has its own website (www.oversightboard. com), which sets out its membership, functions, activities, recommendations and decisions. Individuals may make complaints to the Oversight Board and Meta itself may refer matters to the Oversight Board for review.

Meta has taken these steps for two reasons. First, as an attempt to persuade law-makers (particularly in the US Congress) that self-regulation can address the problems of fake news and disinformation which had driven concerns that section 230 needed to be reformed or replaced. And secondly, to persuade its billions of users (to say nothing of the advertisers who underpin Meta's business model) that Facebook, Instagram and the rest are safe and reliable places to be – or, at least, that they are as safe and reliable as they can be and that Meta is investing and is very publicly seen to be investing in policies and in implementation and enforcement practices designed to make its platforms as safe and reliable as possible. This is not to say that the steps Meta has taken should be denounced as mere public relations, driven by self-interest, commercial necessity and consumer demand. That would be overly cynical. But, at the same time, one should not be overly naive. How, then, might we measure the success (or otherwise) of the steps towards more transparent self-regulation Meta has taken? One element of the transparency is the publication of regular reports on what (for example) Facebook is doing by way of closing accounts and removing content.

These reports do not reveal much about the nature of what is being shut down, but they do at least tell us something of its scale. To put the numbers in context, the most recent figures suggest that Facebook users share some 4.75 billion items each day (worldwide). In the region of 350 million photos are uploaded to Facebook every day; something like 293,000 status updates are made every minute. On Twitter/X there are about 500 million tweets every day (worldwide), or 350,000 tweets every minute. Those are all global figures. In the European Union, Facebook has about 261 million active users. Meta's most recent transparency report to the European Union discloses the following.[46] In the six months from October 2023 to March 2024 Facebook received 2,089 requests from Member States to take action against unlawful content (more than three-quarters of which came from Germany). In the same period, Facebook received some 601,000 notifications from users that content posted to Facebook was unlawful. In the same period, Facebook removed 69.8 million posts on its own initiative. These figures relate just to the European Union. Of the nearly 70 million posts which Facebook took down, 19 million were spam, 2.4 million were adult nudity, 1.1 million were hate speech, 950,000 were bullying or harassment, and 700,000 were violence or incitement. In addition, in the same period, 18.6 million posts were demoted, 13.8 million of which for what Meta referred to as 'fact-checked misinformation'. During the six-month period, some 56 million Facebook accounts were terminated. During the period, 2.3 million complaints were made to Facebook concerning the removal of posts, resulting in 667,000 posts being restored. Again, all of these figures are for the European Union alone.

What can be gleaned from figures such as these is limited. But one matter is clear: the vast majority of what is removed from Facebook – of what is censored – is removed at Facebook's own initiative. Excluding Germany, only 500 requests to remove content were made across the whole of the European Union in the six months between October 2023 and March 2024, whereas nearly 70 million items were taken down at Facebook's initiative, the vast majority being removed via automated processes (those algorithms again) without any direct human input or evaluation. More than a hundred times more content is taken down at Facebook's own initiative than is reported or notified to it by users. Whilst there is transparency about the numbers of posts removed (at least in the European Union) and about the general 'community standards' under which such removal practices are set up and operated, there is far less transparency about what is actually taken down. It is this opacity which has led some to voice concerns, as we saw above, that platforms such as Facebook may be suppressing content they disagree with and promoting content they approve of.[47]

---

[46] The report is available via the webpages of Meta's 'transparency centre'.
[47] See Genevieve Lakier, 'The Limits of Anti-Discrimination Law in the Digital Public Sphere' in Bollinger and Stone (n 4) 179. At 188 Lakier refers to the 'censorship' platforms

It is at least partly in response to such concerns that Twitter/X has moved in a different direction, at least since 2022.[48] Both Twitter's terms of service and its observable practices seem to allow for a broader range of speech than is permitted under Facebook's community standards. Twitter's definition of hate speech (Twitter uses the term 'hateful conduct'), for example, is markedly narrower than Facebook's. Twitter/X prohibits 'targeting individuals or groups with content that references forms of violence … where the intent is to harass' and 'targeting others with repeated slurs, tropes or other content that intends to degrade'.[49] Such content is likewise banned on Facebook but so, too, are 'statements of inferiority, expressions of contempt, disgust or dismissal, [and] cursing', as we saw above. Twitter/X says that its 'mission' is

> to give everyone the power to create and share ideas and information, and to express their opinions and beliefs without barriers. Free expression is a human right – we believe that everyone has a voice, and the right to use it. Our role is to serve the public conversation, which requires representation of a diverse range of perspectives.[50]

Twitter draws the line at 'abuse' but does not seek to extend the notion of 'hateful conduct' as broadly as Facebook does.

Like Facebook, Twitter/X also reported to the European Union on its content moderation and removal activity for the six months from October 2023 to March 2024. In that period, Twitter/X had 61 million active users in the European Union; 484,000 posts were removed via Twitter's own-initiative content moderation; and 238,000 notifications were made to Twitter of illegal content. Of these, no violation was found in 129,000 cases and action either to suspend an account, to suppress content locally, or to delete it globally was taken in the remaining 110,000 cases. These figures underscore that there is considerably more content removal on Facebook than there is on Twitter. Facebook is nearly five times bigger in the European Union than Twitter/X, but removes on its own initiative nearly 150 times more content than is removed by Twitter/X.

---

deploy as being 'non-transparent and potentially unprincipled'. The point is: it may or may not be unprincipled; as matters stand we have no way of knowing.

[48] Prior to its acquisition by Elon Musk, Twitter was also criticised for inconsistency as to what it removed and what it did not. The House of Lords Communications and Digital Committee was interested in 2021, for example, as to why Twitter had banned Donald Trump's account but not the Ayatollah Khamenei's (the Supreme Leader of Iran), despite the fact that tweets on that account had called for 'armed resistance' to remove 'the Zionist regime' (ie, Israel). See House of Lords Communications and Digital Committee, *Free for All? Freedom of Expression in the Digital Age*, HL 54, July 2021 [68].

[49] See: help.x.com/en/rules-and-policies/hateful-conduct-policy.

[50] ibid.

Notwithstanding such apparent variations in self-regulation, and notwithstanding the problems of non-transparency which it poses, it would seem that self-regulation is destined to continue as the principal means whereby the online eco-system guards against disinformation and fake news. However, it is not the only means. In the United Kingdom, online self-regulation is supplemented by a range of legislative provisions concerned with different aspects of fake news and online falsehood. Between them, these offer a patchwork, rather than an integrated system, of regulation. First, there are the communications offences. We saw in chapter five that section 127(1) of the Communications Act 2003 provides for a series of offences relating to 'grossly offensive' or 'indecent, obscene or menacing' messages. Section 127(2) provided, in addition, that it was an offence, 'for the purpose of causing annoyance, inconvenience or needless anxiety to another', for a person either to send a false message or to send persistent messages. Section 127(2) is still in force in Scotland but for England and Wales it was repealed by the Online Safety Act 2023. In its place, three new offences have been provided for: the offences of 'false communications' (section 179); 'threatening communications' (section 181); and 'encouraging or assisting serious self-harm' (section 184). The elements of the false communications offence are that a person sends a message, which the person knows to be false, where the person intends the message 'to cause non-trivial psychological or physical harm to a likely audience', where the person has no reasonable excuse for sending the message. A 'message' may be any electronic communication (whether written or oral) or any letter or package.

There are as yet no reported cases on the section 179 offence of false communications, but we do know that arrests have been made under it. In July 2024 three children were stabbed to death and ten other people (eight of them children) were injured in a horrific attack in Southport, Merseyside. Misinformation about the attacker spread immediately on social media: it was claimed that the attacker was a Muslim asylum seeker (when, in reality, the person arrested for the attack is a young man born in Cardiff whose parents were from Rwanda). The misinformation spread quickly, seemingly propagated by a news aggregation website, now closed down, that had a history of spreading false information. A woman, Bernadette Spofforth, was arrested for tweeting on the day of the attack that a Muslim asylum seeker, whom she named, was responsible for the attack. Her tweet was deleted an hour later, but the false information it contained went viral. On the day after the attack there were serious anti-immigration riots in Southport. Property was damaged and police officers were injured. Over the course of the ensuing days there were similar riots elsewhere in England and also in Belfast. More than one thousand arrests were made. Spofforth was arrested for an offence under the Public Order

Act and for the false communications offence contrary to section 179 of the Online Safety Act. In September 2024 it was announced that the charges against her had been dropped, and that the police would take no further action.[51] There was no doubt that she had sent the tweet – indeed, she publicly apologised for it – but there was 'insufficient evidence', the police said, presumably about the other elements of the offence (that the person knows the information to be false and that the person intends to cause harm by sending the message).

As we shall see in the next section, the main focus of the Online Safety Act is on harms other than those relating to falsehoods and misinformation. There are two further provisions, though, in addition to section 179, which relate to this particular aspect of speech online. Section 152 requires Ofcom to establish an advisory committee on disinformation and misinformation.[52] At the time of writing (more than a year after the Online Safety Act was enacted) no such committee has yet been established. Section 165 of the Act imposes a new duty on Ofcom to 'take such steps, and enter into such arrangements, as they consider most likely to be effective in heightening the public's awareness and understanding of ways in which they can protect themselves and others' when using online services. These are examples of 'soft power'. If appropriately resourced they may be all the more effective for that. As suggested above, one of the surest means we have to diminish the effectiveness of fake news and disinformation is a more educated, more aware and less credulous audience. There is a clear public interest in pursuing such an ambition. To harness Ofcom's power to its pursuit can only be a welcome step.

It was noted above that an early concern about disinformation in US politics related to allegations of Russian interference in the 2016 presidential election. Similar concerns have been expressed in the United Kingdom. Parliament's Intelligence and Security Committee reported on them in 2020.[53] The committee described Russia as an 'established threat' to the UK's security[54] and outlined how Russia's 'malicious cyber activity' was particularly aggressive:[55] it is a matter of 'grave concern', the committee warned, 'and poses an immediate and urgent threat to our national security'.[56] Much of the report is redacted, its published version

---

[51] As reported in the *Times*, 18 September 2024.

[52] Ofcom – the Office of Communications – is, as we saw in ch 4, the UK's statutory regulator for broadcasting, telecommunications and online safety. Its powers and functions, already considerable, were extended significantly by the Online Safety Act, as discussed further below.

[53] Intelligence and Security Committee, *Russia Report*, HC 632, July 2020. See further on the *Russia Report*, ch 4.

[54] ibid [1].

[55] ibid [13].

[56] ibid [15].

being little more than skeletal in places. But the committee referred to 'widespread public allegations' that Russia 'sought to influence' the 2016 EU referendum[57] and to 'credible open source commentary' that Russia undertook 'influence campaigns' in relation to the Scottish independence referendum in 2014.[58] Driven by concerns such as these, the National Security Act 2023 provided for new offences designed to criminalise 'foreign interference' in political processes in the United Kingdom.[59] Section 15 of the Act specifies that making a 'misrepresentation' is included within the scope of the new offences. Thus, if a person makes a misrepresentation 'for or on behalf of a foreign power', intending thereby to 'interfere' with an election or referendum, that is now an offence in the United Kingdom.[60]

IV. Protection from Online Harms

When the Online Safety Act was passed in 2023 – after an unusually long and protracted parliamentary passage – the UK government claimed the legislation would make the United Kingdom 'the safest place in the world to be online'.[61] The harms against which the legislation purports to offer protection are, in the main, different from those considered in the previous section. Fake news and disinformation played only a background role in the deliberations which led to the Online Safety Act (OSA). The Act was the coming together of two, initially quite different, strands of work. The first was the Law Commission's work on modernising the communications offences, outlined in chapter five. The second was work, led by the Carnegie Trust and by the National Society for the Prevention of Cruelty to Children (NSPCC), on keeping children and young people safe online. This work was inspired by tragedies such as Molly Russell's. Molly took her own life in 2017 when she was only 14 years old. The coroner reported that 'she was suffering from depression and the negative effects of online content'. The coroner said the following about the circumstances of Molly's death:

> Molly subscribed to a number of online sites ... some [of which] were not safe as they allowed access to adult content which should not have been available for a 14-year old child to see. The way that the platforms operated meant that Molly had access to images, video clips and text concerning or concerned with self-harm ... The platforms operated in such a way using algorithms as to

---

[57] ibid [39].

[58] ibid [41].

[59] National Security Act 2023, ss 13–14.

[60] For expert commentary on the Act, see Paul Scott, 'State Threats, Security and Democracy: the National Security Act 2023' (2024) 44 *Legal Studies* 260.

[61] HM Government press release: 'Britain Makes Internet Safer', 19 September 2023.

result, in some circumstances, of binge periods of images, video clips and text some of which were selected and provided without Molly requesting them … Some of this content romanticised acts of self-harm … The sites normalised her [depressive] condition focusing on a limited and irrational view without any counter-balance of normality.[62]

The NSPCC started a campaign – 'Wild West Web' – to make the internet safer for children. At the same time, commencing with a series of blog posts hosted by the Carnegie Trust, Lorna Woods and William Perrin began to outline a new approach to online safety which would impose legal duties of care on platforms and service providers, similar in some ways to those found in other areas of law such as health and safety or occupier's liability. The idea took hold and its influence spread quickly. In January 2019 Woods and Perrin refined their work and presented it as a policy paper, *Internet Harm Reduction*, which the Carnegie Trust published.[63] In March 2019 the House of Lords Communications Committee published a report which supported Woods' and Perrin's recommendation that online services should be under a duty of care designed to manage online risks. The committee considered that the duty of care should be enforced by a statutory regulator such as Ofcom.[64] In April 2019 the UK government published its *Online Harms* White Paper, a policy and consultation document that set out ministers' thinking as to how to make the internet safer.[65] At its core was a commitment 'to establish a new statutory duty of care on relevant companies to take reasonable steps to keep their users safe and tackle illegal and harmful activity on their services'.[66] This duty of care would be enforced by an independent regulator, it would require platforms and service providers to take reasonable steps to keep users safe and, as a new regulatory regime, it would be governed by the principle of proportionality.[67] All of these features found their way into the Online Safety Act.

The White Paper was a hybrid document, jointly sponsored by two government departments: the Home Office; and the Department of State for Digital, Culture, Media and Sport (DCMS). The concerns of the two departments were quite different from one another. The Home Office was worried about crime and, in particular, about how the internet facilitates its commission. Child sexual exploitation and abuse (CSEA), terrorist

---

[62] The Coroner's Service, *Molly Russell – Prevention of Future Deaths Report*, 13 October 2022 (available via www.judiciary.uk).

[63] See: carnegieuktrust.org.uk/publications/internet-harm-reduction/.

[64] House of Lords Communications Committee, *Regulating in a Digital World*, HL 299, March 2019 [205]–[206].

[65] HM Government, *Online Harms White Paper*, CP 57, April 2019.

[66] ibid [3.1].

[67] ibid [3.2]–[3.4].

crime, gang violence and the sale of drugs were all highlighted in the White Paper as aspects of crime in which there is a significant online element. None of the Home Office's concerns poses a problem for freedom of speech (any more than would be posed by concerns about expression offline relating to CSEA, terrorism or other serious criminal activity). The DCMS, on the other hand, was worried about cyber-bullying, self-harm and suicide, screen time and, to a lesser extent, the manipulation of information and the abuse of public figures online. The White Paper acknowledged that some of these harms (broadly, the Home Office's concerns) were unlawful and that others (broadly, the DCMS's concerns) were not unlawful but were harmful nonetheless. This distinction – between unlawful activity online and lawful-but-harmful speech online – found its way into the Online Safety Bill and, as we shall see, proved to be both problematic and controversial.

Four and a half years were to elapse between the publication of the White Paper (in April 2019) and the eventual passing of the Online Safety Act (in October 2023). It was an unusually turbulent time in British politics and it was a period during which a great deal of the government's bandwidth was consumed first by Brexit negotiations and then by the Covid pandemic. That four-and-a-half year period saw four prime ministers[68] and no fewer than six secretaries of state at the DCMS.[69] None of the secretaries of state remained in office for more than 19 months. Two years after the White Paper, a draft bill was published in May 2021. An actual bill followed in March 2022. And, after an 18-month legislative passage during which the bill was significantly amended, the legislation was finally passed in October 2023. The most important amendments were made in November 2022. They were made at the instigation of the government, once Michelle Donelan had replaced Nadine Dorries as secretary of state (and once Rishi Sunak had become prime minister).

The OSA imposes a complex series of duties on two sorts of internet platforms: user-to-user services and search services. The former term captures services online where users view content that has been generated or uploaded by other users of the service. Evidently, this includes all social media platforms. Duties are imposed in relation to illegal content, in relation to protecting children and in relation to adults. It was this last category of duties that was controversial (and much amended) as the legislation was going through Parliament.

Neither the duties in relation to illegal content nor those in relation to protecting children are particularly problematic from a free speech point

---

[68] Theresa May, Boris Johnson, Liz Truss and Rishi Sunak.
[69] Jeremy Wright, Nicky Morgan, Oliver Dowden, Nadine Dorries, Michelle Donelan and Lucy Frazer.

of view. As to the first, user-to-user and search services are under duties to assess the risk of illegal content on their services[70] and to take 'proportionate measures relating to the design or operation' of their services to prevent users from encountering 'priority illegal content' and to mitigate and manage the risk of services being used for the commission or facilitation of a priority offence.[71] User-to-user services are also under a duty to minimise the length of time that 'priority illegal content' is online and to take such content down 'swiftly' once they become aware of it.[72] The 'priority offences' are listed in Schedules 5–7 to the Act (and 'priority illegal content' is defined as content relating to a priority offence).[73] They are: terrorism offences (as listed in Schedule 5); child sexual exploitation and abuse offences (as listed in Schedule 6); and such other offences as are listed in Schedule 7. These other offences include assisted suicide, certain public order offences, certain drugs and firearms offences and human trafficking, as well as others.

As far as the protection of children is concerned, user-to-user and search services are again under two sorts of duties: duties to assess the risks their services pose to children;[74] and duties 'to take or use proportionate measures relating to the design or operation of the service effectively to mitigate and manage the risks of harm to children ... and to mitigate the impact of harm to children' presented (as the case may be) by content on the service or by search content.[75] User-to-user services are under a specific duty to use 'proportionate systems and processes' designed to prevent children accessing 'primary priority content that is harmful to children'.[76] Search services are under a similar duty, to use 'proportionate systems and processes' designed to 'minimise the risk' of children encountering 'primary priority content that is harmful to children'.[77] 'Primary priority content' includes pornography and content which 'encourages, promotes or provides instruction' for suicide, self-harm, or an eating disorder.[78] Children are to be *prevented* from accessing such material: services' terms of service must additionally set out how children are to be *protected* from

---

[70] OSA, ss 9 (user-to-user services) and 26 (search services).

[71] ibid s 10(2). Under s 27 search services are under a duty not to 'prevent' but to 'minimise the risk' of exposure to priority illegal content.

[72] ibid s 10(3): the duty is to operate the service 'using proportionate systems and processes designed' to minimise the length of time to allow for swift removal.

[73] ibid s 59.

[74] ibid ss 11 (user-to-user services) and 28 (search services).

[75] ibid ss 12(2) and 29(2).

[76] ibid s 12(3).

[77] ibid s 29(3).

[78] ibid s 61.

accessing material which is abusive, which incites hatred, which encourages or promotes violence, or which is 'bullying content'.[79]

It can be seen that the initial Woods and Perrin idea of imposing a duty of care on social media companies and search engines has been broken down in the OSA into a detailed, overlapping and complex series of statutory duties. There are duties on user-to-user services and on search services. There are duties in relation to illegal content and in relation to protecting children. There are duties to assess risks. There are duties to mitigate and manage various harms. There are duties to have systems in place allowing for the swift removal of certain sorts of illegal content. There are duties to prevent children from accessing particular sorts of material. There are duties to set out how children will be protected from other sorts of material. In all of these cases, considerable care has been taken to identify as closely as possible what the harms are which the duties are designed to protect people from. The Act uses phrases such as 'priority illegal content' and 'primary priority content' to undertake this task, these phrases being exhaustively defined in the legislation. The downside is that the Act is hard to read, understand and navigate. This is complex legislation and, like all such legislation, raises questions of accessibility. The upside is that the Act goes to considerable lengths to specify, at least as far as illegal content and protecting children are concerned, exactly what sorts of content are regulated and what are not. From a free speech perspective, this is essential. If we take a harms-based approach to freedom of speech, it is imperative that we nail down as precisely as possible what the harm is before we impose limits on expression. In its impressively detailed provisions on illegal content and on protecting children, the Online Safety Act works hard to meet that challenge.

The same could not have been said, however, for what the Online Safety bill had initially proposed as regards protecting adults. The bill as introduced would have imposed on services two sets of duties in relation to adults: 'duties to assess risk' and 'safety duties'.[80] So far so familiar (this is the same basic architecture as is used for illegal content and for protecting children). Unlike those contexts, however, the harms from which adults were to be protected were never specified. The bill would have imposed a duty on services to include in their terms of service provisions specifying, 'in relation to each kind of priority content that is harmful to adults', what sorts of content could be taken down, restricted, or demoted.[81] That key phrase, 'priority content that is harmful to adults', however, was nowhere

---

[79] ibid s 62.
[80] Online Safety Bill (2022), cls 12–13.
[81] ibid cl 13(3) and (4).

defined in the bill. Instead, the bill would have provided that the phrase 'means content of a description designated in regulations made by the Secretary of State'.[82] Had these provisions been enacted, they would have placed service providers under duties to allow for the removal, restriction or demotion of online content which was perfectly lawful, but which a minister had specified in regulations was nonetheless somehow harmful. This, the bill's critics claimed, was a dangerous incursion into freedom of speech, not only because the 'harms' were wholly unspecified, but also because they could later be defined by a minister whereas, surely, that was a matter for Parliament. The House of Lords Communications and Digital Committee, for example, concluded that the provisions could not be implemented without 'unjustifiable and unprecedented interference in freedom of expression'.[83]

It was these provisions which were removed from the bill in November 2022 after Michelle Donelan had replaced Nadine Dorries as secretary of state. In their place the OSA as enacted substitutes a series of 'user empowerment duties'. Thus, services are under a duty, to the extent it is proportionate to do so, to enable users to 'increase their control' over certain sorts of online content.[84] Such control could take the form of users being able to reduce their likelihood of seeing it, or of an alert appearing before the content is seen. The sorts of content to which the user empowerment duties apply are listed in the Act, as follows: content that encourages, promotes or provides instructions for suicide, self-harm or an eating disorder; content that is abusive on grounds of race, religion, sex, sexual orientation, disability or gender reassignment; or content which incites hatred.[85] It is notable that misleading content, falsehoods, misinformation and disinformation are not cited by the Act in this context. The OSA is not designed to protect adult users from harms which may ensue from fake news and disinformation.

This is reinforced by virtue of the fact that the Act includes a range of carve-outs, designed to protect various sorts of content. Thus, 'content of democratic importance' is protected: 'the importance of the free expression'

---

[82] ibid cl 54.

[83] House of Lords Communications and Digital Committee, *Free for All? Freedom of Expression in the Digital Age*, HL 54, July 2021 [182]. This conclusion was reached in relation to the Draft Online Safety Bill. The Joint Committee on the Draft Online Safety Bill reached the same conclusion, recommending that the provisions in question are 'removed': see its report published as HL 129, HC 609, December 2021 [176].

[84] OSA s 15. These duties apply to 'category 1 services' – the largest user-to-user services in the UK. The exact threshold conditions governing what is a category 1 service are to be set out in regulations made by the secretary of state (OSA s 94 and Sched 11) on the basis of advice from Ofcom. Ofcom will then establish a register of category 1 services (OSA s 95).

[85] ibid s 16.

of such content is to be 'taken into account' when a service makes decisions about how to treat such content or about whether to take action against a user who has generated, uploaded or shared such content.[86] There are accompanying duties to protect 'news publisher content' and 'journalistic content', as defined in the Act.[87] Freedom of expression is given more general protection in section 22 of the Act, which provides among other matters that 'when deciding on, and implementing, safety measures and policies', services are under 'a duty to have particular regard to the importance of protecting users' right to freedom of expression within the law'.[88] In cases of doubt, the OSA appears to direct services to err on the side of allowing content to remain, rather than on the side of removing it.

Whilst there are differences of emphasis, the basic regulatory approach taken by the OSA is similar to that adopted in EU law under the Digital Services Act (DSA).[89] Both the OSA and the DSA are focused mainly on processes, requiring services and platforms to have systems in place which enable them to assess risk, to remove content and to allow users to protect themselves online. The legislation is designed more to support self-regulation than to replace it. As the DSA states, nothing in this law 'should be construed as an imposition of a general monitoring obligation or a general fact-finding obligation, or as a general obligation for providers to take proactive measures in relation to illegal content'.[90] The scheme of the DSA is founded on the twin pillars of regular transparency reports, in which providers account for the content moderation in which they engage, and facilitating 'notice and action' procedures, whereby providers can be notified of unlawful content so that they can consider what, if anything, to do about it.[91] The DSA does not go into the same level of detail about online harms as the OSA but it does identify four 'categories' of risk, which services – especially 'very large' services – should assess and, where appropriate, mitigate.[92] These risks are: 'the dissemination of illegal content'; 'the actual or foreseeable impact of services on the exercise of fundamental rights'; 'negative effects on democratic processes and civic discourse'; and 'negative effects on the protection of public health, children or mental well-being'.[93] Some of these terms are very vague. It might be said, though,

---

[86] ibid s 17.
[87] ibid ss 18–19.
[88] ibid s 22(2). We have encountered this sort of formulation before – in s 12 of the Human Rights Act. Whether it will have any greater effect under the OSA than it has had under the Human Rights Act remains to be seen. Experience under the Human Rights Act, though, is hardly encouraging in that regard (see ch 3 and ch 4).
[89] Above (n 2).
[90] ibid Recital [30].
[91] ibid Recitals [49]–[50].
[92] ibid Recital [79].
[93] ibid Recitals [80]–[83].

that a number of the duties the DSA imposes on services appear to be correspondingly light-touch: platforms 'should consider', for example, whether they need to adapt the 'design, feature[s] or functioning' of their services to mitigate such risks.[94]

Such, in outline, is the framework which the OSA and the DSA set out. Whether or not the stated aims of the enactments are realised in practice now largely depends on how the legislation is implemented and interpreted. As far as the OSA is concerned, the key actor, as well as the services themselves, is Ofcom.[95]

The various duties provided for by the OSA are to be monitored by Ofcom, which is required by the Act to publish codes of practice and guidance as to best practice in performing them. Extensive provision is made in the OSA for Ofcom's powers and responsibilities as regulator under the Act. Since the Act was passed Ofcom has been undertaking an extensive consultation process as it develops its guidance and codes of practice.[96] The success (or otherwise) of the OSA and, in particular, its ability to navigate between protecting people from harm and protecting freedom of online expression, is largely in Ofcom's hands. What we do know is that Ofcom's regulatory role as regards online safety is designed to be very different from its regulatory role as regards broadcasting (which was discussed in chapter four). The public interest in due impartiality – in having as well-informed an audience as possible – lies at the heart of broadcasting regulation in the United Kingdom. Online safety, by contrast, has come to be understood quite differently. This is not because keeping the audience well informed is regarded as unimportant: it is because that task, critical as it may be, is one which for the time being remains a matter of self-regulation rather than legislative stipulation. The services and the platforms have a role to play, but so too do their users. The hope is that as we learn more about the perils of misleading and unreliable information online, we also learn more about how to manage the risks.

A healthy online environment needs media-savvy, literate, intelligent readers. At either end of the argument for an unlicensed press, John Milton

---

[94] ibid Recital [87]. Commentators have expressed concern about how 'very vague' some of the DSA's key terms are but, at the same time, have pointed out how 'the DSA is largely a procedural tool that creates a lot of new evidence about what is going on in the digital ecosystem': see Martin Husovec, 'The Digital Services Act's Red Line: What the Commission Can and Cannot Do About Disinformation' (2024) 16 *Journal of Media Law* 47.

[95] The regulatory framework provided for by the DSA will be the primary responsibility of Digital Services Coordinators, to be appointed in each EU Member State. The Commission will have various oversight functions. For a full analysis, see Martin Husovec, *Principles of the Digital Services Act* (Oxford, Oxford University Press, 2024).

[96] The process is vast: more than 2,000 pages of consultation documentation have been published. For an overview, see: www.ofcom.org.uk/online-safety/illegal-and-harmful-content/guide-for-services/.

and Jonathan Swift saw that the absence of licensing would need readers able and willing to think for themselves. Milton, in whose time the press was uncensored only rarely, was more optimistic about that than Swift, who witnessed first-hand what he considered to be the ill effects of a free press. Mill turned the argument around: he saw that it is freedom of speech which unlocks human flourishing. It is precisely by being exposed to information and ideas which are contrary to received or official opinion that we learn and progress. That, in the end, is what speaking freely is all about: that audiences – the people themselves – should decide what to read and watch and listen to and should decide for themselves what to make of it. The dangers implicit in this radical and once subversive idea may sometimes be considerable, but they are never so great as when the church, the government or the forces of social censure seek to remove that freedom from us and decide on our behalf what we are free to say.

SELECT BIBLIOGRAPHY

David Armitage, Armand Himy and Quentin Skinner (eds), *Milton and Republicanism* (Cambridge, Cambridge University Press, 1995).

Daphne Barak-Erez, *Biblical Judgments: New Legal Readings in the Hebrew Bible* (Ann Arbor, University of Michigan Press, 2024).

Eric Barendt, *Freedom of Speech* (Oxford, Oxford University Press, 2nd edn 2005).

—— 'Statutory Underpinning: A Threat to Press Freedom?' (2013) 5 *Journal of Media Law* 189.

Anna Beer, *Milton: Poet, Pampleteer and Patriot* (London, Bloomsbury, 2008).

Teresa M Bejan, 'Two Concepts of Freedom (of Speech)' (2019) 163 *Proceedings of the American Philosophical Society* 95.

Isaiah Berlin, *Liberty* (Henry Hardy (ed), Oxford, Oxford University Press, 2002).

Lee Bollinger and Geoffrey Stone (eds), *The Free Speech Century* (New York, Oxford University Press, 2019).

—— *Social Media, Freedom of Speech and the Future of our Democracy* (New York, Oxford University Press, 2022).

Susan Brigden, *New Worlds, Lost Worlds: The Rule of the Tudors 1485–1603* (London, Penguin, 2001).

Stephen Budiansky, *Oliver Wendell Holmes: A Life in War, Law and Ideas* (New York, Norton, 2019).

JH Burns (with Mark Goldie) (eds), *The Cambridge History of Political Thought 1450–1700* (Cambridge, Cambridge University Press, 1991).

Arthur Cash, *John Wilkes: The Scandalous Father of Civil Liberty* (New Haven, Yale University Press, 2006).

Cyndia Clegg, *Press Censorship in Jacobean England* (Cambridge, Cambridge University Press, 2001).

—— Cyndia Clegg, *Press Censorship in Caroline England* (Cambridge, Cambridge University Press, 2008).

Linda Colley, *Britons: Forging the Nation 1707–1837* (London, Pimlico, 1994).

Ian Cram, *Liberal Democracy, Law and the Citizen Speaker: Regulating Online Speech* (Oxford, Hart Publishing, 2022).

David Cressy, *Dangerous Talk: Scandalous, Seditious, and Treasonable Speech in Pre-Modern England* (Oxford, Oxford University Press, 2010).

Fara Dabhoiwala, 'Inventing Free Speech: Politics, Liberty and Print in Eighteenth-Century England' (2022) *Past and Present* (supplement 16) 39.

Leo Damrosch, *Jonathan Swift: His Life and His World* (New Haven, Yale University Press, 2013).

Helen Fenwick and Gavin Phillipson, *Media Freedom under the Human Rights Act* (Oxford, Oxford University Press, 2006).

Lara Fielden, 'A Royal Charter for the Press: Lessons from Overseas' (2013) 5 *Journal of Media Law* 172.

Stanley Fish, *The First* (New York, Simon & Schuster, 2019).

Stephen Gardbaum, *The New Commonwealth Model of Constitutionalism* (Cambridge, Cambridge University Press, 2013).

Timothy Garton Ash, *Free Speech: Ten Principles for a Connected World* (London, Atlantic Books, 2017).

Ian Gilmour, *Riot, Risings and Revolution: Governance and Violence in Eighteenth-Century England* (London, Pimlico, 1993).

Mark Goldie and Robert Wokler (eds), *The Cambridge History of Eighteenth-Century Political Thought* (Cambridge, Cambridge University Press, 2006).

John Guy, *Tudor England* (Oxford, Oxford University Press, 1990).

Philip Hamburger, 'The Development of the Law of Seditious Libel and the Control of the Press' (1985) 37 *Stanford Law Review* 661.

Ivan Hare and James Weinstein (eds), *Extreme Speech and Democracy* (Oxford, Oxford University Press, 2009).

Philip Harling, 'The Law of Libel and the Limits of Repression 1790–1832' (2001) 44 *Historical Journal* 107.

Tim Harris, *Restoration: Charles II and his Kingdoms 1660–1685* (London, Penguin, 2006).

Eric Heinze, *Hate Speech and Democratic Citizenship* (Oxford, Oxford University Press, 2016).

—— *The Most Human Right: Why Free Speech is Everything* (Cambridge MA, MIT Press, 2022).

Christopher Hilliard, *A Matter of Obscenity: The Politics of Censorship in Modern England* (Princeton, Princeton University Press, 2021).

Oliver Wendell Holmes, 'The Path of the Law' (1897) 10 *Harvard Law Review* 457.

David Hume, *Essays Moral, Political and Literary* (Eugene Miller (ed), Indianapolis, Liberty Fund, 1987).

Martin Husovec, *Principles of the Digital Services Act* (Oxford, Oxford University Press, 2024).

PBJ Hyland, 'Liberty and Libel: Government and the Press 1712–1716' (1986) 101 *English Historical Review* 863.

Jonathan Israel, *Enlightenment Contested* (Oxford, Oxford University Press, 2006).

Clare Jackson, *Devil-Land: England Under Siege 1588–1688* (London, Penguin, 2022).

Samuel Johnson, *Lives of the Poets, Vol 1* (Arthur Waugh (ed), London, Oxford University Press, 1906).

—— *Selected Essays* (David Womersley (ed), London, Penguin, 2003).

Jeffrey Jowell and Anthony Lester, 'Beyond *Wednesbury*: Substantive Principles of Administrative Law' [1987] *Public Law* 368.

Anthony Julius, 'Willed Ignorance: Reflections on Academic Free Speech' (2022) 75 *Current Legal Problems* 1.

John Keane, *Tom Paine: A Political Life* (London, Bloomsbury, 1995).

Andrew Kenyon, *Democracy of Expression: Positive Free Speech and Law* (Cambridge, Cambridge University Press, 2021).

Andrew Kenyon and Andrew Scott (eds), *Positive Free Speech: Rationales, Methods and Implications* (Oxford, Hart Publishing, 2023).

JP Kenyon, *The Stuart Constitution: Documents and Commentary* (Cambridge, Cambridge University Press, 2nd edn 1986).

Thomas Keymer, *Poetics of the Pillory: English Literature and Seditious Libel 1660–1820* (Oxford, Oxford University Press, 2019).

Terry Kirby, *The Newsmongers: A History of Tabloid Journalism* (London, Reaktion, 2024).

András Koltay, *New Media and Freedom of Expression: Rethinking the Constitutional Foundations of the Public Sphere* (Oxford, Hart Publishing, 2019).

Matthew Kramer, *Freedom of Expression as Self-Restraint* (Oxford, Oxford University Press, 2021).

Sir John Laws, 'Law and Democracy' [1995] *Public Law* 72.

Simon Lee, *The Cost of Free Speech* (London, Faber & Faber, 1990).

Rebecca Lemon, *Treason by Words: Literature, Law and Rebellion in Shakespeare's England* (Ithaca, Cornell University Press, 2011).

Leonard Levy, *Freedom of Speech and Press in Early American History* (Cambridge MA, Belknap Press, 1963).

—— *Blasphemy: Verbal Offense against the Sacred from Moses to Salman Rushdie* (New York, Knopf, 1993).

Anthony Lewis, *Freedom for the Thought that We Hate* (New York, Basic Books, 2007).

Michael Lobban, 'From Seditious Libel to Unlawful Assembly: Peterloo and the Changing Face of Political Crime 1770–1820' (1990) 10 *Oxford Journal of Legal Studies* 307.

John Locke, *A Letter Concerning Toleration and Other Writings* (Mark Goldie (ed), Indianapolis, Liberty Fund, 2010).

Jack Lynch (ed), *The Oxford Handbook of Samuel Johnson* (Oxford, Oxford University Press, 2022).

Diarmaid MacCulloch, *Reformation: Europe's House Divided* (London, Penguin, 2004).

Roger B Manning, 'The Origins of the Doctrine of Sedition' (1980) 12 *Albion* 99.

Forrest McDonald, *Novus Ordo Seclorum: The Intellectual Origins of the Constitution* (Lawrence, University Press of Kansas, 1985).

Jacob Mchangama, *Free Speech: A Global History from Socrates to Social Media* (London, Basic Books, 2022).

John Milton, *The Major Works* (S Orgel and J Goldberg (eds), Oxford, Oxford University Press, 1991).

David Norbrook, *Writing the English Republic: Poetry, Rhetoric and Politics 1627–1660* (Cambridge, Cambridge University Press, 1999).

Suzanne Nossel, *Dare to Speak: Defending Free Speech for All* (New York, Dey Street, 2020).

Andrew Pettegree and Arthur der Weduwen, *The Library: A Fragile History* (London, Profile, 2021).

Gavin Phillipson, 'Leveson, the Public Interest and Press Freedom' (2013) 5 *Journal of Media Law* 220.

Akhil Reed Amar, *The Bill of Rights: Creation and Reconstruction* (New Haven, Yale University Press, 1998).

Richard Reeves, *John Stuart Mill: Victorian Firebrand* (London, Atlantic, 2007).

Cheryl Reid, 'Press Censorship in the 1990s: the Calcutt Report and the Protection of Individual Privacy' (1992) 43 *Northern Ireland Legal Quarterly* 99.

Geoffrey Robertson, *Lawfare* (London, TLS Books, 2023).

Randy Robertson, *Censorship and Conflict in Seventeenth-Century England* (Pennsylvania, Penn State University Press, 2009).

Trevor Ross, *Writing in Public: Literature and the Liberty of the Press in Eighteenth-Century Britain* (Baltimore, Johns Hopkins University Press, 2018).

Jacob Rowbottom, 'To Rant, Vent and Converse: Protecting Low Level Digital Speech' (2012) 71 *Cambridge Law Journal* 355.

—— *Media Law* (Oxford, Hart Publishing, 2nd edn 2024).

Salman Rushdie, *Knife: Meditations after an Attempted Murder* (London, Jonathan Cape, 2024).

Frederick Schauer, *Free Speech: A Philosophical Enquiry* (Cambridge, Cambridge University Press, 1982).

Paul Scott, 'State Threats, Security and Democracy: the National Security Act 2023' (2024) 44 *Legal Studies* 260.

Andrew Sharp (ed), *The English Levellers* (Cambridge, Cambridge University Press, 1998).

Debora Shuger, *Censorship and Cultural Sensibility: The Regulation of Language in Tudor-Stuart England* (Philadelphia, University of Pennsylvania Press, 2006).

Frederick Seaton Siebert, *Freedom of the Press in England 1476–1776* (Urbana, University of Illinois Press, 1952).

Quentin Skinner, *The Foundations of Modern Political Thought* (Cambridge, Cambridge University Press, 1978, 2 vols).

Victor Slater, *Hoax: The Popish Plot that Never Was* (New Haven, Yale University Press, 2022).

Adam Smyth, *The Book Makers* (London, Bodley Head, 2024).

Richard Sorabji, *Freedom of Speech and Expression* (New York, Oxford University Press, 2021).

Walter Stephens, *How Writing Made us Human* (Baltimore, Johns Hopkins University Press, 2023).

Adrienne Stone and Frederick Schauer (eds), *Oxford Handbook of Freedom of Speech* (Oxford, Oxford University Press, 2021).

Geoffrey Stone, *Perilous Times: Free Speech in Wartime* (New York, Norton, 2004).

Nadine Strossen, *Hate: Why We Should Resist It with Free Speech, Not Censorship* (New York, Oxford University Press, 2018).

John Sutherland, *Triggered Literature: Cancellation, Stealth Censorship and Cultural Warfare* (London, Biteback, 2023).

Jonathan Swift, *Major Works* (Angus Ross and David Woolley (eds), Oxford, Oxford University Press, 1984).

—— *Gulliver's Travels* (David Womersley (ed), Cambridge, Cambridge University Press, paperback edn 2022).

JR Tanner, *Tudor Constitutional Documents 1485–1603* (Cambridge, Cambridge University Press, 1930).

Adam Tomkins and Paul Scott (eds), *Entick v Carrington: 250 Years of the Rule of Law* (Oxford, Hart Publishing, 2015).

John Trenchard and Thomas Gordon, *Cato's Letters* (Ronald Hamowy (ed), Indianapolis, Liberty Fund, 1995, 2 vols).

Mark Tushnet, *Advanced Introduction to Freedom of Expression* (London, Elgar, 2018).

Robin Vose, *The Index of Prohibited Books* (London, Reaktion, 2022).

Jeremy Waldron, *The Harm in Hate Speech* (Cambridge MA, Harvard University Press, 2012).

Nigel Warburton, *Free Speech: A Very Short Introduction* (Oxford, Oxford University Press, 2009).

E Neville Williams, *The Eighteenth Century Constitution: Documents and Commentary* (Cambridge, Cambridge University Press, 1960).

John Willinsky, *The Intellectual Properties of Learning: A Prehistory from Saint Jerome to John Locke* (Chicago, Chicago University Press, 2018).

Sheldon Wolin, *Politics and Vision* (Princeton, Princeton University Press, expanded edn 2004).

David Womersley, 'Swift and Free Speech' in Robert Ingram, Jason Peacey and Alex Barber (eds), *Freedom of Speech 1500–1850* (Manchester, Manchester University Press, 2020).

Gordon Wood, *The Radicalism of the American Revolution* (New York, Knopf, 1992).

—— *Revolutionary Characters: What Made the Founders Different* (New York, Penguin, 2006).

Lucy Wooding, *Tudor England: A History* (New Haven, Yale University Press, 2023).

David Wootton, 'Leveller Democracy and the Puritan Revolution' in JH Burns and Mark Goldie (eds), *The Cambridge History of Political Thought 1450–1700* (Cambridge, Cambridge University Press, 1991).

Blair Worden, *Literature and Politics in Cromwellian England* (Oxford, Oxford University Press, 2007).

Paul Wragg, 'Free Speech Rights at Work: Resolving the Differences between Practice and Liberal Principle' (2015) 44 *Industrial Law Journal* 1.

TABLE OF CASES

United States of America

European Court of Human Rights

Other Courts and Jurisdictions

INDEX

* 9 7 8 1 5 0 9 9 7 2 1 0 4 *